T0133936

Professional Security Management

Historically, security managers have tended to be sourced from either the armed forces or law enforcement. But the increasing complexity of the organisations employing them, along with the technologies employed by them, is forcing an evolution and expansion of the role, and security managers must meet this challenge in order to succeed in their field and protect the assets of their employers. Risk management, crisis management, continuity management, strategic business operations, data security, IT, and business communications all fall under the purview of the security manager.

This book is a guide to meeting those challenges, providing the security manager with the essential skill set and knowledge base to meet the challenges faced in contemporary, international, or tech-oriented businesses. It covers the basics of strategy, risk, and technology from the perspective of the security manager, focussing only on the 'need to know'. The reader will benefit from an understanding of how risk management aligns its functional aims with the strategic goals and operations of the organisation.

This essential book supports professional vocational accreditation and qualifications, such as the Chartered Security Professional (CSyP) or Certified Protection Professional (CPP), and advises on pathways to higher education qualifications in the fields of security and risk management. It is ideal for any risk manager looking to further their training and development, as well as being complementary for risk and security management programs with a focus on practice.

Charles Swanson is a professional security and risk management specialist and teacher. He is a Chartered Security Professional, Fellow of the Security Institute, and currently the Senior Tutor on the MSc in Security and Risk Management at the University of South Wales. He has lectured in risk management, counterterrorism, and information security (cyber) to a global audience.

Professional Security Management

A Strategic Guide

Charles Swanson

Routledge
Taylor & Francis Group

LONDON AND NEW YORK

First published 2021
by Routledge
2 Park Square, Milton Park, Abingdon, Oxon OX14 4RN

and by Routledge
52 Vanderbilt Avenue, New York, NY 10017

Routledge is an imprint of the Taylor & Francis Group, an informa business

British Library Cataloguing-in-Publication Data
A catalogue record for this book is available from the British Library

Library of Congress Cataloging-in-Publication Data
Names: Swanson, Charles R., 1942– author.
Title: Professional security management : a strategic guide / Charles Swanson.
Description: Abingdon, Oxon ; New York, NY : Routledge, 2020. | Includes
    bibliographical references and index. | Identifiers: LCCN 2020007320 (print) |
    LCCN 2020007321 (ebook) | ISBN 9780367339616 (hbk) | ISBN
    9780429323065 (ebk)
Subjects: LCSH: Private security services—Management. | Risk management—Planning. |
    Risk managers. | Industries—Security measures.
Classification: LCC HV8290 .S93 2020 (print) | LCC HV8290 (ebook) |
    DDC 658.4/7—dc23
LC record available at https://lccn.loc.gov/2020007320
LC ebook record available at https://lccn.loc.gov/2020007321

ISBN: 978-0-367-33961-6 (hbk)
ISBN: 978-0-429-32306-5 (ebk)

Typeset in Bembo
by Apex CoVantage, LLC

I dedicate this book to two very special ladies, and they are my granddaughters Darcy and Beatrix who have held my heart in their hands since the day they were born. I love you both so much.

Contents

Figures

Tables

Acknowledgements

These acknowledgements are extremely difficult to begin, because since I decided to research and write a book about professional security management, the support I have received has been absolutely overwhelming. My closest friend, John Horrigan, has been urging me to write this book for over ten years, and he has never faulted in his support for my efforts. Thank you John. Another extremely close friend is Dr Stefano de la Salla, who has responded to every email and phone call made, in an effort to ensure that I realised he was always by my side, offering to buy the book before the proposal was accepted. Grazie Stefano. I would like to sincerely thank the following professionals for their total support throughout this project: Andrew Wilson, Doug Cooke, Chris Judge, Di Thomas, Martyn Bird, and all those who took part in the original survey. Of course, central to my efforts has been my wife Elly, without whose total support I would have struggled. Thanks Ell.

Introduction

I have considered writing a book about security management for a number of years, primarily because I was frustrated by the attitudes of non-security personnel, who tend to have a somewhat jaundiced perspective when it comes to security; and security managers, who in my opinion have always been reluctant to stand their corner when it came to defending their profession. Yes, profession, because how can a group of people who devote their careers to the protection of life and reputation not be recognised as professionals?

The problem of course is that security is often a misnomer, a sector that is needed but not wanted; taken for granted, but not fully understood. Nobody, be it public services or private commerce, wants a relationship with security – until when? Yes, you have it; until something goes spectacularly wrong. The closed-circuit television (CCTV) system specified and procured (wrongly) by facilities which after a couple of weeks malfunctions. Who are you going to call? Not Ghostbusters, but of course the security team. The CEO who decides not to follow the ridiculous safety advice given by the security lead (typical security, worrying about the minutiae) when travelling through a hostile environment is kidnapped. Who arranges and managers the kidnap and ransom (K&R) plan? Yep, security!

Frustratingly and unnecessarily, within corporate commerce and industry there are too often levels of subservience by the security manager to other department leads that are incongruous, because (let us argue) the security manager has ten years' experience in the sector, holds an MSc in international security and risk management and an MBA. She is also a chartered security professional, whereas the health and safety manager holds a minor qualification and has been involved in the industry for perhaps five years. The difference here though is board recognition and legislation, because whilst there is a raft of H&S laws in most developed countries, which if broken will mean a term of imprisonment for the perpetrator, there is no equivalent law for security. Whilst the Health and Safety at Work Act (1974) demands an H&S risk assessment for any number of reasons, a security risk assessment is not mandatory; so, the H&S manager tends to have the ear of the board far more acutely than the security manager does.

And of course, beavering away in the background is the criminal or terrorist, armed with the knowledge that there is this political dispute being acted out in the organisation, that the procurement of security systems, by whichever department wins the argument, is likely to be designed and purchased with a certain amount of ego and vanity. The criminal isn't interested in the validity of the site assignment instructions (AI), which are normally out of date anyway. Nor is he or she impressed with the aesthetics of the new batwing access control turnstiles (that allow swipe cards to be used a number of times, because nobody thought of an anti-pass back configuration, or refused to fund such an 'extravagance'). And the professional, seasoned shop thief is unlikely to be overawed by either the bored security officer at the entrance that nobody is taking responsibility for, nor will the thief be deterred by the electronic article surveillance (tagging) barriers, because nobody pays them any attention when they are activated by an expensive dress being moved through the system with a tag attached. "It's OK mate, it's always going off; on you go", says the officer!

Thinking like a criminal

You see, the problem is this: security managers don't think like a criminal. The guy wanting to climb over the perimeter fence unseen isn't interested in the high-tech patrol equipment, which demands that each point has to be interfaced by the security officer during a patrol, meaning the same security officer is only interested in ensuring that all points are 'clocked' in accordance with the AIs, because if they are not, she is in big trouble. So once the burglar is aware that the security officer has touched point number 7 and is on her way to point number 8, he will use that opportunity to breach the perimeter by climbing the fence which he knows is protected by a Perimeter Intruder Detection Systems (PIDS) that has been inoperative for some time, because he has tested reactions to it being struck – and there were no reactions! On looking at the front entrance, our burglar is extremely unlikely to be in fear of the brand new chrome and glass turnstiles, because during a recce he noticed that the batwings when closed are 18 inches from the ground, so he or a slim accomplice can easily slide under them. As for the bored, overweight security officer at the entrance to the shop, the young, fit shoplifter knows that should he be challenged by the guard on the door, there is no way he will be apprehended after a chase. As one shoplifter said to me during a research exercise, on seeing the big guard at the entrance "That fat bastard won't catch me".

So, in many ways the poorly designed and installed security equipment actually attracts the criminal, offering encouragement by virtue of the fact that no thought had been given to the operational requirement, but more importantly, no members of the security team are thinking like him. Whereas they should always be . . . THINKING LIKE A CRIMINAL.

Aims

Formally, the aim of this book is to:

> Examine exactly what is required of the professional security manager in a demanding and fast-changing business-orientated sector.

Informally, in order for the professional security manager to achieve this, he or she needs to critically understand risk and strategic business awareness and should have a good working knowledge of a number of skills required for him or her to carry out their roles professionally in the eyes of their peers and employers. You see, in certain corporate environments – and this is not easy to swallow – the security manager is often seen as no more than a security officer wearing a suit; the person who mans the 'no desk', someone who is believed to be a business disabler as opposed to being capable of supporting business growth. And that has to stop.

Ironically, there are more experienced and qualified security professionals, certainly in the UK, today than ever before. No more than eight years ago, the Security Institute introduced the Register of Chartered Security Professionals (RCSyP), despite negative resistance by disenchanted security colleagues who argued that we were not professional enough to be recognised as chartered. Today there are 138 CSyPs on that register, and the number is growing.

Just a thought

In your opinion, is it more important for a security manager to have a great understanding of the security industry, or to understand management?

Security management

Bamfield, when writing in Gill (2014) about the business of management argues that:

> The management of security, like all management including corporate security teams and security suppliers, covers many tasks and responsibilities: recruiting, training and controlling employees; planning future outcomes; budgeting; setting standards and monitoring performance; interacting with other departments and corporate senior executives; making department policy and strategic corporate wide choices; and working with others outside the corporation, such as law enforcement, local crime prevention bodies and national and international vertical cooperative security groups in the same industry or sector to exchange information and work together to combat risks and losses.

Is that any different to other management functions within an organisation?

Before you begin to read this book, I would like you to take part in a one-to-one challenge.

Take ten minutes or so to give some thought to policing, the private security sector, and the security manager.

Ask yourself the following questions:

1   What roles do the police carry out, particularly in the UK?
2   What roles and responsibilities do the private security sector have? What does that sector do today, in comparison to let's say, 20 years ago?
3   Define the roles and responsibilities of today's security manager (wow).

Prior to being commissioned to write this book, I was in a constant state of flux, never really understanding if this beast referred to as the 'security manager' actually existed. We see job profiles for loss prevention managers, cyber security managers, and security customer and talent relations manager (what?); even the lesser known corporate security compliance manager (wow). However, where in this complicated, dynamic, organic, seismic sector does the good old security manager fit in? It is my considered opinion that we – yes, we – need to identify a role within the security sector that is all-encompassing, understands the business he or she is in, and has the courage and communications expertise to announce and argue the importance of professional security management. There, I've said it now, rant over.

Chapter 1 of the book considers the history and evolution of the private security sector and the development of the security manager.

The first area of the chapter will examine the emergence of policing and law enforcement, primarily in the United Kingdom and the United States. In this section I will explain the introduction of public policing, focussing on the Metropolitan Police Service (MPS) and the influence that force had on policing in the US, which historically ran along similar paths in terms of law enforcement but in reality now bears little resemblance to policing in the UK.

Moving on, we will examine the impact that police number reductions in 2008/09 had on crime and its prevention after a major financial crisis that came close to the beginning of a global depression. This was a period when, depending on who you believe, between 17,500 and 21,000 police posts were slashed whilst crime continued to increase, particularly knife crime, which during the period 2013/14 to 2017/19 grew from 26,000 incidents to over 40,000.

Interestingly, the commissioner of the MPS was inclined to argue that there was a correlation between reduced police numbers and an increase in crime, whilst the government of the time denied such a claim as inaccurate, stating criminal conditions had changed from street crime to cyber offences and a new type of police officer was required. Ironically, during the course of writing this book there was a Conservative Party leadership election, with both candidates promising an increase in police numbers to those available before the credit crunch (so called) in 2008/09. The new Prime Minister Boris Johnson immediately began a police recruitment programme, promising to pay for 20,000 police officers between 2019 and 2022. Interesting.

The chapter will then go on to look at the emergence of the private security sector and the introduction and growth of the private security company (PSC), explaining in detail how PSCs have filled a number of vacuums left by public policing, and how the sector has developed over a very short space of time.

Finally, in this chapter, we will examine the role of the professional security manager.

Chapter 2 will cover security risk management and strategic business awareness. In this chapter we will first examine the results of a survey carried out whilst researching the book, and it will be seen that there are a number of very interesting points of view from security professionals with decades of experience in the sector.

After the survey we will discuss the security professional and his or her role in risk management, and we will examine a number of areas, such as new build projects, travel security, and so forth, where I argue that the security manager and his or her team should be more effectively utilised by the organisation they represent. We will follow this up by arguing that the security manager and the security function must grasp new technology or be left behind. The next area to be examined in this section is how security is involved in crisis management and disaster recovery. Once again we will scrutinise the responses to the survey where respondents are asked for their opinions about the capabilities of the security manager and his or her team in crisis management, and how they believe senior management looks at security in terms of their suitability to sit on the crisis management team.

The chapter will contain research into strategic business awareness and the security manager, answering questions about why security managers are very rarely included in strategic business programs. Here there is information gleaned from a survey carried out by Professor Martin Gill, when he spoke to a number of board directors about their views of security management and its ability or otherwise, to be involved at the highest levels of an organisation (i.e. the executive board of directors). This is probably the most important chapter in the book, because although it is relatively small in terms of word count, it is an absolutely critical area for today's security manager to be conscious of. That is, conscious of the fact that the security sector must be able to demonstrate that it is no longer purely interested in the protection of assets, but it and its cohorts have the ability to, and must be included in overall business objectives, as business enablers, not security officers in suits with a two-dimensional view of business.

Completion of Chapter 2 will be achieved by examining how today, the security function or department must be able to operate, and be seen to operate, as an income generator as opposed to a cost centre.

Chapter 3, is what I have termed critical security areas, and there are seventeen sub-chapters that cover disciplines that I believe all security managers must have at least a good working knowledge of. The chapter will cover the following disciplines:

- Security risk management
- Crime prevention through environmental design and situational crime prevention
- Physical and electronic security systems
- The security survey and security audit
- Business resilience

  - Risk management
  - Crisis management
  - Disaster management
  - Business continuity management

- Physical and information security management
- Cybercrime
- Critical national infrastructure
- Terrorism and counterterrorism
- Aviation and maritime security management
- Supply chain security management
- Hostile environment awareness
- Strategic business awareness
- Fraud investigations
- Retail loss prevention
- Workplace investigations
- Academic and vocational qualifications.

The aim of the chapter is not to naively believe that the book will overnight produce subject matter experts (SMEs) in these seventeen sub-chapters, but there will be sufficient information for the reader to have a competent understanding of the subject and further information which will guide them, for operational and academic purposes, when carrying out research into any of the sub-chapters.

Exercise Brave Defender

At the end of each sub-chapter you will work with Exercise Brave Defender. The exercise will evolve during the course of the book, and at the end of each sub-chapter you will be introduced to a number of confirmatory tasks that will be relevant to the sub-chapter that you have just read. There will be a synopsis which will introduce you to the chapter issues and then a task or set of tasks.

The aim of Brave Defender is to give you the chance to confirm learning from the previous sub-chapter.

Enjoy and learn from this book.

1 Private security and the development of the security manager

Pause for thought

Take a couple of minutes to give some thought to the term 'private security'. What do you believe it means?

Abrahamsen and Williams (2011) ask:

> When you think of private security and international politics, what is the first image that springs to mind? The answers have been remarkably uniform, usually revolving around burly men in combat fatigues, wrap-around sunglasses and automatic weapons.

Notwithstanding this perception, for us to have a sound understanding of the evolution of the private security sector and the development of the security manager, we must first establish the origins of both entities.

Academics, scholars, and practitioners in the fields of policing and security generally agree that there is and has been for some time a symbiotic relationship between public policing and the private security industry, certainly in the United States and the United Kingdom. The first recognised law enforcement agencies consisted of what we now refer to as privately paid security officers. This is almost a 'chicken and egg' situation: what came first, the police officer/law enforcer or the security officer?

I intend to bite the bullet, take the bull by the horns, or whatever other metaphor I can use, by first of all studying the origins of private policing in the United Kingdom and the United States. I will then examine the perceived metamorphosis from public policing to private security before moving on to describe the evolution of the security manager.

Further, I will be arguing throughout the book that the security manager involved in business today has a lot of catching up to do, in terms of strategic business awareness, before they will be accepted by their organisation's peers as professionals.

Whilst writing this book, I delivered a number of level four and five security management training courses in the United Kingdom. Included in the curriculum of all courses was a session devoted to the cost-benefit analysis (CBA), with an emphasis on return on investment (ROI), and whilst I appreciate the fact that this is an anecdotal snapshot, a huge percentage of those UK security managers participating in the training courses had little or no knowledge of either of the two very basic business concepts (CBA and ROI).

Policing and law enforcement

The United Kingdom

There is no intention for this chapter to capture the global history of policing, because although a number of other countries established policing systems in various formats, it is generally agreed that the evolution and development of police provision in the UK from about 1829, when the Metropolitan Police Service was commissioned, was influential in the progression of policing across the US. This is of particular importance as the focus for police evolution throughout this book, and ultimately the development of private security and the rise of the professional security manager will be focussed within the UK and the US.

The first part of this chapter will focus on how British police forces emerged, particularly the Metropolitan Police Service. Once again, for the purpose of this book, the focus will be on the police services of England and Wales, because Northern Ireland and Scotland formed individual police services with circumstances unique to those parts of the United Kingdom.

There are currently 43 police constabularies in England and Wales, with 42 of the 43 forces headed by a chief constable, the exception being the Metropolitan Police which is led by a commissioner of police. According to a House of Commons Briefing Paper (2018) in England and Wales on 31 March 2018, there were 125,651 police officers in England and Wales. This is around the same number as at September 2017. The two largest constabularies today are the Metropolitan Police service (31,088 police officers) and the West Midlands Police (6,581 police officers).

The British police officer, or 'bobby', has always been viewed as different, perhaps a special breed of law enforcement officer, when compared to police officers serving in other countries, significantly in terms of accessibility and defence. As far as recruitment and accessibility are concerned, there are four methods of entry:

1   There is the standard entry route, in which an applicant will attend a number of assessment days, and if found suitable will serve a probationary period of two years.
2   The applicant may be allowed to join the force if he or she holds the professional degree in policing, which will have been achieved before the application stage, then entering the service as a two-year probationer.
3   There is the degree holder entry route, which means that the applicant will be in possession of a bachelor's degree and will be required to serve a two-year probation period.
4   Finally, there is the three-year degree apprenticeship, which means that the probationer will study for his or her degree whilst serving the initial stage of their service.

No British police officer, as a matter of course, other than specialist armed units, carries a weapon during his or her tour of duty.

During a duty shift, a British police officer will be armed with some form of baton, pepper spray and handcuffs, with the option of being trained to use a taser gun (which electrically disables the criminal for a short period) but will not carry a firearm. Interestingly, only law enforcement officers in countries such as the Republic of Ireland, Iceland, New Zealand, and Norway equally do not routinely carry firearms on their person.

The Metropolitan Police Service (MPS)

Policing in London is dynamic, with two powerful (if varying in size) police forces: The Metropolitan Police Service and the City of London Police. Presently they operate with entirely separate and individual strategic aims and objectives.

The Metropolitan Police Service was founded in 1829 by Robert Peel under the Metropolitan Police Act 1829, and on 29 September of that year the first constables of the service appeared on the streets of London. In 1839 the Marine Police Force, which had been formed in 1798, was amalgamated into the Metropolitan Police. In 1837, it also incorporated with the Bow Street Horse Patrol that had been organised in 1805.

In 1999, the organisation was described as "institutionally racist" in the Macpherson Report. Just under 20 years later, police leaders said that this was no longer the case, but that the service would be "disproportionately white" for at least another 100 years.[1]

The Metropolitan Police were directly answerable to the home secretary until the year 2000, when the Metropolitan Police Authority was created (MPA). The Metropolitan Police also had responsibility for the policing of the Royal Dockyards and other military establishments–Portsmouth, Chatham, Devonport, Pembroke, and Woolwich from 1860 until 1934, and Rosyth in Scotland from 1914 until 1926.

It is often argued that because of its ancestry and sheer size, the Metropolitan Police Service has been hugely influential in the development of policing in the United Kingdom, and has also spread that influence abroad, particularly in relation to the evolution of policing in the United States.

The US

The United States inherited England's Anglo-Saxon common law and its system of social obligation, sheriffs, constables, watchmen, and stipendiary justice. As both societies became less rural and agrarian and more urban and industrialised, crime, riots, and other public disturbances became more common. Yet Americans, like the English, were wary of creating standing police forces. Among the first public police forces established in colonial North America were the watchmen, organised in Boston in 1631 and in New Amsterdam (later New York City) in 1647. Although watchmen were paid a fee in both Boston and New York, most officers in colonial America did not receive a salary but were paid by private citizens, as were their English counterparts.

The first police department in the United States was established in New York City in 1844 (it was officially organised in 1845). Other cities soon followed suit: New Orleans and Cincinnati (Ohio) in 1852; Boston and Philadelphia in 1854; Chicago and Milwaukee (Wisconsin) in 1855; and Baltimore (Maryland) and Newark (New Jersey) in 1857. Those early departments all used the London Metropolitan Police as a model. Like the Metropolitan Police, American police were organised in a quasi-military command structure. Their main task was the prevention of crime and disorder, and they provided a wide array of other public services.

Picking up this theme, Spitzer (1979) argues that the development of policing in the United States closely followed the development of policing in England. In the early colonies policing took two forms. It was both informal and communal, which is referred to as the 'Watch', or private-for-profit policing, which is called the 'Big Stick'.

In the United States today there are approximately half a million police officers, and like the UK there is no national police force; rather there are state troopers and local sheriffs.

There are essentially three types of law enforcement agencies in the US: local, state, and federal. Local law enforcement agencies include police and sheriff departments. State agencies include the state or highway patrol. Federal agencies include the FBI and the US Secret Service.

Of course, whilst policing has always been the subject of academic review, for this book it is the foundation for the analysis of the private security sector, intrinsically because both entities have altered their approach and strategic evaluation of policing and security. However, before we move on to look at the development of the private security sector, it is important to examine a particular time when, certainly in the UK and more than likely in other developed countries, when police levels were markedly reduced, with politicians arguing that because crime has changed from the opportunist burglar to the cybercriminal, this reduction was irrelevant.

The UK police post-2008/09

There are constant arguments about why the private security sector has emerged as a contender for the capture of many policing roles believed to be the domain of public law enforcement agencies. Perhaps of relevance is the fact that there are now approximately 232,000 private security officers in comparison to just over 125,000 police officers (reduced from approximately 143,000 police officers in 2010) in the UK, and there are 1.1 million security officers in the US, where 500,000 government law enforcement officers are employed. The Indian government employs 1.4 million police officers, whilst there are 7 million private security officers in existence. This is a trend throughout most industrial countries in the world.

But in terms of the United Kingdom, has this reduction in police numbers impacted crime figures?

The next great recession

Having shrunk by more than 6% between the first quarter of 2008 and the second quarter of 2009, the UK economy took five years to get back to the size it was before the recession.

As the economy got smaller, lots of people lost their jobs and employers stopped hiring. By the end of 2011, almost 2.7 million people were looking for work. The quarterly unemployment rate reached 8.4%, the highest rate since 1995.[2] This of course meant that public services throughout the UK were going to be decimated, and police constabularies in England and Wales were to be unprotected from this perfect financial storm.

How did the recession in the UK impact police numbers, and did the subsequent reduction in police cover have any impact on UK crime figures? Let us take a look at that.

Total police officer strengths in England and Wales increased year-on-year between 2003, when there were 132,000 officers, and 2010, when there were just over 143,000. Since 2010, the number of police officers has fallen each year. On 31 March 2018 there were just 125,651 police officers operating within England and Wales. This was a reduction of 10,000 police officers compared to 2003, and a decrease of just over 17,500 police officers from 2010.

The dark figure of crime

Crime statistics, as announced by the Home Office, on an annual basis consist of offences, designated as crimes, that have been reported to and recorded by the police. There are occasions when a crime may be reported to the police, but it is not recorded, for whatever reason. Of more concern are those instances when a crime is committed, perhaps a husband assaulting his spouse, and for reasons best known to the wife, the attack is not reported to the police.

Criminologists refer to the above as the 'dark figure of crime': criminal acts that are either reported but not recorded, or unreported acts of a criminal nature.

Notwithstanding the dark figure of crime, according to the British Crime Survey (BCS), crime committed during the period 2010/11 was down, with 4.2 million offences being committed, in comparison to 2009/10, when 4.3 million crimes were committed – a reduction of some 4% over the period.

During the period 2016/17, 4.32 million offences were recorded, and by the time figures for 2018 had been collated, 4.89 million crimes had been committed for that period. That reflected an increase of 8.6% in comparison to crimes committed in 2010/11 (4.2 million).[3] See Table 1.1.

Keep in mind the fact that it was 2010 when police officer numbers began to be cut, and from then on there was a relentless increase in annual crime rates throughout the UK. This has been exacerbated over the last five years by the extremely high rate of knife crime. According to the House of Commons Library, in the year ending March 2018 there were around 40,100 (selected) offences involving a knife or sharp instrument in England and Wales. This is the highest number in the eight-year series (from the year ending March 2011), the earliest point for which comparable data are available. Table 1.2 pertains.

Of course, there will naturally be mass speculation about the relationship between knife crime and the reduction in police numbers, with the media leading this particular charge.

Table 1.1 Crime rates during the period 2010 to 2018

2010/11	4.2 million crimes
2016/17	4.32 million crimes
2017/2018	4.89 million crimes

Table 1.2 Knife crime in England and Wales

2013/14	ca. 26,000
2014/15	ca. 26,000
2015/16	ca. 29,000
2016/17	ca. 35,000
2017/18	ca. 40,000

The commissioner of the Metropolitan Police Service, Cressida Dick, was quoted by the BBC on 5 March 2019 as saying "there is 'some link' between falling police numbers and a rise in violent crime", although Ms Dick went no further in attempting to prove her point.

On 1 April 2019, the head of the Police Federation, John Apter, is quoted in the *Independent* as saying that "Theresa May bears personal responsibility for rising violence in Britain after overseeing years of 'unforgivable' cuts to policing".

Quoted in the *Guardian* on 4 March 2019, UK Prime Minister Theresa May argued that "there was 'no direct correlation between certain crimes and police numbers', the former home secretary said. 'What matters is how we ensure that police are responding to these criminal acts when they take place, that people are brought to justice.'"

Home Secretary Sajid Javid argued in response that all police forces must be given the correct tools to combat violent crimes.

History will no doubt write the verdict about police cuts in the UK and the surge in crime figures, but for now we must continue to investigate how this has led – if indeed it has – to the development of the private security sector and the birth of the professional security manager.

The private security sector

It is impossible to argue definitively when public policing relinquished the reins of so many critical tasks, or indeed when the private security sector took on the perceived mantle of a 'private policing agency'. However, it is difficult to ignore the fact that the private security sector now carries out a significant number of duties that were once the realm and responsibility of public police forces. In this chapter we will examine the change in the balance of public and private security responsibilities using case studies and historic emphasis to support such arguments.

However, it isn't as simple as merely attempting to describe this transition as though it was a smooth extrapolation from public to private policing; rather we need to examine current arguments about the transformation before we move on to examine historical and global connotations of this critical movement of policing responsibilities.

Key to these discussions are the debates surrounding public safety and the community policing role that is seen to be critical in terms of establishing credibility in the eyes of the population. Today, despite (or perhaps because of) the recent brutal dismantling of constabularies by government, the importance of the 'bobby on the beat' still lies at the heart of community policing. It is difficult to persuade the public at large that policing, in terms of reduced numbers, has had to change in accordance with the dynamics of criminal activity.

Despite the fact that the perception of policing in the US, the UK, and Europe has altered over the years, there is still the vision of a uniformed force either walking the beat or carrying out mobile patrols in the community.

To the average person in the street, probably the most common forms of crime committed are domestic burglary, car theft, and street robbery; perhaps today there is more of a likelihood that credit card fraud and identity theft are a little more commonplace than they were 10 to 15 years ago.

However, to the majority of people, certainly in the UK, the likelihood of being the victim of any form of cybercrime (with the exception of card fraud and identity theft) is minimal, because they don't see themselves as being legitimate cyber targets.

The argument is that cybercriminals attack banks, whilst cyberterrorists target critical infrastructure and the military. So there is still a need for community policing, as banks and the military are able to, and should, protect their assets.

Leishman et al. (2000) in Abrahamsen and Williams (2011) argue that the police in many countries have had to adapt to the demands of the 'new managerialism' and strategies of new public management for cost efficiency, results, and effectiveness. Public-private policing partnerships have proliferated, and the widespread adoption of community policing is in large part a response to such pressures. A key tenet of community policing is the mobilisation of private actors in policing. The strategy was clearly articulated in the British government's 2001 statement, Criminal Justice: The Way Ahead:

> There has always been a wide range of people contributing to community safety in various forms. These include park keepers (some with constabulary powers), security guards in shopping centres, car park attendants, neighbourhood wardens, night club bouncers and the private security industry (of course it should be argued that night club Door Supervisors are part of the security industry). The issue for policing is how these various activities can be coordinated to make the most effective contribution to making safer communities.

Of course, the transition from public policing to private security responsibilities hasn't been a leap of faith (well, not totally). There have been several initiatives aimed at the release of semi-public duties to the private sector.

Private security companies (PSC)

Case study – the growth and influence of the private security company

Scenario:

Picture the scene. An inner-city park, somewhere in the UK, which during the weekend, is usually busy with family's making the most of time and space, youngsters playing football, and these days, a multitude of runners competing in the weekly 'park run'.

A couple are witnessed arguing with raised voices adjacent to the lake, and the male is seen to strike the female with some form of weapon, perhaps a piece of iron, three times to the head. She falls to the ground, and he makes his escape. A young boy, 15 years of age, who saw everything calls 999; an ambulance and the police are despatched to the scene. On arrival, the paramedics confirm that the woman has died because of her head wounds, and we are now in a full-blown murder investigation.

At this stage, the scene and the incident are 100% the responsibility of the emergency services, but all that is about to change.

Of course, the priority is the removal of the corpse; however, after that any evidence at what is now a scene of crime must be protected before being processed for onward transmission to the forensic science laboratory. The two police officers who have been despatched to make initial investigations don't have the luxury of hanging around waiting for scientific support, so they are replaced by a single police community support officer (PCSO), whose sole responsibility is to protect the crime scene.

A representative of the police Scientific Support Team, a retired police scenes of crime officer (SOCO) who is now employed as a civilian scenes of crime officer, arrives at the scene to process and remove all evidence pertinent to the offence, leaving the PCSO to tidy up the area.

Investigations begin, and the case file is handed over to a former police detective, who is now a civilian police investigator. There is sufficient forensic evidence available at the scene, and there are a number of witnesses who are prepared to sign statements in which they describe the assailant with great detail. He is a local guy who is well known, and it isn't very long before the suspect is located and arrested for murder.

The arrested person – let's call him John Beck – is taken to a police station where he is processed by a civilian administrator before being placed in a police cell awaiting trial the following day. During his short incarceration within the police station, he is observed by two civilian detention officers before he is transported in a private security company vehicle the following day, escorted by two security officers. Once inside the court, he is escorted and detained by another couple of civilian detention officers.

He is found guilty by a jury of 'twelve good men and true' (mixed gender, of course), and he is sentenced by a court judge. He is once again transported in a private security company vehicle to a private prison, where John Beck is incarcerated for 15 years, during which time it is likely that he will be guarded by civilian prison officers.

From the moment he committed the crime of murder to the day he is released from Her Majesty's Prison (HMP), John Beck will have interacted with a public servant (the police officer who arrested him) once!

So, let's look at the rise and rise of the private security sector.

Over the years there have been a number of private security companies claiming to have been 'first in class': companies such as ADT, who were originally a cable delivery firm, and Brinks Home Security, who first of all delivered their business model through transportation. Both of these companies have diversified significantly in an effort to remain active in the private security sector. Today ADT is recognised as probably the largest electronic security systems provider in the world, specialising in intruder detection and central monitoring systems (IDCMS). Brinks employs about 165,000 people in over 100 locations worldwide.

By far the largest private security company (PSC) today is G4S, with a worldwide footprint of over 100 countries, currently employing about 585,000 people.

G4S was founded in Denmark in 1901 and was shortly to be known as Group 4 Falk (as in Falcon). By the year 2000, the company was recognised worldwide as the largest private security company, dealing in manned guarding and predominantly electronic security systems. In 2006, the group was re-branded originally as Group 4 Securitas, but then once again re-branded, and today the company is known as G4S.

The growth of the company has been phenomenal, and in 2018, G4S generated a revenue of £7,289 million – an increase of 1.1% since trading in 2017, showing a continuous growth vector.

The 2012 London Olympics

However, despite stable financial growth, G4S has been plagued with operational problems, perhaps because the business grew so quickly, and the senior management teams failed to develop resources in line with growth. Over the years there have been numerous examples of companies failing to manage business growth in line with customer expectations, but probably none with a higher profile than security at the London Olympics in 2012.

Depending on the resources available for research, it appears that G4S made a commitment, and won the contract to provide a workforce of some 10,000 personnel to manage security and risk at the 2012 Olympic Games in London.

On 11 July 2012, only 11 days before the Olympics were due to begin, G4S announced that the company was unable to provide the full complement of security personnel as agreed in the contract, and it was likely that a maximum of 7,000 G4S employees would be available. The London Organising Committee of the Olympic Games (LOCOG) would have to look elsewhere to ensure the safety of 10,500 athletes and potentially 8.8 million spectators (that was the number of tickets sold). Fortunately, the British Ministry of Defence (MOD), after trawling through UK resources, were able to provide and deploy just over 3,500 soldiers, sailors, and airmen. The games were safe, which was more than could be said for the brand and reputation of G4S.

Whilst the ultimate aim of this chapter is to examine the unique relationship between public police and the private sector, primarily in the US and the UK, we must first of all examine the phenomenon referred to as the private security company (PSC).

The term 'PSC' has largely been related to in terms of international organisations that have thrived in war-torn areas such as Central Africa, Iraq, and Afghanistan, where they have regularly been referred to (mostly inaccurately) as mercenaries. Generally, armed PSCs have stepped in to fill the void where local warlords, in the case of Central Africa, or post-war conflict governments in Iraq and Afghanistan have needed armed support from experienced and organised former soldiers.

However, the term as read in the US and the UK is not translated as such a militaristic phenomenon. During this chapter, we will examine a number of areas where the private security sector has been influential and has to a certain extent created a pathway and a niche, seemingly unrivalled by the public sector.

Below are a number of sectors in which the PSC has grown.

- *Manned guarding and technical security systems*

  As mentioned earlier, there are approximately 232,000 security officers in the UK, but that number represents security officers holding a Security Industry Authority (SIA) licence, which all contract front-line security officers are obliged to do. However, it is worthy of note that organisations, mainly in the corporate sectors, such as banking, accountancy, and so forth often prefer to employ their own security officers rather than outsource to a contract security company. There are a number of reasons for this preference, such as accountability, more efficient communications, and so on, but the main reason is that such organisations, particularly banking, require loyalty and integrity. It is often argued that outsourcing, which is perhaps the easiest option because the officers are managed by a third party, does not bring with it loyalty to the client in the same way that pay as you earn (PAYE) does.

  The range of responsibilities covered by security officers bears no resemblance to those handled 10 or 20 years ago, when the most important duty carried out by a security officer or guard might have been raising the front barrier, or perhaps patrolling a construction site.

  Security officers will still be responsible for access control, but it is likely to be from a security control room where all systems are electronic. He or she may still patrol internally and externally, but they will be augmented and supported by CCTV and patrol management systems. Whilst on duty, the security officer may be responsible for operating and managing advanced electronic alarm systems, such as intruder detection systems (IDS), automatic access control systems (AACS), and CCTV, all of which are likely to be computer based, which the security officer will also use to send and receive emails, or sign in to the company intranet. How things have changed.

- *Security technology*

  Remaining on the theme of security technology, it is probably safe to say that electronic systems have begun to dominate the security sector, with the vast majority of organisations relying on such systems as CCTV, access control and IDS. We will deal with the descriptions and specifications of physical and electronic security technology later in the book, but for now I would like to conditionally explore an area that perhaps may be the subject of another book, and that covers the argument about the possibility of security technology replacing physical manned guarding.

Pause for thought

In your opinion, will security technology ever replace physical manned guarding?

I have asked this question on numerous occasions, in a variety of environment and diverse cultural teaching facilities, always to security personnel, and generally with a resounding "No chance. What can a system do that a security officer can't?"

The problem here is that it is often a self-defence mechanism, almost going into denial to make a decision which isn't based on evidence. My answer to such stubborn resistance is to ask my students to stop and think about the advancement of technology, and instead of seeing it as an enemy, believe that it can be an ally. As I write this book, it is only 70 years since the first single camera CCTV system was used, which was developed to observe Nazi rockets being deployed to attack the UK. Today we have CCTV, though analytics is almost in a position to learn from its own mistakes and forecast movement before it occurs. Swipe cards, which went some way in replacing keys, were invented in 1970, and their total level of operation was to open doors – no more, no less. We have microwave perimeter intruder detection systems (PIDS), and radio frequency identification (RFID) chips implanted in our cats and dogs in the event they stray from home. We have RFID tags embedded in high-value products in the hope that they will be detected before leaving the store if stolen.

However, we still need security officers to monitor CCTV, security officers to investigate a breach of the perimeter, and security officers to intervene when an RFID alarm activates at the main entrance to Sainsbury's or Marks and Spencer.

Contrary to the preceding argument is the use of security officers or receptionists at front of house. It has been a common site when entering a business address to see a receptionist waiting to help you, sometimes aided by a security officer. However, certainly in the UK we are now seeing buildings, particularly in business parks, where there is no receptionist or security officer; rather as the visitor enters the building on the ground floor he or she will be met by a desk supporting a telephone, accompanied by a directory. The visitor will call the appropriate number, and will be put through to the person they are visiting, and he or she will descend to the ground floor where they will issue a visitor's badge and act as a host for the remainder of time that the visitor is on the premises. No need for either a receptionist or security officer, who in fact at that time will be monitoring the CCTV system and PIDS alarms, or may be on patrol using a patrol management RFID system.

So the question isn't as straightforward as it seems, but what is irrefutable is the fact that certain systems will take the place of security officers, but we have no idea about what that will take nor when it will happen.

- *Private maritime security companies (PMSC)*

On 1 July 2004, a piece of maritime legislation, primarily driven by the US, was internationally accepted, and the impact was felt throughout the global maritime community.

The International Maritime Organisation (IMO), defined this new regulation on its website, saying that:

The International Ship and Port Facility Code (ISPS Code) is a comprehensive set of measures designed to enhance the security of ships and port facilities, developed in response to the perceived threats to ships and port facilities in the wake of the 9/11 attacks in the United States. . . . in essence the Code takes the approach that ensuring the security of ships and port facilities is a risk management activity and that to determine what security measures are appropriate, an assessment of the risks must be made in each particular case.

(Berube and Cullen, 2012)

As the IMO explanation briefly mentions, the ISPS Code – after being discussed as a Resolution of the Conference of Contracting Governments to the International Convention for the Safety of Life at Sea (SOLAS), 1974, which was adopted during an IMO conference in London in December 2002 – was introduced as a direct result of the horrific terrorist attacks carried out by al-Qaeda on 11 September 2001. Consequently, the fear, which was not supported by any credible evidence was that al-Qaeda, having been so successful in attacking the Twin Towers, would perhaps next time turn their attention to a high-profile maritime target.

Fears were rampant of a cruise liner being attacked with resulting mass causalities, or perhaps a liquid natural gas (LNG) tanker being hijacked and used as a weapon, or a floating oil rig being attacked and destroyed. It was this fear that justified the introduction of the ISPS Code.

So you are probably now thinking, what on earth has this to do with private security?

Before answering that question, we will continue to examine the ISPS Code and how it developed.

The ISPS Code is part of Safety of Life at Sea (SOLAS), so compliance is mandatory for the 148 contracting parties to SOLAS – and bearing in mind the financial strength of one of the major signatories, the US, what state can afford not to agree to the terms and conditions of the ISPS Code?

The Code sets out strict guidelines for risk-based security of the following types of ships engaged on international voyages:

- Passenger ships, including high speed passenger craft
- Cargo ships, including high speed craft of 500 gross tonnage and upwards.

The Code also applies to:

- Mobile offshore drilling units.
- All port facilities serving such ships engaged on international voyages.[4]

In relation to management and governance of the Code, the onus is on what is referred to in the Code as the contracting government – nation states – to ensure that all vessels sailing under the flag of that government and all port facilities servicing those ships must meet the standards of the Code.

In essence that means that all ships and port facilities applying for ISPS Code certification must be risk assessed and surveyed (Ship Security Assessment (SSA) and Port Facility Security Assessment (PFSA), and as the result of the assessment and survey process, those vessels that meet the required standard will be awarded an International Ship Security Certificate (ISSC), with corresponding port facilities being certificated to trade by the contracting government.

The result of the SSA and PFSA inevitably mean that risk treatment measures such as physical security systems, electronic security measures, and manned guarding security have to be purchased and installed on board vessels and at port facilities.

Added to this is the fact that all shipping lines deploying ISPS Code–certificated ships must employ at least one company security officer (CSO) for their fleet, and all vessels sailing with that line must employ a ship security officer (SSO), normally the ship's master or the chief engineer. Equally, every port facility, in accordance with the Code, must employ a port facility security officer (PFSO), who will generally report to either the captain of the port or the port authority.

None of this is free, so of course the first question asked by governments and shipping lines after the introduction of the ISPS Code was, "Who exactly is going to pay for the extra security measures required to meet the standards of this Code?"

Using the UK as an example, the government at Westminster, through the Maritime and Coastguard Agency (MCGA), made it very clear indeed that ports, port facilities, and shipping lines, as commercial operators, would be 100% responsible for the procurement and installation of all ISPS Code mandated security measures.

So, by the time the Code was introduced on 1 July 2004, there was the potential for global maritime turmoil and pandemonium. Also, this was an opportunity for forward-thinking PMSCs to move quickly to fill a vacuum, because national governments had neither the resources nor the enthusiasm to carry out this extra workload. However, the threat to the maritime community was real, and a mere three years earlier, the world had been traumatised by 9/11, and in 2003/04, the global maritime community was beginning to witness the embryonic establishment of piracy in the Straits of Malacca and around the waters of Somalia.

Added to this threat was the polemic potential for a relationship being struck between up-and-coming piracy groups and terrorist organisations such as al-Shabaab, with nation state governments announcing to shipping lines and port authorities that liability for safe and secure ships and ports was the total responsibility of the commercial maritime organisations.

It could therefore be argued that 9/11 was the catalyst, not only for critical aviation and maritime security adjustments, but it was also perhaps the birth of private maritime security management on a scale never measured prior to that horrendous and never forgotten day in 2001.

The introduction of private maritime security companies

As mentioned earlier, the ISPS Code demands the contracting government take ownership of the codes of governance for shipping lines and port facilities within its sphere of influence. This of course relates to the fact that the contracting government must ensure that all certificated commercial organisations and companies under its jurisdiction meet the rigorous standards of risk management within the Code. That in turn means that all SSAs and PFSAs must be carried out under the auspices of the contracting government; and that presents an almighty problem for said governments, because they are of course public institutes with limited resources in terms of technical expertise and financial capacity (they would have us believe!). Enter the recognised security organisation (RSO).

An RSO is defined as a private organisation with appropriate expertise in security and anti-terrorism matters recognised by the administration (contracting governments) and authorised by it to carry out assessment, verification, approval, and certification activities, required by SOLAS Chapter XI-2 or by Part A of the ISPS Code, on its behalf.

So of course, in the early days of ISPS Code implementation, private companies such as Lloyds, MUSC, and others were extremely quick to realise that this was an absolutely massive business opportunity, and as the result of the 2002 conference in London they were successfully vying for ISPS Code contracts on a global scale. This really was the beginning of private maritime security company involvement, which was later to evolve to a situation where a significant percentage of merchant vessels sailing in high risk areas would be carrying, as part of the ship's company, a detachment of trained armed guards to protect the vessel and its crew against the threat of piracy.

Somalia

Murphy (2011, 1) says that according to the International Maritime Bureau (IMB), the commercially funded organisation that maintains what are generally recognised as the most reliable piracy statistics – the number of attacks off Somali – had by 2006 grown to such an extent that they exceeded those for any other state, for the first time since their records began in 1991.

Somalian piracy probably hit its peak around 2009, primarily as the result of a number of high-profile hijackings, the most prominent being the takeover of the Maersk *Alabama* on 8 April. The *Alabama* is a container vessel, formerly known as the MV *Tygra*, and with a full complement of officers and crew she was held until 20 April, when she was freed after a raid by the US navy.

Although the ship's crew navigated the vessel in a defensive pattern for three hours, combating the pirates with the use of high-pressure water hoses (versus Kalashnikov AK-47s!), the vessel was eventually boarded by the pirates and a hostage situation ensued. On 12 April 2009, US Navy Seals boarded the *Alabama*, killing three pirates, taking one alive, and rescuing the crew.

The waterborne attack against the *Alabama* by pirates off the coast of Somalia was certainly not the first of its kind, but from political and media perspectives it was the highest-profile piracy incident in Somali waters.

Why was this allowed to happen? Where was the navy?

Of course, in an ideal world, navies belonging to nation states such as the UK or US would have Royal Navy and US navy fleets here, there, and everywhere if there was any intelligence of hostile maritime activity. However, for a number of reasons, notwithstanding cost, national naval forces cannot involve themselves in the territorial waters of another state unless requested to do so.

Snoddon in Lehr (2011) argues that there is no doubt that navies such as the Royal Navy and the US Navy would assist in apprehending pirates, providing that it happened on the high seas and not in territorial waters. If the incident is one of maritime armed crime and taking place in littoral waters, then there is no legal precedent or authority for these navies to get involved. The Royal Navy is committed to providing support to any vessel which may be subject to pirate attack. However, this commitment does not allow for hot pursuit into the territorial waters of any nation. So unless there is activity outside territorial waters, international naval bodies are somewhat restricted in their defensive activities.

Pause for thought

What is meant by the term 'cybercrime'?

- *Cyber*

  In the United Kingdom, the government is reliant on the Government Communications Headquarters (GCHQ) and the National Cyber Security Centre (NCSC) to protect the population and business from cyberattacks. In the US, the reliance is on the National Cyber Security Division (NCSD), whilst in the European Union, member states, even though they have their own centres, are covered by the European Cyber Security Organisation (ECSO). Certainly, in the UK, the resources and outreach of GCHQ and the NCSC are restricted to the protection of national critical infrastructures, whilst also to the best of their abilities offering advice and guidance to commerce and industry. However, even the advice offered is restricted, so private industry must be in a position to defend its own interests; to that end, the security manager is critical. Today there are myriad cybersecurity qualifications, such as certified information systems security professional, information systems security architecture professional, and so on. The onus is on the security manager to make a determined effort to understand exactly where he or she sits in terms of cyber security, whilst employers must offer the maximum level of support for the security team that leads the fight against cybercrime and even cyberterrorism.

- *Supply chain security*

  The global supply chain today is referred to as the intermodal supply chain, which refers to the fact that products are moved around the globe by air, sea, and land. Whether the information technology (IT) component produced in China, with the destination being London, is moved by air or sea, with perhaps supplementary movement on land in the UK, it will be a purely private operation. It may be flown on a FedEx aircraft or a Maersk container vessel before being moved by container vehicles on UK motorways. There will be no government involvement, with of course the exception of border controls.

- *Intelligence*

  Once the domain of national military and security service authorities, there is now a greater involvement of private intelligence agencies than ever before.

  In an article titled 'The Era of the Private Intelligence Agencies', Ioannis Michaletos (2009) says that private intelligence services are non-state actors involved in the sector of intelligence and are primarily collecting and analysing information by outsourcing public funding and by providing assistance to large multinationals.

  In recent years, and after the terrorist attacks of 9/11 in the US, individuals have gained wide access to government services as subcontractors and partners and now operate a very important part of the funds available for the 'War against terrorism'. In quite a few cases, the same companies and agencies are recruiting mercenaries and generally provide a trend towards the formation of ultra-companies that undertake public roles globally in the crucial field of security and information.

  Currently a large number of companies offer intelligence services, and some of them have acquired considerable influence.

  Most of these organisations are based in the US, Britain, and Australia and are staffed by knowledgeable employees of the intelligence apparatus who retire seeking work in the private sector, which in general provides high fees. Due to the strong turnover growth in recent years, there has been large-scale recruitment of individuals that possess enviable skills as well as other collaborators from all walks of life and professions.

  It should be noted that in recent years the private institutions are outsourcing key areas such as recruitment and training of the personnel. Generally it can be assumed that the dividing lines between the state and the business world have blurred to a great extent over the past few years. Clearly the 9/11 attacks have revolutionised the manner by which intelligence operations have being conducted since.

Cussack, McNight, and McPhereson, writing in the *Harvard Business Review* (2010), examine the relationship between public and private security agencies and companies, with the emphasis being on what public and national intelligence agencies can learn from the private sector.

Since 9/11, the need for increased collaboration and information sharing within the military and intelligence communities has become a constant requirement. As marine intelligence officers in Iraq and then as analysts at national-level security organisations, each of us has directly witnessed failures caused by weak communication and poor information sharing practices. These experiences have pushed us to look to the private sector to understand how the military can most effectively leverage innovation in information collection, management, and analysis to support the national security mission.

These three former intelligence officers argue that there are two illustrative areas where the private sector is needed:

- *Failure to share information*

  The flow of intelligence information is generally poor between insular military units with overlapping mandates and between military and civilian intelligence organisations. Even knowing where to find information is tough and time-consuming. It is frustrating how often analysts who have been working on a particular region or target for long periods of time will come across new information that they did not know existed because there is minimal interaction between two different organisations.

- *Failure to identify and hold accountable the relevant centres of expertise*

  Right now, hundreds of analysts are churning out virtually identical slides and memos for their respective bosses within the 16 intelligence agencies and the 10 military combatant commands. When things go wrong, the blame is easy to diffuse because so many different people in many different places *could* have caught the problem. Duplication dilutes responsibility. Additionally, during our time in civilian security organisations we sometimes observed senior analysts treat solving a complex puzzle with real national security implications like an academic exercise.[5]

A recent publication from the University of St Andrews says that according to a *New York Times* article, 70% of the US intelligence budget now goes to private sector intelligence companies – making it a $56 billion a year industry. In the US alone, 500,000 private contract workers currently have top-secret security clearance.

This is a relatively new phenomenon and does not hold true in the UK to that degree. Most people spend many years working in intelligence in the public sector, including typical agencies such as the CIA or MI6 but also military or police operations, before transferring to the private sector. Many private firms were actually established by retirees from the public sector. It's now common for public sector agencies to contract out of a lot of the work they used to accomplish in-house to private consultants. The private sector can also often offer higher compensation than government jobs on average – a heady temptation to successful public sector employees.

The private intelligence sector can be harder to break into than public intelligence. Private intelligence operators either originate from the armed forces, some other recognised public service, or the banking sector.

- *Executive protection*

  Private executive protection, sometimes referred to as close protection, is one of the major growth areas in the private security sector. There are a number of reasons for this, but it is primarily to meet the following criteria:

  - VIPs

    With police services, not only in the UK, but certainly in the US and Europe being particularly stretched in terms of manpower and resources, it is impossible for them to offer protection to non-governmental principals.

    Non-governmental principals (as VIPs are known), may be corporate chief executives, or perhaps pop stars or even footballers may be required to hire some form of protection, depending on individual circumstances. Perhaps the CEO of a corporation is carrying out a visit in what intelligence calls a hostile area, and his or her security advisor has counselled the CEO to accept a certain level of protection; that may include his family coming under the same protection umbrella. In the UK, such protection would entail an unarmed team of executive or close protection officers accompanying the principal, perhaps on a 24/7 basis, dependent upon the threat.

  - Government officers

    In war-torn regions such as Iraq or Syria, there may be a requirement for private close protection to accompany a government official or minister if local military forces in situ cannot guarantee their safety. Under those conditions, and in accordance with local laws and regulations the close protection team will be armed, and are very likely to consist of former soldiers, perhaps special forces because of their levels of professionalism. They will of course be restricted to national rules of engagement (ROE).

- *Criminal detection*

  The Pinkerton National Detective Agency, was founded by Allan Pinkerton, a native of Scotland who emigrated to the USA in 1850, where he became a police officer in Illinois. Pinkerton really had no idea in which direction his career was moving until he began Pinkerton, initially and tentatively involving himself in theft investigations, but later his company moved into the area of executive protection where it thrived.

  In the UK there has never been an equivalent of Pinkerton, although private investigators existed long before the beginning of the twentieth century. What is interesting about the evolution of private security in terms of criminal detection, certainly in the UK, is the recent use of civilian detectives in police services and constabularies. Once again, because of the austerity measures introduced in 2010, a number of police forces in England and Wales began to decrease the levels of detective investigators, finding it more cost-effective to make current roles redundant, whilst recruiting the former detectives, who were now receiving a pension, at a lower salary. Apparently, that was seen as a win–win all round.

The development of the security manager

Pause for thought

What is the core responsibility of a security manager?

Management

Before we begin to examine the roles and responsibilities of the security manager, we need first of all to study what is known as classical management theory, because whether a person manages a security function or a human resources (HR) department, the skills of classical management are required. The intention of this section is not to deliver an essay on the history of classical management theory, rather it is to emphasise the importance of effective management, and that of course applies to the security sector.

The Cambridge Dictionary defines management simply as "the control and organization of something".

Fayol (1916) in Cole (1997) argues that "To manage is to forecast and plan, to organise, to command, to coordinate and to control".

These clinical definitions serve as a good foundation for understanding the general approach to management, but what makes a good manager stand out? Or rather, what makes an effective manager?

Pause for thought

Think of the managers you may have encountered during your career and write down the name of your most and least favoured managers. Then take a little time to describe, from your perspective, what was good and perhaps not so good about two managers.

The definition of an effective security manager is provided by Sennewald and Baillie (2015): a person who can create an environment conducive to the proper performance of acts by others to achieve personal as well as company goals.

Management is not an activity that exists in its own right. It is rather a description of a variety of activities carried out by those members of organisations whose role is that of a 'manager', that is someone who has formal responsibility for the work of one or more persons in the organisation, or who is accountable for specialist advisory duties in support of key management activities. These activities have generally been grouped in terms of planning, organising, motivating, and controlling activities. These groupings describe activities which indicate broadly what managers do in practice, primarily in terms of their inputs. They apply to supervisory and junior management positions as well as to middle and senior management roles.

The groupings of management activities can be summarised as follows:

- *Planning*

  Deciding the objectives or goals of the organisation and preparing how to meet them.

- *Organising*

  Determining activities and allocating responsibilities for the achievement of plans; coordinating activities and responsibilities into an appropriate structure.

- *Motivating*

  Meeting the social and psychological needs of employees in the fulfilment of organisational goals.

- *Controlling*

  Monitoring and evaluating activities and providing corrective mechanisms (Cole, 1997).

Security management

Security management is a field of study and practical application that has developed particularly over the last three decades or so, and in my opinion it is neither fully understood nor appreciated. I suspect if a cross section of security practitioners were asked to define security management, the answer would be something like, "Security management is the practice of ensuring the safety of the assets belonging to an organisation". If you were to challenge the same cohort to categorise the said assets, they would likely be as follows:

- People
- Property
- Infrastructure
- Information and data
- Finance
- Brand and reputation.

The core responsibility of the security manager is to ensure that all of the above are safe and secure from attack.

Alternatively, if academics and scholars in the field were asked to define security management, I believe the explanation would revolve around the following statement:

> Security management is reliant on the underpinning theory of criminological studies and has to involve a strategic appreciation of all risks to the organisation, particularly inclined towards an understanding of all business operations. It is not merely crime prevention, locks and security officers.

This may sound like an obvious response, but I believe that the current professional security manager must have the skills to ensure that the organisation's assets are secure, and that he or she is competent in relation to understanding the business operations of the company that employs them, or the public establishment that they represent. But what does this professional security manager look like?

The cultural debate

In 1993, Dr (now Professor) Martin Gill, Adrian (now Emeritus Professor) Beck, and Ken Livingstone (not the former Mayor of London) introduced what was to be the beginning of academic recognition of the security industry in the United Kingdom. The Centre for the Study of Public Order (later to be the Scarman Centre, named after Lord Scarman) at the University of Leicester began delivering a master of science (MSc) degree in security management and IT. This was an absolute revelation, for several reasons.

In the first instance, the vast majority of security management positions were held by former police officers or members of the armed forces who generally left a particular service with little or no academic qualification, but based on military and police training sold themselves on their organisational and communications skills (I certainly did!). Of course, this was a very attractive proposition for security employers in the late twentieth century, because in the main security managers were expected to supervise a security workforce, generally consisting of a number of untrained security guards, and guarantee the security of the client's premises from those with criminal intent. Easy.

But, in effect, Gill et al. created an uproar because they had the audacity to suggest – no, argue – that security managers in the 1990s needed to be fluent in criminology, workplace crime, and of course IT. This gallant triumvirate also offered those with no formal academic qualifications but an ability to research and write the opportunity to study at a level never envisaged before. This was either going to end in tears or change the face of the security industry in the UK, and later on a global perspective for good. Thankfully, as it turned out, the bravado of the three academics, supported by an extremely forward-looking educational institute, introduced a new breed of security manager not reliant on little black books and contact banks. Neither was the former regimental sergeant major or chief inspector reliant upon shouting and cajoling their workforce; rather they were expected to pay attention to service delivery and customer awareness. Wow!

Prior to this game change, employers, as stated, would hire former soldiers and police officers because 'they got things done'. However, what was becoming apparent was that such security managers had a shelf life; they could only call on favours and (illegally) use the Police National Computer (PNC) for so long. After that, what use were they?

Another issue that business was beginning to recognise was the fact that soldiers and policemen (yes, once again, predominantly men!) may understand security (although that was debatable), but they failed to recognise the importance of the culture of the business that they were about enter and support.

The MSc, on the other hand, taught students the importance of understanding why crime was committed, and how this impacted on the organisational culture of the company employing them. The students were taught the rudimentary elements of IT and IT security, such as being able to interrogate databases and construct spreadsheets – skills never envisaged before this degree.

So here we had the perfect storm. A university that was prepared to re-educate a cohort unprepared for this step change in their employment skills, and an industry arguing that this new breed of security managers was not only needed, but critically, the culture of the security industry had to change, and change quickly.

Today there are a number of universities in the UK and elsewhere in the world, predominantly the US, offering security related qualifications, such as risk, crisis and disaster management; international security and risk management; corporate security and cyber awareness, and so on. There are more security managers holding academic qualifications, certainly in the UK and the US than ever before, ranging from bachelor's degrees to doctoral status.

Gone are the days (hopefully) when the security manager was purely responsible for the security of assets belonging to a corporate entity, whilst writing guard rosters and ensuring that staff were wearing their ID cards around their necks. In the twenty-first century, the professional security manager has to stand equal to his peers in other functions, conscious of the fact that the security team within an organisation is of critical importance not only for ensuring the safety of an organisation's assets but also for being pivotal in the business growth of the company. In Chapter 2 we are going to examine exactly how the professional security manager should immerse himself or herself in all forms of business operations, risk management, and strategic awareness.

Notes

1 https://en.wikipedia.org/wiki/Metropolitan_Police_Service, accessed on 24 January 2020.
2 The Office for National Statistics (ONS) April 2018. www.ons.gov.uk.
3 Home Office Statistical Bulletin (HOSB: 10/11); Chapple, Flatly and Smith (2011).
4 ISPS Code (2003) International Maritime Organisation (IMO).
5 https://hbr.org/2010/11/intelligence-failure-what-the.

2 Security risk management and strategic business awareness

Pause for thought

In your opinion, why is it important for today's security manager to have a good working knowledge of risk management, and why does he or she need to be business aware?

In Chapter 1 we focussed on policing and the relationship between public law enforcement agencies and private security companies. We examined the development of the private security sector, and we analysed those areas where it appears that private security has taken over or at least become more involved in a number of roles that were previously the domain of public police forces. We then went on to discuss the roles and development of the security manager. In this chapter we will first concentrate on security risk management and then examine the role of the security manager from a strategic business perspective.

However, before we look at those two extremely critical areas of security management, it is worth mentioning that prior to the commencement of this book, I carried out a qualitative survey to try to understand how security managers see themselves and where they fit into the business which they support. The respondents to the survey are all currently employed in some form of security business–related role, with a high percentage having achieved a security and risk management related academic qualification. The sectors involved are international communications; cyber management; commerce; and retail and public services.

During the survey, the following ten questions were asked with an extremely varied and interesting snapshot of the responses received.

1   Are you involved in security management in any form, and if so, in what capacity?

   All recipients of the survey are currently involved in security management. Predominantly employed in either a middle or senior management position.

2   If you answered in the affirmative to the previous question, how long have you been involved in security management?

The average length of time served in the security management arena is 28 years.

3   In your opinion, what are the five most important skills that a security manager should possess?

Quotes:

- Business acumen, customer orientation, *effective communication*, organisation skills, *servant leadership*.[1]
- Knowledge and skills including qualifications in security management, basic level training and licensing, that is SIA, management ability and good commercial understanding, crisis management and media training, *very good IT and communication skills*.
- Observation, *communication* (including listening!), empathy, creativity, and versatility.
- Leadership skills, *written and verbal communication skills*, security functions (one CSO), that is physical, cyber, investigations, intelligence, resilience, good listener, good emotional intelligence levels.
- General management/leadership, understanding the business of his enterprise, agility in terms of flexibility and openness for change, assertiveness, risk management.

This was a particularly interesting response, as 80% argued that effective communications are critical.

4   What advantages/disadvantages are there when employing former police/military officers as security managers?

Quotes:

The military bring a huge amount of experience and knowledge to the Security function, but they need to be able to adjust to the challenging world of commercial management.

Ex-members of the armed forces or police tend to have a sense of ownership of the role.

Most service personnel in my opinion come to the private sector indoctrinated by their past, and this often takes some time to correct and "soften the edges".

Missing business acumen, resulting in security being perceived as an inhibitor rather than an enabler.

Good traits are exposure and experience of working in high pressure modes, individually or as a team, whilst achieving the overall aim. Disadvantage: can have an entrenched egotistical perception of self, which may detract from the core team focus and function.

5   In your opinion, how important is it for the security manager to have at least a working knowledge of the operational and business aims and objectives of the organization?

Quotes:

Essential and something former uniformed personnel struggle to comprehend and really adapt to.

Probably number 1 on my list of importance. A competent security manager/leader must have a good/thorough understanding of all business-critical processes.

This is what I call the big picture. *It is vital for success in business* that security managers are an accepted part of the business and contribute to the team effort that drives the enterprise to meeting their goals and aspirations.

It's crucial. Security management must be integrated into business processes. Security must also "talk business" in order to achieve higher acceptance.

This is absolutely critical. Without understanding the business, one cannot understand the risks a business faces and thus cannot present effective mitigation strategies. Also, without this knowledge security managers aren't really taken seriously and can't win a chair at the table where important decisions are being made.

6   Are there any advantages in the security manager holding a high-level academic qualification? Would you recommend a security and risk management-based qualification, or a business orientated qualification? Please qualify your answers.

Quotes:

Most definitely yes. Apart from subject matter learning, it also enables the learner to apply critical thinking and analytical skills.

It demonstrates a level of professionalism and commitment and puts the security management function on the same level as other professions.

I think both are important; however, it depends which role you are in and how senior. A MSc in security management is great for middle-level positions but a business-related qualification (MBA) would also provide credibility if you are a true CSO.[2]

I would recommend any security and risk management-based qualification but only if it included a significant element of business management.

Academia is one of the keys to allowing the security manager not only to define his or her position but also to gain recognition from leadership that their opinions, recommendations, and beliefs are driven by more than anecdotal evidence from oft-times unique circumstances.

7   To what extent should the security manager be involved in risk management, crisis management, and disaster recovery?

Quotes:

The term risk management is used throughout a commercial business and relates to all areas of business activity. There is often a senior manager appointed as head of risk.

The head of risk should ensure that all areas of risk are identified and addressed by experts to a similar formula. This is complicated and often misunderstood.

Security risk management is one such area that must be addressed and only by security specialists. Security risk management is further divided due to the distinct variations within the term security, so there might be cyber risk, fraud risk, information and data risk, physical risk, travel risk, etc. All face different threats and have different vulnerabilities and definitely different impacts.

Therefore, should security managers be involved in security risk management as part of the overall business risk management – absolutely.

It makes perfect sense in my opinion for the security manager to be at the core of all three practices, after all he or she is vital in the mitigation of risk and the prevention of crisis and disaster that may affect the business.

That depends on whether a specialist is already employed in that role. It is difficult to be a master of all trades but invariably, it is often the case that a SM is expected to be all of these roles because that appears to save money.

Risk and crisis management and disaster recovery are key components of what a security manager should have knowledge of and in turn apply that knowledge in the design of relative plans and policies regardless of the organisation, whether profit or non-profit, commercial, government, or charity. The security manager should be a key person an exec team can rely on in such circumstances.

8   Should the security manager sit on the crisis management team? Please qualify your answers.

Quotes:

This would really depend on the role that the security manager has to play in crisis management. To some extend this also depends on the seniority of the security manager in the organisation.

Most definitely yes, but in my experience of having been engaged as a crisis management advisor to several blue-chip organisations, they rarely are, other than at a basic operational level. The security manager should be skilled and trained to operate at a strategic level and be a main member of a CM Team.

Yes. This is exactly what the security manager should be involved in. It's likely that their training will mean they can think of what may go wrong to assist with planning and prevention and when a crisis does occur be able to co-ordinate an appropriate response and recovery.

Not mandatory. In many cases it will be reasonable to involve security, but sometimes it may be more important to have other functions on board (e.g. a financial crisis).

9   What organisational pathways should be available for the aspiring security manager?

Quotes:

Interesting. The government is currently looking at the same question. Consideration should be given to both the security operative becoming a manager. Equally, consideration should be given to the business route where a mainstream officer is appointed security manager. The background, skills, and motivation of the applicant should be taken into account.

None should be unavailable. Personnel should be judged individually, not on their job title but upon their ability, performance, and contribution to the business.

I would be advising any aspiring security manager to map out their personal pathway that prioritises the need to learn about the commercial world, about laws, regulations and standards affecting security, understanding threats, and then developing specialist security prevention skills.

I don't think there is one size/path fits all. I know security managers who have original background in finance, internal audit, and even marketing.

The security manager should be able to spend time in different departments to understand the unique challenges and deliverables each dept has, so that the service security provides can be as supportive and least obtrusive as possible. He should be supported by the business to continue to develop his management skills and security knowledge annually.

10 Should the head of security sit on the executive board? Once again, please qualify your answer.

Quotes:

This is a question asked by many people as they see it as ideal, but actually the executive board is there to manage the business, not security. They can always ask the security manager to attend. In any event, most security managers will report to the company secretary or similar senior member so they would be represented anyway. So, I think not.

Yes of course, this should be someone who perhaps is looking after LP,[3] security, compliance, etc.

This long-standing question doesn't have an absolute answer.

The security manager/head of security should sit on the executive board if the business requires it. This would depend largely on the critical risk factors for that business. For example, it would be a surprise to me if the head of security was not represented at the highest levels of a critical infrastructure business or major event venues.

This would depend on the size and nature of the business. There is no reason why not if they have the right business acumen.

Yes undoubtedly, at the very least the head of security can act as a safety valve and prevent poor security practices from being put in place by uninformed C-Suite personnel and also promote the security practices that can help negate the need for activation of the CMT. I sit on the exec board of my company and regularly contribute for the greater good of the business with advice and guidance that others do not necessarily take into consideration when planning for the future.

This is not a question of whether they "should", but rather what they can/are able to do in terms of demonstrating their value to the business to be *invited* to the board.

Just a thought

Answer the questions in the survey, and compare your answers to those given by the respondents.

The security professional and risk management

> The underlying mission of security management is to provide protection and security for assets, people and reputation, allowing the organisation to continue trading successfully into the future.
>
> McCrie (2007)

McCrie (2007) in Gill (2014) says that the protection of assets from loss always mattered to profit-making organisations; guards, regular patrols, and watchmen were tasked to protect private property from theft, fire, and vandalism based on early payroll records.

As McCrie correctly argues, for centuries the leading role of any security function has been to offer protection of the assets owned by the company employing the security team, although not necessarily offering advice on risk management.

The evolution and development of physical and electronic security systems has greatly assisted the security manager and his or her team in carrying out this protective role, and it is reasonable to say that the security manager of today is comfortable and competent in specifying the most appropriate systems that are fit for the purpose of asset protection.[4]

However, in this chapter I will be arguing that it is not only the ability of the security manager to research and specify exactly what systems are of operational benefit to his or her organisation; rather there are now business complications that must be taken into consideration before any procurement and commissioning of equipment and systems takes place. I believe this discussion goes to the heart of all business debates surrounding the professionalism of today's security manager.

When considering their roles and responsibilities in relation to the protection of company assets, security managers very often have to examine the feasibility of a number of security systems, including manned guarding – an extremely expensive security asset to deploy – and the installation of very advanced, predominantly IT-based security technology.

As previously mentioned, security managers today, through a mixture of experience and training qualifications, very often have the expertise to research and specify those systems that are operationally fit for the purpose of asset protection, with this process being carried out as the result of a *risk-based* decision. It is incredibly difficult if not impossible to specify any form of deterrence if the risk to the organisation has not been assessed, analysed, and measured.[5]

What we need to look at next, bearing in mind the fact that we will be covering risk and risk management in detail in Chapter 3, is where the security manager today fits into the overall picture relating to the risk management of his or her organisation.

Risk management responsibilities

The risk landscape of an organisation is incredibly complex, and it would go beyond the scope of this book to cover all risk functions within a public or corporate body. For the purposes of this part of the chapter, we will concentrate on how the security manager today should be involved in risk management and in fact should encourage the recognition of effective security risk management within his or her levels of influence.

The security function or team, led by the security manager, should be in a position where it is integral to the strategic planning of all security protection needed by an organisation, and there are several distinct areas where it should play a critical role in the planning of individual programmes and strategies, all of which require an appreciation of risk and risk management.

*   *New building projects*

    This is certainly an area where the security team should be involved. Far too often security systems are procured as an afterthought, or perhaps as a necessary evil for insurance purposes, and once again far too often this procurement policy, normally carried out by those unqualified to specify a system, fails because of a lack of risk management and operational requirement appreciation. In any forward-thinking organisation, the security team should be involved at the architectural stage of any building project, where it is believed there may be a threat to assets – either people, infrastructure, or brand and reputation. Sadly and worryingly, this is rare, as non-cost-effective and inefficient retrofitting, for whatever reason, is normally the preferred choice.

    In the initial stages of a new building project, after consultation with the designing architect, the security department should embark on a series of risk assessments, which include the identification of all assets belonging to the company, threats to the organisation, and known vulnerabilities. Once a risk analysis has taken place and an impact assessment has been agreed, the security team should begin to investigate the most effective means of protecting the organisation through a recognised risk management process. This will include the identification of mitigation and prevention strategies to treat the risk.

    An aid to this approach is the use of some form of operational requirement (OR). There are many forms of OR, but the most common, and in my opinion the most effective are the ORs recommended by the Centre for the Protection of National Infrastructure (CPNI). CPNI describe the OR as an essential tool to enable an organisation to produce a clear, considered, and high-level statement of their security needs based on the risks they face.

    A well-defined OR increases the likelihood of success in any security project and reduces the risk of commissioning expensive unnecessary work. The involvement of key stakeholders in the OR process will greatly increase executive buy-in for the project, simplifying any organisational change required.[6]

    Once all systems have been tested and commissioned, it should then be the responsibility of the security department to ensure that levels of security achieved at this stage do not deteriorate over time. It is at this stage that the previously negotiated service level agreement (SLA) and key performance indicators (KPI) are scrutinised and maintained.

*   *An increased or new threat*

    Since 9/11, the threat of terrorism has been with us on an ever-increasing scale, either in reality or perhaps through perception. Between 2015 and 2016 a number of high-profile terrorist attacks took place in Europe (France, Belgium, Germany, and the UK), with increasing difficulty for national police forces to be able to deploy the correct levels of protection for the population, never mind commerce and industry. Equally, the threat and velocity of cybercrime and arguably cyberterrorism have taken the world by surprise, with a number of attacks that have been extremely difficult to defend against, certainly by public bodies such as the police, and latterly in the UK by the NHS.[7]

So from a cyber perspective, a relatively new approach to this area is that of threat modelling. Threat modelling is the proactive process of detecting possible risks to an organisation's online architecture and thereafter creating and testing a variety of appropriate countermeasures (Petters, 2018).

There is a range of methodologies available to security management teams who have responsibility for the cybersecurity of an organisation, including the Process for Attack Simulation and Threat Analysis (PASTA) and Visual, Agile and Simple Threat (VAST) modelling (Ambler, 2018).[8] Both of the named methodologies are risk-based approaches to cybersecurity and focus on a trilogy of assets, threats, and vulnerabilities (Petters, 2018).[9]

The term "threat modelling" has become quite popular recently. Microsoft has published a book about their process and includes threat modelling as a key activity in their secure development lifecycle (SDL).

A threat model is essentially a structured representation of all the information that affects the security of an application. In essence, it is a view of the application and its environment through security glasses.

It is in this environment within an organisation that the security department should be constantly carrying out risk assessments to ensure that all assets are safe from such attacks. If the focus is on the cyberthreat, this is when the physical and IT security functions must converge to offer the most effective defence.[10]

- *Travel security*

The problem with travel security, generally, is the attitude of the person who is travelling, because on far too many occasions he or she will declare: "Typical security, you worry about everything. Nothing is going to happen to me".

Just a thought

Take a couple of minutes to think about what risks there are to travellers in potentially hostile locations. What do you think the main threats are?

Whether we are discussing kidnap, assassination, or perhaps general crime, there has to be some form of risk assessment carried out prior to the travel taking place. However, before we begin to examine who the competent party is to carry out such an assessment, let's take a look at what is probably the greatest threat to personnel travelling to and in hostile locations: K&R.

Kidnap and ransom is a lucrative business, one in which various global criminal organisations including the Mafia and Baader Mainhof, the West German terrorist organisation that thrived in the 1970s. Today K&R is still rife in South America and a number of African countries, with the kidnappers always being on the front foot, as they know when they are going to strike, and therefore have a major advantage.

There are a number of commercial organisations that can offer K&R advice, and any traveller contemplating movement in potentially hostile areas should take professional guidance.

• *New operations*

When considering new operations, any organisation, let's say an oil company wishing to extend its area of operations, is unlikely to select a location, in terms of geographical attraction or business potential, on a whim!

There are a number of critical considerations to take into account before any commitment is made, such as the geopolitical situation and the economic outlook of the region to be developed. Social considerations will need to be examined, as will the technology required to carry out and complete any drilling and processing operations. Finally, there are of course legal arguments to be heard, and environmental conditions must be thoroughly scrutinised. The tool to assist in carrying out this form of survey is referred to as PESTLE:

- **P**olitical
- **E**conomic
- **S**ocial
- **T**echnology
- **L**egal
- **E**nvironmental.

Of course, the executive board will listen to the preceding considerations from a security risk management and business development perspective, but the prime consideration of the chief executive officer (CEO) has to be the safety and security of his or her people, who may be asked to work in what could be a hostile environment.

Case Study – Amenas, Algeria

On 16 January 2013, it is believed that an al-Qaeda-affiliated terrorist group attacked the Tigantourine gas terminal, close to Amenas in Algeria. During the attack it is calculated that 841 oil workers were taken hostage at gunpoint, and by the time Algerian Special Forces were in a position to assault the location, four days later, 39 foreign hostages had been murdered by the terrorists.

There was of course a major investigation carried out, and one of the first questions that will have been asked was who carried out the security risk assessments, and what recommendations were made in terms of a potential terrorist attack.

This book has neither the intention nor the capacity to comment on the described attack, but it is relevant to this section, and it is certainly worthy of research.

The fact of the matter is this; before any operations are carried out, in tandem with a health and safety risk assessment, there has to be a security risk assessment, and just as it is logical for a H&S expert, or rather, competent person to carry out that assessment, it is imperative that the company security function should carry out the security risk assessment. If that means investment in security risk assessment training, then it is funding well invested.

- *New technology*

    Probably the most prominent technological system in use today is CCTV which was first used by the military in Germany in 1942, having been invented by the German engineer Walter Bruch. It was used for monitoring Luftwaffe (air force) flights, and it wasn't until 1949 before the system could be developed commercially.

    Today, in the UK alone, depending who you believe, there are between 2 and 6 million CCTV cameras deployed, with advanced technological developments such as advanced analytics, video motion detection (VMD), Internet Protocol (IP) transmission, multi-element cameras, and so on.

    In terms of access control, where once we were reliant on the key locking system, there are now proximity card readers and biometric scanners, with the former being capable of architectural adjustment and the latter (at the time of publishing) being able to scan a human retina or fingerprint to allow access to secure locations.

    And of course, it is now standard practice, perhaps under certain circumstances, for company employees to be issued smart mobile phones with almost the computing power of an original space shuttle. The smartphone also has a number of features that allows it to be interrogated, to produce evidence of not only communications information, but also the movement of the user, their Internet history, and the strength of their hearts!

    How on earth is this information related to the security manager? Easy. Back to systems procurement. If the organisation makes a strategic decision to upgrade the multi-site CCTV system, or have access control re-designed and deployed, or even spend huge amounts of cash on security-related smartphones, what company function or department is the logical choice to research, have procured and commission such systems? The security function of course. But why, you ask?

    The answer is extremely logical. Taking the UK as an example, every year there are a number of security trade exhibitions and conferences held throughout the length and breadth of the country. The International Fire and Security Exhibition (IFSEC) is held in London and is probably the largest security and fire trade exhibition in Europe. The strategy behind IFSEC is for manufacturers and designers to showcase their products, which mainly consist of state-of-the-art security systems, designed to capture the imagination (and of course the cash) of security professionals who are potentially in the market for security upgrades and replacement systems. If it was the sole remit of any other department, it is likely that procurement would be dependent on cost alone, with little thought being given to the risks involved, or the OR for the deployment of such systems.

    However, when the security team is involved in this process, team members will of course take into consideration cost, but will also select the correct system(s) based on their ability to meet the demands of the risk, for which they must be fit for purpose. Another extremely important part of the security procurement strategy is the assurance that chosen security systems will be accepted by the end user. It is of course a major advantage to have the automatic access control systems (AACS) configured in such a manner that the card and supporting software has a 'no pass back' facility. That is to say, the card may only be able to be used once to enter the building, before it used again to exit; meaning that if a member of staff forgets their pass card, they cannot use a colleague's card, once it has been used for entry. The card cannot be 'passed back'. The problem with this system, of course, is that if staff are not made aware of the necessity to have a 'no pass back' card, which reduces 'tail gating', they only see the card system as an inhibitor to their convenience.

Although this part of the chapter has concentrated on the security professional and risk management, another area that shares a symbiotic relationship with risk management is crisis management and disaster recovery.

Crisis management and the security manager

> ### Pause for thought
>
> In your opinion, what is a crisis, and how is it managed?

Until recently, the prospect of, for lack of a more effective title, a corporate security manager being included in any crisis management or disaster recovery planning would have been slim, to say the least. However, when researching for this book, and as part of the qualitative survey, I asked a number of my professional colleagues the following question:

> Should the security manager sit on the crisis management Team? Please qualify your answers.

The answers were extremely interesting.

> This would really depend on the role that the Security Manager has to play in Crisis Management. To some extent this also depends on the seniority, in the organisation, of the Security Manager. In my last role for example I was responsible for the Crisis Management Team, so I was a key player in that team. There is also a relevant point here that senior managers are not necessarily very good at Crisis Management and quickly become uncomfortable managing the situation. In any event in a crisis people look for good leadership and management and this will often come from the security Manager. So yes, they should sit on the Crisis Management team.
>
> Most definitely yes but in my experience of having been engaged as a crisis management advisor to several blue-chip organisations, rarely are, other than at a basic operational level. The security manager should be skilled and trained to operate at a strategic level and be a main member of a CM Team.

Yes – This might, however, depend on the size of the company. For an SME the crisis team might be a small team and often the security manager might head the crisis team. For larger commercial businesses a crisis team is often headed by a senior executive but including the security leader as a key member.

Yes. As much as an HR manager, Communications manager, IT operations manager, Finance manager, PR spokesperson, Customer service manager. CMT is a cross-functional body and if they're supposed to manage the organization's operations in times of crisis, all critical internal functions shall be represented, incl. security.

Not mandatory. In many cases it will be reasonable to involve security, but sometimes it may be more important to have other functions on board (e.g. financial crisis). Nonetheless there will be always at least indirect effects on security. That's why security must be informed and consulted about security related crisis management decisions.

The average length of time spent by the above respondents in the security industry is 28 years, with security environments varying from retail to international communications, corporate investigations, and crisis management. All respondents agree that there is a place for the security manager on the CMT, but one or two argue that it is not mandatory, and that it depends upon the business in question, and indeed the range of skills held by the security manager.

Of course, I won't enter into a dispute with my learned colleagues, and I do believe that it certainly isn't the God-given right for any security manager to be automatically included in a crisis management team. However, strategically forward-thinking corporations are now beginning to identify strengths and skill sets in the security manager that perhaps weren't so noticeable until recently. The strengths and skill set that allows him or her to dispassionately and objectively advise the executive board on matters relating to security risk and crisis management – which if it were for argument's sake a terrorist attack – would be invaluable.

The modern security manager does, or at least should, understand the business he or she is involved in and must be in a position to contribute to its safety and of course security from a crisis management perspective. Maybe the executive board is cognizant of the fact that a crisis is generally identified as a poorly managed risk, and perhaps the best function or department to deal with risk issues is security.

Most importantly, one of the greatest threats to a business and its people today is the threat of a terrorist attack. Generally, the security manager will have, or should have established good working relations with the local police service, and he or she is then ideally positioned to communicate effectively with law enforcement before, during, and after a crisis.

So, I would argue that it is common sense to include the security manager when organising a crisis management team.

Strategic business awareness and the security manager

The expertise previously mentioned may often be a stumbling block when it comes to procurement because, perhaps in the eyes of the finance director (FD) or chief finance officer (CFO), quality and operational effectiveness are not necessarily acceptable substitutes for, nor do they complement, cost effectiveness!

It is my experience, through consultancy and the delivery of training, that even today, when given the opportunity, those security managers involved in procurement projects tend to select protective systems for a number of diverse reasons:

1   Selection may be decided upon because "We have always used that supplier, and there has never been an issue".
2   Selection may be the result of persuasion through media outlets, such as security magazines and so forth, or perhaps examples of systems demonstrated at trade exhibitions, such as the International Fire and Security exhibition (IFSEC), where delegates are bombarded with subliminal and overt sales strategies by exuberant sales executives.
3   The security manager may have contacts with manufacturers and suppliers who are prepared to 'do a deal', whatever that means.
4   Of course, selection and procurement may be the objective result of an operationally based security risk assessment (SRA) and cost benefit analysis (CBA), and that is the ideal approach.

That said, security managers often base their selection purely on the quality of the product, and perhaps the fact that it meets the demands of an international standard.

This is the crux of the matter.

If little or no regard is given to the financial benefits to the company, when systems procurement is being considered it is highly unlikely that such an application will win the approval of the CFO or FD, who are quite correctly seeking a ROI, not merely injecting more cash and investment on the whims of security departmental needs. The financial senior management team need re-assurance that the security management team, and certainly the leader of that function, understands business operations and the importance of financial robustness and investment.

Unfortunately, because of this perceived shortfall in business understanding by the security function, the executive board will too often delegate security systems procurement, as though the company was buying stationary from the cheapest wholesale supplier. It may be facilities management (FM) or estates within the organisation that is delegated to manage the security systems procurement programme, but of course the argument made here is that FM or estates do not have the security expertise to operationally select the correct equipment or manage the manned guarding contract. Whilst delivering a security management training course, I overheard a facilities manager boasting that she had recently been involved in the procurement and commissioning of an 'advanced analytic CCTV system', but when asked to explain the system she was unable to, because of course the systems specifications were drawn up by the service provider (i.e. the salesperson).

Consequently, as has happened on too many occasions, the security equipment fails or the manned guarding company is difficult to manage, and the internal company security function is instructed to rescue the situation.

This has come about because the board believes that the security function is incapable of understanding financial matters and tends to have too narrow a perspective of the strategic business requirements of the organisation. I wonder how accurate that belief is in your organisation.

This is certainly a major issue in the eyes of a number of academics who have written about the need for the security manager to be more business aware.

In the *Handbook of Security* (2005), Professor Martin Gill argues, and quite correctly in my opinion:

> In many ways security suffers from being a grudge purchase, too often associated with the unattractive features of a "locks and bolts" approach.
>
> Measures can be functional, but they are not always viewed as attractive and it is not always obvious to all parties what benefits they generate.
>
> *Perhaps the real limitation of modern security management is that it has, in general, failed to talk the language of business not least in showing how it systematically impacts (positively or negatively) on the bottom line.*

Drucker (2007)[11] makes no distinction between different types of manager when he argues that a manager's job should be based on a task to be performed in order to attain the company's objectives. It should always be a real job – one that makes a visible and, if possible, a clearly measurable contribution to the success of the enterprise. He goes on to say what managerial jobs are needed, and that each of them should always be determined by the activities that have to be performed – the contributions that have to be made to attain the company's objectives. A manager's job exists because the task facing the enterprise demands its existence – and for no other reason. The manager should be able to point at the final results of the entire business and say, "This part is my contribution".

In my opinion, the security manager is no different. But of course, there are issues.

One of the greatest stumbling blocks for security managers today is perception. Perception perhaps that the security manager is little more than a security officer in a suit, a manager who doesn't understand management – certainly not strategic management. Perhaps a means of confirming this self-fulfilling prophecy – and of course this is where the security industry does not help itself – is to examine recruitment adverts.

For the last decade or so, the security sector has been trying to raise the profile of the security officer and the security manager – with pay and conditions being at the forefront of the strategy – attempting to constantly increase the pay of security officers to ensure that it is above the minimum living wage, which is set at £8.21 for adults over 25 years of age.[12] Today the average hourly pay for a security officer is £8.31 – ten pence above the minimum wage. That in itself is quite scandalous, but the point of this argument is that, with a few honourable exceptions, security officers are still paid by the hour, as they have been for decades. All that is missing is a brown envelope, paid over a table on a Friday afternoon, with a cut taken out for the boss! One would assume that the approach to paying the salary of the security manager is quite different; indeed, a more civilised and mature annual salary – sadly, not necessarily so. A recent advert spotted by the author of this book on a well-respected recruitment web site announced when advertising for a security manager. . .

> [Company] are seeking an experienced *Security Manager* (Static Manned–Guarding) required for a client site based in Tadcaster, North Yorkshire, working on a Full Time and Permanent basis averaging 56 Hours Per week on a working a Day Time only – (7 On, 4 Off and 7 On, 3 Off) shift pattern 06:00–18:00 Hours / 12 Hours Shifts, some flexibility will be required to work the occasional mixture of Nights and Weekends to include Public/Bank Holidays.

This excellent and exciting new opportunity will require a suitable candidate whom has a first class customer centric approach applied to the heart of their routine operation and must be frequently willing to go above and beyond (Going the Extra Mile) in what is required of them in their day to day activity and must lead a team of like-minded Security Officers to adopt those values and behaviours in everything that they do during their activities and duties. In return we offer a generous pay rate and great working conditions including a good work/life balance.

The duties and responsibilities of this role in addition to what is required of a Security Manager in this setting will include (*but not limited to*) access and egress control, logging and recording visitor/contractors, authenticating right of access, conducting Internal & External patrols, following site specific procedures, assisting in all emergency incidents and management of those incidents, manage onsite administration and security systems including various other facility related support functions and ultimately providing and maintaining the highest standards of security service and Customer Care.

For the above roles and responsibilities, the successful candidate will be paid the princely sum of £9.75 per hour, and of course the role relates not to that of a security manager as befits the definition in this book; rather it describes a static security supervisor or senior security officer.

Besides the fact that this very busy security manager will be paid a massive £1.44 per hour more than a security officer, I wonder how many other managers in various sectors are paid such a low wage and paid at an hourly rate. What signal does that send?

Interestingly, Gill (2014 p. 986) asks what skill sets are needed to be an effective security manager. This is essentially about whether one sees security's function as protecting assets (security skills) or enabling a business to make a profit (business skills).

In the opinion of the author of this book, comparing the two skill sets described will lead to the dilution of one of those functions: asset protection or business enablement. That of course is potentially disastrous for the security manager and the organisation he or she is supporting.

There is no doubt in my mind that companies expect and demand the security manager to lead in terms of asset protection and crime prevention, notwithstanding a commitment from the security manager to cooperate with business growth. I cannot understand how asset protection and crime prevention can negatively impact business enablement. It makes no sense whatsoever to have to choose A or B.

In a similar vein later in his book, Professor Gill compares and contrasts security management skills and business management knowledge. As with the argument about asset protection and business skills, the discussion surrounding security management skills versus business management skills is misplaced and naive. Today's security manager must be able to manage the protection of assets whilst assisting in the growth of the business. To enable, not to impede.

The arguments made by Gill and those authors supporting him would appear to be based on the pretext that a significant percentage of senior security managers who may aspire to gain a seat at the executive board, perhaps with lofty dreams of CEO appointment, are former senior police officers or members of the armed forces. And why shouldn't they?

Even if we are to be persuaded that such candidates do not possess the appropriate strategic thought process – and I have yet to see any compelling argument to support such a view – are we not ignoring other vocationally and academically qualified security management director–level applicants who do not originate from the police or armed services. This is, I believe, at the heart of the discussion.

We need to try to understand exactly why there are barriers to security managers, former armed forces or otherwise, being appointed to the executive board. Gill (2014 p. 988) argues that having interviewed a number of board directors about the feasibility of security managers ever being promoted to the executive board, he received comments such as:

1 "I have never seen one that could reach that level. There is not the ability there. Also, there is not the route".

   I find this view extremely narrow, incredibly subjective and without substance. To argue that "*there is not the route*", is not a criticism that should be levelled at the aspiring security management candidate. Rather, the focus must be on the organisation's strategic approach, which should ensure diversity and inclusiveness.

2 "They come from too narrow a perspective. As I said earlier, they are uncompromising, and that comes from a different background, a police or military one, that is fit for purpose, fit for being a security role, but not an overall business role".

   In the first instance there is the perception by this executive board member that all security managers originate from a public services background. That may have been relatively accurate 25 to 30 years ago, but it is certainly unsubstantiated today.
   A particular international telecommunications company that I worked with for a number of years were forward-thinking enough to place an embargo on appointing former police and servicemen based purely on their former careers as police officers or soldiers. The recruitment strategy was formed around the risk management and business awareness skills that the security team candidates possessed. That is not to say that the company would not recruit from the police or armed services, but those candidates from such backgrounds had to prove during the recruitment assessment process that they could bring added value to the business as opposed to merely the protection of assets. The same company very often seconded internal managers from functions outside of security in the knowledge that they would be adding to the security function because they understood the culture of the company. Many of them were being groomed to take up senior positions in the company, which would at some stage in the future see them competing for places on the board.

3 "In this massive organisation the skill set required is so broad, I just don't think that security gives broad enough access to the way the business is run".

   Once again, the perception that the security function has too narrow a focus is not the fault of that department. The organisation must examine its recruitment and strategic development programme to understand whether it is inclusive, or if perhaps there is a bias against the security team. If, for example, there is a graduate recruitment scheme, which potentially leads to strategic advancement, is it open to applicants with academic qualifications in, let us say security manager; risk, crisis and disaster management; or international security and risk management? If it is not open to such graduates, whose fault is that?

So whilst there may be merit in the argument that former police officers or service personnel initially may not conform to the strategic thought process required to sit on the executive board, it cannot be logically argued that such a restriction is relative to a member of the security team who is strategically and academically qualified and has the potential skill sets to meet board requirements.

In relation to the previous section, one of the questions posed in the qualitative survey carried out before embarking on this book was:

> "Should the head of security sit on the executive board? Once again, please qualify your answer".

This was asked because of some of the comments made in response to questions asked by Gill.

Several answers I received were extremely interesting.

> Yes undoubtedly, at the very least the Head of Security can act as a safety valve and prevent poor security practices from being put in place by uninformed C Suite personnel and also promote the security practices. . . . I sit on the Exec Board of my company and regularly contribute for the greater good of the business with advice and guidance that others do not necessarily take into consideration when planning for the future. (head of security for Dyson)
>
> This is not a question of whether they "should", but rather what they can/are able to do in terms of demonstrating their value to the business to be *invited* to the Board. (head of security with an international auditing company)
>
> It depends on the respective business. Security should be represented on the board if security plays a crucial role for the business. (International lawyer and head of compliance for a multinational telecommunications company)
>
> Yes, but as a non-executive member until a C+ grade when they can assume the same position as HR; Legal; Finance; etc. (Country CSO)

4   So the argument about whether a Security Manager is competent enough to sit on and be accepted by the executive board is ongoing, and my opinion is that there has to be an open and transparent selection process that encourages potential executives from all functions within a business. The process must not discriminate on the grounds of non-evidence-based subjective opinion, with statements and arguments such as "they come from too narrow a perspective. As I said earlier, they are uncompromising, and that comes from a different background, a police or military one, that is fit for purpose, fit for being a security role, but not an overall business role".

Another interesting perspective when examining the role played is that the security function within an organisation is often perceived as a cost centre, that is to say that at the beginning of a fiscal year, security will be handed a budget, designed to ensure that the department can carry out its function within the company; that of securing the assets of the organisation. Historically the security department has had no need to create sales, or help with business growth, until now.

Income generation

Arguments in the preceding section do not make comfortable reading from the perspective of the security manager who is very honestly carrying out the task of protecting assets to the best of his or her ability; to be informed that despite best efforts, there was still a gap in terms of what was required from their department. However painful and unpalatable this may seem, the security manager must, in a similar vein to other department heads, be cognisant of the fact that organisations live or die by performance results.

As part of a recent consultancy package, when I was advising a government department on security risk assessment and the security survey, the same department received an instruction that rocked them to their foundations, and from a crisis management perspective they didn't see it coming.

For this particular example, I would like to introduce you to a group of security professionals, working for the British Foreign and Commonwealth Office (FCO), who achieved worldwide recognition for their unique skills in ensuring the security and safety of assets belonging to Her Majesty's Government (HMG). Their role was/is to protect such assets from hostile government agencies, and in that respect, they were/are incredibly successful. Added to this global success, and the acclaim received, was the fact that all team members were civil servants, and therefore expected this euphoria to continue until the day they claimed their civil service pensions.

However, one day a bolt out of the blue was received, with substance that was to change their professional working lives forever.

Whilst attending a strategic management conference, the head of the team was handed a written instruction from the security department at the FCO, it would appear heavily influenced by HM Treasury, informing him that with immediate effect, he and his team were to produce a three-year plan, mapping a strategy which would transform the department from a cost centre to an income-generating function. Wow!

As I am sure you can imagine, this threw the team into total disarray, with our experts putting forward a compelling argument, from their perspective, about their remit, which was as previously described to ensure the security of HMG assets worldwide. They further argued that they were in possession of evidence that they were carrying out their tasks at the highest levels of excellence. They were confident that the evidence offered to the Foreign and Commonwealth Office (FCO) was sufficient for them, to maintain the status quo.

As you would expect, the mandarins within the FCO received this plea with grace and understanding, informing our team of experts that they were indeed performing magnificently, but they were still, at the end of the day, a cost centre. Game, set, and match to HMG!

This narrative has now been replicated on a global platform, with security functions serving major corporations being informed that unless they adjust the manner in which they perform, no longer attracting criticism as cost centres, the alternative will be to outsource all security services to organisations that understand finance and the criticality of a return on investment.

Of course, one of a number of arguments put forward by individual security departments is that through their diligence, and refined crime prevention strategies, the incidence of criminal activity within the organisation has reduced, thus saving the company money in terms of the reduction in crime. The answer from the board has been "well done, but that is what you are paid to do. You are now required to generate an income or be absorbed".

Just a thought

Do you think this is a sign of things to come, or merely a storm in a teacup?

Notes

1 Servant leadership is a philosophy built on the belief that the most effective leaders strive to serve others, rather than to accrue power or take control.
2 Chief security officer.
3 Loss prevention.
4 This will be covered in detail in Chapter 3.
5 Risk and the risk assessment will be examined in Chapter 3.
6 www.cpni.gov.uk/operational-requirements.
7 The WannaCry cyber-attack that swept through dozens of hospitals across the country in May 2017 cost the NHS a total of £92m, new research has revealed. A report published by the government estimates the ransomware virus caused approximately £19m of lost output and £73m in IT costs. Some £72m was spent on restoring systems and data in the weeks after the attack. Doctors and nurses were forced to cancel around 19,000 appointments after the virus locked down computers in 80 "severely affected" trusts in May 2017. The UK and US have since attributed the virus to North Korea, but the EternalBlue exploit that the hackers leveraged had originally been built by the US National Security Agency (NSA). https://tech.newstatesman.com/security/cost-wannacry-ransomware-attack-nhs.
8 S. W. Ambler (2018) *Security Threat Models: An Agile Introduction* [Online]. Available at www.agilemodeling.com/artifacts/securityThreatModel.html, accessed on 19 April 2019.
9 J. Petters (2018) *Threat Modelling* [Online]. Available at www.varonis.com/blog/threat-modeling, accessed on 19 April 2019.
10 Enterprise security risk management (ESRM).
11 *The Practice of Management.*
12 www.gov.uk/national-minimum-wage-rates.

3   Critical security areas

The aim of this chapter is to cover a number of key skill areas that I believe are critical for all professional security managers to have at least a good working knowledge of. The chapter will cover a distinct array of security management skill sets, with links and tips that will offer you the opportunity to research each sub-chapter at your leisure.

At the end of each sub-chapter, you will be offered the opportunity to take part in an exercise pertinent to the content of the section. Here you will assume the role of a fictional character and will be presented with a synopsis for which you are encouraged to find a solution.

For instance, after sub-chapter 3.1, which focusses on security risk management, you will play the role of a corporate global security and resilience manager. You will have the opportunity to analyse a relevant security risk to the business, and you will be expected to provide control measures and strategies to mitigate that risk.

3.1 Security risk management

In Chapter 2 we discussed the security professional and the concept of security risk management, and we examined the need for risk analysis and assessment when the security manager is involved in the procurement process. In this sub-chapter we are going to examine what is meant by the simple term 'security' before we delve into the areas of risk and risk management.

Security

Where do we start?

The Oxford Dictionaries define security as:

> "The state of being free from danger or threat" or "The safety of a state or organization against criminal activity such as terrorism, theft, or espionage".

Gill (2014) develops the theme by arguing that the importance of security derives from its potential to protect people and their assets, in particular from malicious actions.[1]

However, even Gill's explanation requires further clarity, because security is multi-disciplined, and it certainly isn't confined to two-dimensional definitions such as human or state security. Newsom (2014) argues that security has many levels: saying that a useful scale would run through the personal, provincial, national (sovereign government), transnational, international (between sovereign governments), and supra-national (higher authority than sovereign governments).

In an excellent publication, Wood and Sheering (2007) ask precisely what 'security' is, what it should mean, and what should be done to guarantee it, arguing that the answers to these questions have always been contested. Criminologists continue to re-enforce the distinction between 'objective' and 'subjective' senses of the term, particularly given the impact of fear of crime on collective sensibilities and security-seeking behaviour. Zedner writes, for example:

> Security is both a state of being and a means to that end. As a *state of being*, security suggests two quite distinctive objective and subjective conditions. And as an *objective condition* it takes a number of possible forms. First, it is the condition of being without threat: the hypothetical state of absolute security. Secondly, it is defined by the neu- tralisation of threats: the state of 'being protected from'. Thirdly, it is a form of avoid- ance or non-exposure to danger. . . . As a *subjective condition*, security again suggests both the positive condition of feeling safe, and freedom from anxiety or apprehension defined negatively by reference to insecurity.
>
> (Zedner, 2003 p. 155)

So, whilst it is tempting at times to classify security as a means of ensuring safety at a per- sonal level, it must further be understood that security is multi-dimensional, encompassing personal, national, international and supra-national levels.

International security

As this book is being written, events are happening in the Middle East which could impact security at every level.

Timeline

13 June 2019: Two oil tankers were attacked near the Strait of Hormuz while they transited the Gulf of Oman. The Japanese *Kokuka Courageous* and Norwegian *Front Altair* were attacked, allegedly with limpet mines or flying objects, sustaining fire damage. It was also suspected by a number of national intelligence agencies that the Iranian Revolutionary Guard Corps[2] carried out the attack, possibly using under- water drones armed with high explosives.

4 July 2019: The MV *Grace 1*, which is a 30,000-ton Panamanian flagged crude oil tanker, chartered by the Iranian government, and carrying approximately 2.1 mil- lion barrels of oil, was seized by British Royal Marines off the coast of Gibraltar. The *Grace 1* was allegedly carrying oil to Syria, breaking EU sanctions. At the time of writing, the crew of the *Grace 1* were being held under arrest in Gibraltar.

19 July 2019: The *Stena Impero*, a 50,000-ton UK-flagged chemical/oil tanker, was seized by the Iranian Revolutionary Guard Corps in the Strait of Hormuz, a key shipping route in the Gulf. The Iranian government accused the Captain of the *Stena Impero* being involved in an accident with an Iranian fishing vessel, with the UK-flagged ship refusing to stop to render assistance. The vessel was seized and escorted to an Iranian naval port, where the crew were held. The confrontation is ongoing, and it encompasses all level of security concerns.

Personal security – extrapolating from above section

On a personal level, the attacks in the Gulf of Oman could quite easily have injured or killed a number of crew members. Also, the crew of the Iranian ship being held in Gibraltar and the crew of the UK-flagged vessel being held in Iran are at the mercy of perceived hostile governments. Their safety is not guaranteed.

National security

Tensions between Iran and the UK have escalated recently, and there is a perception, certainly portrayed by the media on both sides, that such tensions could easily escalate further, with the possibility of more vessel seizures, and perhaps a military confrontation between the two nation states.

International security

Both countries have military links with other international actors. Iran receives military hardware from Russia, whilst the UK is an active member of NATO and an extremely close ally of the US. There is once again the possibility of an escalation of the situation, a military confrontation into which other nation states may be drawn. There is also the importance of the Straits of Hormuz, where it is reported that in recent years the US and Iranian navies have had numerous tense encounters in the Persian Gulf, where almost one-third of the world's crude oil passes through the Strait of Hormuz daily. An intentional or inadvertent incident at sea could quickly escalate into a direct military confrontation, and risk shipping through the critical energy chokepoint.

On 3 January 2020, as the result of a US drone attack at Baghdad International Airport, General Qassem Soleimani, head of the Iranian Revolutionary Guards, was killed in what has been described as an assassination. The Iranian government swore revenge, and on 8 January 2020, 15 ballistic missiles fired from Iran landed at two US airbases in Afghanistan. Fortunately there were no casualties.

On 11 January 2020, Iran admitted to accidentally attacking and destroying a Ukrainian airliner shortly after take-off, killing all of the 176 people on board.

Globalisation

I suspect the way to approach this section is to first of all to be comfortable with the term 'globalisation' before examining how globalisation impacts international security.

In *Global Transformations* (2016), Held et al. argue that globalisation may be thought of initially as the widening, deepening, and speeding up of worldwide interconnectedness in all aspects of contemporary social life, from the cultural to the criminal, the financial to the spiritual. The computer programmers in India now deliver services in real time to their employees in Europe and the US, while the cultivation of poppies in Burma can be linked to drug abuse in Berlin or Belfast, illustrating the ways in which contemporary globalisation connects communities in one region of the world to developments on another continent.

In terms of international security, the greatest threat must come from cyber, because just as the computer programmers in India now deliver services in real time to their employees in Europe and the US, so too does the cybercriminal who can hack any computer system, anywhere in the world, any time of day. However, although the computer programmers in India, New York, or Beijing will be restricted by when the markets are open and operating, the cybercriminal works on a 24/7 schedule, as and when it pleases him or her.

But where did it all begin?

A potted history

Man first begun to contemplate security when he rose on his hind legs and realised that in terms of survival, it was either him or the giant Apatosaurus (the dinosaur previously known as Brontosaurus), which was once thought to weigh 40 or 50 tonnes.

Pretty quickly, man began to understand that if he didn't protect himself and his family, they would in no time become extinct; so he had to make a plan that would ensure their safety and *security* before they were attacked (by a Apatosaurus or a fellow *Homo sapien*!).

The individual protection of our *Homo sapien* and his family quite soon developed into a protection strategy for ensuring that the whole family was safe. He then protected his property and offered protection to the other residents of the village where they lived (contract security in its earliest form!).

But how was this to be sustained?

Walls and castles

One of the earliest and indeed most effective means of providing community security and safety for the lord of the manor was the concept of defence in depth, with the inner sanctum of the castle being the ultimate target that, no matter what, had to be protected.

Simon Woodside[3] in 2016 wrote an interesting piece articulating the concept of defence in depth, in which he described a medieval lord, ensconced in his chambers in the centre of the castle, sitting by a blazing fire confident in the fact that any attackers would need months to penetrate the layers of security that stood between him and the wilds of Middle Age Europe. His protection went beyond a simple reliance on thick stone walls; he was protected by a specific, proven approach to security known as defence in depth.

Defence in depth is the simple principle that while no security is perfect, the presence of many independent layers of defence will geometrically increase the difficulty of an attacker to breach the walls, and slow them down to the point where an attack isn't worth the expense it would take to initiate it. Each layer multiplies the effects of the previous layer. If the outer wall deters 90% of attacks, and the inner walls deter 90% of attacks, then in combination they deter 99% of attacks. Defence in depth places the core assets behind layers of varied and individually effective security, each of which has to be circumvented for an attack to be successful.

So, in the lord of the manor we had the equivalent of the CEO in a corporation who is tasked to ensure the safety and security of the assets of the organisation. In Woodside's explanation, the single asset that required protection, at least in the eyes of the medieval lord, was himself. He didn't necessarily care about the members of his family, his staff, or the people who lived in and around the castle; there was only one asset, and that was his lordship.

However, the theory and practice of defence in depth was and is very successful, in that the attacker, whether he or she is attempting to breach the vault of a bank or the digital hard drive of an IT system, has to defeat a number of defensive layers without being apprehended or thwarted. This is where what is known as the building blocks of security are particularly important. They are also referred to as the three Ds and one R: deter, detect, delay, and respond.

- *Deter*

    In terms of defence in depth, or any other security defensive system, the control measures are designed in such a manner as to make them very obvious to the potential attacker, in the hope that he or she will carry out their own risk assessment, and making use of rational choice,[4] will decide whether not to carry out the attack, as the risk of failure or being apprehended is significant. As far as the walls and castles are concerned, the attacking forces could easily recognise the fact that the castle was robustly constructed and defended on high ground. There was also 360-degrees dead ground 500 metres before reaching the castle ramparts, making the attacker vulnerable to an onslaught from defending troops, and so on; thus, effecting deterrence.

    Today the criminal can easily see that surrounding the location he or she has targeted is a strong, welded-mesh three-metre fence, which is effectively illuminated and is supported by CCTV, with an alert security officer attending for duty on a 24/7 basis.

    Deterrence.

- *Detect*

    Should the attacker not be deterred by the defensive mechanisms in place, the systems are designed to detect, at the earliest moment, an attack before it takes place. There may have been observation posts (OPs) strategically located around the castle, and watchmen on the castle ramparts 24 hours a day, so the attackers could be observed long before they were in range of their own weapons systems. The arrows fired by archers could fly approximately 400 metres, and a catapult could propel its 80 kg boulder about 250 metres. So the attacker was easily observed before the first arrow was fired or first boulder was slung.

    Our criminal today may be identified using CCTV, supported by radar and video motion detection software, with an image signalled to an alarm receiving centre that can deploy a reaction force extremely quickly and efficiently.

    Detection.

- *Delay and response*

    Here is where it gets somewhat tricky!

    Let us assume the castle attackers were not deterred by the myriad of defensive systems and had not been detected by either the OPs or the (possibly asleep) watchmen in the keep and have confidently decided to attack. However, the first obstacle they meet will be a moat that is 15 metres deep and 20 metres wide. Should they successfully cross the water under a hail of arrows, they will be met by a fortified building with solid stone walls 20 metres high and 3 metres deep. By now they are in danger of being engaged in close quarter battle (CQB), which meant that they would either be met by armoured cavalry before they organised their forces after crossing the moat, or upon reaching the castle walls they would be the subject of an attack from above consisting of flaming arrows being fired and boiling hot tar poured from the ramparts.

Our modern-day attackers will have met the three-metre high welded-mesh fence, which if you recall is supported by lighting and CCTV. The first layer of the fence is protected by a taught-wire perimeter intruder detection system (PIDS), and as soon as pressure is applied to the fence, the PIDS will silently activate, encouraging a response from the security team inside. Should the response fail, and our attackers successfully breach the first layer of the fence, as soon as they set foot inside, they will activate the buried PIDS, which will once again alert the internal response team, who it now appears are either elsewhere or fast asleep! Assuming they manage to manoeuvre across the buried PIDS, they will be met by an inner electrified fence, which is, yes you guessed it, alarmed; and this time the security team responds, whilst at the same time alerting the local police force to the fact that a burglary is in progress.

Delay, response and apprehension.

Having written an appreciation of a minimalistic or potted history of security, there are two aspects of the concept that I would now like to focus on: globalisation and domestic security. By domestic security I am referring to security at a national level that encompasses corporate and commercial environments.

Risk

Just a moment

In your own words (without googling it!), what is meant by the term 'risk'?

Threat and insecurity have always been among the conditions of human existence; in a certain sense this was even more the case in the past than it is today. The threat to individuals and their families through illness and premature death, and the threats to the community through famines and plagues were greater in the middle ages than today. From this kind of threat, we must seek the semantics of risk associated since the beginning of the modern period with the increasing importance of decision, uncertainty and probability in the process of modernisation. The semantics of risk refer to the present thematization of future threats that are often a product of the success of civilisation.

The two faces of risk-chance and danger-became an issue in the course of industrialisation, starting with intercontinental merchant shipping. Risk represents the perceptual and cognitive schema in accordance with which a society mobilises itself when it is confronted with the openness, uncertainties and obstructions of a self-created future and is no longer defined by religion, tradition or the superior power of nature, but has lost its faith in the redemptive powers of utopias.

(Beck, 2007)[5]

This passage, retrieved from the acclaimed book *World at Risk* (2007), sees Beck introducing the geo-societal aspects of risk, and how on a global perspective risk introduces us to the realities of chance and danger and the likelihood of adverse events occurring. This is of course a momentous publication dealing with social and philosophical aspects of risk, and it is certainly recommended reading.

The book you are reading now, whilst appreciating the importance of philosophical risk, intends to narrow the concept by studying security and risk from a business perspective.

First, we must define risk.

Much like the definition of terrorism, there are many versions of the definition of risk. However, for the purpose of this book, and from personal experience, I will lean towards the Royal Society, who define risk as

> the probability that a particular adverse event occurs during a stated period of time, or results from a particular challenge.

An *adverse event* is an occurrence that produces harm.[6]

Engemann (2018)[7] develops this definition by adding:

> Unanticipated crises can lead to immense negative consequences for businesses. Analysing these risks and making appropriate decisions regarding them is very challenging but necessary to generate requisite security.

Adams (1995) quotes Thompson et al. (1980), who argue that risk is culturally constructed; where scientific fact falls short of certainty, we are guided by assumption, inference, and belief. In such circumstances, the deterministic rationality of classical physics is replaced by a set of conditional, probabilistic rationalities. Risk throws up questions to which there can be no verifiable single right answers derivable by means of a unique rationality.

So by quoting Thompson et al.'s arguments relating to scientific fact falling short of certainty, Adams is immediately introducing one of the most disputed areas and probably most asked questions about risk: is risk real or perceived? Is it subjective or objective?

Adams once again throws himself into this argument by quoting the Royal Society for the Prevention of Accidents (1983), where the 1983 report distinguished between *objective risk* – the sort of thing the 'experts' know about – and *perceived risk* – the lay persons' often very different anticipation of future events.

We will return to the expert versus lay person debate when we discuss risk communication.

Risk perception

Arguably, the most important facet of risk and risk management, intrinsically linked to risk communication, is that of risk perception.

Just a moment

What do you believe is meant by the term 'risk perception'?

Risk perception refers to the "subjective assessment of the probability of a specified type of accident happening, and how concerned we are with the consequences" (Sjoberg, Moen & Rundmo, 2004 in Cho et al., 2015, p. 11).

Pidgeon et al. (2003) defined risk perception as "people's beliefs, attitudes, judgements and feelings, as well as the wider social or cultural values and dispositions that people adopt, towards hazards and their benefits", arguing that risk perception is not simply an individual process but has to be understood against the societal and cultural background (see also Kasperson et al., 2003).

However, whilst we are presented with two very good definitions of risk perception, we still need to understand the influences that explain how risk perception is categorised. A critical influencing factor for understanding risk perception is known as optimism bias.

Bodemer and Gaissmaier (in Cho et al. (2015)) argue that when asked about their risk comparison to the average risk, people often show unrealistic optimism. They believe themselves to be better off and less likely to experience negative life events (or more likely to experience positive events) than others. Optimism bias, also termed the *above-average effect* and *comparative optimism*, serves as an explanation of why people often do not take precautions, and instead simply discount their personal risk (the famous saying being, *It won't happen to me*).[8]

The media are often believed to be a strong influencing factor when it comes to risk perception because of the almost right and left tribal elements of society that take all forms of media as the absolute truth. If the *Sun* newspaper announces that Jeremy Corbyn is going to bankrupt the nation if he is sworn in as prime minister, it is likely that such a risk will be believed by the readers of that newspaper. Should the *Guardian* announce that a Tory government will take us to war, that is also likely to be believed by readers of that newspaper.

However, arguing against such persuasion, the *Journal of Risk Research*[9] (2011), in an article titled "Risk Perception and the Media", Wahlberg and Sjoberg argue that the media are diverse in content and often not as biased in their (news) reporting as is commonly thought. Although many take the media's influence for granted, the evidence points the other way: even for heavy media users, media are probably not a strong causal factor in (especially not personal) risk perception. Risk perception may be affected by the media via availability (more information gives a stronger effect), but the effects are lessened by impersonal impact: general risk perception is more easily changed than personal risk perception. Risk perception is often thought to cause behaviour, but this is still uncertain, and caution is necessary as to this possible connection.

Age is often cited as a critical influencing factor in relation to risk perception, and it is sometimes argued that younger generations tend to hold a different approach to risk perception based on bravado or ignorance. For example, a young child is likely to cross a busy road because they are either totally fearless or incredibly naive, whereas an adult will probably approach the same traffic flow with great caution, because he or she is either frightened or more experienced.

There is this widely held but unsupported belief that adolescents engage in risk behaviour because they feel invulnerable. In fact, the opposite may be true. Quadrel, Fischhoff, and Davis (1993) in Cho et al. (2015) found adolescents are less inclined to optimism bias compared with adults. In addition, adolescents provide higher risk estimates than adults for various natural hazards and behaviour-linked outcomes (Millstein & Halpern-Felsher, 2002) and overestimate their risk of dying in the near future (Fischhoff et al., 2010).

Moving on from age, of critical importance when discussing risk perception is the distinction between the expert and the layperson. Hertwig and Frey in Cho et al. (2015) argue that experts and the lay public are often at odds with each other when assessing risks. A common explanation for such disagreements in expert and lay opinions is that experts tend to operate on the basis of a technical ('objective') definition of risk. This definition is generally based on a risk's detrimental consequences (e.g. fatalities, injuries, disabilities) weighted by the probability of those consequences. Laypeople's assessment of risk – and particularly their perception of risk – does not simply follow this metric. Instead, they include other qualitative characteristics of the hazards, such as whether exposure to the risk is voluntary, how controllable the risk is, its catastrophic potential, or its threat to future generations (cited by Hertwig and Frey in Cho et al., 2015).

Thinking about a business environment, in many ways the relationship between the security manager and the business development manager may reflect the expert versus layperson argument when it comes to risk. However, you are probably asking the question, "Exactly who is the expert and who is the layperson?"

Interestingly, in my opinion, this is a hybrid situation in which both managers believe themselves to be the expert, and the other party the layperson! The security manager may believe that the business development manager totally misunderstands risk as he or she has a cavalier approach, basing all of their risk calculations on Return on Investment (ROI), with no thought given to the security and safety of the business. On the contrary, the business development manager is of the opinion that the prehistoric security manager worries only about locks, bolts, and security guards, with little professional devotion to growing the business. A conundrum!

Risk perception case study: 9/11

The attacks carried out by al-Qaeda against the World Trade Center in New York are well documented, and it is believed that approximately 3,000 people were killed as a direct result of the acts of terrorism on 11 September 2001.

Interestingly, it is my opinion that had members of the US intelligence community or the person on the street been asked about the risk of two heavily populated commercial aircraft being consciously flown into the Twin Towers by a high-profile terrorist group, the answer would have been something like this.

> What are you crazy, we have the most powerful air force on the planet. There is no way that two planes could breach our air defence system. Impossible; they would be blown out of the sky long before they reached New York.

However, according to the 9/11 Commission Report (2004), throughout the early part of 2001 there had been high levels of terrorist activity, specifically by al-Qaeda, who it appeared from various intelligence sources were credibly planning a high-profile attack against targets in either Saudi Arabia or Israel. Rome was mentioned as a potential target, but there was no evidence to support any thoughts or arguments about an attack against the US.

That is, not until 31 July 2001.

On 31 July 2001, a Federal Aviation Administration (FAA) circular appeared alerting the aviation community to "reports of possible near-term terrorist operations . . .

particularly on the Arabian Peninsula and/or Israel". The circular warned that the FAA had no credible evidence of specific plans to attack US civil aviation, though it noted that some of the "currently active" terrorist groups were known to "plan and train for hijackings" and were able to build and conceal sophisticated explosive devices in luggage and consumer products.

It appeared that the landscape had begun to change.

During the spring and summer of 2001, President George W. Bush had on several occasions asked his briefers whether any threats pointed to the United States. Reflecting on these questions, the Central Intelligence Agency (CIA) decided to write a briefing article summarising its understanding of this danger. Two CIA analysts involved in preparing this briefing article believed it represented an opportunity to communicate their view that the threat of a Bin Laden attack in the United States remained both current and serious. The result was an article in the 6 August 2001 presidential daily briefing (PDB) titled "Bin Laden Determined to Strike in the US". It was the 36th PDB item briefed so far that year that related to Bin Laden or al-Qaeda, and the first devoted to the possibility of an attack in the United states.

It now appears that there were rumblings and whispers relating to a terrorist attack against the US, and possibly hijack preparation, but no solid evidence.

It would be totally unprofessional to insinuate that US intelligence operations were in disarray leading up to 9/11, but there is little doubt that prior to the attacks against the Twin Towers by al Qaeda, the perceived risk of such an outrageous and daring attack was believed by experts (US intelligence) to be extremely low.

So what of the layperson?

In 2001, the US Air Force flew a total of 1,840 of the world's most advanced fighter aircraft, with I suspect a proportionate percentage of air squadrons on 24/7 standby to protect the air space over major conurbations. So with the US media focussing and reporting on terrorist activities in the Middle East and Europe, the population of New York City (the laypeople) could be forgiven for believing a terrorist threat against their homeland to be very low, if not non-existent.

Then 9/11 happened!

This is perhaps a rare example of experts and laypersons agreeing on the level of risk, but for very different reasons.

The consistent agreement counselling that "It will never happen to me!"

The arguments about risk perception have and will continue to rage on within the academic community for a long time to come – probably without an outcome. So I suppose the obvious question now is, "How does this affect the security manager?" From personal experience, risk perception is one of the most potent subjects of debate in any organisation.

Within a business environment, the security function will view risk in terms of the damage that may be done to the business by either human-made or natural crises and tends to be rather risk averse, for obvious reasons. On the other hand, the business development manager is concerned about the risk of constrained business growth and he or she tends to be risk tolerant; they are more likely to take a risk in order to achieve financial growth through contract development. The executive board, of course, is reliant on advice and guidance from both parties.

Another critical component of risk is the risk assessment, and as with risk communications, there is an element of risk perception here.

Just a moment[10]

Within a corporate organisation, for example, who owns any risks to the business?

The security risk assessment

Just a moment[11]

What is the aim of a security risk assessment?

If you use a search engine to define the term 'security risk assessment', the vast majority of descriptions unearthed will relate to either information security or cybersecurity (both of which will be covered later in this book), with very little reference to physical security.

Now this is a conundrum, because what you should be asking yourself now is, "What is the difference between an IT security risk assessment, and a physical security risk assessment?"

I will let you determine the answer to that question at the end of this section.

Competent persons and the security risk assessment

As mentioned earlier, formally the aim of this book is to

> examine exactly what is required of the professional security manager in a demanding and fast changing business orientated industry sector.

Informally, in order for the professional security manager to achieve this, he or she needs to critically understand risk and strategic business awareness and should have a good working knowledge of a number of skills required for him or her to carry out their roles professionally in the eyes of their peers and employers.

One of the skills required by the professional security manager is the ability to carry out a security risk assessment, and following this section you will be introduced, perhaps for the first time, to the two distinct types of risk assessment (quantitative and qualitative). The section will also explain the meaning of different component parts of risk, and how they should be considered when assessing risk, prior to recommending risk treatment options. All of that should fall within the comfort zone of a competent security manager.

However, one area of the security risk assessment that has proved to be a stumbling block over the time that I have been practicing and teaching the security risk assessment process is subject matter expertise. At the beginning of a risk management seminar that I was running in 2019, the delegates were asked if they had any experience of assessing risk; with indignation, all 22 security managers boasted that they carried out security risk assessments on a daily basis as this was an important skill within their roles as security managers. The seminar lasted two days, and at the end, the delegates asked me if I could develop and deliver a bespoke security risk assessment course for them. Hmm!

Because of the diversity of security and risk management, it is not at all unusual for the security manager to be asked to carry out a security risk assessment within an area that may not necessarily fit into the skill set of that security manager. He or she may be competent in all matters of generic security, but if asked to carry out a security risk assessment of a ship, for example, they may struggle, as they might not be able to tell the difference between the bow (front pointy end) and the stern (round back end). So how does the security manager begin to carry out the assessment when they may have never heard the term 'ship security assessment' (SSA), and probably have little experience of maritime security and its cultural values?

One of the many maritime threats encountered may be attacks by a group of pirates in the South China Sea, for which a certain amount of research can of course be carried out to understand that type of threat. However, when it comes to risk treatment, what knowledge of maritime weapons systems and emergency communications does the land-based security manager have? I suspect very little.

In a similar vein, the example security risk assessment used later in this sub-chapter is to measure the likelihood and consequences of an attack against an IT system, but if the security manager commissioned to carry out the assessment has a poor understanding of IT security, where does he or she begin?

Just a thought

In the above situation, how does the security manager measure likelihood and consequence?

Subject matter expertise

It is probably safe to assume that the IT system in question is owned by a corporate body – let us assume a city bank – and that institute will have its own IT systems engineering and management department or team that one presumes will be intimate with the operational capabilities of the network. Who better, then, to question about the likelihood of an attack and the consequences should an attack take place? Now you may think this is abrogation of responsibilities by the security manager who is being paid to carry out the security risk assessment and not the network engineers, but I would dispute that argument.

There is a phrase which may be used under these circumstances, and that is "Jack of all trades, master of none", and I don't mean to be harsh on the security manager here, not at all. I am merely making best use of resources at my disposal.

The network engineers, knowing the capabilities and frailties of their system, will be best placed to understand and explain exactly what vulnerabilities within the network will attract the attacker, because the security manager has asked them to "think like a criminal" and decide what course of action they would take if they were the potential perpetrators. The network engineers, understanding the vulnerabilities and limitations of the system, will also be able to advise on the consequences or impact of an attack. The next stage in the IT network security risk assessment is to decide on the risk treatment required to safeguard the systems against attack, and therefore reduce the risk score (more of that later). Once again, who is ideally positioned to give this advice? Yes, of course: the network engineers.

The professional security manager must have a good working knowledge of areas related directly to security, but he or she is unlikely (not guaranteed, of course) to be a qualified IT engineer (or a ship's master). So, the security manager must always be cognisant of the fact that he or she may require assistance from other 'experts', and that professionals in all fields may be subject matter experts in their own domain, but nobody is a master of all domains.

Moving on, the security risk assessment. My definition of a security risk assessment is this:

> A process that identifies organisational assets, the vulnerability of and threats to those assets, and the likelihood and impact of a successful attack against the assets.

It is generally agreed that there are two types of risk assessment, both being related to individual research models:

- *Quantitative risk assessment*

  A quantitative risk assessment requires an examination of the likelihood and impact of a known threat, resulting in a probabilistic risk value.

  Visually, this type of risk assessment normally takes the form of a mathematical calculation within a risk matrix, with a weighted result. See Figure 3.1.

  As a result of the security risk assessment, it was decided that on a scale of 1 to 5 (1 being the least likely), the likelihood of the IT system being attacked was estimated at 3, whilst the impact would rate a score of 4. This calculation offers us a score of 12 out of a total 25 marks (5 × 5).

  If this form of quantitative risk assessment was to be used in conjunction with what is referred to as the RAG (red, amber, green) approach, the risk assessment value of

	Impact	1	2	3	4	5
Likelihood						
1						
2						
3					12	
4						
5						

Index

Red	Act
Amber	Document
Green	Observe

Figure 3.1 The quantitative risk assessment risk matrix in relation to the threat of an attack against an IT system

12 would be placed in the amber zone in accordance with the assessment index, which would be part of the risk register, and there would be an obligation to document the score in accordance with organisational procedures.

*   *Qualitative risk assessment*

    While the assessment of risk in quantitative terms is usually preferred in the security sector, it is sometimes neither practical nor possible. There may be no mathematical data or research evidence available to arrive at a calculated score, so the risk value is qualitatively defined as either low, medium, or high, or described within the RAG approach, which means the risk value falls into either the red, amber, or green sectors. Normally, the value within the green sector requires monitoring; in the amber sector it will need to be recorded; and in the red sector action is required to treat the risk.

    Figure 3.2 illustrates a qualitative risk assessment matrix, showing a severity scale of low likelihood but high impact. An example of this may be a terrorist attack in a suburban area of the UK. Intelligence supports the fact that the likelihood of such an attack is low; however, because of the density of population and critical infrastructure located close to the populated area, the impact would be high, as there is likely to be mass casualties and fatalities, and potentially severe damage to critical national infrastructure.

Risk component parts

Earlier in this sub-chapter we examined the definition of the term 'risk', and I believe we accepted the definition argued by the Royal Society:

> The probability that a particular adverse event occurs during a stated period of time, or results from a particular challenge.

Very often when teaching risk management, I would challenge my students to define risk for me, and on a number of occasions – after an extended concerned look of pain on the majority of learner faces, who are trying meaningfully to define a four-letter word that is used every day – I receive answers such as:

"The threat"
"The vulnerability"

	Impact	Low	Medium	**High**
Likelihood				
Low				X
Medium				
High				

Figure 3.2 The qualitative risk assessment

"The impact"
And so on.

In fact, what they are describing are the component parts of risk; because risk is a theory, it is a concept that is in effect an umbrella for its component parts.

So, let us examine the various component parts that constitute risk.

Assets

> Something of value, in financial terms, owned by an organisation and requiring some form of protection.

Added to this definition is the fact that an asset should have some form of protection.

Just a moment

In descending order, most important first, list the five most important assets in your life or perhaps your business.

Of course, in a similar vein to risk, asset prioritisation is very subjective, and you will have your own views about the importance of assets in either your personal life or business operations. However, below is a list of assets that you may recognise as having some importance, and subjectively this is my order of priority:

- People
- Brand and reputation
- Infrastructure
- Information
- Policies, plans, and procedures.

My belief is that people are irreplaceable and are therefore at the very summit in terms of my priorities.

Brand and reputation come a close second, because it generally takes a lifetime to build a trustworthy reputation, and that can be destroyed in a heartbeat.

Brand and reputation

British Petroleum, or BP as it is now known, has always been recognised, it can credibly be argued, as a forward-thinking, environmentally friendly company; one that has invested millions of dollars in corporate social responsibility (CSR). In 2010, the integrity, brand, and reputation of the company were tested to the limit when an environmental disaster as never seen before struck the Gulf of Mexico.

Case study: Deepwater Horizon

The Deepwater Horizon oil spill, also called the Gulf of Mexico oil spill, the largest marine oil spill in history, was caused by an explosion on 20 April 2010 on the Deepwater Horizon oil rig –located in the Gulf of Mexico, approximately 41 miles (66 km) off the coast of Louisiana – and its subsequent sinking on April 22.

On the night of April 20, a surge of natural gas blasted through a concrete core recently installed by contractor Halliburton in order to seal the well for later use. The rupture of the concrete core allowed crude oil to flow, which it did for 87 days, releasing 4.9 billion barrels (205.8 billion gallons) of oil into the water. Before the explosion, there were 126 crew members on board, 11 of whom were never found, suspected to have died during the explosion and consequent fire. Seventeen crew members were seriously injured. In financial terms, the total settlement is believed to have been approximately $124 billion, but a precise figure is impossible to calculate.

This was a lesson in how not to communicate a disaster.

The BP CEO at the time was Tony Hayward, who is alleged to have commented that the spill was relatively tiny compared to the very big ocean. This was one of the most disastrous spills in history, with the damage to wildlife and the environment being almost immeasurable. As mentioned, it appears that 11 crew members were killed, but at the height of the crisis, the CEO took a sailing holiday, asking the media to give him his life back.

Hayward was replaced as CEO on 1 October 2010.

Threats: capability combined with intent

> A threat is based on a combination of capability and intent, in relation to the aggressor.

Although this is a relatively straightforward concept, in terms of the risk assessment we are looking at threats to the organisational assets – perhaps the threat of kidnapping the CEO for ransom, or maybe the threat to set fire to a business building (arson). However, the greatest threat to business and the community today, in my opinion, emanates from the cybercriminal and cyberterrorist.

The cyberthreat today is far more advanced than it has ever been, with the cybercriminal always on the front foot.

Of course, the perpetrators won't just randomly attack the CEO or the building. There will generally be a great deal of planning, and part of that preparation will be the identification of any inherent weakness in the defences of the organisation. They will be looking for a vulnerability.

Vulnerability

> Vulnerability is a weakness in the system, or the measurement of exposure to some form of risk.

Using the analogy of the CEO kidnapping scenario, the potential attackers will be looking for an opportunity borne out of a weakness that they believe will offer the opportunity to commit the crime. It may be that the potential victim is picked up at home every day at the same time and uses the same route to the office. Equally it may be that on certain days the CEO walks to work unprotected. Both situations will alert the kidnappers, and they will be seen as weaknesses that allow or even encourage the attack.

Whilst travelling on public transport or perhaps staying at a hotel overseas, the CEO is likely to have his laptop with him, and here is another vulnerability or series of vulnerabilities that the attacker is looking for. Of course, the mere factor that the executive is in possession of his laptop doesn't necessarily constitute a vulnerability; rather, it is the way in which he takes care of it – or perhaps not.

Just a thought

In your opinion, what are the main vulnerabilities in terms of carrying a laptop or any other mobile communications hardware?

Take a look at the following list of common vulnerabilities when carrying a laptop:

- *The laptop*: In the first instance, security of the laptop itself is critical. If not in use, it should be placed in some form of secure location; maybe a lockable cabinet, or a secure desk drawer. If it is going to be left within an insecure room, perhaps on an open desk, then it should be secured, using a reliable cable and locking system.
- *Laptop software*: Absolutely no organisational data should be downloaded onto a company or public service laptop. That is an easy rule, but it is one that is too often circumvented.
- *Public transport*: It is far too easy, when travelling on public transport, particularly the train, for the laptop user to be immersed in whatever they are working on during the journey, failing to see the passenger next to him constantly scanning the laptop, and making notes about what he or she sees. This lack of security awareness also sends out the signal that the user of the laptop is either disinterested in security or maybe just unaware. However, the potential attacker is now perhaps looking for an opportunity to steal the laptop, if it is left unattended, which is quite likely.
- *Private transport*: Whilst there is a different threat plane here, the threat is nonetheless real. The central difference between the two scenarios is of course that whilst driving, the CEO is not consulting his or her laptop; that is until he or she stops at a service station, or overnight at a hotel, when once again the threat is from the perceived casual observer, or from the burglar during lunch or dinner, and the laptop is left insecure in the hotel room.

  However, on too many occasions laptops and tablets have been left insecure in an observable location in the car, normally on the rear seat, just before they have been stolen. Be under no illusion that a secure vehicle will deter the potential thief if he or she can see the device in open view. If the vehicle is parked at a location where there is little surveillance, either in the form of a security officer presence or CCTV, and the lighting may be poor, there is every likelihood that the rational choice criminal will break into the vehicle to steal the device. What does he or she have to lose? If they are successful in their efforts, at the very least they will probably be in possession of an expensive tablet or laptop that can be moved on; but if they strike lucky, they have in their possession layers of information and data that the organisation employing the CEO cannot afford to lose.

- *Bars and restaurants*: The next time that you are enjoying a meal at a city centre restaurant, take note of the number of diners who are completely engrossed in either their laptop or tablet. They are likely to be using the machine, not merely before the meal is served, or whilst waiting for their sweet; but probably while they are eating. So what, you may ask? That is the fast pace of life we live today, and of course you are correct, inasmuch as it is totally acceptable to carry a laptop or tablet into a bar or restaurant, it happens all of the time. The problem, of course, is that because the machine is in constant use, and is almost surgically attached to corporate businessmen or woman, there comes a time when the bond has to be broken; generally, after a couple of pints of beer, or a few glasses of wine, when the bladder has its way. Now of course you would be correct to argue that the professional user of such equipment will take it with them everywhere they go. They will of course, when nature calls, disconnect the power, remove any plug-in devices, and take the laptop with them to the loo! Perhaps that is a standard operating procedure (SOP) in a parallel universe, but my experience on planet Earth tells otherwise. On too many occasions I have sat and watched as business people either dash off to the restroom, casually hiding their device under their jackets (like that is going to help), or stupidly leave the laptop on the table in the hope that it will still be there when they return. And of course, it will, because it is always somebody else who's going to be stolen from (I don't think!). Probably the worst-case scenario here is when the businessman has to face the call of nature, and all of a sudden the guy on the table next to him, who incidentally is not using a device, is a trusted companion, who will of course defend the device with his very life.

  We hear our CEO saying, "I say old chap, would you be kind enough to keep an eye on my laptop whilst I dash off to spend a penny?" Well of course he will. He will keep both eyes on it as he casually leaves the restaurant so as not to cause too much of a fuss. When other diners are asked by the police for a description, the silent grey man has made his exit unseen, with the company's five-year financial plans on his newly acquired device. Bingo!

- *In a hotel*: For some obscure reason, people staying away from home on business at times believe that they are impenetrable and will not be the target for a criminal or terrorist; and I have no idea why that is. As with senior managers eating in restaurants and bars, there is the impression that everyone is their friend, and will, at the drop of a hat look after their laptops with their lives; and unfortunately the criminal knows this. Notwithstanding eating in the hotel restaurant (which is covered in the previous section) the security of laptops is most compromised during three distinct periods.

- *Entering the hotel*: From my experience, business managers tend to enter the hotel in a state of flux, because they are using their cell phones, that are trying to pay the taxi driver whilst the hotel door person is trying to wrestle their bags from them to take to their rooms. They then have to check in, whilst probably still engaged in a telephone conversation, and it is far too easy to place the laptop on the floor by their feet; and that is what the thief wants and expects. One loss of concentration and the laptop is gone.

- *When the laptop is in the hotel room*: Our friend from the previous section has managed to fight off the door person, pay the taxi driver, check in and make it to his room. However it is now eight in the evening and his colleagues are waiting for him in the bar with a cold pint of beer and the promise of steak and chips courtesy of the company credit card. He or she will probably either throw the laptop bag on the bed or place it on the dressing table and rush off to the bar. The criminal has been watching this harassed businessperson and has a copy of the room swipe card. He or she can now say goodbye to the laptop, or the data it contains.

- *When leaving the hotel*: Here we go again. Still using the cell phone, whilst rushing to check out, because there is a plane or train to catch in thirty minutes. Once again, far too often the laptop is the last priority.

Case study: TSB data loss in 2018

On 20 April 2018, TSB began to migrate all of its customer data from their current system to an IT system used by their new owners, Sabadell. Customers were optimistically informed that that they would be able to access their accounts on 22 April 2019. However, on 22 April 2019, TSB customers began to complain that services were erratic. Balances were incorrect, transactions had been cancelled, and a number of customers informed the bank that they could see the details from other accounts. That should have been a critical warning to the bank's security function, because if accounts were accessible, fraud was just around the corner.

By 24 April 2019, 1.9 million TSB customers were locked out of their accounts, with the bank at that stage only able to apologise profusely.

Despite being informed by the bank on 26 April 2019 that the problems had been solved, customers after seven days were still having problems accessing their accounts, and worse was to come, as it appears that whilst the bank was attempting to solve the IT problems, fraudsters were taking the opportunity to attack TSB customers.

According to a BBC report on 6 June 2019,[12] fraud has become a problem, with confused customers being tricked into allowing access to their accounts.

Mr Pester (TSB CEO) said that 70 times the normal level of attacks were seen from criminals attempting to "exploit" the problems TSB were experiencing.

Yet the FCA said that TSB had failed to refund their money quickly enough having initially been "overwhelmed" by the weight of cases. Some 10,600 alerts about cases of potential fraud were identified. TSB said in 1,300 cases money had been taken from accounts.

At times, only 1 in 10 calls about fraud were answered, but TSB said, as a result, it put in a new dedicated fraud line.

Among the unhappy customers is photographer Paul Clarke, who could not use online accounts. Then in the confusion he was defrauded of more than £10,000 and spent days arguing on the phone to get TSB to say it would pay the money back.

"I've lost all confidence now that TSB have got a grip on this. I don't know the situation on my accounts – I can't get in there. I have no confidence in their ability either to answer phones or to get my account back into a secure position", he said.

One TSB customer told BBC Radio 4's *You and Yours* in November 2019 that he watched thousands of pounds in wedding savings being stolen from his Internet account as he waited on hold for the bank's fraud department.

Ben Alford, from Weymouth in Dorset, said it took more than four hours to get through to TSB, by which time most of the money had gone. TSB said it had put in "additional resources" to support customers.

The *Guardian* reported on 19 November 2019 that an independent report into the bank's 2018 meltdown found that the board of TSB lacked "common sense" and shifted customers to a new IT platform before it had been fully tested.

The report, commissioned by the bank and carried out by law firm Slaughter and May, said the board failed to ask its contractor key questions ahead of the launch, which resulted in nearly 1.9 million customers being locked out of their accounts.[13]

This was almost a disaster waiting to arrive and should have been foreseen in a credible risk assessment carried out before the migration. But whether we are talking about cyber, terrorism or general crime, part of the risk assessment for the business is to understand the probability of such an attack; the likelihood.

Likelihood

The probability of an incident occurring, in the knowledge that such an occurrence is not certain.

In terms of the risk assessment, this stage is arguably the most complicated, in that, in my opinion, it is subjective. Attempting to estimate (because that is exactly what it is: an estimation) the likelihood of an event is of course attempting to predict the future, and as far as I am aware, as yet there is no analytical software that can do that with 100% certainty, so it's up to you and me!

Just a moment

In your opinion, during the course of a security risk assessment, how should likelihood be estimated?

Once again, referring to my training days, when asked how to ascertain the likelihood of an event in the context of a security risk assessment, very often my students would opt for an examination of past instances:

Well, if there have been ten burglaries, in the same street, carried out at roughly the same time, during the day, it is likely that similar crime will be committed in the future.

I have no issues researching statistical historic crime patterns and using that data as part of the likelihood estimation, but I would argue that the use of such information alone is flawed. My question to the same student would be this:

> OK. Does it therefore correlate that no historical crime activity in that street means that there will be none in the future?

Of course, that would be totally inaccurate because there is insufficient evidence to support such an argument.

So in terms of likelihood measurement, the first issue to consider is the asset which is being protected. As an example, ask the following questions in relation to the company IT system:

- Is the asset critical to the organisation, and what benefits would theft or damage of the asset be to an attacker? Your business has recently invested heavily in R&D of a programme that is beneficial to the UK defence communications sector in terms of secure communications; hostile states are naturally eager to determine the construction and commercial/defence benefits of the programme.
- Is the asset vulnerable in such a way that would offer an attacker the opportunity to steal or clone the programme? For instance, is there 'end-to-end' encryption of all data used by the programme?
- What are the current threats to the asset, and from where do they originate? Perhaps the current and most concerning threat is espionage or a cyberattack, and that threat comes from a perceived hostile state.
- What intelligence sources are at your disposal for analysis of current threat patterns? Perhaps, as the programme is to the benefit of the defence industry, you will be able to call on government intelligence agencies to carry out a threat analysis for you.

Of course, there is also the question of context and the use of subject matter experts, particularly if the person being asked to carry out the risk assessment is not an expert in that field.

In terms of threats to a company's IT system, whether it is espionage or cyber, it is always advisable to consult those professionals whose task it is to manage the network. Not only are you more assured of receiving the most professional advice, but you will also reach out to peers from divergent functions, offering them the opportunity to involve themselves in a project that directly impacts them.

Impact

> The result of a successful attack, or the result of an action against an entity. Two things coming together will create an impact.

In terms of the security risk assessment, in which the asset is a very sensitive IT programme, the impact would be a successful attack and theft or destruction of the programme. Whereas the measurement of likelihood is complex, the determination of the impact is relatively straightforward, but once again I would strongly advise you to consult a subject matter expert for an accurate assessment or impact analysis.

Risk treatment and control measures

It is generally argued that risk per se cannot be eliminated. I tend to use the approach that risk is a probabilistic concept, a theory strongly related to mathematics and philosophy, and to that end it will always be with us in some form or other.

Bamfield writing in Gill (2014) says that an organisation can adopt one or more of number of generic strategies to deal with identified risks. Risks may be *avoided* for example, by the organisation ceasing practices or ending production of goods or services that carry particular risks. Reduction may involve improved staff training, the use of safer equipment, or better procedures to ensure that the likelihood and the effect of the event will be lowered. Risks may be *spread* so that information systems data may be continually backed up to other sites, or assets held in several locations to prevent a major corporate failure occurring as the result of a catastrophe at a specific location. Risk *transfer* occurs when the responsibility for some types of risk is shifted elsewhere for example, to an insurance company or third party outsource provider; and risk *acceptance* involves the organisation acknowledging that whatever changes are made, there will always be some residual elements of risk. Risk management principles and guidelines for use within an organisation are classified by the International Standard ISO 31000: 2009 (ISO 2009).

To minimise risk, these generic strategies need to be combined (rather than each risk being seen as requiring only one solution) in order to have the greatest effect (Gill, 2014).

Reduce the risk

Figure 3.3 in this sub-chapter illustrates a quantitative risk assessment matrix, in which it has been determined that the likelihood of a criminal attack against our IT systems shows a severity level of 12/25. In order to reduce the risk, we must introduce a range of IT control measures (stronger password regime; more rigorous firewalls; up-to-date patches, etc.) which will hopefully deter the criminal from attacking the network. This should reduce the likelihood of an attack and hopefully reduce the impact if an attack takes place. This will potentially produce a score of 6 (2×3), which means the risk is reduced by 50% and is moved from documentation to observation. See Figure 3.3.

Avoid the risk

Operationally and from a business perspective, the only logical means of avoiding risk is not to carry out the proposed operation. Of course, in business that option is never as simple as it may seem.

Impact	1	2	3	4	5
Likelihood					
1					
2			6		
3				12	
4					
5					

Figure 3.3 Quantitative risk assessment matrix before and after control measures have been applied

Using the maritime environment as an example: a shipping line may have a contract to move heavy diesel oil from Djibouti, which is west of the Gulf of Aden, to Yemen, a sea journey of approximately 620 kilometres. Under normal circumstances this would be a very straightforward journey north-east, with a sailing time of about 30 hours. However, recent history has identified the Gulf of Aden as being what is referred to by mariners as a high-risk area (HRA) because of the intense threat of attack by armed Somalian pirates. The method of operation of such piracy groups is to take over the vessel, kill members of the crew if necessary (with the exception of key personnel such as the master, the chief engineer, etc.), and hold the ship to ransom until the ship's owners pay a substantial amount of money, normally several million US dollars.

Any professional shipping line in this situation will carry out a due diligence risk assessment, taking into consideration all factors such as the attractiveness of the asset, current intelligence, and the strength of any potential adversaries. It is highly likely that the assessment will show a considerably high risk factor for that journey at this present moment. There are no mitigation strategies, such as armed guards or fortified areas of the ship that will deter the pirates, so the most obvious decision to make is to avoid the journey.

However, in today's maritime economic climate, it is also highly likely that the option of cancelling such a lucrative contract as this will not be taken without due care and consideration about the development of the business, and the cost of no sale. Certainly, the business development director and probably the chief executive officer will need to be convinced by the security department that the only option is to cancel the operation, or else put the lives of the crew and the possession of the ship in severe danger. If the operation is cancelled, then of course the risk is avoided. Reality tells me that the debate with business development will be long and hard, and is certainly not to be taken lightly.

Risk transference

> Risk transference is when the risk is moved to a second party. A good example is when a car is insured, where the risk is managed by the insurance broker.

The shipping line involved in transiting the HRA would not have the financial resources to cover every type of risk that besets a vessel on the high seas, and whether the risk is from severe weather or a possible attack by a group of pirates, the ship must be insured. The largest and most famous maritime shipping insurer is of course Lloyd's of London, who have been involved in insurance brokering since 1668. When maritime insurance rates are discussed, this is in reality an agreement that the insurance broker will accept responsibility for all risks agreed in the insurance contract.

Residual risk

> Residual risk is the threat remaining after all means of mitigation have been applied.

Despite very intelligent advice offered by the security department, the owners of the vessel in the preceding scenario have decided to continue with the journeys across the high-risk area in the Gulf of Aden.

The company has decided to have all fleet vessels fitted with a citadel. A citadel is an armoured space, normally either in the engine room or close to the bridge, where the crew can take refuge very quickly and securely. Also, it has been decided at board level to deploy contract armed guards for every sailing. Normally recruited from national armed forces, every armed guard will carry a self-loading rifle (SLR) and will be conversant with all rules of engagement (ROE) in the event of an attack by armed criminals. Extra deck and overboard lighting will be installed, and whilst under way the ship's railings will be protected by razor wire. The precautions taken will lower the risk factor, because it is anticipated that the majority of piracy groups will not attack a vessel at sea which is so visually defended. However, that is not to say that piracy groups desperately in need of finance, or perhaps merely not deterred by razor wire and rifles, will not carry out an attack; so, the risk is still there – that is residual risk.

Risk acceptance

The level of risk that is deemed acceptable when risk treatment has been considered.

Risk acceptance, or as it is sometimes referred to as the 'risk appetite', appears to be such a simple definition of what a straightforward process should be. The risk assessment is carried out by a competent person, and the risk factor for the organisation is announced, offering the board the opportunity to either reduce the risk, avoid it, transfer it, or accept it. Here is where company politics far too often take over, particularly if the risk assessor, who is (let us say) the security manager, is inexperienced.

Why is that important, I hear you asking?

To the inexperienced risk assessor, the idea of accepting any risk is anathema. Why on earth should the company be prepared to put itself in jeopardy by accepting a risk that may harm or damage not just the infrastructure and operations, but also the brand and reputation of *his* or *her* business? He or she demands the board make sufficient efforts to target harden, defend in depth, guard, write more effective procedures ... do anything, at no matter what cost is involved to protect the company. "What do you mean we need a cost benefit analysis", he or she says. "Just purchase the systems recommended, and then we will all be safe". Possibly, but how about safe and bankrupt?

An experienced risk assessor would realise that carrying out a risk assessment is no more than compiling evidence in relation to assets, threats, vulnerabilities, and so on before passing that evidence on to the board for their consideration. The risk belongs to the business, and if the executive board, acting in the best interests of that business, its staff, and its shareholders, decides to accept the risk for whatever reason, it is their decision. That in essence is what risk acceptance is; a board-level decision based on the good and benefit of the organisation. And of course, critical to this is the manner and way in which the risk is communicated.

Risk communication

Just a moment

In your opinion, what is risk communication, and how important is effective risk communication to an organisation?

Risk communication is having the ability to manage two-way communication in order to ensure that all parties involved are aware of risk that may pertain to them and their organisations. Central to this is the relationship between the expert and the layperson.

Whilst still in its early developmental stage as an academic field, risk communication has largely emerged from earlier work in the area of risk perception (Pidgeon et al., 1992 in Borodzicz, 2005). This happened for two reasons. First there was concern about the passing of quantitative information about risks to laypeople from expert analysts. Ordinary people would find it increasingly difficult to understand the types of highly technical information that experts are very good at producing. Second, this is often further complicated by the use of an abstract, and is difficult due to comprehensive (and overly complicated) argot in which such information is presented (Slovic, 1002; Covello et al., 1986; Covello, 1991).

However, it doesn't end there. Some risk communication theorists even suggest that experts cannot agree among themselves as to what constitutes a risk. For example, in a case study of the *Exxon Valdez* oil spill on 24 March 1989, it was found that a situation of 'multiple realities' existed among the expert decision makers responding to the event. In particular, there was some considerable confusion among the response staff about whether the crew should have been airlifted from the stricken vessel so quickly. It was argued by some response staff that the vessel could have been diverted from its collision course with the rocks if there had been a crew on board (Browning and Shetler, 1992 in Borodzicz, 2005, p. 34).

The sociologist Brian Wynne suggests that a serious dialogue between expert and layman has yet to be embarked upon if risk communication is to become an effective framework for establishing rationality in risk management (Wynne, 1989 in Borodzicz, 2005).

Can you think of an example of risk communication in which the 'expert' struggles to explain a technical concept to a layperson?

Reflecting on the section in which we discussed risk avoidance, in terms of transiting the Gulf of Aden, you will recall the dilemma faced was the security function attempting to communicate the risk of moving through a high risk area, whilst the commercial department was doing its best to convince the Executive Board that this was a risk worth taking because of the potential (nothing is certain) huge return on investment. Whilst the company has a requirement to show due diligence in relation to the safety and security of its staff (i.e. the crew of the vessel), the lure of commercial return will always be a strong negotiating tool. So how do we tackle this problem? How do we effectively communicate the risk of sailing a ship through a high-risk area?

We could always gather legal defence material, arguing that should any of our vessels be attacked, resulting in casualties or even fatalities, the executive board, as it is a UK-flagged vessel, will be liable for prosecution under the Corporate Manslaughter and Corporate Homicide Act 2007, which warns that companies and organisations can be found guilty of corporate manslaughter as a result of serious management failures resulting in a gross breach of a duty of care.[14] This may frighten the board, and perhaps the transits will be cancelled until the area is safe, or such a threat may alienate the directors, convincing them that security will always be a business disabler, with no business acumen whatsoever.

I am not for one second advocating leaving the board in the dark until it is too late; we as security professionals have a duty to ensure that we offer the best possible legal advice, but in an appropriate manner. We need to think very carefully about our risk communication strategy.

While every situation is different and needs a different type of response depending on the specific circumstances, there are five separate elements to consider:

1   Whether it is risk communication or any other element of security risk management, preparation is critical. Worst-case scenarios have to be considered, and they will emanate from the original risk assessment.

  In terms of our maritime scenario, there are a number of crises that the shipping line security function will need to be prepared for. Assuming the worst-case scenario is that the executive board elects to accept the advice from the sales team, and no matter what the risk assessment illustrates, the transit is going to take place, come hell or high water (excuse the pun!). Potentially even more concerning would be the situation in which the board was not prepared to finance physical security (reducing the risk), allowing purely for insurance cover (risk transference).

2   Another crucial area to be aware of when planning any form of risk communication delivery is understanding who the recipient is and what might be their expectations. Are there any personality issues, do you have allies, and who are your competitors?

  The security function is at a major disadvantage in terms of this piece of advice; in that the sales team are represented by the sales director (who has the ear of the CEO) on the board, whilst the security team is represented by the HR director! Quite obviously the chief executive needs as much information as possible in relation to all aspects of the transit. Whilst they may be swayed by the personal relationship they have with the sales director, the security function lead will need to not only diligently research the risk implications of the transit, they will have to ensure that their risk communications are impeccable. Ensuring their conduit, the HR director fully understands the information that they have to communicate to the board. This may take several briefings prior to the next board meeting.

3   It is always tempting to make spectacular announcements, but the problem, of course, is that often extravagant communications may bear little resemblance with a situation that can change on a regular basis. A promise broken can have disastrous results, with honesty and integrity being devalued in the eyes of the recipient.

  This aspect of risk communication relates to the dynamic risk assessment. Prior to the board decision about whether to accept the transit through the Gulf of Aden or not, the security function lead must analyse the risk to the transit on a 24/7 basis, and it is likely that the situation will be changing constantly, as this is a pirate-infested high-risk area, and quite literally anything can happen. The board must be constantly updated, but there must not be an atmosphere of fear, because that will lead to poor leadership and management, which is the last thing that is required at this moment in time.

4   Moving on from point 3, honesty is always the best policy, and whilst it is advised to be cautious, it is crucial to be absolutely honest and transparent. It is easy to communicate all of the good aspects of risk, but it may be difficult to tell the board something that maybe they don't want to hear.

  Perhaps this where the expert versus layperson is emphasised most effectively. The board wants – no, demands – as much information as possible; they want it when it happens, and they need it communicated in a manner that they can understand. They demand honesty without complication.

I recall answering a risk management question for my first line manager not long after graduating with an MSc in security management. I recall with some embarrassment citing a scholarly answer that bore no resemblance to the question asked. My manager, John Roke, who was the group security controller – who had no academic qualifications but had been discharged from the Royal Marine Commandos as a regimental sergeant major – looked at me rather scarily and said, "Charles, when I ask you a question about a jar of pickles, I need to know how to unscrew the lid; not the relative density of the liquid inside!" Lesson learned.

5   Post-crisis communication is generally about understanding where the team excelled and where lessons have to be learned. No situation is going to be a 100% success throughout, and sometimes the security manager delivering the risk or crisis communication may have to 'take it on the chin'. It's all about honesty and integrity.

In this fictitious scenario, the board has decided to listen to the sales team and continue with the transit across the Gulf of Aden. The senior directors have also acquiesced to the risk mitigation advice offered by the security function, primarily surrounding the deployment of armed guards and the installation of a robust citadel.

During the transit, the vessel was attacked by three groups of armed pirates deployed from a mother ship five miles from the coast of Yemen, south-west of Aden. Fortunately, the pirates identified the ship as being protected by skilled, armed personnel, and after an initial skirmish, during which warning shots were fired by the guards on board the tanker, the potential attackers decided to seek an easier target.

The vessel reached its destiny, the port of Aden, without damage or injury, but of course the incident had occurred, and it had to be communicated to the executive board. This is an opportunity for the security team to produce a concise post-incident report highlighting details of the incident, including the success of having armed guards on board, and any lessons learned.

Now at the end of this sub-chapter you are invited to engage in an ongoing exercise that will develop and evolve throughout the remainder of the book.

Exercise Brave Defender: security and risk management

Scenario

For the purpose of the overall exercise, you are the designated global corporate security manager employed by a multi-national telecommunications company, with a corporate global footprint encompassing 22 countries.

Britcom UK: 1 Canada Fields

Britcom is a multinational telecommunications company, with its headquarters located in the heart of the UK's financial district, Canary Fields. At 1 Canada Fields, Britcom occupies the first ten floors, and through contractual agreement, manages access to the 35-floor building by subcontracting Canary Fields Security plc. There are approximately 600 full- and part-time members of staff and management, including the executive board, with the boardroom being located on the tenth floor. There is no public access to the Britcom floors except by appointment.

The building is operational on a 24/7 basis, and within the same footprint on the ground floor is a shopping mall facility, with direct links to the London Underground system.

There is also an underground car park for staff parking and goods inward delivery to the shopping mall outlets, with entrances to the east and west of the building; the car park is also open on a 24/7 basis, with security of the car park being supplied by Canary Fields security plc.

Security systems at 1 Canada Fields

- *Manned guarding*

  Canary Fields security works a three-shift system, which consists of:

  - 0600hrs to 1400hrs: Ten security officers manning the ground floor
    Two security officers manning the security control room Four security officers manning the underground car park One supervisor
    Subtotal: 17 security officers/supervisor
  - 1400hrs to 2200hrs: Ten security officers manning the ground floor
    Two security officers manning the security control room Four security officers manning the underground car park One supervisor
    Subtotal: 17 security officers/supervisor
  - 2200hrs to 0600hrs: Two security officers manning the ground floor (and patrolling inside only)
    One security officer manning the security control room Four security officers manning the underground car park One supervisor
    Subtotal: 8 security officers/supervisor
  - Rest day: Seventeen security officers/supervisor
    Senior security supervisor working days Monday to Friday
    Total: 42 security officers/supervisor
    In total there are 60 security officers and supervisors working the early, middle, and late shifts, with one shift on rest day. All security officers hold a front-line SIA licence, all are fire marshal trained, and at least one security officer per shift is first aid trained.
    Every security officer will be conversant with the on-site assignment instructions (AI), which are written by the Canary Fields Security plc management, and owned by Canary Fields plc.
    All four security supervisors hold a level four qualification in security management, and the senior supervisor has a bachelor's degree in security risk management.

- *Closed circuit television (CCTV)*

  - Cameras: There are total of 48 analogue/digital static cameras installed at the following locations:

    - Internal: Ground floor

      - 2 x cameras observing the reception area from the main entrance.
      - 2 x cameras observing the front door from the reception area.

- 3 x cameras located behind the reception area observing that location and the route from the main door to it.
- One camera observing each of the four lift doors.
- Two cameras observing the access control turnstiles.
- Six cameras located in the underground car park and goods inward.

- External: Ground floor

  - Eight cameras offering 360-degree cover of the building.
  - Four cameras covering the four fire exits.

- Internal: Floors one to ten

  - Four cameras covering the lifts.
  - Two cameras covering the stairs.

- Internal: Floor five – data halls

  - Four cameras covering the lifts.
  - Two cameras covering the stairs.
  - Two cameras covering each (2) hall entrance.
  - Six cameras inside the halls.

There are total of 48 cameras installed within the ten floors, and external to the building.

Cabling telemetry is by means of category 5 fibre-optic cable, and power is supplied by the national grid feed. There is a uninterruptible power supply (UPS) and standby generator in the event of a power outage.

Controls for the CCTV system are located within the data halls, and all monitors (monochrome and colour) are installed within the security control room. Access is by privileged status only.

The CCTV system is ten years old and is overdue for an upgrade.

Access control

- *External to internal:* There is a single, two leaf inwards-swinging glass entrance that is open during daylight working hours.

  There are four single leaf outward-swinging steel fire doors to the rear of the building; both are secured from the inside with standard crash bar fixing. All doors are alarmed when secure, and all entrances are covered by the building CCTV system.

- *Internal:* Throughout the ten floors occupied by Britcom, access control is by means of a dual proximity card reader/PIN system. All members of staff and management are issued an identity card with an appropriate access control card included, and every card can be amended by the security function, including deletion if required. For entry to the data halls, which is IT privileged only, complementing the proximity/PIN access control is a thumbprint biometric system installed on each door.

  All visitors and contractors are issued a temporary pass whilst on site, and passes must be surrendered when the holder exits the building.

- *Underground car park and goods inward area*: Staff will use their identity cards for access, and all contractors and visitors will be issued a temporary pass which must be surrendered upon leaving.

  When a member of staff leaves the organisation or is dismissed, his or her pass will be deleted from the system within an hour of departure.

Intruder detection system (IDS)

Office spaces on floors 1–4 and 6–10 are protected by a passive infrared (PIR) volumatic IDS, which when activated signals to the security control room on the ground floor, and there will be an immediate response from the patrolling security officers.

On the fifth floor where the data halls are located, the floor space outside of the lift is protected by a PIR IDS, and all doors have contact IDS which activate if the door is forced. The doors to the data halls are also contacted and are fitted with a door hold open alarm, which activates if the door is left open for more than 60 seconds. Inside the data halls, the space is protected once again by a volumatic PIR IDS, signalling to the security control room.

The building is locked down at 2200hrs, and all entrances are contact alarmed.

Britcom plc

Mission statement:

> Our mission revolves around a total dedication to the quality of service and experience our customers receive from us: Britcom Plc is a customer-centric distribution business that will grow shareholder value and deliver an excellent, continuously improving, customer experience.

Unique selling point

The unique selling point (USP) is cloud-based secure communications. Unlike other telecommunications organisations that offer cost effective, user-friendly cloud communications, Britcom bases its reputation and business growth on the ability and capacity to securely manage all of its customer data and communications information.

Britcom plc is a truly multinational telecommunications company, with a global footprint representing 25 countries in Europe, the Middle East, and Africa as well as the US and Russia. The company currently employs approximately 100,000 people, and in the fiscal year 2018/19 generated a net income of just over £2 billion.

Britcom sells and delivers all forms of telecommunications including land-based communications systems and cloud networking, and is constantly seeking business growth in areas untapped by other communications companies.

Current delivery platforms by geographical location.

- Europe

  Britcom's strongest area of activity, with current robust business platforms in the UK, Germany, France, Portugal, Croatia, Holland, and Belgium.

- The Americas

    Developing markets in the US, Canada, Mexico, Brazil, and Argentina.

- The Middle East

    Developing markets in United Arab Emirates (UAE), Bahrain, Qatar, Saudi Arabia, and Oman.

- Africa

    Developing markets in Egypt, Algeria, Tunisia, and Kenya.

- Russia

    Britcom is currently in negotiations with the Russian government in an effort to become the major shareholder in the Russian telecommunications conglomerate, Russtel. The main problem here is the complex political situation in the Russian Federation. Britcom is placed to win a number of major contracts in the country but is facing strong opposition from Chinese telecommunications group Tai Chi Comms.

Risk

There is considerable risk in the Russian venture, mainly because it is unchartered waters for Britcom, having never operated in such a restricted and regulated country where the opposition is formidable and where corruption is extremely embedded in all aspects of commerce and industry.

With risk comes context, and context is subjective and very strongly related to perception. There are no particular formula for measuring context, which is usually arrived at through discussion and debate. However, once the context is agreed, there are two well-used analysis tools that can assist an organisation in measuring its capabilities and capacity within each context.

In order for the executive board to clearly understand the context of this particular risk, two analysis tools will be used: SWOT and PESTLE. SWOT is generally used in the internal context and PESTLE in the external context. In the internal context, an organisation measures its own abilities, and in the external context, a company examines the environments in which it hopes to operate.

Internal – SWOT

- *Strengths*

    This is when an organisation examines its own inner strengths in order to understand capabilities and capacities.

    - Britcom

        Britcom is a multinational, leading-edge telecommunications organisation with excellent technical capabilities and the political and fiscal weight to launch the development of a new business strategy. It also has very strong links with a number of nation state government departments and a reputation that very few companies in the field can equal.

- *Weaknesses*

  What weaknesses can be found in terms of how the company performs, and are they weaknesses that can exploited by the opposition in any way, shape, or form?

  - Britcom

    Britcom has never operated in such a political or corrupt environment. Whilst comparisons can be made in a number of nations perhaps less advanced than the UK, there is no direct comparison to the environment and atmosphere found in Moscow.

- *Opportunities*

  In a commercial environment, the obvious opportunity will be business growth, but of course there are other areas such as the fostering of close business relations, and the possible influence of political decisions that may work to the advantage – in this case, Britcom plc.

  - Britcom

    Russia has a population of about 145 million people and a gross domestic product (GDP) of over $1.5 trillion. In many ways Russia is one of the fastest technologically developing countries in the world, however communications infrastructure for Russian citizens and Russian commerce and industry is far from those standards found in western nations.

- *Threats*

  What threats might a company face prior to embarking on a particular path? The threats may come from internal politics, or perhaps the fact that cash flow and financing capabilities are weak, threatening the advancement of business strategies.

  - Britcom

    The executive board of Britcom is split in terms of developing the Russian markets, with the risk and compliance function demanding caution and the business development functions pleading for the freedom to invest. There is the threat of deadlock, which may fracture the board.

External – PESTLE

- *Political*

  What are the current political circumstances in the country or region where development is about to take place? Is there political stability, or is there a potential for levels of political instability that may impact the development of business operations?

  - Britcom Russia

    Russia is an enigma in that although it is ruled by a singularly powerful and inflexible governing body, which declares itself to be a democratic republican government, it is well known that contracts are won or lost through contacts with the Kremlin. Relations between the UK and Russia are at quite a low ebb at the moment, and that may make it difficult for Britcom to have negotiated contracts awarded through government channels.

- *Economic*

    Whilst the organisation wishing to begin operations may be financially sound, what of the country or region where the development is to take place? The company will probably have to invest in not only research and development (R&D) and possible corporate social responsibility (CSR); it may also have to shore up a national government under circumstances that such an investment may show no return and potentially bankrupt the developing organisation.

    - Britcom Russia

        Although the Russian Federation may have a GDP of just over $1.5 trillion, levels of poverty and corruption are amongst the highest in the world. Britcom may face a situation where the company is not only investing in corporate social responsibility, but it may have to consider covert 'taxes' from local and national government sources. Sensible levels of return on investment (RoI) will have to be clearly communicated to all departments before the beginning of any business operation or exploratory discussions.

- *Social*

    As already mentioned, circumstance may dictate that a huge investment is made in terms of CSR. This normally takes the form of investment in the local community, perhaps introducing schooling, education or medical facilities to counter any inconvenience due to ongoing development of operations.

    - Britcom Russia

        The vast majority of Britcom operations and business activities will take place in heavily populated conurbations, such as towns and cities, so CSR should not be an issue of significance. However, British expatriates and Britcom UK–based staff and management may have to embed in Russian society, so there will be a need for extended levels of social awareness and interaction.

- *Technological*

    Whatever the potential operations may be, perhaps drilling for oil and gas or searching for rare elements, there will always be a requirement for technological support. Whilst the developing organisation may be able to provide limited technology for local operations and its own requirements, will there be the regional or national technological spine to support such operations? As an example, it is pointless drafting in high-tech equipment halfway across the globe if the electricity supply is inadequate, or if national communications capabilities fall short of what is required.

    - Britcom Russia

        This is another Russian enigma, in that although the Russian government and media will quickly declare the state to be technologically one of the most advanced nations in the world, this is not necessarily that accurate given it is generally based on Russian military technology. It is true that Russian military hardware is extremely advanced to a point, primarily because of the disproportionate funding spent on military research and development compared to other sectors such as health and education. However, there are still vast swathes of Russia where there is no electricity grid, and horse and cart are the prime movers in terms of local transport.

- *Legal*

  History is strewn with examples of corporations failing to take into consideration the local and international legal requirements of operating on foreign soil, and repercussions to be felt if transgressions of those laws are proven.

  - Britcom Russia. The legal system in Russia is still recovering from the tribulations conceived during Cold War years, and is relatively difficult to navigate.

- *Environmental*

  Woe betide any organisation in the twenty-first century that ignores the requirements to protect the environment. A global issue, environmental awareness and protection are always the first two issues on the agenda when new business is being discussed, particularly if such business impacts the local environment and how it affects close communities.

  - Britcom Russia

    Russia is the largest country in the world, with a land mass area of over 17 million square kilometres and a population of almost 146 million inhabitants, so it isn't surprising that there is great diversity in terms of the environment. Whilst the telecommunications business doesn't have the same environmental impact as, perhaps, drilling for gas and oil, from the moment any foreign operations begin they will be under the microscope to ensure that they are not transgressing any environmental laws or regulations.

Exercise Brave Defender – task 1: risk management

Synopsis

The current terrorism state in the United Kingdom and Northern Ireland has been raised to critical, which means that an attack is highly likely in the near future.[15] This has raised a number of concerns with the executive board, who understand that they have a duty of care to everyone using their premises, for whatever reason.

Task

You have been tasked with carrying out a security risk assessment of 1 Canada Fields to include the first ten floors, the shopping mall, and the underground car park and goods inward areas. The executive board has instructed you to focus squarely on the threat from terrorism.

The task is to be divided into two distinct areas:

1 The risk assessment and risk control

    Carry out a security risk assessment as mentioned earlier, taking into consideration the likelihood and impact of a terrorist attack against 1 Canary Fields. The type of security risk assessment (qualitative, quantitative, or semi-quantitative) is entirely your decision. The board has already decided that in terms of treatment, the risk will be reduced (remember, the risk belongs to the business, not you), so once the level of risk has been ascertained, you are to describe the measures to be taken in order that the risk may be reduced.

    Remember, subject matter expertise is critical in terms of carrying out an effective and robust security risk assessment. If you have little or no experience in the field of counterterrorism, whom should you speak to in order to accurately estimate likelihood and impact?

2 Risk communications

    Once the risk has been measured and reduced, you are to decide on a strategy in relation to how the risk will be communicated to the business. Here you should give thought to whom you intend to communicate with and how you intend to communicate.[16]

3.2 Crime Prevention Through Environmental Design (CPTED) and Situational Crime Prevention (SCP)

CPTED and SCP are two quite relatively new security theories that function in ways that complement each other. CPTED utilises the built environment, whilst SCP focusses on the offender and how he or she may be dissuaded from carrying out a criminal offence.

CPTED

CPTED originated from one of the most notable crime prevention books written in this century, *Defensible Space*, written by Oscar Newman in 1972. Newman referred to the theory as Crime Prevention Through Urban Design, with subtitles such as:

- An alternative to the fortress apartment
- An investigation of how architects can affect the attitudes and actions of tenants
- A proposal to design crime-free urban housing.

The likes of Lawrence Fennelly looked at what Newman had to say and very ably adapted the theory of defensible space to the protection of all areas of occupation, not just urban housing. Newman focussed on urban redevelopment in the US, but his argument can be extrapolated to include almost any occupational environment in any developed country. When discussing urban crime, Newman argued that the crime problems facing the US will not be answered through increased police forces or firepower. We are witnessing a breakdown of social mechanisms that once kept crime in check and gave direction and support to police activity. The small-town environments, rural or urban, which once framed and enforced their own moral codes have virtually disappeared. We have become strangers sharing the largest collective habitats in human history. Because of the size and density of our newly evolving (this was 1972)[17] urban megalopolis, we have become more dependent on each other, and more vulnerable to aberrant behaviour than we ever have been before.

Newman identified the importance, indeed criticality, of the architect as a means of designing out crime through the use of the environment. In the same book, he argued that architecture is not just a matter of style, image, and comfort. It can create encounter – and prevent it. Certain kinds of space and spatial layout favour the activities of criminals. An architect, armed with some understanding of the structure of criminal encounter, can simply avoid providing the space which supports it.

Why is one property robbed and vandalised while its neighbour remains crime-free? When louder alarms, increased police surveillance, and stronger locks fail to prevent crime? The answer to these questions of environmental security may be found in *defensible space design* living areas structured to inhibit crime and increase the community's control of its living (and working)[18] space. Fennelly and Clarke, recognising the work carried out by Newman, argue that

> the CPTED concept, is the proper design and effective use of the built environment that can lead to a reduction in the fear of crime and the incidence of crime, and to an improvement in the quality of life.
>
> (Jeffery, in Fennelly, 2013)

> The theory of Crime Prevention Through Environmental Design (CPTED) is based on one simple idea: that crime results partly from the opportunities presented by the physical environment. This being the case, it should be possible to alter the physical environment so that crime is less likely to occur.
>
> (Clarke, in Fennelly, 2013)

The first question asked in Fennelly's book, *Crime Prevention Through Environmental Design* (2013) is, "What is CPTED and how does it differ from traditional approaches to crime and loss control?"

Fennelly argues that CPTED is a natural approach to crime and loss control. CPTED differs from traditional approaches by placing most of its emphasis on human activities and how they become exposed to crime and loss. Traditional approaches to crime control centre on the offender, the offence, and the offender's background.

CPTED is not an alternative to other crime prevention methods; rather it is a means of complementing such strategies, including target hardening.

Target hardening is a theory that is generally bandied about rather loosely, sometimes meaninglessly, even though it is an excellent way of describing an increase in physical security such as stronger and more robust walls and doors, more effective locking systems, better perimeter protection, and so on. CPTED complements target hardening; it does not take its place.

CPTED is normally based on five central principles, which are:

- *Natural surveillance*

  The theory and argument behind natural surveillance is the idea or premise that criminals do not like being seen. The fact that the observer may not be in a position to carry out any form of crime prevention action is irrelevant; the observer probably has no idea that the person who has just had eye contact as they walked into the shop may be a criminal, but that doesn't make it any easier for the criminal. As far as he or she is concerned, they have been seen, and that means their features have been captured for future use, perhaps even passing on their descriptions to the police. A criminal entering a shopping centre, for instance, will stay close to the wall, and will not venture to walk across an open, well-lit area, once again for fear of being 'clocked' or observed. So, if it is agreed that criminals do not like being under observation, can you think of any areas or locations where the offender may perhaps feel uncomfortable?

Probably a good example of this type of natural surveillance environment is an airport departures lounge, which normally consist of straight lines with minimal obstructions, ample glazing, and of course chairs designed and installed in a manner that forces travellers to face each other without being too intimate. To the opportunist criminal, the prospect of crossing a clear room to sit opposite a total stranger is his or her worst nightmare. You may be thinking that I haven't mentioned CCTV; but surveillance cameras are not considered to be intrinsically natural, and they will be covered separately when we examine situational crime prevention.

Another excellent example of natural surveillance is what is known as the 'meeter/greeter', sometimes employed at large retail outlets. The member of staff referred to as a meeter/greeter generally stands at the entrance to the store, and he or she may simply be there to say 'hullo' and 'good morning/afternoon' to members of the public entering the shop. Alternatively, it may the same member of staff offering coupons to shoppers, and both are of course very legitimate activities, not at all out of the ordinary – unless of course one of those members of public is entering with nefarious thoughts. Whilst a law-abiding member of the public receives such staff activities with total acceptance, if perhaps a little inconvenient "Oh no, not more coupons" or "I really am in a rush" (aren't we all!), the potential criminal will perceive the member of staff as being a means to observe and remember his features for future use, and may decide not to enter the store.

- *Natural access control*

Natural access control is more than a high block wall topped with barbed wire. CPTED uses walkways, fences, lighting, signage, and landscape to clearly guide people and vehicles to and from the recognised entrances. The goal of this CPTED principle is not necessarily to keep intruders out but to direct the flow of people while decreasing the opportunity for crime.

It is relatively easy to direct people in a semi-autonomous manner, and if you shop in a certain Swedish flat pack furniture shop, you will fully understand what I am saying! Heaven help those that dare to walk against the flow of traffic or infringe the floor arrows ordering them to walk one way, and one way only. Equally today, if you move around a modern distribution centre you will see very few human beings. You will however notice sets of painted parallel lines, for visiting humans to walk within (don't stray from the path).

Of course, the preceding examples are predominantly pertinent to law-abiding citizens only, and I suspect that a person intent on committing some form of heinous crime will not be deterred by fellow shoppers and painted icons. However, if you imagine a very robust three-metre steel perimeter fence protected by perimeter intruder detection systems (PIDS), CCTV, and movement detection lighting, probably the easiest way for even the most determined criminal is to attempt to illegally enter the premises by blagging their way past the security officers on duty. If that is the case, then natural access control has been successful.

- *Territorial reinforcement*

  Territorial reinforcement is often referred to as territoriality and is described by Newman (1972) as the capacity of the physical environment to create perceived zones of territorial influence.

  In terms of CPTED, this territorial reinforcement or territoriality is used to help to prevent crime, in that it encourages members of staff to take ownership of their organisation's property and infrastructure. It is far too common for staff to reply that "It's not my responsibility, I'm not security", and that of course is an absolute abrogation of responsibility, because as the saying goes, "Security is the responsibility of everyone in the organisation". That is, however, too simplistic.

  Territoriality is all about claiming territory, and it is a process that is carried out at all levels.

  Territorial behaviour is characteristic of all human and even all animal existence. Humans establish hierarchies of territories, or turf, that range from private to semi-private, semi-public, and public space. Humans in particular have a need to establish both temporary and permanent ownership of space. That a person's home is his castle is a universally recognised concept and legal tradition. Experts in crisis intervention know that even the most minor offence that involves an intrusion into one's abode is a major stress producing event for the residents. Police are trained to be sensitive to an individual's concerns and resultant fears about even minor burglaries. It is common knowledge that the meekest person is fiercely protective of the home front.

  Dogs defend their turf vigorously, even when they are outsized. Interestingly, other animals tend to acknowledge turf identities and respond accordingly. Humans mark their turf using fences, signs, and plain border definition. Common law requires that turf or property be identified as prerequisites to the defence of property rights (Fennelly, 2013).

  There are also subliminal territorial messages that are sent by the property defender and received by the potential offender. In areas such as Canary Wharf, London, or the Champs-Élysées, Paris, it is not unusual to see chairs and tables outside of cafes and bars, or even spread outside the entrance to multi-storey buildings in other city centres, and during the day such accommodation will be occupied by either customers enjoying a glass of wine, or members of staff taking a break, with coats over chairs and bags placed on tables, standing in a defensive posture with either a drink or a cigarette in hand, in effect barring the entrance to *their* territory.

  However, once again to the horror of the would-be burglar, the members of staff and customers represent 50 pairs of eyes staring at him, protecting their territory, for one reason, and one reason only; to observe his movements, and report him or her to the authorities at a later date. Once again, the offender may decide to go elsewhere, to an area or location where territorial behaviour is not so fierce. I'm sure you can see the subtle but critical link here between natural surveillance and territoriality.

• Maintenance and management

The broken window theory is a contentious concept that has been discussed from a criminological perspective for a number of years, and the framework is as follows.

Picture in your mind's eye an abandoned cotton mill (let's say) residing close to a canal. The building has been designed to allow as much natural light in as possible, and to that end there are dozens of small glass windows. A group of bored young-sters passing by the mill one day throw a stone at the building, smashing one of the windows. They immediately run off in fear of attracting the attention of a security guard or perhaps a police officer. The following day the same happens, and there is no pursuit. Over the weeks and days, the youths, now feeling very confident that they won't be caught, break every window on the mill. Their confidence is extremely high, so their next course of action is to see what is inside the building, and they achieve that by breaking down the rear fire exit, still unchallenged. In their final act of bravado, they enter the mill and start a fire, which burns down the building. So, for the sake of non-repair of one small pane of glass, the mill has been destroyed.

This can be extrapolated to the workplace, where what may seem like minor issues such as staff turnover and absenteeism, if tackled at an early stage, can be prevented from growing to point where they are unmanageable – the equivalent of the mill being burned down.

How about the hole in the fence theory?

Under normal circumstances, maintenance and management of systems are carried out in order to ensure that they are fit for purpose. In terms of security, we are looking at technology that has the ability to ether deter, detect, or delay (or per-haps all three) a potential criminal. Remember, the criminal is hopefully deterred by the expansive array of security on show, such as CCTV, lighting and security officers. Failing that, upon attempting to commit a crime the offender is detected by CCTV, access control, lighting, intruder detection systems (IDS) or security officers. Finally, although he has not been either deterred or detected, he has been delayed by the three-metre wall, which is topped with barbed wire.

However, what about the real world, where the criminal searching for a weakness in the system comes across a small hole in the fence, and three days later the fence is still in disrepair. What thoughts do you think are going through the head of the criminal?

Put yourself in his shoes.

The fence has required a low level of repair for some time, but no action has been taken. You must think, "Why is that?"

Either the owners of the fence have yet to notice the gap, or there are no funds avail-able to carry out repairs.

In terms of the first option, an ignorance of the problem is highly unlikely because since you discovered the breach, you have maintained observations on the fence line, and you have witnessed security officers stopping at the hole before using their radio, presumably to report it.

As far as the second option is concerned, that is more likely. Whilst carrying out your observations during the hours of darkness, you have noticed that several of the perimeter lighting units are not operating. You are now convinced that funding for security systems repairs are probably not available, and even more interesting; if there is insufficient funding for perimeter protection, what level of security is likely to be found inside? Probably very low, and so in terms of risk, it is worth taking the chance of breaching the fence, because you are assured that you are not going to be apprehended inside the grounds or premises.

- **Image**

  Anybody flying into New York prior to 11 September 2001 would have observed two spectacular pieces of architecture that stood over 1,300 feet high, comprising 110 floors and housing over 14,000 occupants, people like you and me going about their normal daily lives. In terms of image, one can only imagine the envy and hatred being contemplated by Osama bin Laden every time he saw them on the news, or any other form of media. The image to Bin Laden portrayed the US as being the dominant world force that was, to the so-called leader of al-Qaeda, attempting destroy his religion, his culture, and his very way of life. The Twin Towers epitomised everything that Bin Laden loathed about the US in particular, and the West in general. They had to go, and if that meant the deaths of over 3,000 people, so be it!

  After the second Gulf War in 2003, the world's media captured images of Iraqi civilians attacking anything related to their former ruler, Saddam Hussein. Statues were toppled and destroyed with a vigour never before seen in that country. Paintings of the tyrant were destroyed, in some cases by people wielding shoes and knives, and as if to eliminate history, all visages of Hussein were removed in an effort to cleanse the soul of Iraq.

  In areas of West Belfast, Northern Ireland, there are murals on the sides of tenement houses, portraying, to the occupants of that part of the United Kingdom, heroes such as Gerry Adams, the former commander of the Provisional Irish Republican Army (PIRA), and Bobby Sands, who was the first martyr to the cause. Sands died after going on hunger strike whilst incarcerated in the Maze prison, Northern Ireland on 5 May 1981.

  The introduction of a large grouping of new buildings of distinctive height and texture into an existing urban fabric singles out these buildings for particular attention. If this distinctive image is also negative, the project will be stigmatised, and its residence castigated and victimised.

  Government-sponsored housing developments, for a variety of reasons, seldom articulated are designed so that they stand out and are recognised as distinctly different residential complexes. It is contended that this differentiation serves in a negative way to single out the project and its inhabitants as 'easy hits'. The idiosyncratic image of publicly assisted housing, coupled with other design features and the social characteristics of the resident population, makes such housing a peculiarly vulnerable target of criminal activity (Newman, 1972).

  In terms of CPTED, image is critical, and there may be times when images and characteristics have to be altered in order to maintain a low profile, and thereby discourage attacks from either wanton criminals or even perhaps deluded terrorists.

CPTED as adapted for Newman's original concept is a cost-effective and often aesthetically pleasing means of reducing crime, and the effects of crime, but it does not and should not stand alone. We have already examined, or at least mentioned target hardening, which refers to an increase in physical security methods, such as more robust doors and windows and better locking systems. However, there is another criminological theory that often accompanies and complements CPTED, and that is situational crime prevention (SCP).

Situational Crime Prevention

It was the British criminologist Ron Clarke who ventured to make use of Routine Activity and Rational Choice Theories by researching and then delivering what are often referred to as the tenets of Situational Crime Prevention. The four tenets are:

- Increasing the effort by the criminal
- Increasing the risk of being caught
- Reducing rewards
- Removing excuses.

Increasing the effort by the criminal

Making it more difficult for the criminal to achieve his or her aims.

- *Target harden*

  Target hardening refers to an increase in physical security to protect a property, and is generally related to the strengthening of the fabric of the building and upgrades to areas such as doors, windows, and the perimeter. It can also include the installation or upgrading of systems such as CCTV, access control, intruder detection systems, and so on.

- *Control access to facilities*

  This refers to the installation or upgrading of the location's access control system. This may be by electronic or physical means, or it may mean the use of manned guarding.

Table 3.1 The 4 tenets were extended to 24 in tabular format

Increasing the effort by the criminal	Increasing the risk of being caught	Reducing rewards	Removing excuses
Target harden	Extend guardianship	Conceal targets	Set rules
Control access to facilities	Assist natural surveillance	Remove targets	Post instructions
Screen exits	Reduce anonymity	Identify property	Alert conscience
Deflect offenders	Utilise place managers	Disrupt markets	Assist compliance
Control tools/ weapons	Strengthen formal surveillance	Deny benefits	Control drugs and alcohol

- *Screen exits*

  Having dealt with access control, screening exits amounts to monitoring and under-standing who is leaving the premises.

- *Deflect offenders*

  Otherwise known as displacement, deflection means upgrading all security systems in order that the criminal decides it will be too difficult to attack the location, and through rational choice, he or she will select a weaker and more vulnerable target.

- *Control tools and weapons*

  Probably the simplest section to define is having the ability to control tools and weapons. I believe that Clarke meant those tools that can be used for or adapted to be used for the commission of a crime. Weapons refers to any implement that do harm to a person or persons.

  Increasing the risk of being caught

  Ensuring the criminal, through rational choice, is more aware of the risks of being apprehended.

- *Extend guardianship*

  Although a common mantra is often "security isn't my business", an extension of guardianship relates to security engagement by non-security staff, ensuring that all employees and management take ownership of the safety and security of the organisation.

- *Assist natural surveillance*

  To assist natural surveillance means to ensure that there are no areas where the offender can hide. If you recall CPTED practices, straight lines, good natural lighting, and room design were mentioned as concepts that make the criminal feel ill at ease.

- *Reduce anonymity*

  The criminal naturally wishes to remain anonymous, to be allowed to blend in without being seen; in a number of high street banks there may be a sign requesting motor cyclists to remove their helmets. This is so they can be observed by staff and possibly CCTV, making the potential offender very nervous.

- *Utilise place managers*

  In a similar manner to the extension of guardianship, the utilisation of place managers means making the most of resources at hand. It maybe that during a security incident, fire wardens are given the responsibility of cordoning off an area or perhaps securing entrances to stop unauthorised personnel entering the building.

- *Strengthen formal surveillance*

  This is relatively straightforward inasmuch as formal surveillance may be strengthened by the installation of CCTV, or it may mean harnessing the services of extra security staff to monitor an area.

Reducing rewards

Even if the criminal is successful, he or she is unlikely to reap the benefits of their illegal actions; there is no return on their investment.

- *Conceal targets*

  This means minimising the likelihood of the criminal being able to attack, and potentially steal or damage all of the targets that he or she has acquisitioned. It may be feasible to display the less valuable items, and if the criminal observes them, he or she is likely to make off with products that are not so critical, leaving important assets concealed.

- *Remove targets*

  This is the simplest strategy available. If no targets exist, there is nothing to steal or damage. A clear desk policy means just that; ensuring that at first glance there is nothing to see.

- *Identify property*

  Whereas ten years ago property would be overtly identified with bar codes and serial numbers that could easily be removed, today there is the option of identification through the likes of smart water, which can only be identified under ultraviolet light. Whilst the name of the owner is not present, the thief would have to justify being in property that is covered by smart water.

- *Disrupt markets*

  In terms of situational crime prevention, market disruption means making it difficult for the criminal to sell stolen goods. An example of this was introduced in the United Kingdom when scrap dealers were prohibited from buying scrap metal that may have been stolen, by the use of cash. In order to be able to buy scrap metal the dealer has to use some form other than cash, perhaps bank transfer of funds that can be audited. If the scrap dealer is found in possession of metals that may have been stolen, he or she will have to prove to the authorities that the transaction was legitimate and above the law.

- *Deny benefits*

  Working on the hypothesis that the criminal will at some stage be successful in (let us say) stealing from a retail outlet, particularly when designer clothes are so expensive and easy to move, there has to be a strategy to ensure that the stolen goods are sold on the legal market. In terms of clothing, a typical crime prevention method is the electronic article surveillance (EAS) or tagging system, with installed vertical barriers at the exit to a store. Should an article of clothing be moved through the tagging barriers with a tag attached, the EAS system will activate and it should alert a member of staff. However, certain criminals are prepared to rip off the tags in the changing rooms, allowing safe passage through the EAS. As a last resort, staff may be forced to use ink tags, which if removed by force will spill ink over the expensive article. There is no return on investment for the criminal, because who is going to buy an expensive pair of jeans covered in ink, even on the black market? Nobody with any sense. However, when did criminals ever employ sensible thinking?

Malcolm

An off-duty retail clothing security manager, let's call him Malcolm, was walking home a number of years ago, choosing to visit an outside market en route. Within the market area he noticed a trader with a number of trestle tables that were full to the brim with jeans that were doing a roaring trade. As he approached the market trader he noticed that the Wrangler and Levi's look-alike jeans that were disappearing off the tables were covered in ink, which astounded Malcolm, because why on earth would anybody buy jeans covered in ink. Malcolm wasn't thinking like a criminal, so he was totally out of his depth, despite the fact that he was a former detective, and had been in the retail industry for a number of years.

After convincing the trader that he was neither police nor trading standards, he asked why on earth people were buying ink-corrupted jeans, only to be told that they were a badge of honour to the youths of the area because they were stolen. Thinking like a criminal is critical.

Removing excuses

Rule breakers will inevitably argue that they were ill informed: "It's not my fault".

- *Set rules*

  In any organisation it is critical that all members of staff and management are aware of the regulations and laws relating to the protection of company assets, and what the penalties are for breaking those rules. The security manager in liaison with HR has to be responsible for ensuring that all laws, rules, and regulations are communicated in a manner that is crystal clear to all stakeholders. Rules have to be set, and they have to be clearly communicated and understood. Criminals will be looking for the opportunity to exploit the system, and when cornered they are likely to say, "I didn't know that, nobody told me that I had to, I wasn't allowed to".
  Clarity is critical.

- *Post instructions*

  When Clarke published his first draft of situational crime prevention, no doubt he envisaged the posting of instructions to take the form of posters being strategically pasted to walls around a factory in the hope that staff would read and abide. However, today we live in the age of social media, the Intranet, the World Wide Web (WWW) and the Internet of Things (IoT); the potential for effective communications has never been better. There is absolutely no excuse today for the security manager to hide behind the defence of not being able to communicate with his peers and stakeholders.

- *Alert conscience*

  Alerting conscience refers to staff and management being aware of criminal issues, and potentially having knowledge of who has committed a crime. This the opportunity for the security manager to appeal to the conscience of the workforce, emphasising the fact that any impacts of crime will affect everybody, and that now is the opportunity to put an end to the criminal issues.

- *Assist compliance*

    Assisting in compliance means ensuring that the security manager and his or her team exist to assist in compliance with security rules and regulations, as opposed to being the department that can only facilitate punishment.

- *Control drugs and alcohol*

    Drugs and alcohol in the workplace should not be tolerated, and it is the role of the security function, in liaison with HR, to ensure that such dependencies are not consumed.

Situational Crime Prevention activities

It is often argued that situational crime prevention (SCP) is founded on two academic principles, those of Routine Activity Theory (RAT) and Rational Choice Theory (RCT), both of which will be explained before we continue.

Routine Activity Theory (RAT)

Routine Activity Theory is an intrinsic element of situational crime prevention, being heavily influenced by time and space continua. Clarke and Felson (2008) argue that the routine activity approach states three minimal elements for direct contact predatory crime: a likely offender, a suitable target, and the absence of a capable guardian against crime. A likely offender, it is argued, is anybody who for any reason might commit a crime. How this likelihood might vary has been avoided, since that would bring up the forbidden issue of criminal motivation.

A suitable target of crime is any person or object likely to be taken or attacked by the offender. The third minimal element of direct contact predatory crime, the capable guardian, is not seen to be a policeman or security guard in most cases. The most likely persons to prevent a crime are not policemen (who seldom are around to discover crimes in the act) but rather neighbours, friends, relatives, bystanders, or the owner of the property targeted.

An example of Routine Activity Theory could be characterised by a member of staff (with debt problems) who every day, as part of his regular duties, delivers mail to the cash office, when the end of day cashing up is taking place by the accounts supervisor, and the door to the safe is always either open or observed to be unlocked with the key in the door lock. One particular day the member of staff arrives at the cash office to drop off mail, and notices that the key to the safe is in the safe-door lock, but the accounts supervisor is nowhere to be seen.

This is an opportunity for the likely offender (the mail delivery operator) to attack the suitable target (steal cash) because there is no suitable guardian (the accounts supervisor is away from her desk).

Rational Choice Theory

The Rational Choice Theory had its beginnings in work on situational crime prevention, which seeks to block opportunities for crime by environmental change (Clarke, 198). By comparing benefits against punishment, the criminal is presented with a number of options, and rational choice criminals do exactly that: they make a choice because they are able to. In many respects it is feasible to argue that rational choice criminals carry out a risk assessment in which they internally compute the risks of being apprehended, facing a term of imprisonment, against the rewards and benefits of committing the crime. Very quickly, in terms of, say, theft, they will consider the assets to be stolen, the threats to themselves (e.g. alert staff or the police), vulnerabilities when attempting the crime, and the likelihood of being caught. Is it worth doing the time for committing the crime?

Therefore, the combination of CPTED and situational crime prevention offers the professional security manager the opportunity and the means to combat all forms of crime against his or her organisation, by the natural defence of space, and the increase in risk presented to the potential offender. Routine Activity Theory and Rational Choice Theory are pivotal for the development of situational crime prevention.

Exercise Brave Defender – task 2: CPTED and situational crime prevention

Synopsis

The Britcom executive board have decided that the global headquarters in Canary Fields requires a number of upgrades in terms of Crime Prevention Through Environmental Design (CPTED), and furthermore, after consultation with a number of crime prevention advisory consultants, has decided to adopt situational crime prevention (SCP) as the baseline security standard through its global portfolio. Your next tasks are as follows:

1   Prepare a paper for the executive board outlining the importance of Crime Prevention Through Environmental Design (CPTED) and situational crime prevention (SCP).
2   Within the paper, detailing both concepts, explain how CPTED and SCP may be introduced initially to the headquarters building at Canary Fields and then ultimately across the business.

3.3 Physical and electronic security systems

In this section we will study a number of physical and electronic security systems which support a concept known as defence in depth, and we will examine the following areas:

* The surrounding environment
* The perimeter
* Dead ground
* Building fabric
* Reception area
* Target location.

Defence in depth (DiD)

The picture conjured up by the majority of people when the terms physical and electronic security systems are mentioned I suspect would be a huge security officer monitoring a CCTV system, or maybe the same security officer rattling padlocked doors on a building site, or perhaps a docks area. The issue of course is how the media tends to project the security industry in a negative light, and being perfectly honest the industry does itself no favours in terms of some of the disastrous public relations incidents that hit the newspapers far too often. Physical and electronic security systems today are extremely sophisticated in terms of research and design, and the standards of professional installation and maintenance are at higher levels than they have ever been.

For the purpose of this section I would like to introduce you to a concept that has been in use for a long time, and today is the basis for integrated security. The concept is referred to as defence in depth.

Defence in depth (sometimes referred to as layered security) is a term that has been used by military forces, effectively since World War II, and recently adapted for private security use.

In a layperson's terms, this would be defensive concentric circles, protecting a military asset, perhaps a divisional headquarters where senior military personnel are stationed, with the defensive layers eventually sapping the strength of the attacking force, which would be either militarily defeated or would retreat before it was too late.

Defence in depth is used extensively within the global security industry, but interestingly if the term is placed in a search engine, the vast majority of answers will refer to either IT or cybersecurity. However, for the purpose of this book, we will initially in this section concentrate on the use of defence in depth as it is supported by physical and electronic security systems, including human response. Figure 3.4 illustrates the concept of defence in depth, showing the configuration from the extended perimeter or perhaps the environment; through to the immediate ground and perimeter; followed by the building at which the fabric, design, and maintenance of the building is critical; and finally the inner sanctum and target for the criminal.

The idea behind the concept is a configuration which does not allow for a single point of failure, because if an individual layer is breached, the perpetrator will be faced with a second hurdle, then a third and so on. The argument being that through integration of systems such as CCTV, lighting, access control and intruder detection systems, the criminal is going to be constantly monitored and challenged before he or she reluctantly accepts defeat or is apprehended.

Of course, the standards of research and development for security systems and the related specifications used within a layered security system are achieved by security systems

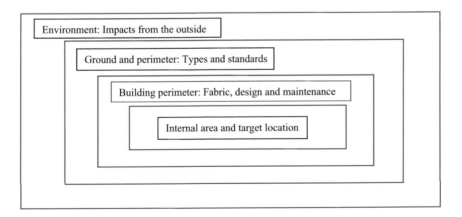

Figure 3.4 Defence in depth from the environment to the target location

specialists; they are generally designed to match proportionate risk whilst following a particular operational requirement. This means that they must perform to the standards and requirements for which they were intended. However, the single point of failure (SPF) here is that very often they take on the appearance of a one-way mirror, seen only from the perspective of the 'good guys', the security industry. Why, I am sure you are asking, is that an issue? Well there are two factors to take into consideration here.

- In the first instance, the security industry is striving continuously to be as high tech as possible, with a continual reliance on IT-based platforms. Whether it is an automatic access control system (ACS), CCTV, or an internal/perimeter intruder detection system (IDS), the majority of specifications today are configured to an IT-based platform, with control processing units (CPU) and radio frequency identification (RFID) being at the heart of the system.

  The problem here of course, without sounding like a Luddite (which I don't think that I can be justifiably accused of), is that the more sophisticated a system is, the more prone it is to fail, and the costlier it is, and more complicated repairs tends to be. Systems designers will from a technical perspective argue against this attitude, but to me it is totally logical. I am not for one second advocating the return, totally, of lock and key in favour of the proximity card reader or biometric scanner, but I am arguing for recognition of the fact that over sophistication and micro-engineering are not always the answer to the client's needs.

- The second consideration, which to me is far more concerning, is the fact that systems designers and installers, as argued earlier, tend to see crime through a one-way mirror. You only need to attend security seminars such as the International Fire and Security Conference (IFSEC), which is held in London annually, to understand the levels of self-congratulation in terms of design, and the adornment of the microchip, which is hailed as the answer to all of our crime prevention needs. There are companies from all over world plying their goods, with the use of high-tech displays, both aurally and visually, regurgitating specifications and statistics, designed to utterly dumbfound those non-technical attendees who are blinded by sound and vision. I may be wrong, but I don't believe there are many burglars or robbers attending IFSEC, and if they were to be seen wandering around the stands, I suspect nobody would ask their opinions; well, why would you?

  I once asked a young, well-heeled business development manager (BDM) if he had ever sought the opinion of the criminal fraternity about what they thought of his taught-wire perimeter intruder detection system (PIDS), and I believe he came close to requesting security to eject me from the conference for asking such a heretical question. But how do you know how successful a system is at deterring crime unless you ask those potential criminals who are intent on defeating that system?

Just a moment

If this book is designed with the professional security manager in mind, why is it important for him or her to think like a criminal?

Professor Martin Gill, the renowned criminologist, whilst speaking to a number of criminals several years ago about particular crime trends and the related systems to enhance deterrence of crime, was accused of not thinking like a criminal. He was discussing the use of sophisticated CCTV systems to either deter crime or detect and recognise criminals, arguing that even if CCTV didn't deter the criminal, they would be arrested some time later, and as a result of the use of CCTV footage would likely be convicted and spend some time at Her Majesty's pleasure. He was met with disdain and scorn, being told: "You see Martin, you are not thinking like a criminal. At the moment I am, in your words commissioning a crime, I don't care what will happen to me in two or three weeks' time, I am only interested in carrying out the crime, and making good my escape". What an eye-opener that was.

So from now on, I would like you to take on board that short lesson learned, and when looking at or examining a security system, instead of polishing the ego of the BDM, take a step back, look at the system from all angles, and think to yourself, "How can I evade that CCTV system, or perhaps bypass the IDS, or even maybe evade the security guard who is completely disinterested and bored, easily?" Only then will you be thinking like a criminal.

Complementing examination of the theory of defence in depth, we are now going to look at a series of physical and electronic security systems and measures that the security professional uses, probably on a daily basis, to protect the assets of the organisation that he or she is supporting. Bear in mind the fact that although this book will offer advice and guidance on systems configuration, this is a specialised area that must be led by a subject matter expert.

It is also critical that you appreciate at this juncture four points that all security professionals must be cognizant of when specifying physical and electronic security systems:

- *Risk and proportion*

   All security systems must be specified as a result of the risk level that is proportional to their choice and use. In terms of financial risk, it is pointless investing significant expenditure to protect an asset that costs less than the measures chosen to protect it. In purely financial terms, putting aside brand and reputation and other non-tangible costs, why would you spend, let us say, £10,000 to protect a small stationary cupboard with a value of perhaps £2,000 or £3,000. That doesn't make a great deal of financial sense. All security systems must be risk based and proportionate in terms of their selection.

- *Operational requirement*

   A good way of thinking about an operational requirement when purchasing a piece of equipment is to ask yourself, "Does it do what it says on the side of the can?" The meaning of the term 'operational requirement' will be covered in greater detail elsewhere in the book, but suffice it to say that all security systems must conform to the exact requirements of the client and end user – no more and no less.

   However, there is a problem here, because that is not how the BDM sees it. The BDM in the first instance is likely to have sales targets that he or she must meet to achieve bonus status and also to ensure that they keep their job; there is no easier way of putting that. Of course, the BDM wants to enhance his or her salary, and commission generated from sales is the favoured route. Let me explain.

When selling a piece of equipment, be it a CCTV system or perimeter intruder detection, the salesperson will of course enhance and maybe embellish the positive nature of the product he or she is attempting to sell. For instance, the CCTV system being discussed has excellent definition, and there is a pan, tilt, and zoom option that allows the operator to control all cameras by use of a simple joystick. It looks great and will blend in with any building aesthetic; unfortunately it has a poor day/night capability, so the building lighting must be enhanced! This will of course increase the overall cost. Therefore, one very simple question should be asked at the earliest opportunity, and that is, "What are the limitations of the system?" If you are informed that the system being discussed has no limitations, show the BDM the door because either he or she is not telling the truth, the whole truth, and nothing but the truth, or they do not understand the product they are trying to sell you!

Does it do what it says on the side of the can?

- *Competency of use.*

When viewed at a security conference or a trade exhibition, security systems, particularly electronic systems, are portrayed by expert operators as being simple to use and understand. However, once installed and commissioned, and after the installers have disappeared, the outlook tends to be somewhat more complicated. Security managers who may be used to operating sophisticated digital CCTV systems or automated access control systems often struggle, but without technical training or support how is a client with little or no technical acumen going to cope with a sophisticated biometric system that may require micro-management and maintenance?

Of course, the argument could be made that such a client, be it a solicitor or accountant for example, should employ this technical rarity known as the security manager, but there may be no budget. Therefore, when physical and electronic security systems are being chosen, the skills of the end user must be taken into consideration. Never rely on on-the-job training or a systems handbook that may have been printed in in a distant country, and once translated makes very little sense. *Ensure that all systems procured have some form of training program built into the sales contract.*

- *Cost-benefit analysis (CBA)*

The cost-benefit analysis is a process by which expected costs are weighed against expected benefits to determine the best (or most profitable) course of action. The CBA is always expressed in monetary terms and can be used for capital expenditure (Capex), when a one-off payment is expected, or for operational expenditure (Opex) to cover ongoing payments such as monthly or weekly expenditure.

CBA case study – access control

As the result of a security survey, the access control system at one of Britcom's small distribution centres (DC) has been classified as operationally inefficient and not cost-effective. The DC operates on a Monday to Friday basis and is open between 0800hrs and 1700hrs. The current system requires a security officer to operate an external manual barrier which he or she lifts to allow access once identification has been verified. It is envisaged that this system will be replaced by an automatic single barrier, which will be equipped with a proximity card reader system, communications with the reception area in the main building, and a single camera signalling back to a monitor at reception. Members of staff will use their company identification card to access the area, whilst visitors will activate the communications system and, if appropriate, will be granted access by the receptionist or security officer. This will be covered by capital expenditure.

In order for the CBA to be valid, a number of sections of the process have to be competed in terms of costs and benefits. They are as follows.

Costs

Costs are divided between the following areas:

* *Development costs*

    This refers to any development of a product and may include research and development costs.

* *Operational costs*

    Operational costs may include payment for the operation of equipment.

* *Recurring costs*

    Examples of recurring costs may be equipment leasing, travel, training, and so on.

* *Non-recurring costs*

    This may include procurement and planning, installation services, and so forth.

Benefits

Benefits are divided as follows:

* *Recurring benefits*

    This may include reduced stock loss, reduced staffing costs, or greater efficiency and productivity.

* *Nonrecurring benefits*

    This category may include one-off benefits such as terminated contracts that are no longer necessary, increased use of technology, and so forth.

For the purpose of this exercise, we will use the following calculations in Table 3.2.

Table 3.2 CBA costs and benefits

Costs		
Development	Nil	
Operational	Installation of equipment	£2,000.00
Recurring	Nil	
Non–recurring	Cost of equipment	£13,000.00
Benefits		
Recurring	Nil	
Non–recurring	Termination of guarding contract	£60,000.00

We now need to calculate what is referred to as the CBA ratio.

Total costs: £15,000
Total benefits: £60,000
Benefits (£60,000) divided by costs (£15,000): £60,000/£15,000 = 4

This provides us with a positive CBA ration of 4:1, meaning that for every pound spent, there will be a return on investment of four pounds (£4:£1).

Defence in depth (continued)

The surrounding environment

We should work on the premise that prior to a criminal attempting to breach the security of our site, he or she is extremely likely to carry out some form of reconnaissance. The aim of the reconnaissance, or 'recce', is to visit the destination prior to the attack in order to examine critical target defence tactics. From a criminal perspective, they need to know what systems are in place that may be able to deter, detect, or delay him or her. What responses should the criminal expect if he or she is detected?

Of course, the first concern the criminal will always have is being apprehended and arrested by the police, and to that end he or she may carry out acts of low-level crime in order to observe the rate and quality of response from the law enforcement agency. This will give him or her an idea, and that is all it is, of how long they will have to carry out the crime.

During the recce phase, the criminal will take into consideration all possible routes to and from the location they intend to attack, noting the shortest and quickest routes in and out.

At the site itself, the criminal is likely first of all to circumnavigate the location, in order to have a better idea of the exact point to breach the security. They will initially study the front entrance, and they will be looking for bad habits, such as member of staff 'tailgating', that is having forgotten their own pass, they will ask a colleague to give them access to the building by leaving the door open, or asking to use their colleague's pass for entry purposes.

Perimeter

After giving due consideration to the environment and topography surrounding the area of the location to be security surveyed, there has to be an assessment of how the perimeter is going to be protected. Before that, however, we must have a consensus of why a perimeter exists in the first instance. The perimeter is not the three-metre-high steel fence or the five-metre-high concrete wall; rather it is that point where two areas of ground meet. It is the point of delineation, normally between two properties, and it may be the line that separates public and private space. The steel fence and the concrete wall are two of the many means of protecting the integrity of the perimeter, and they are symbolic of area defence measures.

The perimeter of a site is one of the key locations where physical security measures and controls can be applied to protect both users and facilities. Without proper thought, the perimeter can become a significant vulnerability. The criminal is likely to examine the entire perimeter, looking for any form of vulnerability that will allow him to breach the fence or wall – perhaps even an insecure gate.

This section explains what properly implemented perimeter security measures can deliver, and how to identify what is needed.

Fencing

As with all physical and electronic security systems, perimeter protective measures must take into consideration risk to the property. The fence or wall has to be commensurate to the risk. So let us now take a look at some of the more common perimeter protection systems on the market.

- *Fencing*
  - *Chain link*

    Chain link fencing tends to be the weakest form of perimeter protection, and it is easily breached. Generally, it is stand-alone, that is to say that it is not dug in and is constructed from low-grade small-wire gauge (SWG) steel which is easily cut. However, in comparison to other forms of perimeter protection, it is low cost in terms of purchase and installation.

  - *Expamet (XPM)*

    Expanded metal fencing (known as Expamet or XPM fencing) is used extensively within the retail environment and at distribution centres where high value cages are required. This type of fencing, because it is normally constructed from a tough alloy and is flattened, is difficult to breach. Expamet is costlier than chain link, but it is far more robust.

  - *Welded mesh*

    Welded mesh fencing is the choice for the majority of public locations, such as schools, parks, and so forth, because it is relatively easy to install, and is quite vandal resistant.

  - *Palisade*

    Palisade is probably the most robust form of fencing commercially available. It consists of a series of vertical standing metal posts, normally 2.3 metres high, with each post being no more than 100 centimetres from the next post. Palisade is the costliest of the standard types of fencing.

  - *Electrified*

    Electrified is the costliest form of fencing, but it has the lowest breach rates and is probably the best deterrent. In the UK at least, this form of barrier has to be an inner fence so that innocent members of the public are protected. Electrified fencing, once again in the UK, must not have any form of topping attached.

- *Topping*

  There are a number of types of fence toppings, with those below being the most popular.

  - *Barbed rape/razor wire*

    As the name suggests, the barbs on this form of fence toppings consist of hundreds of extremely sharp steel strips that are designed to inflict as much damage as possible on anybody attempting to breach the perimeter, should they climb the fence.

- *Barbed wire*

   Whilst not designed to inflict as much damage as razor wire, the steel barbs in barbed wire will still cause discomfort and may inflict serious harm to anybody attempting to climb over or through it.

- *Rota spikes*

   Freely rotating, anti-scaling, anti-climb security fencing topping which is designed to roll when pressure is applied. Some Rota spikes are merely anti-climb and will not cause harm. However, some spikes are very sharp, and they will cut or puncture the skin when pressure is applied.

   Go to www.google.com/search?q=Fence+topping&tbm=isch&source=univ&sa =X&ved=2ahUKEwjpx9C785LnAhXllFwKHe7VDLcQ7Al6BAgFEDs&biw =2021&bih=826 for images of fence topping.

Security lighting

For obvious reasons, the criminal and the terrorist in the main prefer to carry out their attacks under cover of darkness. That is not to say that crime is not committed during daylight hours; indeed there is statistical evidence that would support the argument that bolder criminals will carry out crimes of, for example, burglary and car theft during the day, if it suits their modus operandi (method of operation).

However, it is logical to believe that criminals feel safer and more secure in carrying out crime when the environment is poorly or not illuminated. Of course, the type, size, and location of the lighting system will vary in accordance with the risks involved and also the types of business being operated.

External access control

Often, when external access control is spoken about or discussed, a picture is painted which depicts a three-metre-high welded mesh fence, with razor wire connected to the top of the fence, supported by CCTV, lighting, and perimeter intruder detection systems (PIDS).

The robust fence line will often in itself support an entrance to the location which may consist of a sliding steel gate, also supported by integrated systems and either manned by or monitored from within a security control room by a security officer.

However, whilst such systems are critical in terms of external access control, and they will be examined in greater detail in the sub-chapter which covers physical and electronic security systems, external access control begins before the criminal has the site in his or her vision. It begins in the surrounding environment.

Building fabric and construction

Having covered security in relation to the environment and the perimeter, the next phase of the defence in depth model is security of any buildings contained within the perimeter.

Buildings within the UK are usually constructed using a structural frame, typically steel, concrete, or timber, or are built from unframed masonry. There are many different types of walls and floor systems that are used within buildings, but together these elements play an important role in protecting occupants and assets from the effects of blasts and other security threats. For many, a primary security concern is for the building to remain standing, or for damage to be limited to defined zones, following an attack involving explosives, impact, and/or fire.

Designing structural framing, walls, and floors for structures so that they incorporate physical security requirements from the outset will help deliver robust and resilient business operations.

All buildings constructed in the UK must meet minimum standards, and that will be reflected in other countries. Building regulations are the minimum standards for design, construction, and alterations to virtually every building. The regulations are developed by the UK government and approved by Parliament.

The Building Regulations 2010 Act covers the construction and extension of buildings and these regulations are supported by Approved Documents. Approved Documents set out detailed practical guidance on compliance with the regulations.

There is no legislation which mandates levels of security cover; however, insurance brokers will demand a set of standards that, in their opinion, provides the appropriate level of security cover for the buildings being insured.

Physical security standards

There are a number of national and international standards that can be applied to the security cover of any installation, including the security of individual systems such as IT (ISO 27001), CCTV (NSI Code of Practice NCP 104), intruder detection systems (BSEN5036), access control (BSEN 50133), and so on.

However, www.opensourcedworkplace.com offers some extremely good guidance in terms of overall standards, suggesting the following classification of buildings and facilities.

- *Class A facility*

  A designated "Class A" facility is defined as a data centre that houses data and systems. Data centres are further divided as primary and backup facilities.

- *Class B facility*

  A designated "Class B" facility is defined as a facility that houses a critical function for business operations and affiliated business operations, has a high reputational impact, and has employee headcount in excess of a particular number, depending on the organisation.

- *Class C facility*

  A designated "Class C" facility is defined as an office building with noncritical business operations and has a particular employee headcount (organisational dependent).

- *Class D facility:*

  A designated "Class D" facility is defined as an office building staffed to support business operations and has a small employee headcount.

Reception areas

Once inside the building, it is likely that the criminal will have access to some form of reception area, and this is likely to be the final hurdle before he or she is free to move unhindered around the building. The reception area can be an extremely vulnerable location, particularly if the receptionist is alone. What follows is a mini–case study of a fictitious confrontation between a very angry customer and a receptionist.

Mini–case study scenario

Dan Jones has been a loyal customer to Britcom plc for 15 years, during which time he never made a late payment, and indeed he renewed his mobile phone contract on 1 January every year since taking delivery of his old Nokia 3310 in 2005. However, Britcom plc customer service has deteriorated over the last six months, and despite a number of phone calls in relation to his monthly bills, which have been inaccurate for the last three calendar months, today he received a letter threatening legal action for an unpaid bill. This was the final straw, and he is off to the head office in Canary Fields where he is going to "sort this out once and for all". To say that he is angry is a wholesome understatement.

Of course, the head office in Canary Fields is on the second floor of 1 Canada, and Mr. Jones must first of all access the building via the front entrance and be processed at the reception area by a Britcom plc receptionist.

By the time Mr. Jones reaches the reception area of 1 Canada, having read his *Final Notice* ten times on the overcrowded, very hot London Underground, he is incredibly angry, and who is he going to confront first? Yes of course, the receptionist.

Now you may be thinking, "What is the problem with that, the receptionist can't possibly be held accountable for the actions of the Britcom plc accounts department", but of course that is not how Mr Jones sees it. As far as he is concerned, the young, very nervous female receptionist is wearing the livery of Britcom plc, and she represents the organisation that has threatened him, wrongly of course, with court action; and she is going to get both barrels.

The reception area of any organisation, whether it is a corporate building such as in the above scenario, or perhaps a hospital, even within a building housing a Magistrates or Crown court, is an incredibly vulnerable area. In terms of security risk management, it may be the single point of failure, because in general terms a reception area by its very nature is open and accessible to members of the public, who may at times be volatile.

Of equal importance is the fact that criminals contemplating an illegal entry into the building will first of all study the main entrance, which normally houses the reception area, and they will be looking for any signs of vulnerability which will allow them to breach the security of the building.

When carrying out a security survey of a building, whether it is a city centre corporate enterprise or a data centre in a business park, the first area that I always recce is the main entrance and reception area, and the reason for this is that a similar approach will be made by the potential aggressor who needs to see where the vulnerabilities of access control lie.

In the same vain as my approach, the criminal may sit quietly somewhere, perhaps in a café opposite the building, or an adjacent location where he or she can quite clearly observe access control procedures at the building he or she is targeting.

They will be observing the actions and procedures of staff entering the building, perhaps being made aware that there is no 'anti pass back' facility configured in the access control system, because quite clearly staff are handing their passes to colleagues who may have forgotten theirs. Tailgating may be prominent, with staff holding open the door for colleagues or visitors, thus demonstrating a lack of security awareness and an extremely weak security culture.

Again, as I would, the criminal is likely to carry out some form of practice attack, using his or her own version of defence in depth, in that they will, if possible, move from the local environment, having established escape routes and alternative approaches, to an access point, perhaps the main door, which will allow them entry to the target building.

Once inside the entrance or reception area, the criminal will begin, at a pace suited to his or her needs, and dependent upon the security awareness of security officers and reception staff inside, to covertly examine the physical security systems deployed to protect the building and its assets. He or she will begin a detailed inspection of the following:

- *Personnel*

  It is recognised by most academics and policing practitioners that the vast majority of crime is committed because the opportunity to carry out a criminal offence is blatant, and once that crime has been committed, the perpetrator wants one thing, and one thing only, and that is to escape. So when the potential criminal enters the building, the first line of defence they will examine will be the human element of physical security (i.e. security officers and staff). What the criminal does not want to find is an integrated security system, led by security personnel and staff, who are alert, communicative, and obviously security aware and well trained.

  The criminal will be hoping to find a hopelessly overcrowded area, with security officers and staff who have other things on their mind and have neither the time nor inclination to pay any attention to a stranger whose presence may be unauthorised. The criminal will choose a time of day, either first thing in the morning or perhaps during lunch break when the area is extremely busy, and he may open an alarmed fire exit, or encourage a member of his team to do so, in order to monitor the response from security staff.

  He or she may commit a minor crime in order to measure the time it takes for a police presence to appear, if indeed there is going to a police response; there may not be, and of course that will strongly encourage the criminal to escalate the attack.

- *Access control*

  As mentioned earlier, the criminal will probably view the building from a distance to understand the levels of access control, and unfortunately it is often far too easy to gain access to a building, even where there is a security access control system. The criminal is regularly offered two choices; he or she can either place themselves at a safe distance where they can view the access control PIN being entered, and then enter the building by use of that code, or they can position themselves to appear at the door just as a member of staff is entering the building, say 'good morning' with a smile, and as the legitimate member of staff is entering, they will often hold open the door to allow the 'very nice young man' to enter the building. If the staff member is ever asked who it was, they allowed access to the building, they will say, "I don't know, he seemed pleasant enough, but security is your job, not mine". Too easy.

Once inside, access may become slightly more complex for the criminal, but the fact that he is now actually inside the target building will increase his confidence, because he is very aware that even despite the fact that he is not wearing a pass, or he is aimlessly wandering around the reception area, the chances of him being challenged are limited, because "security isn't my job!" Of course he or she will be very wary of being alerted to the security team, whose job it is to challenge suspicious persons, so the criminal will keep an extremely low profile, and he or she will blend in with their surroundings as much as possible.

They will mentally make a note of the different types of access control systems that are in use, whether they are plain swipe systems, proximity card reader systems, or biometric configurations. The criminal will be looking to see how they can be replicated for their next appearance.

- *CCTV*

  Of course, CCTV should act as a deterrence for all types of crime, or at least that is what CCTV systems providers want us to believe. Making use of defence in depth, from his or her point of view, the criminal will already have made a note of the locations of the external cameras before entering the building. Once inside, he or she will covertly examine the internal camera locations, and a decision will be made as to whether the CCTV system can be evaded. I am not for one second attempting to devalue CCTV, because like every physical or electronic security system it has its place in the configuration of integrated security, and it is often very successful in ether deterring or detecting suspicious activity, and if designed, commissioned, maintained, and used correctly it is an excellent tool. However, that is exactly what it is, a tool – not the panacea that it is far too often argued to be. A well-configured CCTV system in the reception area or main entrance will no doubt send a signal that the risk of detection and ultimately apprehension for the potential criminal is high, but it is not an infallible standalone crime prevention system; it must be integrated and professionally managed, and the criminal knows that.

- *Lighting and natural surveillance*

  As mentioned already, there is no panacea in terms of crime prevention, and integrated security at all levels is always recommended, but a strong argument can be made for criminals not feeling comfortable in well-lit environments. That is not to say that crime only takes place during the hours of darkness, when the criminal believes that he or she is unseen, as statistically most domestic burglaries take place during the day (perhaps when the home is unoccupied), and then at night (when the homeowners are on the premises). It is fair to say, however, that the criminal does not enjoy being seen, and natural surveillance, which includes open spaces with straight lines and good viewpoints for security staff often increases the perceived vulnerability of the criminal.

Reception areas and main front entrances can always monopolise lighting and natural surveillance in an effort to ensure maximum discomfort for the potential criminal, but this must be achieved in conjunction with security awareness training for all staff and members of the security team. Staff need to know what actions are required should they observe anything unusual.

• *Intruder detection systems (IDS)*

Intruder detection systems (IDS) to the untrained eye are not particularly easy to identify, however, a seasoned criminal will know that ground floor fire exits will be alarmed on a 24/7 basis, and that if the building is locked down at close of business there is likely to be some form of IDS in existence. Linked to this is the fact that configured into most newly constructed buildings will be an automatic fire alarm system, that if activated, will disengage the IDS on all ground floor exits, allowing undetected movement. There is therefore the danger that in collusion, with perhaps a member of staff, the criminal can wait outside of a fire exit, and then make his way into the building once the IDS is deactivated and the door is insecure.

Pause for thought

If you were about to hire a security officer, what qualities would you be looking for?

• *Manned guarding*

The vision or perhaps more accurately the perception of a security guard/officer is that of a low-paid, poorly educated and trained member of staff, whose only interest is in ensuring that the rules of the organisation are followed or enforced no matter what the circumstances may be. Historically, the security guard has been employed to secure an entrance, to perhaps a building site or a maritime dock area, by whatever means possible; part of the perception is that he will be a huge, perhaps elderly man in a poorly fitting uniform, who tends to utter a monosyllabic grunt when asked a question.

Of course today, in the vast majority of circumstances that is far from the truth, because more security officers are better educated than they have ever been, will hold a Security Industry Authority (SIA) licence (which means that they have received a basic level of training) and if managed and supported effectively will be aware of the importance of good customer service.

The role of the security officer has also changed dramatically over the last 20 years or so, with security officers now being expected to support the business that employs him or her by adding value to their terms and conditions of employment. It is probably as recent as the late '90s when the thought of a security guard provoked a scene in which a somewhat dishevelled male in a uniform was sat in a rundown shed, purporting to be a security lodge, with his feet on the desk, a copy of a tabloid in one hand and a cup of tea in the other. The only time the guard was disturbed, and was therefore reluctantly forced to move, was when he either had to lift the access control barrier or attempt to answer the telephone in a manner that was understood. Under duress, he was also expected to be able to make a legible, pen written entry into a daily occurrence book (DoB), which nobody read, but he went through the motions anyway. Formal training was never written into the contract, and terms such as service level agreement (SLA) and key performance indicator (KPI) had yet to be added to the vocabulary of the security industry.

Today it is far from uncommon for a security officer (not guard) to be seen wearing the corporate attire of the high street or city organisation that he or she (yes, she) is contracted to protect the assets of. Duties will include internal and external patrolling whilst interacting with staff and the general public, monitoring advanced electronic security systems such as CCTV, automatic access control (AAC) and intruder detection systems (IDS). Equally, the security officer is expected to add value to the contract by perhaps carrying out maintenance patrols during the quiet hours, saving the company expenditure from leaks, unnecessary lighting, and running machinery that should have been shut down at close of business. In terms of education and training, all front-line security officers must, by law (in the UK), hold a valid Security Industry Authority (SIA) licence, which entails police background checks, and a mandatory four-day training course, which includes security duties, customer service and conflict management awareness. As Dylan said, "The times they are a changin'".

Licencing

The Private Security Industry Act 2001 was a huge milestone for the United Kingdom private security sector, and its introduction sent reverberations globally. The central aim of the legislation was to form and introduce the Security Industry Authority (SIA), which would be an arm of the Home Office and would hence be responsible for the legal requirements of all aspects of the UK private security sector.

Central to the legislation was licensing, and in particular it was the licensing of all contract security officers, who after a period of regulated training and vetting would be issued with a Front-Line Security Licence. Any organisation from 1 January 2003 found to be employing and operating a non-licensed security officer would be subject to the full force of the Act and would likely be subject to a heavy financial penalty, and perhaps closure of its operations. The same could not be said for security officers directly employed by an organisation on a PAYE basis, otherwise known as 'in house'. In-house security officers were not subject to the Act, and as at November 2019, it is likely that the status quo will remain.

However, there is a mass of debate surrounding the employment of licensed and non-licensed security officers – to outsource or to in house, that is the perennial question!

In house versus outsourced

It is generally agreed that the greatest advantage of directly (PAYE) employing security officers is their perceived loyalty, as they see themselves as part of the 'team', accepted by peers and managers alike. They understand the culture of the organisation and believe, as is often the case, that they can add to the culture of the company, seeing a pathway to progression and promotion.

It is likely that an in-house team of security officers will be more expensive than their licensed counterparts who are employed by an external organisation. Costs such as recruitment, training, sickness and National Insurance will have to come out of the security manager's budget.

Contracted security officers are more likely to be cost-effective, as all running costs (recruitment, training, etc.) will be met by the service provider, the security company. Also, if there are problems with rostering, for example a security officer calling in sick, the service provider is contracted to ensure that gap is filled – a task not so simple for the company security manager when an in-house officer is unable to attend for duty. Of course, there is the issue of loyalty, or a lack of it in relation to contracted security officers, as their company pays their salary and not the client. Another advantage of considering the selection of an outsourced option is the fact that contract security officers are licensed, and with licensing comes a certain level of training and awareness. That said, it is not uncommon for large organisations who directly employ their security officers to have those members of staff attend an SIA licensing course because of the regulated standards. It is also a means of recognising staff by offering them the opportunity of security education, which may be the first rung on a learning ladder for future career development.

For more information about licensing, go to www.sia.homeoffice.gov.uk/Pages/home.aspx.

Electronic systems

Closed circuit television (CCTV)

The first rudimentary CCTV system was invented in in 1942 during World War II. Walter Bruch, a German engineer, wanted to be able to monitor V2 rocket launches and hence designed the world's first CCTV system, enabling him to watch the rocket launch from a different location.

CCTV is probably the most contentious and controversial element of security equipment to be introduced to the market since it was first used commercially in the late 1970s.

There has always been an element of distrust surrounding video surveillance, with issues of privacy and allegations of the 'big brother' state controlling the movement of entire populations, and it doesn't help when unsubstantiated statistics are introduced, such as that a person will be filmed 300 times as they move across London.

There are political and philosophical arguments to be made for and against CCTV, but the aim of this book is to remain politically neutral, focussing on the operational role that CCTV can play in the protection of organisational assets, including personnel.

Closed circuit television is composed of a number of individual component parts, and as a concept it is continually evolving. However, for the purpose of this book we will examine those component parts that are critical for every CCTV system.

- *Cameras*

  The camera is arguably the most important component within a CCTV system, and there are a variety of CCTV cameras available for use today, ranging from an individual static unit to a remotely controlled Internet Protocol (IP) pan, tilt, and zoom (PTZ) camera. Below are the descriptions of the most common forms of CCTV cameras being used in commerce and industry.

- *Dome encased static or PTZ*

   'Dome cameras' as they are commonly known, were originally designed to hide the camera encased within a PVC dome, in order that criminals could not determine which direction they were facing. The dome cameras will be strategically located within the area being protected, and they will normally be viewed remotely from a security control room or an alarm receiving centre. Internet Protocol (IP) cameras can be accessed using a cell phone from anywhere where there is an Internet connection.
   Dome cameras are also aesthetically designed to fit in with the environment in which they have been installed, so they blend with the background.

- *Static*

   Probably the simplest type of camera used within a CCTV system is the static unit, which is quite literally installed in an area to capture images in a field of vision that does not change. The static may be covering a lift area in a high-rise building, or it may be located behind the reception desk offering protection to those working in that area, whilst covering the main entrance.

- Pan, tilt, and zoom (PTZ)

   The PTZ camera, as the name suggests, allows the operator, using either a joystick or mouse, to either pan (sweep), tilt (up and down movement), or zoom (in or out). It is a major asset if the CCTV system has to cover a large area of land, such as a car park or perhaps a container terminal. The problem of course is that whilst the PTZ is being operated, its field of vision can be assessed by a criminal who will of course attempt to avoid it.

- *180-/360-degree cameras*

   The 180-degree camera can cover a large field of vision (180 degrees) and is normally used to cover areas such as the outside area of a distribution centre, a large room or even a bank vault.
   The 360-degree camera will be installed in a roof area, looking down on its field of vision, and it may be used to survey an office or a bank.
   Definition of both the 180-degree and the 360-degree cameras is normally poor when compared to either a static or PTZ unit.
   An option to the 180-degree camera is the multi-sensor camera that has a number of sensors and lenses built into a single enclosure. Multi-sensor cameras are more expensive than a 180-degree camera, but definition is normally a higher grade and the camera will have a greater field of vision.

- *Day/night cameras*

   Day/night cameras operate like any other camera in good natural daylight, but once the light deteriorates and the lux levels drop, an infrared element of the lens will activate, allowing the camera to operate in total darkness or poor illumination.

For images of CCTV cameras, go to www.google.com/search?q=CCTV+cameras&source=lnms&tbm=isch&sa=X&ved=2ahUKEwi18pD2_JLnAhUtUBUIHZeXCF0Q_AUoAnoECA8QBA&biw=2021&bih=826.

- *Telemetry*

  Telemetry refers to how an image is transferred from being captured by a CCTV camera to either a monitor or a storage and recording device, such a hard drive. The following two types of cable are the most common used for CCTV transmission:

  Coaxial cable is a type of transmission line used to carry high-frequency electrical signals with low losses. It is used in such applications as telephone trunk lines, broadband Internet networking cables, high-speed computer data buses, and cable television signals, and also to connect radio transmitters and receivers to their antennas. It differs from other shielded cables because the dimensions of the cable and connectors are controlled to give a precise, constant conductor spacing, which is needed for it to function efficiently as a transmission line.[19]

  Cat 5 cable. Alternatively referred to as an Ethernet or LAN cable, a cat 5 or category 5 cable is a network cable that consists of four twisted pairs of copper wire terminating in an RJ-45 connector. Cat 5 has a maximum length of 100 metres; exceeding this length without the aid of a bridge or other network device could cause network issues.[20]

- *Monitors*

  Monitors are the devices used for viewing activity captured by CCTV cameras and signalled by whichever system telemetry has been deployed. The CCTV monitor is one of the most important elements of CCTV systems, providing real-time feedback from CCTV cameras and security surveillance equipment. The CCTV camera's digital signal needs to be converted into a visual picture, and this can happen thanks to the specially designed monitors.[21]

- *Recording devices*

  The traditional way of recording until probably a decade ago was the analogue VHS system that used magnetic tape. This was a laborious means of recording images, as the tapes generally had to be changed and cleaned every 31 days, and they tended to stretch, making them unserviceable. There was also a painstaking process of having to review each tape from start to finish in order to find an incident.

  The analogue recording system has since been replaced by digital systems that will continue to record until the hard drive is full, so a greater capacity hard drive will afford the system's owner longer periods of recording. Also, because the system is digital, there is no need for the use of magnetic tape. If an incident needs to be searched for, the operator merely inputs the date and time, and when the system is located it can be burned to disk. That is to say, it can be recorded onto a blank CD or DVD and used as evidence if necessary.

- *Input/output devices*

  An input device is a peripheral piece of hardware which can be used to enter data into a computer. For example, keyboard and mouse are input devices.

- *Video motion detection (VMD) and video analytics (VA)*

   Video motion detection (VMD) through the use of pixel matching is a system which activates and can alarm when pixels within a frame alter (either fill or empty), warning that an image has moved into the camera's field of vision.

   Video analytics (VA), on the other hand is far more proactive, allowing for preemptive action by forecasting an alarm activation before an action occurs. VA is less prone to false alarm activations and is far more flexible than VMD. It is also more expensive.

- *Lighting*

   Although a growing number of CCTV systems are now using day/night cameras, there is no substitute during the hours of darkness for strong lighting, with LED being the best source of lighting support.

   For images of security lighting, go to www.google.com/search?q=security+lighting&source=lnms&tbm=isch&sa=X&ved=2ahUKEwivtpqiiZPnAhVUoXEKHcOGAywQ_AUoAnoECBAQBA&biw=2021&bih=826.

Perimeter intruder detection systems (PIDS) and intruder detection systems (IDS)

A major contribution to the protection of locations and buildings is the intruder detection system deployed to detect unauthorised persons. There are two distinct configurations for such a system:

- *Perimeter intruder detection systems* (PIDS) are further divided into three types:

   - *Barrier-mounted systems*

      One of the main advantages of using any form of barrier-mounted PIDS is the presence of a barrier which provides a physical delay to the intruder's progress. Introducing a delay can assist in the verification and response processes which are initiated following an alarm.[22]

      Barrier-mounted PIDS are generally reliant on some form of taut wire running through the fabric of the fence or the gate, and if the barrier is attacked in any way, either by cutting or an attempt to climb the barrier, the wire will be disturbed and will activate, causing an alarm.

   - *Underground intruder detection*

      The greatest advantage of the underground intruder detection system is that it is covert to a certain extent. There are of course electronic systems that will detect an underground PIDS, but for most of the time they will lie undetected by the opportunist criminal. They act as an early warning system if located at a distance from the target being protected, allowing the reaction force time to deploy and interdict any attack.

   - *Free-standing PIDS*

      The main advantages of a free-standing PIDS system are reduced installation cost due to no requirement for a physical barrier and a lower level of groundworks. They do not hinder legitimate activity, such as the movement of vehicles, and if required, installations can be designed to be discreet/covert.[23]

As opposed to barrier-mounted PIDS, free-standing configurations do not require attachment to any form of barrier, allowing free movement of legitimate traffic. However, because there is no physical barrier, reaction to an alarm activation has to be swift because the intruder will be inside the grounds very quickly.

The most common forms of this type of system are:

- Active infrared
- Passive infrared
- Doppler microwave
- Dual technology
- Laser scanner.

Go to www.cpni.gov.uk/system/files/documents/2c/80/Guide-to-PIDS.pdf for further advice about PIDS.

- *Internal intruder detection systems* (or *intruder alarms*) are usually configured to protect either the perimeter of the building or individual indoor areas (rooms, vaults, etc.). Perimeter protection is usually supported by the following systems:

  - *Door and window contacts*

    Door and window intruder detection systems use what are known as reed switches. A reed switch consists of a set of electrical connectors placed slightly apart, and once a magnetic field is introduced to the two plates it will pull them together and close the circuit, making the contacts active. Should the plates be forced apart, the circuit will collapse and the alarm will activate. Quite a basic system, but it does what it should do!

  - *Magnetic locking systems*

    An electromagnetic lock, magnetic lock, or maglock is a locking device that consists of an electromagnet and an armature plate. There are two main types of electric locking devices. Locking devices can be either 'fail secure' or 'fail safe'. A fail-secure locking device remains locked when power is lost. Fail-safe locking devices are unlocked when de-energised. Direct pull electromagnetic locks are inherently fail safe, and the door should be secure as soon as the magnet makes contact with the plate.

  - *Glass break detectors*

    A glass break detector senses the sound of different forms of breaking glass, whether they are plate, tempered, laminated, wired, coated, or sealed insulating glass. The system uses a microphone to listen for a frequency that is generated by breaking glass. Ideally, glass break detectors should be compatible with the type of glass that is installed. It will have a range of approximately 20 metres.

  - *Passive infrared (PIR) intruder detection system*

    A passive infrared sensor is an electronic sensor that measures infrared (IR) light radiating from objects in its field of view. They are most often used in PIR-based motion detectors. PIR sensors are commonly used in security alarms and automatic lighting applications.

As the name suggests, the PIR is not active, and it does not produce any form of infrared signature; rather it is activated when it receives an infrared notification.

PIR sensors detect general movement but do not give information on who or what moved. For that purpose, an active IR sensor is required.

- *Active infrared (AIR) intruder detection system*

Active infrared sensors are the types of detection sensor that requires an infrared signature that is picked up by a bespoke receiver. The IR is emitted by a IR light-emitting diode (LED) and received by photodiode, phototransistor, or photoelectric cells.

During the process of detection, the radiation is altered between the process of emission and receipt, when an object is in a position to block the signal.

Internal access control

Internal access control refers to entry into any room or location within a building, beginning with those entrances at the perimeter, and in this section, we will discuss common forms of access control used today.

- *Keys and key suited locking mechanisms*

A lock is a mechanical or electronic fastening device that is released by a physical object (such as a key, key card, fingerprint, RFID card, security token, coin, etc.), by supplying secret information (such as a number or letter permutation or password), or by a combination thereof or only being able to be opened from one side, such as a door chain.

A key is a device that is used to operate a lock (such as to lock or unlock it). A typical key is a small piece of metal consisting of two parts: the *bit* or *blade*, which slides into the keyway of the lock and distinguishes between different keys, and the *bow*, which is left protruding so that torque can be applied by the user. In its simplest implementation, a key operates one lock or set of locks that are keyed alike, a lock/key system where each similarly keyed lock requires the same unique key. The key serves as a security token for access to the locked area; only persons having the correct key can open the lock and gain access. In more complex mechanical lock/key systems, two different keys, one of which is known as the master key, serves to open the lock. Common metals include brass, plated brass, nickel silver, and steel.[24]

Locks and keys were a stalwart security system until the invention of the swipe card. Locks and keys have found to have been reliable, and if produced securely are extremely difficult to replicate. However, once a key was lost, it meant the replacement of all locks it was suited to.

The replacement for the lock and key has no such inadequacies.

- *Swipe card*

There are a number of reason why the simple swipe card was easily preferred to the lock and key, and I suppose the central reason was if a card was lost, electronically it could be deleted from the system, which meant that it could not be used to open an electronic lock; it was useless. The swipe card, which uses a simple aligned magnetic strip to open the lock, in the main is far less expensive than a complex, difficult to produce (even today) lock and key.

Also, and this is one of the main reasons why swipe cards began, in the main, to replace lock and keys; they could be audited. That is to say, the swipe card software creates a record for every time the card is used. The system will announce electronically when interrogated that by using his swipe card, Charles Swanson entered room A at 1000hrs, room B at 1100hrs and room C at 1200hrs; but did Charles categorically enter those rooms? Not necessarily. The system knows that the card belonging to Mr Swanson, card number 09 was used at those times, but there is no irrefutable evidence that it was Charles, who incidentally loaned his card to his friend John Horrigan who had left his card at home but needed to access rooms A, B, and C at the times stated.

- *Proximity card reader system (smart card)*

This really is where automatic access control made its name: the smart card.

A proximity card or prox card is a contactless smart card which can be read without inserting it into a reader device, as required by earlier magnetic stripe cards such as credit cards and contact type smart cards. The proximity cards are part of contactless card technologies. Held near an electronic reader for a moment, they enable the identification of an encoded number. The reader usually produces a beep or other sound to indicate the card has been read.

The term 'proximity card' refers to the older 125 kHz devices as distinct from the newer 13.56 MHz contactless smartcards.

Second-generation prox cards are used for mass and distance reading applications. Proximity cards typically have a read range up to 50 cm, which is the main difference from the contactless smartcard with a range of 2 to 10 cm. The card can often be left in a wallet or purse and read by simply holding the wallet or purse near the reader.[25]

These early proximity cards can't hold more data than a magnetic stripe card, and only cards with smart chips (i.e. contactless smartcards) can hold other types of data like electronic funds balance for contactless payment systems, history data for time and attendance or biometric templates. When used without encoding data, only with the card serial number, contactless smartcards have similar functionalities to proximity cards (Wikipedia, 2020).

Often proximity cards are supported by a personal identification number (PIN) second-stage security system, which means that the proximity card must be shown to the reader, and a PIN must be keyed before the lock will open. This is referred to as double verification.

- *Biometric access control*

There are myths and legends about biometric systems, mainly spread by people who have read headlines but have never carried out any evidence-based research. So, before we begin to examine the different types of biometric access control systems available today, we will consolidate the true meaning and definition of the technical term referred to as biometric.

When combined with another form of security control, such as a PIN or perhaps proximity card readers, biometric systems are the most secure systems used. However, let us have a definition of biometric.

There are a number of commercial biometric systems available today, and they are designed to recognise biological features of an individual before access is granted. The systems are in fact verification systems that use personal characteristics to verify identity. Such systems are currently fraught with problems, however, relating to the fact that physical characteristics of people do change with physical injuries, stress, and fatigue.

The three most common forms used for access control are:

* *Fingerprint recognition*

  They optically scan a chosen fingerprint area and compare the scanned area with the fingerprint on file of the person wishing to be admitted.

* *Hand geometry recognition*

  This system uses the geometry of the hand. The system measures finger lengths and compares them with those dimensions on file.

* *Eye retina recognition*

  The system analyses the blood vessel pattern in the retina of the eye. These patterns vary wildly, even between identical twins. The chance of false identification using this system is rated at one in a million (Fischer *et al.*, 2013).

  There are other systems such as signature recognition, speaker verification, and facial recognition, but they are less widely used.

Radio frequency identification (RFID)

The final electronic system to be examined in this section is radio frequency identification (RFID). RFID uses electromagnetic fields to automatically identify and track tags attached to objects. An RFID tag consists of a tiny radio transponder, a radio receiver, and a transmitter. When triggered by an electromagnetic interrogation pulse from a nearby RFID reader device, the tag transmits digital data, usually an identifying inventory number, back to the reader. This number can be used to inventory goods. There are two types. *Passive tags* are powered by energy from the RFID reader's interrogating radio waves. *Active tags* are powered by a battery and thus can be read at a greater range from the RFID reader, up to hundreds of metres. Unlike a barcode, the tag doesn't need to be within the line of sight of the reader, so it may be embedded in the tracked object. RFID is one method of automatic identification and data capture.[26]

RFID is used extensively today, with the following sectors using the system constantly and consistently.

* *Logistics*

  RFID is used to tag goods and pallets. The system can instantly inform the user about what goods are available, how many there are, and how much space they occupy in the warehouse or back store as they are entered.

- *Inventories and warehouses*

  The main reason to use RFID is to increase the efficiency of warehouses by reducing work and logistic costs. One can obtain an instant, accurate inventory of goods with all kind of details, like size, quality, country of origin, and so on. Physical inventory counts which are expensive and inaccurate are no longer necessary.

- *Identification of animals*

  Tagging animals with RFID is an important tool for a farmer in order to identify each animal with information such as its origin, pedigree, and medical details. With the help of software, the information can be updated by uploading the new information during veterinary visits.

- *Surgeries*

  RFID technology in hospitals is present in many forms, from tracking surgical tools to tracking persons – patients, visitors, and staff. There are several important reasons to use RFID technology in the healthcare industry – anything from reducing medical errors to lost essential surgical tools or forgotten surgical sponges within patients.

- *Access control*

  The RFID access control system works to identify who the card with RFID belongs to, and where and when it has entered a building or a room. It is useful to have information about individuals in an organisation or event like a sports match or music festival, and also to allow or deny the entry of individuals in particular places.

- *Passports*

  Passports with an embedded RFID tag are called biometric passports, e-passports or digital passports. This tag has biometric information that is used to authenticate the identity of the passport holder. The information stored in RFID tags of e-passports depends on the country's policy. Data usually stored are name, date and place of birth, sex, nationality and a digital version of the photograph. Data about the passport are in the tag also, such as the number, issue date and place, and the expiry date. The standardised biometrics used for identification systems are facial recognition, fingerprint recognition, or iris recognition.

- *Libraries and museums*
  RFID is being applied in the museums, libraries, and other related settings mostly in three ways:

  - *Objects tracking*: Managing full inventories of collections is a huge and time-consuming process.
  - *Security systems*: Protecting assets from theft is an essential issue in museum galleries. RFID provides security by automatically tracking the movement of objects tagged, which can be located instantly.
  - *Visitor experience*: There is too much information to put in a single label on the wall. The visitor's experience is complete and amusing if they are directed to a virtual resource linked with a tag.

Exercise Brave Defender – task 3: physical and electronic security systems

Synopsis

The risk assessment recently carried out by you and your team has highlighted a number of areas that have been communicated to the board. The chief executive officer (CEO) and the chief operating officer (COO) have concluded that a number of areas explained in the risk assessment report require attention.

Your next tasks are as follows:

1   Explain to the CEO and the COO what is meant by defence in depth (DiD) and demonstrate how the concept may be applied to the headquarters at Canary Fields.
2   The CCTV system, the automatic access control system (AACS), and the intruder detection system (IDS) now require replacement. Lay down a set of specifications relating to the ideal replacement CCTV, AACS, and IDS systems at Canary Fields.
3   Accompany this set of recommendations with a cost-benefit analysis (CBA) for replacing the current CCTV system, which is ten years old and beyond its warranty. For the purpose of this exercise, all costings may be fictional.
4   The current manned guarding service is contracted to Canary Fields security. The chief finance officer (CFO) has asked you to outline a series of arguments explaining your personal views as to whether security officers should be directly employed by Britcom or remain outsourced to the external service provider.

3.4 The security survey and the security audit

Pause for thought

In your opinion, what is the difference between a security survey and a security audit?

Before we address that question, it is important to understand that there is a process here; a journey that must be followed, because otherwise the component parts are completely out of synchronisation.

In my experience, stretching over almost four decades (wow), there is an impression of people involved in security management to have an almost God-given understanding (some might say rightly so) of what a security survey or a security audit is. Unfortunately, that is generally far from the truth, for a number of reasons.

I suppose that is what this book is all about.

In my opinion, if a security professional does not understand the rudiments of extrapolating the findings of a security risk assessment to a credible security survey, we as a sector have immense problems.

So, for the remainder of this section we shall explore the relationship between the security risk assessment, the security survey, and the security audit.

In my opinion, there has to be what I reluctantly call the risk journey, depicted in Figure 3.5.

The risk assessment, previously covered in this book, offers the security manager or whoever is carrying out the security survey the opportunity to understand the levels of risk pertaining to the location under survey. You may recall that one of the means of treating risk after an assessment is to reduce the risk factor, whether the assessment is in either qualitative or quantitative format. One method of reducing the risk factor is to introduce physical and electronic security systems that are fit for purpose.

The security surveyor is not and must not be perceived to be a salesperson, nor is he or she an auditor.

The security survey, once the risk factor is known, is a comprehensive analysis of a company's premises, systems, and procedures. There are three primary objectives for performing a security survey:

- Examine the security systems in situ.
- Examine any security plan in existence and peruse possible previous security survey reports.
- Have an understanding of what security systems are required to mitigate the identified risk.

The security survey is an opportunity to examine all security systems on site in an effort to understand if they are fit for purpose. 'Fit for purpose' means that those systems under

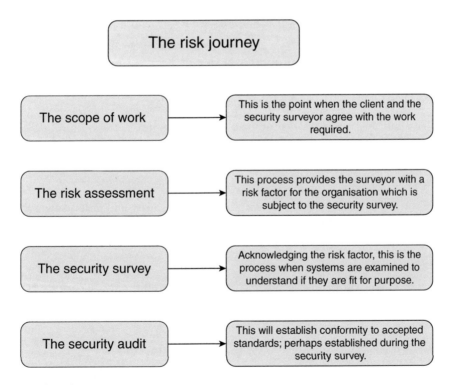

Figure 3.5 The risk journey

scrutiny meet the conditions of an operational requirement, affording protection to the organisation in terms of the result of the risk assessment.

In my opinion, this is the opportunity to have 'boots on the ground', with the surveyor asking questions in relation to the systems deployed that have perhaps not been asked before; and whilst a physical penetration test is not a prerequisite, the surveyor should challenge access control methods deployed to see if it is possible to enter restricted areas unauthorised and undetected. The surveyor must not be afraid to get his or her hands dirty.

The security survey and its meaning are relatively straightforward to understand, and if you search for the term 'security survey' in most search engines, you will be offered a definition quite close to the preceding definition.

However, attempting to analyse the meaning of the term 'security audit' is far from straightforward, and once again this is an indication of the confusion currently embedded in a number of security definitions. Equally as important is the fact that most search results for security audit will default to computing and IT.

For example, I searched for security audit in Google, and here are a number of examples of the results of the search.

- www.quora.com/What-is-a-security-audit

  "A security Audit is a Complete procedure to identify and fix all the security flaw in a computer, or may be network, or may be any system application or web application".

- www.latestdictionary.com/word/meaning/Security+audit

  "The protection of information and information systems against unauthorized access or modification of information, whether in storage, processing or transit, and against denial of service to authorized users".

- www.thelawdictionary.org/security-audit

  "The audit that is used to determine a systems computer access control procedures against unwanted attacks and intrusions from criminals and any unauthorised personnel".

- www.locknet.com/

  This site offers a checklist which refers to physical security, and in so many ways mirrors what I argue is a security survey.

The security survey

In this section we will cover the physical aspects of carrying out a security survey, and there is a logical means of doing that, but there are a number of issues that must be covered first.

- *Why carry out a security survey?*

  In an ideal world, the executive board of a corporation will be risk forward-thinking, and after commissioning a security risk assessment will better understand the assets, threats, and vulnerabilities pertaining to the organisation. Being aware that risk reduction is required, the board will order a security survey to be carried out by a competent person at the earliest opportunity.

However, in general terms that is not how business applies itself to security risks that may impact the organisation and its operations, including staff and management.

Just a moment

Can you think of two or three reasons why a security survey may be commissioned by the senior management team?

There are several reasons why a security survey may be commissioned, with the most common being listed below:

- *Compliance*

    In order to meet the requirements of a company's insurers, or perhaps to comply with the terms of a particular international standard, the executive board may create a mandate whereby a security survey (or perhaps several) are carried out annually. The survey(s) must be carried out by a competent person (more about that later), with the findings being completely transparent.

- *Organisation review*

    Under circumstances such as the takeover of a corporation or the inclusion of a number of new functions, the executive board may order a security survey of all new locations to ensure that physical security systems on site at the recently acquired locations are fit for purpose and to ensure that all systems are compatible with those in the rest of the group.

    This is often the case with ICT data centres. It may be that a relatively minor data centre has been acquired to store unique data, and the group executive board must ensure that all physical systems are compliant with group requirements and standards.

    Whilst discussing ICT, if an organisation decides to apply for ISO 27001 accreditation (Information Security Management Systems), all physical security systems and measures on every site must comply with the requirements as laid down in the international standard.

- *Regulations and initiatives*

    The intermodal global supply chain is a very good example of circumstances when regulations and initiatives may demand physical security surveys, but perhaps in another guise.

    In 2004, as a direct result of the terrorist attacks on 9/11, when al-Qaeda attacked the Twin Towers at the World Trade Center in New York, the International Ship and Port Facility Security Code (ISPS Code) was enacted.[27] As a result, certain vessels and port areas (facilities) had to be physically security surveyed (referred to as security assessments, I believe from an American perspective) to ensure that they complied with a global standard.

A spin-off from this set of regulations was a number of initiatives devised by nation states to ensure that the logistics chain was secure. In the first instance, ISO 28000 (2007) was introduced, and this allows those organisations involved in the global supply chain to meet a physical security standard that is compliant with global best practice. As with all international standards, it is of course voluntary.

Related to the effects of 9/11 and indirectly related to the ISPS Code came the introduction of an initiative named the authorised economic operator (AEO) scheme. This ensures logistics companies have unrestricted access to European Union borders unhindered. Part of the criteria for acceptance onto the AEO scheme is the level of physical security of all aspects of the logistics company, particularly vehicle parks and distribution centres. Such locations are subject to a high-level security survey by revenue bodies before accreditation is granted.

- *As the result of a criminal attack*

  Unfortunately, the dilemma faced here is that by far the most common reason for a security survey to be requested is as the result of a criminal attack. This makes very little sense.

Just a moment

In your opinion, why is it that a considerable number of organisations wait until they have been attacked before they have their on-site systems examined in the form of a security survey?

In my experience, there are a number of reasons why organisations tend to wait until they have been a victim of a burglary, an assault, or a terrorist attack before they are prepared to finance a security survey.

- *Unnecessary concern*

  "Typical security, you worry over everything. When was the last time we were attacked – never, in fact? Show me the evidence that we will be attacked, and I will sign the cheque".

  In this scenario, the finance director advising the CEO is of the opinion that his company won't be hit – why should it be? It has never been attacked before, and we 'security experts', in his or her opinion, are using speculative fear to enhance our standing in the eyes of the senior management team. We are using guesswork and subjective opinion, as opposed to evidence-based argument.

- *A lack of finance*

  Unfortunately, the security budget (if one indeed ever existed) has been exhausted for this financial year, and expenditure will not be discussed until the next fiscal period. So "Put a business case together and present it to me next March".

- *No legal requirement*

In terms of health and safety in the UK, the law is quite straightforward.

The Health and Safety Executive (HSE) says risk should be assessed "every time there are new machines, substances and procedures, which could lead to new hazards".

The HSE guidelines are quite vague, but suffice it to say that a risk assessment should be carried out when the following circumstances prevail:

- If a new task or role is being contemplated (e.g. a new manned guarding site), a risk assessment to ensure the safety of all staff must be carried out before the work commences.
- If there is evidence of a changing situation, for example the introduction of new machinery or working practices which it appears may lead to greater staff discontent.
- If an employee is about to participate in what may be deemed a high-risk role.

This is not the case when examining security requirements and operations. Irrelevant of crime levels and threats to an organisation, there is no legal mandate to have a security risk assessment or survey carried out, so in the words of the finance director, "I'm not forced to pay for a security survey by law, so why should I?"

Ludicrous.

Competency levels

So now let us assume that for whatever reason, the executive board has taken a command decision to have a security survey carried out at its new distribution centre. The question now of course is, who is going to carry out the survey?

Just a moment:

In your opinion, what qualifications should a person hold before being allowed to carry out a security survey?

In terms of the risk assessment, the Health and Safety Executive (HSE) in the UK says that as an employer or a self-employed person, you are responsible for health and safety in your business.

You can delegate the task, but ultimately you are responsible. You will need to make sure that whoever carries out the risk assessment is *competent* to do so. But what does that mean? There are a number of health and safety (H&S) qualifications available, such as:

- NEBOSH National Diploma in Occupational Health and Safety
- British Safety Council Level 6 Diploma in Occupational Safety and Health

- City & Guilds Level 5 (NVQ) Diploma in Occupational Health and Safety Practice
- NCRQ Level 6 Diploma in Applied Health and Safety.

So, to carry out an H&S risk assessment, the assessor merely has to prove 'competence', and that is generally measured by qualifications and experience. However fragile this proof of competency is, at least it is a baseline; but no such term of reference is required to carry out a security risk assessment or a security survey.

I have been teaching recognised level 4 risk assessment and survey courses for about 20 years, and I am constantly surprised and at times disappointed by the number of students who are currently carrying out security surveys as part of their professional role without any formal qualifications.

When asked about the template used for his security surveys, a former student of mine, who at that time was a serving member of the armed forces, replied, half joking: "The back of a fag packet".

I suppose that is one of the many reasons why I was determined to write this book.

Credit should be given to the Health and Safety Executive for setting a standard in terms of who should be carrying out the risk assessment. In my opinion, the same level of professionalism should be replicated by the security sector.

This is where it becomes slightly complex and somewhat aspirational, so please bear with me.

The security surveyor

In an ideal world (again) there would be a security professional referred to as a security surveyor. The security surveyor would be mandated to hold relevant security qualifications, perhaps a degree or diploma, and because of the sensitivity of his or her work, some form of licence.

Licencing is another area that increases my passion for professionalism and common sense.

Once again, reflecting my experience not just as a tutor but also as a security surveyor with several hundred surveys that make up my portfolio, I have had the privilege of carrying out security surveys at the British Museum, BT Tower, the South Bank, Venice, Athens, New York, and many others – and I have loved every task. However, during this extremely interesting career, I have never had to prove my honesty or lack of criminal activity.

I wandered around the British Museum wearing only a visitor's badge (figuratively speaking of course), and in the Hayward Gallery, which was showing Andy Warhol works, all I was carrying was a clipboard and a camera. Embarrassingly for the UK, I was allowed to carry out several security surveys at MOD list X sites which are responsible for the construction of secret weapons systems without any form of vetting being carried out. I security project managed/surveyed the new construction of a very high-profile bank in Knightsbridge, London – once again, unchecked. How can that be?

Security officers who may man an access control barrier for eight hours per shift, and door supervisors who control access to pubs and clubs, not to forget CCTV operators, all have to hold a Security Industry Authority (SIA) licence before they can practice their trade. In contrast, an inspector who examines often sensitive equipment and documents does not have to be in possession of any form of licence or authority. This is insane.

My vision – the professional security surveyor

If I were to start with a clean sheet of paper, after being requested to specify the responsibilities and qualifications of a security surveyor, it would not be an easy task.

The responsibilities have already been outlined so far in this section, but to summarise: the security surveyor is responsible for carrying out an examination of current systems, physical and procedural, on site to ensure that such systems are fit for purpose. We will discuss how he or she achieves this later in this section.

As mentioned previously, the default word when attempting to describe the requirements of a security surveyor is competency: Is he or she competent enough to carry out a security survey. But the term is very vague, and in many respects it is misleading. If an organisation was attempting to recruit a member of staff, let us say an IT security specialist, there would be a list of competencies and qualifications that every candidate must be in possession of, but the advert in an appropriate trade magazine wouldn't require an IT specialist who is merely competent, because exactly what does that mean?

Registered security surveyor/auditor

If a homeowner or a business requires the services of a gas fitter or an electrician, it is extremely likely that a registered tradesman will be selected. A competent gas fitter is registered on the Gas Safe Register, which demands extensive levels of safety and competency. An electrician will be registered with the National Inspection Council for Electrical Installation Contracting (NICEIC). Therefore, it makes perfect sense for a security surveyor in the twenty-first century to hold some form of accreditation. Similar to paths chosen by chartered security professionals, the security surveyor should be given the opportunity to choose a pathway to professional recognition.

I envisage two parallel pathways that I have named the academic and the apprenticeship pathways. The academic pathway, as the name suggests, is reliant on the applicant holding either a bachelors or a master's degree and a level four qualification in security surveying (or its equivalent). This academic achievement should be supported by at least five years' management experience in the security sector.

The apprentice pathway will require the applicant to have served a two-year apprenticeship in a security related skills area, during which he or she will have studied for a level five qualification in security surveying.[28]

Academic pathway

- Recognised security related qualification

  - A degree or ASIS qualification; and
  - A level four Security Survey qualification.

- Five years' security management experience

Apprenticeship pathway

- Two-year security survey apprenticeship, culminating in a level five qualification in security surveying

  - Two years' practical training

    - Twelve months' level five security survey qualification training (incl.)

  - Twelve months' experience.

Security Survey Methodology

The security survey methodology is not described in any international or national standard, such as an ISO or BS (EN),[29] rather it has evolved over time, in a quite disorganised manner; and the approach will very much depend on organisational culture and perspective, personalities, and subjective judgement. However, I have developed a system that has been very effective over the years, tested in a number of environments, and I refer to it as the five-stage approach to security surveying (I know, not particularly exciting or imaginative, but it does what it says on the side of the can). Here we go.

Stage 1: Preliminary research

As soon as the contract is signed, or perhaps a gentlemen's agreement has been made, preliminary research must begin. Assuming that the contract or agreement is for the security surveyor to act as an external consultant, which is the norm, he or she needs to obtain as much information about the business of the client for whom the survey has been agreed. If the security survey is part of internal compliance, required pre-survey information will probably (although not guaranteed) be easily accessible.

Preparing a security survey for an external client, in my opinion, almost equates to being selected to attend for a job interview; the interviewee needs to understand as much about their prospective employer as his future boss does. Being asked about your knowledge of the company you hope to join and replying, "I don't really know a great deal", may be the death knell to your future prospects of employment. In a similar vein, if the security surveyor arrives on site with little or no client knowledge, he or she is going to appear unprofessional at best and perhaps distinctly disinterested. It is not a great start. We live in an era that allows us unlimited access to global information, with the Internet and social media at our fingertips; there is absolutely no excuse for poor research.

So, there are a number of areas that must be investigated, and certain issues that have to be clarified.

- *Company business operations*

     In order for the security surveyor to have a balanced opinion about the forthcoming security survey, he or she must have a solid understanding of the business his or her client is involved in. I have heard arguments that a security survey is consistent whatever the business operations may be, and as long as the surveyor adheres to a set of recognised procedures, the type of operations carried out by the client are irrelevant. I totally disagree. My argument is that culturally, there is likely to be strong differentiation, because it is impossible to equate, let's say, a retail outlet to a chemical plant, or an airport to a power generating facility. Each site must be judged on its merits.

- *Political, cultural and ethical perspectives*

     The site of the proposed security survey may be located in an area of substantial risk, and there may be cultural and ethical issues pertaining, so an examination of the company's corporate social responsibilities (CSR) will have to be taken into consideration. The politics of the situation will need to be given thought, as will the safety of the surveyor in what may be a high-risk area (HRA).

- *Crime pattern analysis (CPA)*

  The security risk assessment that should have been carried out before the security survey will provide a certain level of criminal knowledge, but it will be applied quantitatively, purely from an incident likelihood/consequence perspective, with little detailed qualitative information or data. With that in mind, the security surveyor should attempt to carry out some form of crime pattern analysis (CPA), as that will give an indication of the types and volumes of crime committed in the area of the survey.

  With web sites such as www.police.uk, there is the option not just to be able to drill down to street level but also investigate local police 'clear up' rates, that is to say, examine those crimes that have been subject to a successful criminal investigation and those that have not.

- *Security survey reports*

  Depending on the relationship between the surveyor and his or her client, it may be possible to examine any previous security survey reports. There may or may not have been previous security surveys carried out, and it is possible that security survey reports have been generated, which may be available. From my experience, there is minimal chance of this. It may be that the survey was carried out, but a report was never produced, or if it was it is no longer available. It is possible that for political internal reasons, the report cannot be shared. There are a host of reasons why the report may not be available, but if the security surveyor is fortunate enough to be able to examine a previous security survey report, it may be invaluable.

  Upon perusal of such a document, the security surveyor must determine if the report has been produced by a competent person, and if so, are the observations and recommendations credible? Next, he or she must investigate the actions of the client, because if the observations and recommendations are indeed viable, with credibility, but the client has failed to action them, the security surveyor has to rhetorically ask why this is.

  From this point on the upmost caution is required, because there may be a number of reasons why the client has chosen not to follow the credible advice of a former security surveying colleague.

  There may be a simple answer, such as at the time of the survey and its subsequent recommendations, there was insufficient funding available for the treatment options recommended. Equally, it may well be that since the security report was produced, there have been a number of changes and alterations within the decision-making section of the company, and the report is still in the pending tray.

  However, there may be deeper rooted political reasons involved, such as internal collusion to cause an offence, or perhaps the report is sub judice in terms of a police investigation, and it cannot be shared. Whatever the reasons for its withdrawal or non-availability, the security surveyor must handle the situation with the highest level of subtlety and diplomacy.

- *Reconnaissance*

> "A day spent on recce is never wasted" is one of the very few phrases that I recall from my military career, but it has paid handsomely since leaving the armed forces and beginning a career in the security industry, particularly as a security surveyor.
>
> A city centre security survey location early Monday morning, with its hustle and bustle, is completely different to the same location at midnight, when illumination may be reliant on streetlamps, and anybody seen loitering is observed with suspicion.
>
> As a rule, whenever possible I will carry out a reconnaissance of the location some time beforehand. It may be the night before the survey, and I will walk 360 degrees around the site, taking photos if possible, whilst maintaining a low profile.
>
> The recce may be next morning when I will perhaps sit at a street café opposite the building in question, enjoying a cup of tea and reading the newspaper, whilst actually studying the front door of the survey location to understand the levels of access control, and to observe security for staff and visitors entering and leaving the premises. I always study the front entrance, because that is where perhaps I will see security officers yawning and paying little attention to the visitor who has just gained entrance by piggybacking a member of staff, who thought it gentlemanly to hold open the door for the obviously honest lady who appears a little confused! I may be able to take a photograph of a member of staff who has rather laboriously, in a very bored fashion used the digital access control panel in full view of everybody passing. "Security isn't my job", he would probably protest if challenged.
>
> "*A day spent on recce is never wasted*".

Stage 2: Planning and preparation

As can be seen from Figure 3.4, the risk journey, the immediate priority for the security surveyor is to understand the scope of work, and this is critical. I have already argued the fact that the entire security survey process is blurred, in that perceptions are different dependent upon who sits where in discussions.

For instance, the client is extremely unlikely to understand what is meant by the term 'security survey' because he or she will have heard terms such as 'security audit' and 'security review' and is unlikely to actually know what they are being expected to pay for. It is during the project inception meeting that the security surveyor must instigate momentum. The surveyor must command the high ground and be in a position to dominate discussions, or initial talks will descend into arguments about the cheapest options available, as opposed to the quality of work required. The surveyor must have absolute clarity at this stage about what the expectations and deliverables are in relation to time and contractual terms and conditions.

Only when this is crystal clear can discussions move on.

I was involved in a complicated series of security surveys in 2012 for a local authority. During the initial discussions, referred to as the 'kick-off meeting', I asked my point of contact what the scope of work was, to which he replied, "You are the security expert, we will leave that to you". I agreed – school boy error!

There were twelve sites to be security surveyed, and the agreement was for me to provide a security survey report after the first survey for us to agree on the levels of service being provided.

I despatched my first survey report to the client, who wrote to me asking for a meeting, which was quite acceptable. When we met he had my report in his hand, and was tossing it into the air, before announcing that the report did not meet the 'weight test'; in his words it was too flimsy and lacking in content, and, wait for it, 'It didn't meet the scope of work'. Bingo, lessons learned. Never walk away from a kick-off meeting without being clear about what the client wants and needs.

Time spent in preparation and ensuring that you have the right tools to do the job is never wasted and will save a great deal of time and potential embarrassment. There are a number of considerations that must be taken into account, and below I have listed a number of preparatory tasks that have to be carried out.

- Maps or GPS

  We live in an age of technology, where to a certain extent GPS has replaced ordinance survey maps, and whether it is a bespoke GPS system such as TomTom or Magellan, it is likely that the journey will be shorter and easier than when having to constantly refer to maps. However, how many times have you read about heavy goods vehicles becoming wedged in a road that is too narrow for them to turn around, or perhaps coming across a barrier that the GPS was unaware of. I use a GPS app on my smartphone, and most journeys run smoothly, but I always carry a road map, just in case.

- Details of the area

  Details of the area where the security survey is about to take place are essential. Issues such as demographics, unemployment rates, similar business in the area and current crime rates by type and volume will provide a very useful backdrop to the survey.

- Authorisation (crucial)

  This would appear to be quite obvious; of course, you need authorisation before beginning the security survey. However, we live in an era of complicated communications and shifting roles and responsibilities, so for the sake of a telephone call, it is always worth checking confirmation of authority before beginning the journey.

- Changes in laws and regulations

  There may be new laws or regulations that impact, not only the security survey, but peripheral procedures to the survey, such as data protection. In 2017 we saw the emergence of General Data Protection Regulations (GDPR) 2018. The EU General Data Protection Regulations (GDPR) replaces the Data Protection Directive 95/46/EC and is designed to:

  - Harmonise data privacy laws across Europe.

  - Protect and empower all EU citizens data privacy.

  - Reshape the way organisations across the region approach data privacy.

  The regulations are not intended to replace the Data Protection Act 2018, rather they are to complement it, and the UK will still adhere to GDPR if it leaves the EU. There are of course other laws and regulations that must be considered, and this should be done at the earliest stage of preparation.

- Social media and social networking.

  Part of the preparation for the security survey may be the consultation of social media sites such as Facebook, Twitter, LinkedIn, and so forth, and of course there are a number of reliable search engines such as Google, Bing, Search Encrypt, and so on. By researching the organisation through social media and networking, the security surveyor is likely to uncover information about the organisation that is perhaps unavailable elsewhere.

- Specific contacts and client relationships.

  By far, one of the most important factors to be taken into consideration when preparing for a security survey is client relationship. The sound working relationship between the Security Surveyor and his or her client is critical in terms of the efficiency and effectiveness of the project.

  This may be anathema to the old and bold within the security sector, who for a number of reasons, haven't exactly covered themselves in glory in terms of customer service over the years and decades. The term "bloody security" is heard far too often, as are the allegations that security personnel understand and are more interested in locks and bolts (business disruption) than how a business operates and grows (business enablement).

  The security surveyor, from day one, must make it very clear to his or her potential customer that the clients' wellbeing and that of his or her business are paramount. This all about customer service, and the highest levels of attention to the needs of the customer must begin with the first hand shake.

  Matthew Odgers, Attorney/Founder, Odgers Law Group recently announced that "The sole reason we are in business is to make life less difficult for our clients". That certainly has to apply to the security surveyor, who must make it clear from day one that his or her task is to cost effectively safeguard the assets belonging to the client on a 24/7 basis.

- Camera (smartphone)

  As an operational security surveyor, it is not unusual for me to take the occasional photograph of a system on site which may perhaps be new to me, or a component of that system that I don't recognise, and send the photo to a colleague who may be a subject matter expert in that field. He or she may be able to recognise the CCTV camera or access control housing and send me an explanation or specification for the component.

  I advocate taking as many photographs as possible, and much like the theory of defence in depth, I will begin with the surrounding streets and roads, moving onto the perimeter and access points before photographing inside the building where the protected asset is located. Finally, I will take a number of photographs of the server room, the communications room, or whatever it is that my security survey is striving to protect.

  The photographs will play a critical role in the security survey report, but they must be introduced correctly and explained logically.

  There is absolutely no doubt in my mind that photography during a security survey is almost priceless, but a word of warning. Always ensure that you have permission to take photographs, because even in a democratically liberal country such as the UK, people tend to become nervous, for reasons unknown to me, when they see photographs being taken – particularly if they are the star attraction! In countries that may be politically unstable, the practice of taking photographs of public buildings or in sensitive areas can lead to arrest.

On 19 March 2016, the *Sun* newspaper revealed that four British tourists were arrested on suspicion of terrorism after taking pictures at an airport in Nairobi. Ian Glover, 46, Steve Gibson, 60, and Eddie Swift and Paul Abbott, both 47, drew the attention of authorities after taking photos from the bar of planes taking off at Wilson Airport, the *Sun* reported. They said they believed they were allowed to do this, but they sparked a terror alert and were taken in for questioning by police in the Kenyan capital. They were charged with trespassing and taking photos without authority.

Kenya criminalised all private photography at airports following the terrorist attack at the Westgate Shopping Centre in 2013, during which it is believed that at least 65 people were killed, with hundreds being injured.

- Identification

  Related to the discussion about photography is the topic of identification. Once again, using the UK as an example, verification of identification is not generally an issue, which is a bonus, as UK citizens are not bound to carry a form of identification on their person. However, in the US, Europe, the Middle and Far East, it is not unusual to be asked to produce some form of identification. Now of course, anybody from outside those geographical areas, by virtue of the fact that they have travelled to them, will be in possession of a valid passport, otherwise they could not have travelled. Returning to the UK, if the security survey is going to be carried out at a sensitive location, such a government building, it may be a prerequisite to be able to prove one's identity. My advice, therefore, is for the security surveyor to always have some form of identification on their person, as this may save embarrassment if they are refused entry because they cannot prove they are who they say they are!

  Remember the six P's: Perfect Planning and Preparation Prevents Poor Performance!

Stage 3: Conducting the survey

Where are we?

The commissioned security surveyors have the necessary qualifications and experience to carry out the security survey, and they have struck up a sound and professional working relationship with their client. They are aware of what is required, the levels of risk and the scope of work, and they have researched and prepared adequately for the forthcoming project.

Boots on the ground – conducting the survey

The next stage of the work is to physically carry out the security survey; the phase is referred to as boots on the ground, and for exercise purposes, this phase will take the form of a fictitious case study. However, before we arrive at the data centre, there are a number of details about the surrounding environment that we must be aware of:

The Crime Pattern Analysis

The location to be security surveyed is a data centre located adjacent to a main trunk road near a busy South of England city.

Employment in the area is higher than the national average, as is crime; with predominant offences being highlighted.[30] The data centre employs 600 full-time members of staff, and before we conduct the survey it is always advantageous to carry out a crime pattern analysis.

Probably the easiest website to use for measuring crime, certainly in the UK is www.police.uk, and from that source we can reveal the following statistics relating to the immediate area where the data centre is located. See Table 3.3.

- Burglary

    With 147 offences of burglary being carried out over the last 12 months, accounting for 5.13% of the overall crime figures for the area, there is of course a concern that the data centre may be targeted, probably by opportunist criminals.

- Criminal damage and arson

    The two crimes (243 offences and 8.48% of all crime) are of concern because the data centre is a high-profile location within the city, and it may draw criminals intent on either damaging or setting fire to the building, or perhaps vehicles in the large car park.

- Vehicle crime

    There are approximately 500 cars parked at the location every day, and they will make ideal targets for car criminals' intent on stealing or stealing from staff vehicles. There were 364 offences of vehicle crime committed during the last year, accounting for 12.71% of all crime committed in the post code.

Table 3.3 The crime pattern analysis

Burglary	147	5.13%
Criminal damage and arson	243	8.48%
Drugs	81	2.83%
Possession of weapons	25	0.87%
Public order	113	3.94%
Robbery	40	1.40%
Shoplifting	184	6.42%
Theft from the person	34	1.19%
Vehicle crime	364	12.71%
Violence and sexual offences	876	30.58%

- Violence and sexual offences

  The data centre is a 24/7 operation, which means that members of staff will be walking to their cars, or perhaps walking home at all hours of the day and night. With 876 such crimes being committed, which is just under one third of all offences (30.58%), this is a major concern.

Emergency services

- Police

  The closest police station is located three miles from the data centre, but it is only open to the public, Monday to Friday, 0900hrs to 1700hrs. The nearest 24-hour police station is approximately 15 miles away from the data centre, with a 15-minute non-emergency response.

- Fire and rescue

  The nearest 24-hour fire station is located eight miles away, with an emergency response time of ten minutes.

- Medical services

  The closest ambulance and A&E facility are six miles from the data centre, with an emergency response time of ten minutes.
  Road communications to and from the data centre are excellent, with access to a number of A roads and motorways.
  The physical security of the data centre is as follows.

- **Perimeter defence**

The perimeter is protected by a three-metre-high welded-mesh steel fence, which is fitted with a taut wire perimeter intruder defence system (PIDS). Should the fence be struck with the same force as a person attempting to climb the fence, the alarm will activate in the security control room. The location of the attempted breach will be highlighted on a monitor in the control room, and a security officer will be despatched to investigate. During daylight and dark hours, a member of the security team, in adherence to the site assignment instructions, will patrol the inside of the perimeter fence five times. The patrolling security officer will have a handheld radio and a 'man down' emergency beacon on his or her person. LED 360-degree perimeter lighting has only recently been installed, and it is very effective.

- **Access control**

There is a single point of entry to the front of the site, with access to vehicles and pedestrians. There is also an emergency entrance to the rear of the site for easy escape, and if necessary, access for the emergency services.

The front entrance consists of an electrically driven, sliding steel gate for vehicle entry, which is approximately three metres in width and two metres in height. The gate is operated from the security control room, which is immediately inside the site perimeter, and from which the duty security officer has full view of the main entrance. In terms of pedestrian access, there are two systems.

- Staff

  All members of staff are issued an identity card, which in actual fact is a photo verification proximity smart card, which they may use for operating the steel pedestrian turnstile. The turnstile allows one-person entry at a time, and each smart card has RFID 'anti pass back' software, which means that it has to pass by an exit reader before it can be used again for entry. This prevents members of staff passing their cards to anybody who is not in possession of such a card. If a member of staff forgets their ID card, they must contact the security team who will verify their identity, make a note of the discrepancy, and contact their line manager before allowing them access.

- Visitors

  There is a two-way communications system that allows visitors to contact the security team in the control room. All visitors must have an appointment, and once access is gained, they will be escorted to the control room, where they will be issued a temporary pass, which must be surrendered on leaving, and their host will be contacted; the host will escort the visitor during their stay on site.

- Rear entrance

  The rear entrance is not manned, but it is observed on the site CCTV system, and it is linked to the PIDS. Should it be forced from the outside or climbed, the PIDS will activate, and the activation will be investigated. From the inside, the emergency exit is opened by means of a standard crash bar, which is also alarmed, signalling back to the control room.

- **Building protection and integrity**

  Once on site, it can be seen that the data centre building is a two-story unit, constructed from pre-cast concrete, steel and glass.

- Doors and windows

  - Front entrance
    The main entrance is to the front of the building, consisting of two inward swinging, single-leaf metal framed, double-glazed doors. Between the single entrances is a metal framed, double-glazed revolving door. All front entrance doors are open and insecure during working hours but have the capacity to be 'locked down' during dark hours, or if required to ensure the safety of staff. Once secure, all doors are linked to the building intruder detection system (IDS).

- Goods inward/loading bay

    The goods inward/loading bay is secured by an aluminium upward moving roller gate, complemented by a single steel, inward pedestrian door. Both doors are secure and alarmed unless being used for the acceptance of product delivery. Both doors are also linked to the building IDS.
- Fire exits

    There are three ground floor fire exits built into the fabric of the building. Each door is of steel construction and is secured from within by a three-point, crash bar opening system. The fire doors are not linked to the building IDS.

Recommendations

It is recommended that all fire doors are linked to the building IDS on a 24/7 basis, and if a door is opened, the alarm will activate and signal to the security control room for investigation.

- All windows are UPVC double-glazed, sealed units, which are protected by the building IDS.

- Roof area

    There is a flat roof on the building under survey, and there are a number of air condition and chiller units located there. There is access from the second floor, consisting of a single internal ladder which leads to a one-metre square steel opening. The steel flap lading to the roof is secured by a single open shackle padlock inside. The access point is not alarmed.

Recommendations

It is recommended that the roof access panel is linked to the building IDS on a 24/7 basis, and if the panel is opened, the alarm will activate and signal to the security control room for investigation. It is further recommended that the roof area should be covered by the building CCTV system.

- Reception area

All visitors and staff enter the building via the main reception area, which is manned during the hours of 0800hrs to 1700hrs, Monday to Friday. During all other times, the main doors are secure, and there is a roving member of the security team.

Upon entering the premises, staff will make their way to the access control turnstiles, where their photo ID proximity card will allow them access to the remainder of the building. There is no anti pass back software installed at this entry point.

Visitors will report to one of the two receptionists on duty and will be issued a temporary visitor pass before their host is contacted.

Because there is constant movement in the reception area, day and night, with the exception of door protection, there is no intruder detection systems (IDS) installed.

There is no CCTV system installed in the reception area.

Recommendations

It is critically recommended that CCTV is installed to protect the following areas:

- *The front doors*
- *The fire exit doors*
- *The reception area*
- *The access control turnstile area.*

All cameras and control equipment must be compatible with current systems fitted on site, with clear instructions relating to their usage.

- Goods inward area

The goods inward area is operational on a 24-hour basis, and there is constant movement of personnel and vehicle traffic. The goods inward doors are linked to the building IDS and are secured when not in use. The interior door within the goods inward area allows access to the remainder of the ground floor, and all other areas of the building. The door is not access controlled, and there is no CCTV in this area.

Recommendations

It is recommended that the internal adjoining door is included on the building proximity card reader access control system, with authorisation limited to those operating in the goods inward area.

It is further recommended that CCTV is installed to offer protection to the main entrance, and the adjoining interior door.

- Data halls

There are two data halls within the data centre, both sited adjacent to each other, in the middle of the upper ground floor. The halls hold all data controls for any client information contained in the hard drives and cloud access.

This is the most sensitive area of the data centre and is business critical.

Entrance to the corridor immediately outside of the data halls is gained by use of a privileged proximity photo ID card. Entrance to the data halls is restricted to those privileged to enter, and this is by means of a twin access control system consisting of a biometric retina scan, and an individual six digit Personal Identification Number (PIN). There is also a 'door held ajar' alarm fitted to each door, and should the door be legally held open for more than 120 seconds, the alarm will activate in the security control room.

The corridor is supported by CCTV from all angles, and inside each data hall there is 360-degree CCTV coverage for all of the control cabinets. There is no duress code built into the six-figure PIN.

Recommendations

It is strongly recommended that a duress code is configured for the PIN, as this will offer a level of safety assurance to members of staff, operating alone in the area. The duress code will consist of an extra digit that is inputted if the member of staff is threatened. The alarm is silent in the data hall area but will sound in the security control room, and if agreed, the nearest police station.

- Guarding

Site guarding is provided by an external provider, and all Security Officers hold SIA Front Line Licences.

Assignment instructions (AI), service level agreement (SLA) and key point indicators (KPI) are current, with negotiations underway in relation to service provision for three years, after 1 January 2020. There are no service level issues, and during an informal survey carried out to understand how security provision is perceived on site, it would appear that the majority of staff and management are happy with levels of service delivered by the current security officers.

The current contract provides for the following service provision.

- There is currently a seven day three-shift system in place, with security officers on duty during the hours of:

  - 0600hrs to 1400hrs: one supervisor and five security officers
  - 1400hrs to 2200hrs: one supervisor and five security officers
  - 2200hrs to 0600hrs: one supervisor and three security officers.

- Duties carried out by security officers include:

  - Site access and egress control
  - Gatehouse duties
  - Alarm response
  - Patrolling (internal and external)
  - Search
  - Immediate incident response
  - Incident report writing
  - Visitor escorts.

All security officers hold an SIA Front Line Licence, and all are first aid trained. No security officers are currently fire-response trained.

Recommendations

It is strongly recommended that all security officers are fire response trained, and this should be carried out by the local fire and rescue service.

- Policies, plans and procedures

During the security survey, permission was requested to view all current security policies, plans and procedures. The following documents were viewed, and there were no issues identified.

- Site assignment instructions
- Fire and evacuations plans
- Search policy and procedures
- Health, Security and the Environment (HSE) policies and procedures
- IT security policies and procedures.

There was no serious incident response plan and procedures, nor was there a bomb threat checklist in the security control room.

Recommendations

It is recommended as a matter of urgency that the following two documents are produced:

- Bomb threat checklist: This should be held on the main desk, in the security control room, so it can be responded to immediately a threat is received.
- Serious incident response plan: In the event of a crisis, man-made or natural, the security team needs to know how to react. The plan should be introduced as soon as possible, and it should be practiced regularly.

Summary

The security survey report should be circulated to relevant stakeholders, and actions and recommendations should be carried out as soon as possible. If further action is required, the author of the report can be contacted on the agreed terms, and by the most appropriate means.

Charles Swanson MSc PG Dip CSyP
Security Surveyor
20 October 2019

Upon completion, and when the security survey findings and recommendations have been accepted, the organisation will have an understanding that the systems and processes in place will be proportionate to the levels of risk being faced. Next, the company must measure itself against the requirements for business resilience.

Exercise Brave Defender – task 4: the Security Survey and Security Audit

Synopsis

The insurance brokers selected to provide cover for 1 Canada Fields in conjunction with the compliance function of Britcom have advised the executive board that a security survey is long overdue, the most recent survey having taken place in 2017. You have been instructed to carry out the following tasks:

1   Write a briefing document for the board, explaining what a security survey consists of.
2   Within the briefing note, describe the five steps required for an effective security survey.
3   Produce a separate briefing note to explain the difference between a security survey and a security audit, as this is often confusing for the layperson.

3.5 Business resilience

> "It is not the biggest, the brightest, the best that will survive, but those that adapt the quickest".
> —Charles Darwin (1809–1892)

Pause for thought

A term is used more today that at any other time, certainly in the security sector. What do you believe is meant by the term 'resilience'?

I am sure to many people the term 'organisational resilience' is not only a new phrase, but it may also be quite confusing. For so long it seems, security professionals have perhaps struggled to come to terms with and master concepts such as risk management, crisis management, business continuity management and disaster management, primarily because those particular management responsibilities were seen as being within the gift only of other functions; perhaps compliance and business risk?

Then, without a great deal of warning (although it began 40 years ago!), came the introduction of yet another concept, with the mandatory standard.

Organisational resilience, which is covered by ISO 22316,[31] is difficult to interpret, but I see it as the overarching concept that focusses its efforts on organisational values and cultures, and the importance of top management and leadership. Annex A to the standard argues that management disciplines can offer organisational resilience support for areas such as asset management, crisis management, business continuity management, and so forth.

Professor David Denyer (2017), in an excellent study titled *Organisational Resilience: A Summary of Academic Evidence, Business Insights and New Thinking*, says that

> Organizational Resilience is the ability of an organization to anticipate, prepare for, respond and adapt to incremental change and sudden disruptions in order to survive and prosper.

He goes on to argue that the thinking behind organisational resilience has evolved over time and has been split by two core drivers, *defensive* (stopping bad things happening) and *progressive* (making good things happen), as well as a division between two approaches that call for consistency, and those that are based on flexibility.

In the same paper he introduces a concept referred to as the 4sight methodology, arguing that it can help those in leadership roles throughout the organisation introduce and sustain organisational resilience by developing four key practices: foresight, insight, oversight and hindsight.

Denyer further argues that the 4sight methodology complements the established Plan, Do, Check, Act (PDCA) methodology. Whilst PDCA provides consistency, 4sight provides the flexibility to deal with the complex issues that abound in modern business.

Howard Kerr, chief executive of the British Standards Institute (BSI), in the same study refers to a global piece of research by the BSI, Cranfield Business School and the Economist Intelligence Unit which took place in 2015. The study revealed that just a third of CEOs were confident their organisations possessed the resilience to survive long term. However, Kerr argued that 9 in 10 saw resilience as the number one priority for their business, while 8 in 10 believed it to be indispensable for long-term growth.

One constant that reappeared continuously during my research into organisational resilience was the strategic importance of risk and its management and the symbiotic relationship between risk and resilience.

To my mind, crisis management, disaster management and business continuity are reliant on sound risk management, and all four disciplines come under the banner of organisational resilience.

I would further argue, and this is supported by academic research, that effective organisational resilience is dependent on effective strategic risk management strategies from board level down.

Risk, crisis and disaster management together with business continuity have key relationships with organisational resilience, and it is those areas that we will examine next.

Risk management

Risk management is the concept that persuades senior management to make a strategic and critical decision: whether to accept the risk or apply controls.

Perhaps through the prism of simplicity, we should identify risk as it applies to our particular situation, that is analyse its impact in terms of how much damage it may inflict on our organisation, before we decide to either accept or control it. If we decide not to accept the level of risk, because it is outside of our 'risk appetite', then we simply need to implement some form of risk treatment or control measure. Easy!

The issue here is that actually it isn't easy, because the arbiters of this particular situation, those who must make an appropriate decision are human beings, and to me the greatest stumbling blocks in any risk situation are the interpretation or perception of risk and how it is communicated. And without doubt, our particular species is not the greatest proponent when it comes to making informed decisions about risk and its management, or how we communicate those risks.

When researching this book, I was able to uncover vast swathes of rainforest that had been torn to the ground in order that thousands of books about risk could be written, published and sold on a global scale. I was able to decipher probabilistic risk calculations, cognitive decision-making strategies, risk from a psychometric perspective, and diagrammatic analysis, and I was fascinated by risk homeostasis. However, those academics and scholars who did venture to stand on their hind legs and propose a definition of risk management failed to actually convince the layman that they, the experts, had a solid understanding of how we actually should in practical terms manage risk.

Let us then take a look at one or two experts in the field of risk, who offer their opinion of what risk management actually is.

Bamfield, in Gill (2014) argues that risk management is a set of actions that the organisation has put in place to address the identified risks (Caralli et al., 2011). As such, risk management naturally forms part of the security domain, but risk managers in many corporations are in separate departments. That is an argument that Bamfield has in many ways identified as one of the greatest flaws in risk management: the lack of either consistency or transparency. Whilst important to security managers, and quite rightly so, risk and its management are spread across not only a plethora of alternative departments but also across the cultural identification of risk.

As we realised earlier, and the problem was highlighted in the maritime scenario, security managers identify risk as a phenomenon that may harm the organisation, or the assets of the organisation; whilst the sales team are concerned about the risk of restricted business growth. Both departments believing that their risk issues are far more important than risk concerns as perceived by any other team or function. And you are probably asking yourself, "Why can't they discuss that in a civilised manner, for the good of the organisation?" Unfortunately, as we have already discussed in terms of risk communication, perception is all; and culturally disengaged departments will often only acknowledge their own risk perceptions. The expert versus the layperson.

You see, if risk management is so simple, why do corporations and governments so consistently get it wrong? I go back to my main argument, and that is the debate about who is right, and who is wrong when it comes to risk identification, and by association risk management. This is more than a conundrum.

Hubbard (2009) defines risk management as:

> the identification, assessment and prioritisation of risks, followed by coordinated and economical application of resources, to minimise, monitor and control the probability and/or impact of unfortunate events.

He goes on to say that there are a couple of qualifications that, while they should be extremely obvious, are worth mentioning, when we put *risk* and *management* together.

When an executive wants to manage risk, he or she actually wishes to reduce it, or at least not unduly increase it in pursuit of better opportunities (unless of course we are talking about risk speculation from a sales perspective).[32]

The Institute of Risk Management has an interesting, if not exciting, definition of risk management, in which they argue that:

> Risk is part of all our lives.
>
> As a society, we need to take risks to grow and develop. From energy to infrastructure, supply chains to airport security, hospitals to housing, effectively managed risks help societies achieve. In our fast-paced world, the risks we have to manage evolve quickly. We need to make sure we manage risks so that we minimise their threats and maximise their potential.
>
> Risk management involves understanding, analysing and addressing risk to make sure organisations achieve their objectives. So it must be proportionate to the complexity and type of organisation involved. Enterprise Risk Management (ERM) is an integrated and joined up approach to managing risk across an organisation and its extended networks.
>
> Because risk is inherent in everything we do, the type of roles undertaken by risk professionals are incredibly diverse. They include roles in insurance, business continuity, health and safety, corporate governance, engineering, planning and financial services.

IRM's mission is to build excellence in risk management, in all sectors and across the world. Read about how some members have benefitted from the IRM.[33]

(The Institute of Risk Management (IRM), 2020)

The International Standards Organisation (ISO) in the standard ISO 31000 (2009) describes risk management as:

Coordinated activities to direct and control an organisation with regard to risk.

It then goes on to describe the risk management process, by stating that it is

a systematic application of management policies, procedures and practices to the activities of communicating, consulting, establishing the context, and identifying, analysing, evaluating, treating, monitoring and reviewing risk.

Although the aim of this sub-chapter is not to replicate ISO 31000, as the standard is easily (if not inexpensively!) available. The above sentence is in effect what risk management involves, and we will now study each section in an aim to better understand the intricacies of risk management, as seen by ISO 31000.

Management policies, procedures, and practices

Clause 3b of the standard advises that risk management is not a stand-alone activity, that it is separate from the main activities and processes of the organisation. Risk management is part of the responsibilities of management and an integral part of all organisational processes, including strategic planning, and all project and change management processes.

Clause 4.3.2 discusses establishing a risk management policy, advising that the risk management policy should clearly state the organisation's objectives for, and commitment to, risk management, and typically addresses the following.

- The organisations rationale for managing risk.
- Links between the organisations objectives and policies, and the risk management policy.
- Accountabilities and responsibilities for managing risk.
- The way in which conflicting interests are dealt with.
- Commitment to make the necessary resources available to assist those accountable and responsible for managing risk.
- The way in which risk management performance will be measured and reported.
- A commitment to review and improve the risk management policy and framework periodically and in response to an event or change on circumstances.

The clause finishes almost casually by saying that the risk management policy should be communicated appropriately, as though risk communication was a non-problematic area!

Communicating, consulting, and establishing the context

Clause 5.2 advises that communication and consultation with all stakeholders should take place during all stages of the risk management process.

The clause argues that plans for communication and consultation should be developed at an early stage. They should address issues relating to the risk itself, its causes, its consequences (if known) and the measures being taken to treat it. Effective external and internal communication and consultation should take place to ensure that those accountable for implementing the risk management process and stakeholders understand the basis on which decisions are made, and the reasons why particular actions are required.

It further argues that a consultative team approach may:

- Help establish the context appropriately.
- Ensure that the interests of stakeholders are understood and considered.
- Help ensure that risks are adequately identified.
- Bring different areas of expertise together for analysing risks.
- Ensure that different views are appropriately considered when defining risk criteria and in evaluating risks.
- Secure endorsement and support for a treatment plan.

Identifying, analysing, evaluating, treating, monitoring, and reviewing risk

Clause 5.4.2 says that the organisation should identify sources of risk, areas of impact, and events (including changes in circumstances) and their causes and potential consequences. Comprehensive identification is critical, because a risk that is not identified at this stage will not be included in further analysis.

Risk identification should include an examination of the knock-on effects of particular consequences, including cascades and cumulative effects. It should also consider a wide range of consequences, even if the risk source or cause may not be evident. As well as identifying what might happen, it is necessary to consider possible causes and scenarios that show what consequences occur. All significant causes and consequences should be considered.

Clause 5.4.3 advises that risk analysis involves developing an understanding of the risk. Risk analysis provides an input to risk evaluation, and to decisions on whether risks need to be treated, and on the most appropriate risk treatment, strategies and methods. Risk analysis can also provide an input into making decisions where choices must be made, and the options involve different types and levels of risk.

Clause 5.4.4 says that the purpose of risk evaluation is to assist in making decisions, based on the outcome of the risk analysis, about which risks need treatment and the priority for treatment implementation.

In some circumstances, the risk evaluation can lead to a decision to undertake further risk analysis. The risk evaluation can also lead to a decision not to treat the risk in any other way other than maintaining existing controls.

Treating, monitoring, and reviewing the risk

According to its definition, risk treatment is the process of selecting and implementing measures to modify risk, and there are a number of options available to the risk manager, such as:

- *To avoid* the risk by deciding to stop, postpone, cancel, or divert an activity that may be the cause for that risk.
- *To modify* the likelihood of the risk by trying to reduce or eliminate the likelihood of the negative outcomes.

- *To try modifying the consequences* in a way that will reduce losses.
- *To share the risk* with other parties facing the same risk (insurance arrangements and organisational structures such as partnerships and joint ventures can be used to spread responsibility and liability).
- *To retain* the risk or its residual risks. This all part of the risk acceptance and risk appetite strategy.[34]

Identification of residual risks

Residual risk is a risk that remains after Risk Management options have been identified and action plans have been implemented. Control measures have been introduced to reduce the risk to the point where it is acceptable. It is relatively straightforward to adopt measures which would in effect transform the location into a building that replicates Fort Knox or perhaps the Bank of England. However, there are two questions which must always be asked.

1   If the building is part of a commercial organisation, does it have the budget for the control measures recommended?
2   If the recommended measures are implemented, can the organisation still trade?

An example of this may be a small, family-run hotel that is reliant on a constant stream of guests perpetually returning because of the friendly ambiance. It is unlikely that such an establishment will have the funding for extensive risk treatment processes, and even if it did manage to raise the cash, would returning guests be as comfortable in this pseudo-military establishment which is now bristling with security guards, cameras, and alarms? I think not. So, the balance has to be struck between acceptable residual risk and the financial lifeline of returning guests.

It is important for the organisation's management and all other decision makers to be well informed about the nature and extent of the residual risk. For this purpose, residual risks should always be documented and subjected to regular monitor-and-review procedures.

Monitoring and reviewing risk

The easy option is to carry out a risk assessment, which includes risk treatment and the identification of residual risks, and then place the assessment on a shelf (electronically or physically) and wait until compliance demand another risk assessment, or even worse, wait for an incident to occur. Risk is never static, and it could be argued that as soon as a risk assessment has been carried out and the results published, it is out of date. The onus is on the security/risk manager to ensure that the risk management framework (i.e. the policies and procedures on which the risk process is based) is robust, and that there are contingencies in place to ensure that it is constantly monitored, and reviewed on a regular basis.

Risk management, as explained earlier, is the final stage of the risk process, and it is a concept that is hotly disputed in terms of approach and understanding. However, one aspect is clear, and that is if an organisation does not have an effective risk management process in place, it will at some stage suffer because of a lack of forethought and due diligence. A crisis is a badly managed risk.

Crisis management

A vast number of textbooks based on risk, crisis and disaster management have been published over the years, and they have complemented, or been complemented by, scholarly study, with academic qualifications. All three elements maintain a bond of relationship, and it is illogical to examine each one from a silo perspective, so we will study this relationship, and notwithstanding the previous sub-chapter, begin with the bond between risk and crisis management.

A crisis is defined by the Cambridge Dictionary as 'a period of *great disagreement, confusion or suffering*', with British Standard 11200 advising that crisis management is "the development and application of the organisational capability to deal with a crisis".

Borodzicz (2005) argues that essentially, a crisis is a poorly managed risk, and that a risk could give rise to a crisis, which in turn could become a disaster. So how is a disaster described?

The Collins Concise Dictionary defines a disaster as "an occurrence that causes great distress or *destruction*".

The Cambridge Dictionary argues that a disaster is "an event that results in great harm, damage, or *death*, or serious difficulty".

Dictionary.com says that a disaster is "a calamitous event, especially one occurring suddenly and *causing great loss of life*, damage, or hardship, as a flood, airplane crash, or business failure".

A risk can be managed, with the threat being prevented from occurring, or the impact of such a threat can be reduced by the introduction of effective mitigation strategies; and a crisis may be prevented at the pre-crisis phase with little or no damage. However, a disaster, often without warning, normally leads to loss of life or the destruction of an incalculable asset, with no way back, except for recovery to a point that is acceptable.

Perhaps because of effective crisis management mitigation, 3,000 people were killed, as opposed to 10,000 within the Twin Towers on 11 September 2001, but it was still a loss of life – a disaster which was far beyond the scope and consequences of a crisis.

Maybe an easier way to describe this triumvirate is to argue that a crisis may be avoided if an effective risk assessment has taken place, and the correct levels of risk treatment or control measures have been applied. Equally, if a crisis is managed in accordance with a robust crisis management plan, there is no reason to believe that the catastrophic effects of a disaster will be felt. Figure 3.6 demonstrates the journey from risk to disaster.

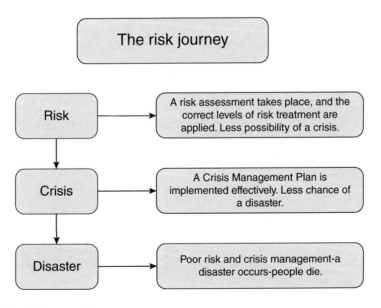

Figure 3.6 The risk journey (2)

Just a thought

What is meant by the term 'crisis'?

The term crisis is so broad that even when considering terrorism and crime, practical examples of crises are all too familiar: fires and explosions in complex nuclear or chemical plants; accidents in the transportation and storage of hazardous products (or ourselves); and tragic fires which sweep through ever more adventurous building structures (Borodzicz, 2005).

Lebinger (1997) in Borodzicz (2005, p. 75) warns that

> as crises become more numerous, visible and calamitous, organisations have no choice but to accept them as inescapable reality that must be factored into their planning and decision making.

Professionally, crisis management is covered by British Standard 11200, which explains that every crisis management situation requires a particular framework, arguing that the development of a crisis management capability needs to be strategically directed from the top of an organisation and implemented through a crisis management framework. One aspect of this is that top management should establish, define and document a policy for crisis management that:

1   Clearly and concisely outlines their objectives in managing a crisis.
2   Describes in broad terms how they intend to realise these.
3   Makes plain the commitment to high standards in crisis management.

In general terms, an organisation requires the following for a crisis management capability:

1   People who are able to quickly analyse situations, set strategy, determine options, make decisions, and evaluate their impact.
2   A common understanding of the concepts that underpin crisis management.
3   Structures and business processes to translate decisions into actions, evaluate those actions and follow them up.
4   Staff who are able to share, support and implement top managements vision intentions and policies.
5   The ability to support solutions by applying the right resources, in the right place at the right time.

Figure 3.7 sets out a general framework for crisis management, identifying the steps necessary to create a crisis management capability, organised around anticipation and assessment, preparation, response, recovery, and review and learning.

In order to be able to meet the anticipated crisis management requirement and capability, the organisation needs to begin to plan for every eventuality as soon as possible.

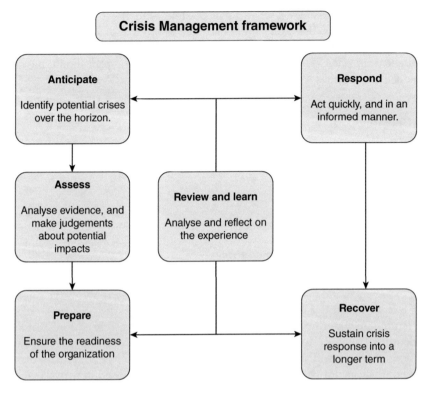

Figure 3.7 A framework for crisis management

The crisis management plan (CMP)

There are numerous commercial organisations that will offer their services to provide you with a crisis management plan template, and if you believe most of the marketing documentation that accompanies such offers, all you have to do is to complete the various sections, and lo and behold, you are now in possession of an effective CMP that will meet all of your demands. However, before you go there, let's spend a little time on examining the CMP before you make any decisions that you may regret.

A crisis management plan is a strategic document that is authorised by the CEO and executive board of an organisation. The plan is used to ensure that the organisation is prepared for all types of crises, and it should be worded and communicated in a manner that is clear to all stakeholders, including of course the crisis management teams (CMT).

The CMP should include a list of all personnel that are critical to the safe running of the organisation, and it should include all contact details of critical personnel, including any reserves that have been identified for particular roles.

The plan, whether in hard copy or in electronic format, should be easily accessible, and it should contain exactly what needs to be done, by whom and in what fashion for every crisis that may impact the safety of an organisation and staff and management. In public and private areas such as sports stadia, museums and art galleries, shopping centres and transport hubs, consideration for the general public is absolutely critical.

The CMP should contain a number of contingencies that are applicable and sufficiently flexible to cover as many 'what-if's' as possible, with worst case scenarios topping the list of considerations. The plan should be tested as often as possible, and there should be maximum participation, particularly from key personnel, including of course the crisis management team (CMT), and after every drill or exercise the plan should be evaluated and amended accordingly.

Phases of a crisis

It is generally agreed that there are three stages to a crisis:

- Pre-crisis
- Operational crisis
- Post crisis.

Pre-crisis – preventing the crisis from occurring

It's interesting.

In my experience, and as the result of years of research, I believe this is the most critical phase of a crisis, because it is at this stage that the impending crisis can be avoided if the correct actions are taken, and taken in a timely fashion. Conversely of course, if the crisis is not identified, or more worryingly, if it is identified but for whatever reason ignored, the full force of the incident will be felt very quickly. There are legitimate reasons for the impending crisis not being identified, or perhaps being missed in reasonable time for prevention and mitigation tactics to be enabled. It may be that the pre-crisis processes adopted by the organisations are ineffective, or perhaps there is a skills gap, and those responsible for monitoring operations critical to the organisation do not possess the skill sets required.

For several reasons, human beings very often make innocent mistakes; errors that may prove costly to the organisation, and perhaps the shareholders, but errors nonetheless. Unintentional!

Of far more concern is the situation, when despite credible warnings of an impending crisis, the decision makers elect not to take the advice they have received. This tends not to be an innocent mistake, perhaps based on immaturity and inexperience, rather it is a conscious decision to ignore credible, evidence-based research, probably in favour of a subjective view based on ego and vanity.

Pre-crisis is also referred to as crisis prevention, and as described above, amazingly it is often skipped altogether, even though it is the least costly and simplest way to control a potential crisis. The problem may be that crises are accepted by many executives as an unavoidable condition of everyday existence, and that they have to be faced some time, so let us ensure that we have systems in place to mitigate the crisis, in order that acceptable levels of damage are conceded, and the company can move on. So short-sighted.

History is littered with crises, that for one reason or another have not been dealt with at an early stage and have consequently impacted business and society with devastating results – none more so than the events that led to what has come to be known as the 'credit crunch'.

The financial crisis of 2008

On 15 September 2008, Lehman Brothers, the giant US investment bank, announced its bankruptcy. According to the UK newspaper the *Independent*, this was the day when global financial stress turned into a full-blown international emergency or crisis. The failure of a systematically important financial institute with some £585 billion of liabilities created a seismic shock to the global financial system. The global money markets froze, and banks and insurance institutes in most of the developed world found that they couldn't borrow money. The chair of the US Federal Reserve, Ben Bernanke, called it the worst financial crisis in global history. "If you can't buy food or petroleum, or medicine for your kids, people will just start breaking windows, and helping themselves . . . it'll be anarchy", said UK Prime Minister Gordon Brown.

However, the newspaper argues that the fall of Lehman Brothers wasn't the cause of what was to be called the 'credit crunch'. Rather, the fall was a result of a weak financial system that had been in decline for some years, but it appears that the so-called financial gurus, not only in the US but on a global scale, had either not recognised the forth coming crisis, or worse still, crossed their fingers and hoped it would go away, as if by magic. However, crises are not magically delivered, they are generally the result of a poorly managed risk. Remember what Borodzicz correctly had to say about that?

To continue. . .

The *Independent* argues that the proximate cause of this stress was a systematic loss of trust amongst financial institutes in the solvency of each other's institutions.

It is likely that the recession, almost a global depression, began in 2006, when according to the *Independent*, the US Federal Reserve increased interest rates, and many homeowners began to default on their mortgages, house prices fell, and these securities were revealed to be, in fact, very risky indeed, and it was clear that there were considerable losses in the system.

What happened when Lehman went under was that the crunch morphed into out and out panic, when everyone more or less stopped lending entirely.

Interestingly, Ben Tue, who is the author of the article in the *Independent*, argues that historically, financial crises have tended to come in unexpected forms. He says that if one knew when, where and how they would happen, one could take early preventive action.

I am certainly no financial expert, but common sense tells me, without being too simplistic, that if the US Federal Reserve had carried out an effective and credible risk assessment, focussing on business resilience, prior to the interest rate rise in 2006, perhaps they would have foreseen the oncoming dark clouds of a global recession, during which millions of innocent people lost their livelihoods, homes and critically in some instances, their lives.

Operational crisis – containment and control

This is the stage in any crisis when the incident or the attack actually happens. The terrorists' explosive device detonates; the dam wall collapses; the IT network fails; or the business is placed in the hands of the receiver. The warning signs have either been missed or ignored, and the only option from here on in is containment; stop the haemorrhaging. Save life; shore the dam and evacuate the area; restrict the use of the network and begin to hope that the company has some form of business continuity or business resilience plan.

Of course, one of the problems here is that the crisis management team, because of the possible failure at the pre-crisis phase, may not be entirely aware of the details of the incident; they don't know what they don't know. In August 2009, Donald Rumsfeld, the former US Secretary of Defense, famously said:

> Reports that say that something hasn't happened are always interesting to me, because as we know, there are known knowns; there are things we know we know. We also know there are known unknowns; that is to say we know there are some things we do not know. But there are also unknown unknowns – the ones we don't know we don't know.
>
> (Google, 2020)

Remember also, that usually the media is pretty disinterested about a crisis until it happens, then they are after blood, and will pick up any snippet of information that may lead to what they refer to as a scoop. I am not for one minute disputing the honesty and integrity of the media, however, perhaps taking the lead from Mark Twain,[35] who once said: "Never let the truth get in the way of a good story". The media are more interested in selling news rather than the truth, the whole truth, and nothing but the truth.

Once again, crisis history is littered with examples of organisations failing to recognise the importance of media speculation when responding to an incident, by either ignoring newspaper and television investigations, or responding with an incorrect level of crisis management.

Two huge PR mistakes were made at the beginning of the Deepwater Horizon disaster, when the CEO, after 11 men had been killed in the action, asked the world's media to let him have his life back. During the same period, the chairman of BP referred to all of the people living in the area of the accident as little people. These were two extremely ill-thought-out remarks that left the press baying for blood.

Norman Augustine, writing in the *Harvard Business Review of Crisis Management* (2000), offers several good pieces of advice in relation to this stage of the crisis management cycle. In the first instance, Augustine argues that the CEO and his or her response is critical. He says that the demand for the CEO to clarify a murky situation might well describe the early phases of most crises. Crisis situations tend to be accompanied by conflicting advice – with the legal department warning, "Tell 'em nothin' and tell 'em slow", the public relations department appealing for an immediate press conference, the shareholder relations department terrified of doing anything, and the engineers all wanting to disappear into their labs for a few years to conduct confirmatory experiments. Augustine advises that his experience has been that it is preferable to err on the side of disclosure, even at the risk of harming one's legal position. Credibility is far more important than legal positioning.

Finally, Augustine offers the following four pieces of advice, which I wholeheartedly endorse.

First, it is wise to have a dedicated group of individuals working full time (the crisis management team)[36] to contain the crisis; others still have a business to operate.

Second, a single individual should be identified as the company spokesperson, the one who makes all of the public comments.

Third, a company's own constituencies – its customers, owners, employees, suppliers, and communities – should not be left to ferret out information from the public media.

Fourth, a devil's advocate should be part of the crisis management team – someone who can tell the emperor in no uncertain terms when he is wearing no clothes.

Crisis containment.

Post-crisis phase

Identifying an oncoming crisis should be relatively straightforward; we look for known crisis triggers, and we act accordingly, in line with the organisation's crisis management plan. If we miss the tell-tale signs of an impending crisis, we are at the crisis containment phase, and it is here that we have to consolidate our crisis management procedures and operations in an effort to ensure that we have the crisis under control. Once this is achieved, we are at the post crisis phase, and we are generally entering unchartered waters, with so many lessons to learn.

The post-crisis recovery phase is one of the least addressed in planning, training, and simulations. This is an area that, if not properly managed, can cost financially, reputationally and operationally. Guidelines for post-crisis recovery are lacking; and many entities lose focus when it comes to discussing post-crisis recovery operations. It may be that post-crisis recovery is one of the most complicated of the business continuity lifecycle elements, and it is extremely likely that no two recovery periods are the same.

However, this is a part of the learning curve that must not be ignored or paid lip service to, because if lessons are not learned from how the organisation dealt with the crisis, there is every likelihood that the same mistakes will be made next time (there is likely to be a next time), and perhaps the impact of the crisis will be greater.

As soon as the crisis management team (CMT) and the board are convinced that the crisis has been brought under control, there has to be some form of debrief, which includes all involved in the incident and its management. Those involved have to be asked and must ask themselves a number of corporate soul-searching questions, and more importantly must be strong enough to take uncomfortable questions and answers on the chin!

Some of the questions that need to be asked post crisis.

Question 1: Pre crisis

- Bearing in mind the crisis could have been avoided at a very early stage. Were any crisis warning signs/triggers recognised?
- Looking back, and with the presence of hindsight, if such triggers were present, why were they not acted upon?
- If they were not identified, what was the reason for the lack of clarity and observation?

Answers:

Recommendations:

Question 2: Operational crisis-containment and control

Once it was recognised that the organisation was in the midst of a crisis:

- Were the original responses in accordance with the company's crisis management plan?
- If not, what was the reason?
- If so, was the plan robust, and was it fit for purpose?
- If not, what recommendations are feasible?

Answers:

Recommendations

Question 3: The crisis management team

- How did the CMT perform?
- Did the CMT respond to developing levels of pressure?
- Were internal and external crisis communications effective?
- Were there any obvious weaknesses in terms of personalities and permeance?
- Was there an immediate post incident debrief?

Answers:

Recommendations

Question 4: Crisis impact

Has there been a quantifiable impact in any of the following areas?

- CMT moral
- Staff and management moral
- Finance (sales and turnover)
- Brand and reputation
- Operations and performance

Answers:

Recommendations

Question 5: Future responses

Is the organisation in a position to face a similar crisis, in terms of impact and response?

Answers:

Recommendations

These five questions and their sub-questions are really only a snapshot of the post crisis phase, and of course organisations will formulate their own post crisis debrief in accordance to their needs and specialist areas.

Throughout all three phases of a crisis, effective communication is paramount, and it only needs a slip of the tongue or a poorly thought-out press release to alter the dynamics of the crisis management approach and impact. *Crisis communications must not be treated lightly.*

The crisis management team (CMT)

Pause for thought

In your opinion, who should lead the CMT?

There is little doubt that an effective crisis management team (CMT) can mean the difference between a crisis being identified and managed at the appropriate time, and in a professional manner, or the crisis through mismanagement very quickly developing into a full-blown disaster. The central issue generally is the make-up of the team, who should be included, and who should not. Should it be led by the CEO, or perhaps the leadership must be delegated to a board director with executive powers? Should there be one team, or perhaps there should be a tiered consistency, covering the headquarters, the operational and communications team; or is a single team robust and flexible enough? When will the CMT be stood to (activated), and by whom, under what circumstances?

Dependent upon the size of the organisation, a decision will have to be made in relation to the strategic, tactical, and operational roles carried out by the CMT.

With a small to medium-sized single site organisation, it may be realistic for a solitary CMT to exist, with all functions being carried out from a specific location. However, there is no 'one size fits all', as every CMT must be selected on the organisational operations and culture in order that the team may be able to respond effectively and as quickly as possible. If the CMT is not alerted and activated until the crisis has reached the operational, containment, and control phase then speed is of the essence, and all of the drills and exercises carried out before this moment will be worth their weight in gold.

Figure 3.8 describes the recommended make up of a single CMT.

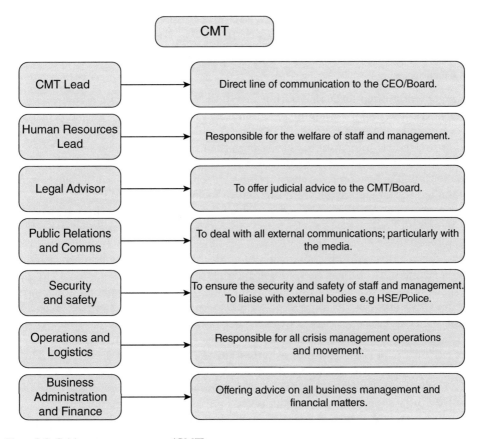

Figure 3.8 Crisis management team (CMT)

CMT members

As can be seen from Figure 3.8, there are a number of critical personalities and roles involved in the CMT, and initially they will constitute the most effective group available for the first stages of the crisis. One problem, however, and this is crucial for any CMT lead to consider, is that his or her people are human, and they need rest and recuperation when fatigued.

It would be ideal if a crisis lasted a matter of hours or days, then perhaps the CMT unchanged may be able to cope; but that is a rarity. According to the *Guardian* newspaper published on 22 July 2010, the BP (Deepwater Horizon) crisis which began on 20 April 2010 lasted for 46 days, and must have taken a great deal of time and effort to ensure the CMT remained effective.

The point being made here, of course, is that there must be a contingency of reserves in the organisation, sourced from appropriate departments (Security and Safety, Legal, HR etc.), who are nominated as replacements to cover for fatigue, illness, holidays, and so forth.

Of at least equal importance is the need for exercises and drills, which can either be desktop exercises or fully-fledged drills that include external agencies such as the police and other emergency services. The exercises and drills must be carried out on a regular basis, they have to be as close to reality as possible, and critically they must be measured, with all lessons learned being recorded, discussed, and taken forward for the next exercise.

Below is an example of the makeup of a crisis management team (CMT), followed by what may represent a desktop exercise called Noble Response, which examines how the security manager may be pivotal during a crisis.

CMT lead

The argument is often made that during a crisis the CEO or MD of the business should be the CMT lead, and that is quite understandable given the complexity and demands of the task; with operational, tactical and strategic decisions having at times to be made with little or no credible information. Equally important of course is the power of the media, and the relentless pressure to provide information about the incident(s) on a 24/7 basis. The media will only accept an interview with the chief executive, even if there is a very professional and efficient public relations person included in the CMT.

There may also be leadership and management skills to be taken into account, and whilst the CEO may be able to drive and grow a multibillion-dollar business, he or she may not be skilled enough to manage a number of very influential personalities with specialist expertise in a crisis situation; when every decision, and the details of every remark, are critical and of course will be recorded and published.

William Snyder, writing for Deloitte in the *Wall Street Journal* (date unknown) argues that the CEO may not always be the ideal choice to lead a response to an unexpected or unusual crisis as it could distract him or her from the day-to-day business and other important matters. In a crisis, other C-level executives, such as the chief operations officer, chief risk officer, or chief legal officer in the case of a major legal challenge, can step forward to lend support, as can an outside crisis manager.

The only caveat that I would add to Snyder's comments is that whoever leads the CMT must have the authority of the executive board to make command decisions or have access to the board on a 24/7 basis in order that such decisions may be made. I would argue for the former option.

Human resources lead (director)

Whilst in smaller companies, HR directors may often take on many of the tasks normally undertaken by HR managers, in larger companies they are usually responsible for the overall strategy and budgeting of the HR department.

Their responsibilities are likely to include (but are not limited to) the following:

- Provide strategic information to the business on global hiring trends, HR-related developments and technological advances, and so forth.
- Monitoring statistics such as sickness/absence levels across the company and liaising with the HR manager to ensure that these figures are reduced/improved.
- Overseeing the HR consequences of company takeovers, redundancies, and buy-outs.
- Allocating the yearly budget for the HR department, and ensuring that this is used effectively and within monetary constraints.
- Attending HR seminars/conferences/networking events as the public face of the company's HR responsibilities.
- Maintain succession plans for each business department, along with exit strategies and hiring policies.
- Act as an experienced point of contact for HR managers and advisors within the business on a daily basis.

HR directors most commonly report directly to the CEO, along with other departmental directors employed by the business.

Depending on the size of the company, the HR director may act as line manager to the legal department where a company secretary or solicitor may be employed.

It is therefore reasonable to argue that the HR lead plays a particularly significant role in any CMT.

Legal advisor

Dependent upon the size of the organisation, the CMT legal advisor may be the company secretary or a fully qualified and practicing solicitor.

The company secretary is often more than just a legal advisor; very often he or she acts as a corporate governance advisor to the CEO and the executive board. The company secretary is responsible for the efficient administration of a company, particularly with regard to ensuring compliance with statutory and regulatory requirements and for ensuring that decisions of the board of directors are implemented.[37]

A significant difference in the two roles is that the company secretary, who, within his or her role may offer legal advice to the executive board, is not required to hold a law degree, nor to have been a practicing solicitor or lawyer. So, whilst a company lawyer can of course represent the organisation he or she is employed by in a court of law, the company secretary cannot.

Both roles offer significant support to the CMT in terms of giving legal advice during all stages of a crisis, because of course, in line with the growth in litigation procedures throughout the developed world, organisations must ensure that they are in a position to combat any efforts to take them through judicial procedures in the aftermath of a crisis. Legal mitigation strategies must be a part of the crisis management plan, overseen by the CMT legal advisor.

The Deepwater Horizon oil spill, also called the Gulf of Mexico oil spill, was the largest marine oil spill in history. It was caused by a 20 April 2010 explosion on the Deepwater Horizon drilling rig, and its subsequent sinking on 22 April began a chain of events requiring the sharpest legal minds that BP could muster.

The oil rig was owned by BP, and as the result of legal action the company paid around $63.4 billion by the end of September to cover clean-up costs and legal fees linked to the largest environmental disaster in US history, where 11 rig workers were killed and untold damage was caused to the immediate environment in the Gulf of Mexico.

BP's legal team will have been critical in terms of offering support to the executive board and CEO during every phase of the oil spillage crisis, and who is to say if they were successful or not, but I believe that BP would have been in a much weaker position had they not employed such a team.

Public relations (PR) and communications lead

Contentiously the most important member of the CMT is the public relations and communications lead because corporate history is littered with examples of how an organisation fails to be positively recognised as managing a crisis by both the media and the public in general. This is far too often due to poor communications and ineffective media management.

Having already discussed the BP Deepwater Horizon crisis in terms of litigation and costs, it is worth revisiting the situation to look at it from a PR perspective.

In 2010, the seal of an oil well in the Gulf of Mexico failed, causing the worst oil spill in history. The Deepwater Horizon oil rig exploded, *killing 11 workers* and causing oil and methane gas to pour into the ocean for 87 days afterward.

BP, the company in charge of the oil rig and responsible for its failure, was blamed for what CNN calls "the worst environmental disaster in history".

But it wasn't just BP's negligence that caused damage to their brand. The company's reaction to the events, including CEO Tony Hayward's thoughtless comment, "I want my life back" (when 11 rig workers had been killed) and subsequent apology, showed a serious lack of organisation and ownership of the situation. However, the easy option is to focus with laser-like precision on what in effect was the sacrificial lamb. Of course it could be argued that as the CEO of a multibillion-dollar corporation, Hayward should have been able to defend his actions and those of his company, but neither he nor any other executive who is untrained in the black arts of PR would ever be any match for the world's media. Where were his advisors?

In his book *Crisis Management: Planning for the Inevitable*, Fink (2002) offers sound guidelines for crisis communication when he argues that if the media can communicate the news the instant it happens, crisis communications dictate that a company must be prepared to respond almost as fast (I would argue *as* fast). The inability to communicate your message skilfully during a crisis can prove fatal. And it would be a totally needless demise, a wrongful death.

Fink invites us to try to envision events in two categories: those over which you are probably not in total control and those over which you are in much greater control. The former is the crisis itself, and the latter is your communication of the crisis to the outside world. And since it's your crisis, you at least have the ability to shape the public's initial (and perhaps total) perception of what has happened or is happening.

But as with everything else, Fink argues, the time to begin is not when the crisis is upon you, but well before.

If you are the CEO of a company with an internal communicator (PR or communications Lead)[38] who does not have direct access to you, who does not have your confidence, who does not have authority, who does not serve in a senior management level position, and who does not actually participate in all strategic planning sessions, then you must ask yourself why? If it's because that particular individual does not measure up to being an advisor to you, one option[39] is to find yourself a replacement immediately. The second option of course is to look at your organisational structure and decide if the fate of the communications manager has been decided because he or she does not meet the standards required, or is it perhaps because they are not receiving the training and support needed for the role. Ultimately if you are the line manager, then standards are your responsibility, or as President Harry S Truman said on 19 December 1952, "The buck stops here", that is, with you.

Security and safety

It is always very tempting to revert to the default position, which sees security and safety (health and safety) as two separate entities, and in many organisations on a global perspective that pertains today. There is the security department, and there is the health and safety team, and woe betide any team members who interact with the old enemy. Fortunately, there are now a growing number of organisations, mainly in Europe and the US, that take a different, it may be said, more mature approach to the issue, and are converging both departments into teams such as Health, Safety, Security and the Environment (HSSE). Thank goodness.

Therefore, it seems logical to argue that forward thinking organisations who make extensive efforts to support a multi-disciplined and professional crisis management team, will include a combined security and safety lead.

However, you may be forgiven for thinking that we have a problem here. Because whilst the HR lead is a single professional from within human resources, and the legal advisor may be the company secretary or company solicitor, who will be well versed in all matters legal, we have a single CMT member who is responsible for two disciplines; security and safety. Hmmmm.

This isn't as critical as it may seem, for a number of reasons. In the first instance, those companies and organisations that have invested in the convergence of security and safety have probably also identified a training gap, and are likely to support the team lead with a variety of subject matter training courses, allowing him or her to achieve a level of credibility in terms of offering advice in both security and safety disciplines.

As a member of the CMT, the security and safety lead will support the team and CMT lead with advice and guidance relating to internal and external security issues, whilst liaising with external bodies, such as the police and if necessary, the military. In terms of safety, the CMT advisor will ensure that all operations carried out by the organisation and its personnel are safe, and at all times conforming to national and perhaps international safety legislation.

Operations and logistics

If a crisis is identified at an early stage of the crisis cycle, it is likely that it will impact in some way or other on the operations of the organisation. It may be some form of banking crisis, which will require the adjustment of day-to-day operations and enforced alterations in working practices. The same crisis may involve changes in the way that cash in transit is operated, and that will be the responsibility of the operations and logistics lead to ensure that all new practices are feasible and robust.

The crisis may involve operations overseas, perhaps a drilling rig somewhere in the Middle East, where the safety environment has deteriorated to a point where staff and perhaps the families will need to be repatriated. At the same time, whilst the board has decided to terminate all operations in the region, from a safety and commercial perspective operations will have to be drawn down in a timely manner as such a termination cannot be achieved overnight. Once again, the tasks of repatriation and the slowing down of operations will fall to the remit of the operations and logistics lead, in conjunction with support offered by security and safety and human resources.

Business administration and finance

A crisis is the ultimate test for any organisation, and in particular it is a critical challenge for the business administration and finance teams. In a similar vein to other team members, business administration and finance team members have to be cognisant of the fact that whilst the crisis is ongoing, the remainder of the organisation has to operate at a level that constitutes the correct standards of service in accordance with client requirements, and perhaps shareholder expectations.

In terms of business administration, the CMT must ensure that all business matters, including business continuity management (BCM)[40] are attended to at the highest levels to ensure that the organisation suffers from minimum exposure to any developing business crisis. Financially, the CMT must ensure that the business is fiscally sound, and that there is, at all times, sufficient cash flow to support all operations. Reverting back to the role of the CMT security and safety members, when there is a requirement to re-patriate staff and possibly their families from a hostile environment, business administration and finance have to ensure that there are sufficient funds to carry out any repatriation operations. Goods and products will still need to be purchased, and people have to be paid!

The role of the crisis management team

Probably the most important question will be, what exactly is the *role* of the crisis management team?

The CMT is a team that has been formed to ensure the safety of an organisation against the negative effects of crisis. The crisis management team prepares an organisation for inevitable threats, with the further aim of ensuring that the crisis does not develop into a disaster where lives are lost and infrastructure destroyed.

Organisations select crisis management teams to decide on future courses of action and devise strategies to help the organisation emerge from difficult times as soon as possible.

The CMT is there to:

- Identify any early signs of a crisis, ensuring that they are neither misinterpreted or denied.
- Highlight any problematic areas in the business.
- Ensure that all crisis communications are clear and effective.
- Interrogate the crisis management plan (CMP) to ensure that it is fit for purpose and up to date.

- Motivate employees and stakeholders not to ensure that standards of performance are away of the highest standard.
- Ensure that all post crisis issues are managed efficiently, and that lessons have been learned.
- Revisit the CMP in order to offer assurance to the organisation that it will be ready when the next crisis appears; which it surely will!

One of the greatest hurdles faced by any crisis management team is gaining support from senior management, and often the most effective means of achieving buy-in by the executive board is to produce and communicate a crisis management plan that is acceptable. Potentially to the point where the board eventually believes that the plan is written by them, and is therefore bound to succeed, because if it doesn't, they may suffer from a distinct lack of credibility and confidence on the part of the shareholders, and perhaps legal action.

The board and other critical stakeholders must have confidence, that in a crisis situation, the combination of a credible crisis management plan, operated by a professional and equally credible crisis management team, will protect the company from a crisis before it develops into a disaster.

Another way of convincing the board that the CMT is worthy of its respect is for the CMT lead to explain the importance of understanding that any crisis consists of three phases, and the crisis management plan, signed off by the board will be equal to the task of meeting the crisis head on at any of the three points in the oncoming crisis.

Failing to prepare is preparing to fail.

Crisis communications

In his book *Crisis Communications Management* (2019), Adrian Wheeler begins by emphasising the importance of preparation and honesty.

Preparation is everything.

The option of doing nothing and saying nothing is not an option. In a crisis, we must be ready to step forward and speak out. If we fail to do this, or if we do it unconvincingly, the consequences are likely to be severe. As far as the media are concerned, silence and confusion imply guilt. This means that however large or small our organisation is, however centralised or dispersed . . . and whether we have a proficient or rudimentary communications team, some level of crisis communications preparation is essential.

There is no hiding place.

Professional communicators know that we live in the media spotlight on a 24/7 basis. It's what Paul Johnson called 'the modern electronic democracy'. He went on to say, "When the media fill a large part of our lives . . . the PR people have to be present at the policy-making stage, when the actions are decided" (*The Spectator*, 1984). If you are the CEO of United Airlines, you will have to answer for the behaviour of airport security personnel (not your employees) within hours, and you will have to get it right. It can be a frightening challenge.

Many CEOs (perhaps most) would prefer things to be different. They would like time to take advice, consult, reach a consensus and then – maybe – issue a statement.

Wheeler argues that the world isn't like that anymore. There is no hiding place, and there is precious little time to decide what to say, and then say it.

Ulmer et al. (2011), in the excellent publication *Effective Crisis Communication: Moving from Crisis to Opportunity*, support Wheeler when discussing surprise and time available to react to and communicate a crisis. The authors argue that much of the intensity of a crisis comes with some degree of surprise. Even in cases where there are clearly warning signs, most people are still surprised when a crisis actually occurs. Thus crises are almost always unexpected events. Because they exceed any planning expectations, they cannot be managed with routine procedures. Once an organisation abandons its routine procedures, its leadership is faced with managing this uncertainty by emphasising either opportunities for growth or renewal, or threat to the organisation's image or reputation in their crisis communication.

Whilst I can to a certain extent empathise with this argument, I still believe that in a high percentage of crisis situations, the organisation, and in particular the crisis management team (CMT) does not have the luxury of arguing that they 'did their best' but were not prepared for the situation. Where I am in total agreement with Ulmer and his colleagues is when they say that crises are accompanied, and indeed driven by uncertainty. Back to risk management.

Every crisis carries with it some form of uncertainty. Whether the crisis is a food-borne illness outbreak or a plant explosion, a crisis communicator has to manage uncertainty. Uncertainty makes communicating complex, because the crisis communicators must speak publicly without always having clear or accurate information. With that in mind, Ulmer and his colleagues offer ten lessons for effectively managing the uncertainty of crisis, and my comments are in italics. They are:

1   Organisation members must accept that a crisis can start quickly and unexpectedly.

    - *There is little or no room for excuses, such as 'We weren't expecting that', because inevitably it is too late then.*

2   Organisations should not respond to crises with routine solutions.

    - *A three-dimensional thought process and worst-case scenario approach is required.*

3   Threat is perceptual.

    - *Like risk, crises threats are subjective; we all think differently.*

4   Crisis communicators must communicate early and often following a crisis, regardless of whether they have critical information about the crisis.

    - *The organisation's representative cannot respond early enough, and certainly must not be perceived to be covering or hiding any crisis related evidence; that is business suicide.*

5   Organisations should not purposely heighten the ambiguity of a crisis to deceive or distract the public.

    - *Honesty is always the best policy.*

6   Be prepared to defend your interpretation of the evidence surrounding a crisis.

    - *The crisis communicator must ensure that he or she has the best and most robust evidence available in support of their arguments. Individual opinion, assertion, and wishful thinking are unacceptable.*

7   Without good intentions prior to a crisis, recovery is difficult or impossible.

    - *Preparedness is everything.*

8 If you believe that you are not responsible for the crisis, you need to build a case for who is responsible and why.

- *However, be very careful not to create a blame culture.*

9 Organisations need to prepare for uncertainty through simulation and training.

- *Everybody who may have a part to play in a crisis must be fully trained and current in all areas of crisis response. An organisation can never 'over train'.*

10 Crises challenge the way organisations think about and conduct their business.

- *Business operations must be flexible in response to a crisis. CMT members and senior management cannot afford to be rigid and unmoving when challenging a crisis.*

Senior management response

There are a number of ways in which a CEO (and ultimately the organisation he or she is responsible for), may ultimately commit professional suicide when involved in a crisis communications situation.

- **Total ignorance.**

  An Internet service provider (ISP) or perhaps a bank has had its IT system hacked, and all customer details have been stolen. The senior management team may decide to gamble as part of the organisation's risk appetite (because that is what it is) on silence, in the hope that the details of the breach will not be made public (at least not any time soon), and that in the fullness of time the crisis will dissipate as though it never occurred in the first place.

  The problem here, of course, is that there will be employees within the organisation that are aware of the situation, and for whatever reason, perhaps revenge against a bad employer, or for financial reasons, may decide to inform the media of the crime.

  The problem now is that the organisation involved also has several internal crises to focus its attention on.

  First, how to contain the original crisis. They may at last decide to face up to the world's media, throw themselves on their sword, and admit the breach; quoting weak media relations structures for failing to come clean earlier. Committing the organisation to 'learn lessons moving forward' (don't you hate that phrase?).

  They will have to face the wrath of their client base, perhaps millions of customers who demand answers, and demand them now. The ISP or bank has to convince its now depleted client base that nothing sensitive has been stolen; there is no evidence that a crime against the customer base has been committed as the result of the breach, and come up with some form of compensation package that will placate the two customers that have naively decided to stay loyal.

  Second, management hesitation. In many ways this is the worst possible option because it displays a lack of moral courage, the inability to make a decision. It is likely that the organisation will go into political meltdown as board members attempt to survive, to save their own skins by refusing to adhere to any decisions that place them in a position of guilt. It could be days or even weeks before the cull of positions and personalities is complete, and by that time the internal crisis may have degenerated to a disastrous situation from which there is no recovery.

Finally, a lack of senior management leadership. Symbiotically related to management hesitation is a lack of senior management leadership. In a crisis situation, the last thing an organisation needs is a democratic leader. There is no time to canvas opinion and hold committee meetings, as the crisis has the organisation in a head lock, and without strong autocratic leadership, the organisation, similar to a ship without a rudder, is going to meander aimlessly, without any effective decisions being made, until it is too late. The media will smell blood and go for the jugular vein of the company, no doubt with disastrous results for staff and shareholders.

- **'Pleading the Fifth Amendment'**

The constitutional right of a person to refuse to answer questions or otherwise give testimony against himself.[41] In other words, 'no comment'. The problem with that approach is that once again, the media will interpret this response as the organisation not telling the truth, the whole truth, and nothing but the truth.

Wheeler (2019), being slightly sympathetic, argues that managers obviously prefer to remain silent when they don't have the facts to hand. It is understandable; managers succeed by being sure of the information they impart. Most managers are not natural or trained communicators. They are comfortable with the 'hard' disciplines rather than the 'soft' arts of communication, public speaking, and stakeholder engagement. In a crisis we *do* have to say something. It must be the right thing, and we have to say it in a way that evokes empathy, sympathy, and support.

The senior management team (SMT) in any organisation constitutes the governance authority for that organisation, and their ability to make command decisions is critical in any situation. The SMT should always be persuasive in terms of any crisis management situation, and it is crucial that the SMT and CMT have full and effective communications at all times during an emergency.

Exercise Noble Response is no different.

Crisis Management: Exercise Noble Response

Synopsis

You are the global security and risk manager for Britcom Plc (details of the company are to be found in the main exercise description earlier in the book). You are also an advisor to the board for all matters relating to crisis management, and you are the liaison officer between the board and the crisis management team (CMT). You are located at 1 Canada, Canary Fields, as is the majority of the executive board.

Please follow and participate in the following exercise, taking into consideration your views about when and how the CMT is going to be alerted and activated throughout the exercise.

Exercise Noble Response

Phase 1

The current terrorism threat level in the UK, according to the Home Office is SEVERE, which means that a terrorist attack is highly likely.

The Metropolitan Police Service (MPS) Counter Terrorism Unit (CTU) and the Cross-Sector Safety and Security Communications (CSSC) have advised all businesses located in London to be on full alert in relation to a terrorist attack, advising them to seek further advice from the Centre for Protection of National Infrastructure (CPNI), and the National Counter Terrorism Security Office.

The MPS CTU have further advised that Canary Fields in particular has been identified as a likely target.

- *What action should be considered?*

Phase 2

Canary Fields security officers have reported increased activity by known suspicious persons. They also believe that hostile reconnaissance operations have taken, and are taking place, as particular vehicles being driven by the same people have been seen driving around Canary Fields continuously, day and night. Two vehicles over a period of 12 hours have attempted to gain access to the underground car park without authority but fled when challenged.

- *What action should be considered?*

Phase 3

Further intelligence has been received from the police, and it appears that the most prominent terrorist threat is either:

- A personnel-borne improvised explosive device (IED). Maybe a suicide bomber.
- A vehicle-borne IED.
- A marauding attack by armed terrorists.

A full executive board meeting is due to take place at 1 Canada Fields in the next 14 days, with the date yet to be set.

- *What action should be considered?*

Phase 4

There is talk on the streets and in the bars about 1 Canada Fields being the target of an attack, but of course they are only rumours and there is no hint of what type of attack is forecast. The security team, however, recommends the rumours to be taken seriously, as in their words, "People know what's going on".

- *What action should be considered?*

Phase 5

The IT department located at 1 Canada Fields have reported that they are currently investigating what they believe to be a series of distributed denial of service (DDoS) attacks against the company network. Network engineers have utilised a number of backup systems but admit that any increase in DDoS attacks will stretch their resources.

Is this perhaps a precursor for further diverse attacks, which may see the wide area network collapse, leaving a distinct shortfall of communications functions throughout the group.

- *What action should be considered?*

Phase 6

The DDoS attacks continue on an irregular basis but appear to be more sophisticated and increasingly difficult to defend against. There is no current evidence of their origin.

Evidence is being provided by the police and the security team about hostile reconnaissance taking place in a number of locations around Canary Fields, and a number of suspicious persons have been seem taking photographs of the entrances and exits of 1 Canada Fields CCTV around the building is also receiving unnecessary attention, as are the activities of the security patrols in the area.

- *What action should be considered?*

Phase 7

Monday morning, and with the threat level still SEVERE, a rucksack has been found semi-hidden within one of the reception areas at 1 Canada Fields, and a number of witnesses attest that a male was seen to drop the bag before moving swiftly out of the building. The entire security team followed him out of the building.

CCTV footage confirms the male person as belonging to the group of people recently believed to have carried out hostile reconnaissance around Canary Fields.

The police have been informed about the suspect rucksack and suspicious person, however, before they arrive, masked gunmen appear at the front and rear entrances. They have entered the building and forced everyone in the reception areas to lie on the ground, with their hands on top of their heads.

The executive board are in situ on the tenth floor.

- *What action should be considered?*

Phase 8

The gunmen seal the ground floor unopposed and begin to move through the building extremely quickly. They enter the tenth floor where the executive board have assembled, taking the directors hostage before sealing the floor.

Demands have yet to be made.

- *What action should be considered?*

Phase 9

The emergency services have arrived, and set up their cordon, incident control point (ICP) and forward control point (FCP), and they need as much information as possible, particularly from you and the external security team.

- *What action should be considered?*

Phases 1 to 7 – summary

Phase 1:

- The threat level is SEVERE.
- Warnings for all businesses to be on full alert.
- Warnings that Canary Fields may be targeted.

CMT alerted/activated   Y/N

Phase 2:

- Increased suspicious activity.
- Potential hostile reconnaissance threat.
- Attempted vehicle breach of the underground car park.

CMT alerted/activated   Y/N

Phase 3:

- Intelligence about the possible MO to be used by a terrorist group.
- Board meeting due in 14 days.

CMT alerted/activated   Y/N

Phase 4:

- Local intelligence about an attack supported by the security team.

CMT alerted/activated   Y/N

Phase 5:

- Constant DDoS attacks against the networks at 1 Canada. . .

CMT alerted/activated   Y/N

Phase 6:

- Increasing sophisticated DDoS attacks.
- Photographs of all entrances and exits at 1 Canada. . .
- CCTV and security patrols being monitored.

CMT alerted/activated   Y/N

Phase 7:

- Suspect bag in reception area at 1 Canada. . .
- Masked gunmen appear at entrances and exits of 1 Canada. . .
- The executive board are in situ.

Problems!

    CMT alerted/activated   Y/N

Phase 8:

- The gunmen have sealed the ground floor.
- The gunmen have taken the directors hostage on the tenth floor.
- They have sealed the floor.

    CMT alerted/activated   Y/N

Phase 9:

- The emergency services have arrived.
- They have set up their ICP/FCP.
- They need as much information as possible.

Reflection on the above

The emergency services have arrived and have taken over the scene, so now is the opportunity to reflect on what we believe should have been the actions taken by the crisis management team during each phase of the operation. At the end of each action there will an indication of which member of the CMT should have been involved or taken the lead.

Phase 1

The CMT have been alerted, and should have carried out the following actions:

- Established the credibility of the intelligence received – *Security and Safety Rep.*
- Ensure that all members of the CMT, and nominated reserves are available and 'In country' – *Administration.*
- Examine the crisis management plan (CMP) to ensure it is available and fit for purpose –*CMT Lead/Security and Safety Rep.*
- Establish and practice command and control procedures – *CMT Lead/Communications/Security and Safety Rep.*
- Check all communications equipment and procedures – *IT/Communications.*
- Check designated ghost locations and equipment – *Administration/IT.*

Phase 2

- Monitor the situation – *CMT Lead/Security and Safety Rep.*

Phase 3

- Activation of the CMT – *CMT Lead/Administration.*
- An immediate meeting to be arranged off-site – *CMT Lead/Administration.*
- The entire CMT to be briefed – *CMT Lead.*
- Executive Board to be briefed – *CMT Lead.*

- Check the availability of the CMT and reserves for the following 14 days.
- Monitor the situation – *CMT Lead/Security and Safety/CISO*.

Phase 4

- Monitor the situation – *CMT Lead/Security and Safety/CISO*.

Phase 5

- Monitor the situation – *CMT Lead/Security and Safety*.
- Remain in communication with the IT department and the CISO – *CMT Lead*.
- Consider and investigate other means of IT through alternative resources – *IT/CISO*.

Phase 6

- Monitor the DDoS attacks, ensuring that CMT communications are operational – *IT/CISO*.
- Report the HR operations that have been observed – *Security and Safety*.
- Peak to security teams to ensure that they are aware of what is happening – *Security and Safety*.

Phase 7

- Ensure that communications are open to the police at all times – *IT/CISO/Security and Safety Rep*.
- Contact the families of all members of staff, and offer them a contact telephone number –*Administration*.
- Deliver a statement to the press – *PR*.
- Establish who is still inside the building – *Security and Safety/Administration*.
- Attempt to establish the motive behind the attack – *Security and Safety Rep*.
- Attempt to establish communications with the Executive Board – *CMT Lead/IT/PR/Security and Safety Rep*.
- Maintain communications with the media – *PR*.
- Ensure that all administration, logistics and communications are available for an extended period – *Operations and Logistics Rep./Administration/IT*.
- Prepare to occupy the ghost location with whatever members of staff are available – *CMT*.

Phase 8

- Monitor the situation – *CMT Lead/Security and Safety Rep*.
- Maintain communications with the police – *Security and Safety Rep*.
- Maintain communications with the media – *PR*.

Phase 9

- After consultation with the police, prepare for the following:

  - Injuries and fatalities.
  - Kidnap and ransom.

Résumé

Terrorist threat level: SEVERE

After a receiving intelligence from the police of a potential terrorist attack against 1 Canada Fields, Canary Fields, suspicious activity was observed by the Canary Fields security team, with possible Hostile Reconnaissance taking place.

The CMT moved out of Canada Fields and began preparing for what may be a terrorist attack (pre-crisis phase?).

As a possible diversionary tactic, a suspect rucksack was semi hidden in the reception area of 1 Canada Fields The security team chased a male person out of the building which was then breached by masked gunmen. The intruders very quickly established control in the building by sealing all entrances, placing occupants on the floor, before moving to the tenth floor and taking the executive board of Britcom plc hostage.

The location is now under the jurisdiction of the police, who have established a cordon, an incident control point (ICP) and a forward control point (FCP).

Phase 10

The gunmen claim to be a Chechnian freedom militia that is fighting for independence from the Russian Republic. They further claim that several hundred of their countrymen are being illegally held by the Russian authorities on false charges of terrorist activity.

The terrorists are currently holding approximately 150 occupants of 1 Canada Fields, including the executive board of Britcom, insisting they will to kill their hostages unless the British government begin negotiations with the Russian authorities for the release of their comrades.

They also require a guarantee of safe passage from the UK if they release their prisoners. They further demand food and water and access to the media.

At this stage, other than ensuring the well-being of their staff, retaining communications with the victim's families, the CMT must be reliant on the actions taken by the emergency services. This is the operational stage of a crisis.

Phase 11

The Russian government has refused to release what they are referring to as enemies of Mother Russia, arguing that this is a domestic issue that the government of the United Kingdom must solve alone. The decision of the Russian government is relayed to the terrorists inside 1 Canada Fields, with the UK government promising to listen to the gunmen's requests, and to continue dialogue with the Russians if the gunmen release their hostages unharmed.

Twelve hours into the siege, and five gunshots are heard from within the building, which is immediately assaulted by UK Special Forces (SF) that have been on standby.

Several volleys are heard, followed by two explosions and more gunfire, before the commander of the SF team radio's that all of the gunmen have been killed, but unfortunately so have four of the hostages.

So, action taken by the police and the military has contained this phase of the crisis, in that the physical threat emanating from the terrorists has been eliminated, but of course that is not total crisis resolution and containment.

Post crisis. There maybe 140 members of staff held in 1 Canada Fields, and in many ways the crisis for them may be just beginning. Besides any physical injury they may have suffered at the hands of the gunmen, it is very likely they will require some form of psychological counselling, and it also must be recognised that they are at severe risk of suffering from post-traumatic stress disorder at some stage in the future.

Britcom plc has a duty of care to ensure that all of its staff affected by the attack are offered support.

Discussion point

In your opinion, what course of action must Britcom now take to ensure that all of its staff involved in the attack are offered the correct levels of support?

Post crisis operations will continue for some time and will only cease when the CMT leader and the executive board agree that there is no more to be done. However, we need to know that lessons have been learned, otherwise the next crisis faced by Britcom may develop into a disaster.

Disaster management

Pause for thought

What is meant by the term 'disaster'?

Whichever definition is chosen, and like all negative events there are various meanings and interpretations, there are also distinct similarities; see the three examples below.

The International Federation of Red Cross and Red Crescent Society's (IFR) argues that a disaster is "a sudden, calamitous event that *seriously disrupts* the *functioning of a community or society* and causes *human, material, and economic or environmental losses* that exceed the community's or society's ability to cope using its own resources. Though often caused by nature, disasters can have human origins".[42]

The United Nations Disaster Risk Reduction (UNDRR) defines a disaster as a *serious disruption* of *the functioning of a community or a society* at any scale due to hazardous events interacting with conditions of exposure, vulnerability and capacity, leading to one or more of the following: *human, material, economic and environmental losses and impacts*.[43]

In the same document the UNDRR goes on to define a number of disasters by typology:

- *Small-scale disaster:* a type of disaster only affecting local communities which require assistance beyond the affected community.
- *Large-scale disaster:* a type of disaster affecting a society which requires national or international assistance.

- *Frequent and infrequent disasters* depend on the probability of occurrence and the return period of a given hazard and its impacts. The impact of frequent disasters could be cumulative or become chronic for a community or a society.
- *A slow-onset disaster* is defined as one that emerges gradually over time. Slow-onset disasters could be associated with, for example drought, desertification, sea-level rise, or epidemic disease.
- *A sudden-onset disaster* is one triggered by a hazardous event that emerges quickly or unexpectedly. Sudden-onset disasters could be associated with, for example earthquake, volcanic eruption, flash flood, chemical explosion, critical infrastructure failure, or a transport accident.

Borodzicz (2005) takes a slightly different approach, saying that a disaster can be defined as a cultural structure of reality. Disaster is distinct from both emergency and crisis only in that physically it represents the product of the former. Disasters are the irreversible and typically overwhelming result of ill-handled emergencies and crises. 'Disasters do not cause effects. The effects are what we call a disaster' (Dombrowski, 1995, p. 242).

What Dombrowski argued is worthy of further research because cause and effect are very often confused when discussing disaster management. I would take the argument further by supporting Professor Ed Borodzicz, who argues that a crisis is a poorly managed risk. My argument is that a disaster often occurs as the result of a poor crisis management approach.

Let us take a look at an extremely high-profile disaster that occurred during a supposedly well-organised football match in the UK.

Hillsborough

On 15 April 1989, a Football Association cup tie was scheduled to be played at Hillsborough, South Sheffield. At approximately 1445hrs, as Liverpool FC and Nottingham Forest FC players were warming up on the pitch, there were problems outside the ground.

Hillsborough football stadium, which is owned by Sheffield Wednesday Football Club has been in existence since 1889, and on 15 April 1989 it was the scene of the worst sporting disaster ever to occur in the United Kingdom.

With 15 minutes before kick-off, it was reported to the grounds authority and the police that there were still several thousand late-arriving Liverpool supporters attempting to enter the ground, which had a mixed seating/standing capacity of 39,000.

Believing that they were facing a crisis, South Yorkshire police, who were responsible for safety on the day, ordered the Leppings Lane exit to be opened, and there was a surge as at least 2,000 Liverpool supporters entered the tunnel to an already crowded standing area of the ground, and for those inside there was no escape, as the pitch was protected by a two-metre-high steel fence.

During the enquiry into the disaster Graham Mackrell, former club secretary at Sheffield Wednesday and the man responsible for the safety at the stadium, admitted to the jury that safety conditions were breached during Liverpool's FA Cup semi-final, including not keeping a record of how many spectators were admitted. Mr Mackrell said, at the time, he did not see any problems with what was in place. *But the jury announced that there was an error in the safety certification for Hillsborough stadium.*

It has also been revealed that Sheffield council's environmental health officer, Paul Jackson, 'may have written' a report in 1988 refusing a safety certificate for the football grounds. The jury were shown a fire service report also written in 1988, recommending the stadium be 'shut down' for breaches of fire safety regulations.

Mr Mackrell, however, said he was unaware of this information.

Mr Jackson reported to the jury that he visited the stadium later that evening on the day of the disaster, where he noticed the spacing between barriers at Leppings Lane Terrace (the entrance for all Liverpool fans) was not compliant with the Green Guide to stadium safety.

So in terms of the relationship between risk and crisis management, let us examine the fact that leading up to one of the greatest disasters to ever befall a sports event in the UK, and perhaps anywhere on the planet, risk and crisis management was non-existent.

It is safe to argue that the game should never have taken place, and that means that the lives of 96 innocent football supporters would not have been lost.

What do we know?

1   There may be evidence that a report was written by Sheffield Council Environmental Health Officer, Paul Jackson in 1988 refusing to issue a safety certificate for Hillsborough.
2   During the same period, a fire service report was written, recommending that Hillsborough be closed down due to breaches of fire safety.
3   Safety at the Leppings Lane area, where the majority of Liverpool fans were, was in breach of recognised standards, in that the spacing in between barriers was not compliant.

A combination of the above three factors makes a compelling argument for a severe risk, which could easily have been avoided had the game been postponed. As it happened, for reasons known only to those officiating on the day, including Sheffield Council and South Yorkshire police, the poorly managed crisis quickly developed into one of the most serious disasters in the history of British, or any other national sport.

RIP YNWA

Disaster management and the disaster management cycle

Having devoted a great deal of time in researching risk and crisis management, I was somewhat surprised to note by comparison that empirical research into disaster management pales into insignificance when compared to the former two pieces of research. A number of well-researched publications, such as *Risk, Crisis and Security Management* (Borodzicz, 2005), *Innovative Thinking in Risk, Crisis and Disaster Management* (Bennet, 2012) and *The*

Handbook of Security (Gill, 2014) pay scant attention to disaster management, without even a thinly veiled definition in any of the three books.

Dillon's excellent publication *Emergency Planning, Crisis and Disaster Management* (2014) is extremely detailed in its description of emergency planning, but disaster management isn't even mentioned in the index.

This is no criticism of several first-class publications, which are unique in their own fields, but it makes me wonder about the emphasis on crisis management, and the lack of enthusiasm in terms of disaster management.

Is there perhaps some confusion when classifying incidents, whether crisis or disaster, or is it perhaps more convenient to allow overlap and individual choice of terminology. For example, the 2011 incident which occurred at a power plant near Fukushima, Japan, has been described as both a crisis and a disaster, despite the fact that hundreds of people were killed.

The International Federation of the Red Cross and Red Crescent (IFR) define a disaster as being the organisation and management of resources and responsibilities for dealing with all humanitarian aspects of emergencies, in particular *preparedness, response and recovery* in order to lessen the impact of disasters.[44] To my mind, preparedness, response and recovery in terms of disaster management bears a great similarity to the three phases of a crisis; pre-crisis, operational crisis and post crisis. If only life was that simple.

Whilst there may be levels of confusion when differentiating crisis and disaster (although the terms are perfectly clear to me), the phases of a disaster are known as the Disaster Management Life Cycle, and despite the very clear statement made by the IFR, it is generally recognised that there are in fact four phases ('oh no', I hear you scream at me – don't shoot the messenger is all I have to say).

The Disaster Management Life Cycle

The Centre for Disaster Resilience, University of Salford have produced a very good open sourced publication titled Disaster Resilience in the Built Environment; a major contributing section being the Disaster Management Life Cycle.[45]

In this paper, the centre argues, not unlike other institutes researching this topic, that there are four distinct stages in the cycle. They are:

- *Mitigation* – This stage allows for mitigation strategies to be identified at the earliest moment and refers to the reduction of the impact that a disaster may bring. For example, houses built in a recognised earthquake zone in Japan are reported to be 'earthquake proof'. I am not convinced that anything is 'proof', but *What's Next*[46] argues that Japan's proximity to the Pacific Ring of Fire and all its seismic activity has contributed to the country's strict building codes for skyscrapers and towers. Thanks in part to materials that are flexible and shock-absorbent as well as modern tools to test and analyse the performance of a building, the architecture and engineering seen in Japan is among the most resilient in the world, with even some older buildings retrofitted to make them more earthquake-resistant.
- *Preparedness* – Policies, plans and procedures. Preparing for a disaster is no different to making preparations for any type of incident, or any perceived crisis; and it requires policy documentation that meets the highest levels of scrutiny and is of course authorised by the senior management team. The strategy then needs to be

accurately communicated to all stakeholders, and all levels of documentation should be tested at regular intervals to prove its effectiveness. Examples being an evacuation plan for a multi-storey high-rise building in a busy city centre that may be susceptible to man-made or natural disasters such as a terrorist attack, or an earthquake.

- *Response* – How an organisation responds to the very early stages of a disaster can determine the long-term impact of that disastrous incident. Of course, successful response is dependent upon a number of issues, with tested mitigation and preparedness procedures being critical. However, as Helmuth von Moltke the Elder said when he was the chief of staff of the Prussian army before World War I: "No battle plan survives first contact with the enemy". Policies, plans and procedures are not necessarily battle plans, and a tsunami or earthquake cannot be described as the enemy, but the theory is the same. No plan is guaranteed to succeed; no matter how sophisticated it is, or how many times it has been tested, because there is always the human element to be taken into consideration (www.salford.ac.uk).

United Airlines Flight 93 – 11 September 2001

United Airlines Flight 93 was a domestic scheduled passenger flight that was hijacked by four al-Qaeda terrorists on board, as part of the September 11 attacks. It crashed into a field in Somerset County, Pennsylvania, during an attempt by the passengers and crew to regain control. All 44 people on board were killed, including the four hijackers, but no one on the ground was injured. The aircraft involved, a Boeing 757–222, was flying United Airlines' daily scheduled morning flight from Newark International Airport in New Jersey to San Francisco International Airport in California.

The hijackers stormed the aircraft's cockpit 46 minutes after take-off. The pilot and first officer took measures, such as de-activating the autopilot, to hinder the hijackers. Ziad Jarrah, who had trained as a pilot, took control of the aircraft and diverted it back towards the east coast, in the direction of Washington, D.C., the U.S. capital. Khalid Sheikh Mohammed and Ramzi bin al-Shibh, considered principal instigators of the attacks, have claimed that the intended target was the U.S. Capitol Building.

After the hijackers took control of the plane, several passengers and flight attendants learned from phone calls that suicide attacks had already been made by hijacked airliners on the World Trade Center in New York City and the Pentagon in Arlington County, Virginia. Many of the passengers then attempted to regain control of the aircraft from the hijackers. During the struggle, the plane crashed into a field near a reclaimed strip mine in Stonycreek Township, near Indian Lake and Shanksville, about 65 miles (105 km) southeast of Pittsburgh and 130 miles (210 km) northwest of Washington, DC. A few people witnessed the impact from the ground, and news agencies began reporting the event within an hour.

The passengers and crew on board Flight 93 were aware that the hijackers were probably armed and dangerous, and the last thing that they would have advised under different circumstances would be to attack the terrorists. However, human beings often act with what appears to be great stupidity and naivety when faced with irrevocable danger, and the passengers and crew on board that aircraft, flying over Stonycreek Township on 11 September 2001 were determined that al-Qaeda were not going to kill any more innocent US civilians on the ground. In that respect, they were successful.

- *Recovery* – This is an attempt to return to activities before the disaster occurred, in as normal a manner as possible – normality, of course, being subjective. The recovery phase is also an opportunity to examine the effectiveness, or otherwise of the proposed mitigation strategies, the levels and adequacy of preparedness and all response activities. This is hopefully the time when 'lessons are learned'. An example of the need to return to life before the disaster can be seen by the efforts made after 7/7.

On 7 July 2005, four young Muslim youths decided, for reasons which are unclear, to attack the London transportation system as suicide bombers. Bombs were detonated on underground trains in or near Aldgate, Edgware Road, and Russell Square tube stations, resulting in the loss of life for 56 people, with 770 being injured. The aftermath of the attack also saw massive disruption to the capital city, with transportation and communications being unstable for some time. Elements of this type of attack would have been practiced and drilled by the emergency services, but as mentioned earlier, once the live attack takes place, policies, plans and procedures are tested to the limit and the recovery phase begins.

As the result of a crisis or disaster, there is always the likelihood that business will be impacted. 9/11, 7/7 and the horrors of Fukushima saw business in New York, London, and Tokyo coming to a grinding halt. Hopefully all those involved were able to invoke an effective business continuity plan.

Business continuity

Pause for thought

In your opinion, what is meant by the term 'business continuity'?

Business continuity is the final component part of organisational resilience, with us having examined the three other areas, risk management, crisis management and disaster management. Essentially business continuity has two constituent parts: business continuity planning, and business continuity management.

> Business continuity is the intended outcome of proper execution of business continuity planning and disaster recovery. It is the payoff for cost-effective buying of spare machines and servers, performing backups and bringing them off-site, assigning responsibility, performing drills, educating employees and being vigilant.[47]

The *Business Dictionary* is slightly more succinct but comes to a similar conclusion as the law dictionary.

> The ability of the key operations of a firm to continue without stoppage, irrespective of the adverse circumstances or events.

Business

On 22 May 2017, at 2131hrs, suicide bomber Salman Abedi detonated an improvised explosive device (IED) at the Manchester Arena. Twenty-three men, women, and children were killed by the bomb, with over 800 being injured.

Business continuity planning and business continuity management are not bespoke strategies that can only be adopted by large corporations and government organisations. On the contrary, small to medium enterprises (SMEs) with extremely tight budgets critically need robust business continuity planning and management, because unlike larger organisations and corporations who have the business capacity to perhaps absorb a financial crisis, SMEs don't! Thinking about the Manchester Arena, where the vast majority of businesses supporting the events location were SMEs, perhaps it could be argued that it was fortunate that only 40% became insolvent.

Business Continuity Planning (BCP) and Business Continuity Management Systems (BCMS)

Business Continuity Planning as part of the overall Business Continuity Management System is critical, but not always easy to 'sell' to the senior management team (SMT) and other stakeholders in the organisation.

It should be remembered that executive boards within major corporations or owners of small to medium enterprises (SME) are constantly bombarded with requests and demands for systems. Whether it is HR demanding ISO 9001 (Quality Management Systems), or the IT function threatening cyber extinction if ISO 27001 (Information Security Management Systems) isn't purchased, there is always a doom monger threatening death and disaster.

However, the lack of a Quality Management System won't threaten the safety and security of the business, and it is unlikely that (although not certain) a cyber-attack will mean the demise of the organisation. On the other hand, if the business is unprepared for such events, it may well cease to exist as a thriving enterprise, with little or no growth expectations.

The standard for Business Continuity Management (BCM) is currently ISO 22301, which says that business continuity is the strategic and tactical capability of the organisation to plan for and respond to incidents and business disruptions in order to continue business operations at an acceptable predefined level.

Business Continuity Management (BCM) is the holistic management process that identifies potential threats to an organisation and the impacts to business operations that those threats, if realised, might cause, and which provides a framework for building organisational resilience, with the capability for an effective response, that safeguards the trust of its key stakeholders, reputation, brand and value creating activities.

How quickly – and painlessly – you manage to get back to 'business as usual' in the event of a terrorist attack, fire, flood or other form of disaster, or any other major interruption, depends on how effectively you can devise, and put into action, your own business continuity management.

The results of a survey carried out by the Chartered Management Institute in 2012 (Sharp, 2012) show that 43% of those organisations involved in the study admitted the reason for them implementing a BCMS was as the result of pressure from corporate governance. Thirty percent of respondents said the reason for their BCMS implementation was because of the insistence of existing clients, and interestingly 34% of those questioned insisted that they were under pressure from new legislation of regulation. See Figure 3.9.

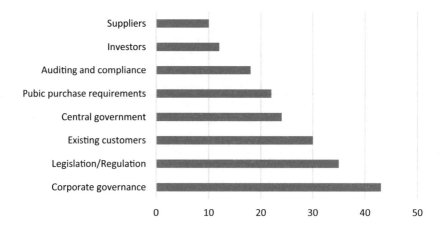

Figure 3.9 Survey carried out by the Chartered Management Institute (2012)

In the UK, the Civil Contingencies Act 2004 requires local government bodies, the National Health Service (NHS) and emergency services to put in place effective BCMS to ensure that they can continue to perform their functions in the event of an emergency. They have to ensure that they can mobilise the functions they need to deal with the emergency, minimise the impact on the responder's day-to-day activity, and maintain vital services for the community at an appropriate level. In addition, local authorities have the responsibility of promoting business continuity to business and appropriate voluntary bodies in support of the concept of a resilient community.

In the UK public authorities and emergency services that are driven by the Civil Contingencies Act are now the biggest drivers of BCMS down the supply chain. Increasingly they are seeing evidence that their partners and suppliers have effective BCMS; in many cases suppliers cannot tender unless they have implemented business continuity Sharp (2012).

The Business Continuity Plan (BCP)

In any business context, planning is critical, whether it is sales or operations, and business continuity is certainly no different. Once the basic tenets of business continuity are established, every organisation has to plan a management strategy that will suit the needs of the business and its client base. So, the first step to be taken in the drive to implement a Business Continuity Management Systems (BCMS) is to formulate a Business Continuity Plan (BCP).

Experience has shown that organisations can be disrupted for many reasons. Business continuity planning has traditionally been based on known threats: loss of IT, loss of buildings through fire, flooding, and so forth. In recent times however, the UK has experienced some unexpected disruptions, including a widespread outbreak of foot and mouth disease, extensive disruptions on the rail network, a national shortage of oil-based fuels, the loss of water supplies for weeks, and a volcanic ash cloud that disrupted flights, impacting the supply chain. In most cases existing plans did not cover these disruptions and the impact they had on the day-to-day operations of organisations.

When developing a Business Continuity Plan it is important that all elements of the organisation are involved – risk management, IT disaster recovery, supply chain management, environmental management, health and safety, human resources, security, and so on. If this does not happen, assumptions may be made about the ability of other parts of the organisation to respond and meet the needs of the plan. For example, if the plan calls for members of staff to work from home, then the IT department must confirm that technical arrangements have or can be made to enable this to happen. The HR department may need to adjust its policies to accommodate working, and health and safety policies may have to be modified.

In response to a business crisis, the plan should provide answers to the following basic questions:

- What is to be done?
- When is it needed?
- Where are the alternative sources located?
- Who is involved?
- How is continuity to be achieved?

The plan should contain the contact details for critical personnel and organisations, such as:

- Key senior management
- Key operational staff
- Emergency services
- Local authorities
- Suppliers
- Key customers
- Utility companies
- Insurers
- Media organisations.

Having completed the plan(s), they must be implemented and tested. Those who hold positions that are named in the plan must be made aware of their role(s) and have the appropriate training to enable them to fulfil their responsibilities.

Business continuity management is critical to all aspects of business resilience, and particularly from a security perspective are the roles played by the chief security officer and chief information security officer.

Exercise Brave Defender – task 5: resilience

Synopsis

The executive board is under pressure to conform to resilience standards, particularly in relation to security, but this is an area that the board is totally unfamiliar with. Your tasks are as follows.

1   Explain how the international standard ISO 22316 pertains to the security operations of Britcom, and how it will be advantageous to the organisation to adhere to the standard.

2   Give a brief description of the following areas, explaining how they may influence, or be influenced by security.

- Risk management
- Crisis management
- Disaster management
- Business continuity
- Organisational resilience.

3.6 The chief security officer (CSO) and the chief information security officer (CISO)

This is probably the most critical delineation of the security functions within an organisation, and whilst there are no direct comparisons in terms of seniority by appointment, it is clear that there has to be an extremely strong working relationship between the two roles, or the security resilience of the organisation will inevitably suffer. So, in this sub-chapter we are going to examine both functions individually, and then reconcile the importance of a combined effort to ensure the security and safety of the company.

The CSO

The role and appointment of chief security officer (CSO) is a relatively new innovation in terms of the overall security strategy of the organisation; introduced because there is a need for the executive board of directors to receive an accurate, reconciled annual security report. But what exactly does the CSO do?

The CSO is the senior security manager within an organisation, and he or she is responsible for the entire security landscape, including physical and cyber functions, and prior to his or her appointment, function leads, such as the security manager or the IT security manager would dominate the security requirements of the organisation, and that was not conducive for effective communications, with 'turf wars' being predominant.

That is exactly the point. However the battle, or turf war was not exclusive to physical and IT security; audit, compliance and sometimes even security business development waged in, with each function desperately trying to catch the eye of the CEO in what amounted to a security department beauty contest that no section was ever going to win. If anything, it allowed other departments to continue to fire barbed comments about the fractionalisation and lack of credible communication in relation to security; a difficult argument to counter.

The appointment of a CSO has been to stabilise the security function, negate historical turf wars and encourage other functions and departments to work closely with security professionals.

The CISO

The chief information security officer (CISO) is the senior manager responsible for all information and data security handled by his or her organisation. Once referred to as the IT security manager, the CISO sits on a similar platform and works closely with the

CSO, and normally reports directly to or works in conjunction with the chief information officer (CIO).

The CISO directs staff in identifying, developing, implementing, and maintaining processes across the enterprise to reduce information and information technology (IT) risks. They respond to incidents, establish appropriate standards and controls, manage security technologies, and direct the establishment and implementation of policies and procedures. The CISO is also usually responsible for information-related compliance (e.g. supervises the implementation to achieve ISO/IEC 27001 certification for an entity or a part of it).

Typically, the CISO's influence reaches the entire organisation. Responsibilities may include, but not be limited to:

- Computer emergency response team/computer security incident response team
- Cybersecurity
- Disaster recovery and business continuity management
- Identity and access management
- Information privacy
- Information regulatory compliance (e.g. US PCI DSS, FISMA, GLBA, HIPAA; UK Data Protection Act 1998; Canada PIPEDA, Europe GDPR)
- Information risk management
- Information security and information assurance
- Information security operations centre (ISOC)
- Information technology controls for financial and other systems
- IT investigations, digital forensics, eDiscovery.[48]

So it is quite clear that there will probably always be overlaps between the roles and responsibilities of the CSO and the CISO, but one issue that is incredibly obvious, is that both appointments must work in harmony to combat crime against the organisation or corporation; with cybercrime and cyber terrorism being the greatest threat to business today

Exercise Brave Defender – task 6: the CSO and the CSIO

Synopsis

The board of Britcom plc has made a strategic decision to have a data centre constructed within a new business park in Croydon, South London. Speaking on behalf of the CSO and the CISO, respond to the following tasks:

1   As CSO, produce a plan that will take into consideration the physical security needs of the new construction; basing your design features on the concept of defence in depth. Cover the following areas:

   a   A crime pattern analysis of the following area: BR33BZ[49]
   b   The perimeter defence
   c   Integrated security systems
   d   Manned guarding.

2   As CISO, advise the board on the following issues:

    a   The physical security standards required to protect the site IT network
    b   Cyber security requirements
    c   Standard Operating Procedures (SOPs) for the use of the network, and for those using the network.

3   Demonstrate how both tasks can be integrated for effective operational synchronisation.

3.7 Cybercrime and the cyberthreat

> I am convinced that there are only two types of companies: those that have been hacked, and those that will be. And even they are converging into one category; companies that have been hacked and will be once again.
>
> (Mueller, 2012).[50]

There is no clearly recognised definition of the term cybercrime, rather the offence is seen as a means of committing crime with the aid of a computer(s). Generally speaking, the term is used to describe criminal offences specifically related to computers and telecommunications, or crimes that have taken place in cyberspace.[51]

When describing cybercrime, Singer and Friedman (2014) arrived at an interesting appraisal by describing how criminologists and police officers may have thought in times gone by. The professionals may have been thinking that there is one kind of crime which may exist in the future – computer crime. Instead of mugging people in the streets, or robbing houses (technically they probably meant burglary as opposed to robbery, but I'm perhaps splitting hairs here), tomorrows criminal may try to steal money from banks and other organisations by using a computer. The computer criminal works from home (as we all do much more now), using his (or her) computer to gain access to the memories of the computers used by the banks and companies. The criminal tries to interfere with the computers in order to get them to transfer money to his computer without the bank or company knowing that it has been robbed.

So whether the computer is used by cyber criminals as a direct weapon, or perhaps when it is the target, that is to say, the aim is to temporarily disable or close the network down; or even if the computer is being used as a recording tool, the threat of cybercrime is self-evident.

The cyberthreat

The National Cyber Security Centre (NCSC)[52] defines the cyberthreat as:

> Malicious attempts to damage or disrupt devices, services and networks – and the information on them.

Without a shadow of a doubt, the cyberthreat to commercial and public entities is greater now than it has ever been, with cybercriminals and terrorists becoming more sophisticated as they gain confidence in their ability to attack systems that are too often unprotected, or certainly lacking in the sophistication required to be adequately defended.

Short of a successful chemical, biological, radiological or nuclear (CBRN) attack by, for example Islamic State, or a resurgent al-Qaeda, the greatest danger to society and business today is the threat from the cybercriminal or cyberterrorist. Cyber resilience is not merely needed, it is absolutely critical, and if businesses do not have adequate cyber risk and crisis management plans in place, with related business continuity plans and disaster recovery strategies, they are going to be susceptible to a form of attack, a threat that can financially strip them to the bone.

The non-profit Information Security Forum, which describes itself as "the world's leading authority on cyber, information security and risk management", warns in its annual study of the cybersecurity landscape (Threat Horizon, 2019) of increased potential for:

- Disruption – Over-reliance on fragile connectivity creates the potential for premeditated Internet outages capable of bringing trade to its knees and heightened risk that ransomware will be used to hijack the Internet of Things.
- Distortion – The intentional spread of misinformation, including by bots and automated sources, causes trust in the integrity of information to be compromised.

The most common cyberthreats today are:

- *Phishing*

   Normally delivered in email format, phishing emails look like official emails from the victim's bank, employer or some other trusted entity. They claim to require some action by the victim, perhaps to correct an account error or see a message on Facebook and fool the visitors into visiting a web page where they are asked to enter their credentials. If the victim enters his or her account details, the attacker can now do anything with that information, from transferring money to reading confidential emails and other communications (Singer and Friedman, 2014).

- *Malware*

   Malware, or malicious software, is normally delivered by phishing means in email attachment form. The malware used in thee attachments is often quite sophisticated. The emphasis is on stealth, so the authors will not only try to hide from traditional antivirus defences but burrow deep into networks and operating systems to avoid discovery, attempting to impersonate legitimate network traffic (Singer and Friedman, 2014).

WannaCry and the NHS

This was a devastating global cyberattack in 2017 that crippled computers in hospitals across the UK costing the NHS £92m, a report from the Department of Health has found.

The so-called WannaCry hack, which shut down hundreds of thousands of computers around the world with messages from hackers demanding ransom payments, hit a third of hospital trusts and 8% of GP practices. Around 1% of all NHS care was disrupted over the course of a week.

The hack caused more than 19,000 appointments to be cancelled, costing the NHS £20m between 12 May and 19 May and £72m in the subsequent clean-up and upgrades to its IT systems.

The cyber attack caused 200,000 computers to lock out users with red-lettered error messages demanding the cryptocurrency Bitcoin. The attack was blamed on elite North Korean hackers after a year-long investigation.

At the time of the attacks, the NHS was criticised for using outdated IT systems, including Windows XP, a 17-year-old operating system that could be vulnerable to cyberattacks.

- *Zero-day exploit*

  Probably the easiest way to describe this form of cyberattack is to say that the attacker identifies a flaw in either the hardware or software and exploits it before the legitimate developer has the opportunity to patch it. By the time the repair is carried out, the damage is done, normally with catastrophic consequences.

Of course one of the problems with cyber is that there are very few cybersecurity 'experts' who have either the opportunity or seniority to convince the Executive Board about the importance of cyber security, because (a) the board doesn't understand, or indeed want to understand cyber security and (b) the board is interested in one topic, and that is business growth. I am not for one second advocating such cybersecurity measures that will inhibit business development, but there have to be risk-managed checks and balances. However, it is not quite as simple as that, because whilst the chief information security officer (CISO) is advocating a robust risk management approach to cybersecurity, which means risk assessment and analysis, the chief information officer (CIO) is only interested in having a smooth flow of information which is not impeded by barriers. So once again the perception is that whilst the business needs to grow and develop, with the use of cyber and information flow at the core of such growth, security once again is unable to help with business enablement.

Evans (2019) in an extremely useful publication named *Managing Cyber Risk* talks about the fact that cyber security was the natural development from information security, which commercial entities were never particularly comfortable with, and the original need for security tools, such as intrusion detection systems (IDS), data loss prevention systems (DLP) and cyber threat intelligence (CTI) tools. He argues that as a result of this interdiction, IT personnel gained more and more power, as they were the sole source of information security. Everything was technically oriented, and risk management was not part of the conversation. IT persons isolated the business and were emboldened by their new power, resulting in a complete disconnect between the risk to the business assets and how cyber was being managed. Today a chief information security officer (CISO) walks into a board meeting with 300 vulnerabilities, and the board is mystified. They have no idea what a MITM (man in the middle attack) or SQL injection means in terms of business risk. This obviously leaves the risk owners (the business) at a serious disadvantage, with a complete reliance on the CISO (who usually has only a technology background) to set the strategy. This is a colossal mistake. Cyber, like any other threat, must be understood in terms of the risk to the business, not only at a technical level. A smart cyber risk management strategy is part of a long-term integrated enterprise risk strategy, not a checkbox or one-time fix.

Within the realms of cyber resilience and response to attack are a number of appointments and critical relationships, that it will be to our advantage to discuss here.

- *The board of directors*

   According to the Institute of Directors (IoD), the board's key purpose "is to ensure the company's prosperity by collectively directing the company's affairs, while meeting the appropriate interests of its shareholders and relevant stakeholders".

   It is generally agreed that all boards of directors have a responsibility to their shareholders for managing the following areas:

   - *Governance*: Comprising all of the processes of senior management, governance, whether it relates to a nation state (governing) or a commercials organisation where the board dictates how the organisation is governed. The rules and regulations that stakeholders must follow.
   - *Strategy*: Strategy is a high level plan to achieve one or more goals under conditions of uncertainty.[53] This allows the board to be in a position where it makes all strategic decisions in relation to the aims and objectives of the organisation.
   - *Risk*: The likelihood or probability of an unknown, usually negative occurrence that may impact an organisation. The board will always have the financial say in matters relating to risk and risk management. Technically, the board owns all risks on behalf of the business.
   - *Talent*: Skills and accomplishments identified in a person or group of people.
   - *Compliance*: This is conforming to a set of rules and regulations, normally set by the board as part of the overall governance package.
   - *Culture*: The culture of an organisation or group of people is an agreed sense of unity that applies to areas that impact that group (e.g. security culture or cyber risk culture). Culture is driven by the board.

   Because the board is responsible for organisational governance, it has to have the final say in all matters relating to cybersecurity on a strategic, tactical and operational basis.

- *Chief information officer (CIO)*

   The chief information officer is arguably the most powerful and authoritative person in any commercial organisation, often formally identified as the IT director. The difference between the two roles is that the IT director was generally a technically qualified senior manager who originated from a purely IT background.

   Whilst the CIO still has the responsibility of oversight of all IT functions, he or she will also be seen as a senior business manager, who generally reports to the chief executive officer (CEO) or the chief operating officer (COO).

- *Chief Information Security Officer (CISO)*

   See previous section.

- *Compliance manager/officer*

   The central role of the compliance manger/officer is to ensure that all functions within an organisation, particularly a corporate organisation are compliant, in terms of following all rules and regulations relating to ethical and legal requirements. The compliance manager usually works alongside human relations or audit, but increasingly they are recruited to support the IT department, particularly in terms of cyber representation. The compliance manager in relation to the cyberthreat will ensure that all cyber stakeholders are adhering to ethical beliefs and legal requirements, often working very closely with the chief information security officer (CISO).

- *Auditor*

  Internal audit has a critical role in helping organisations in the ongoing battle of managing cyberthreats, both by providing an independent assessment of existing and needed controls and helping the audit committee and board understand and address the diverse risks of the digital world.

  In any audit situation, the internal audit team should be used first, primarily because its members will understand the systems being audited and will very quickly be able to identify flaws and abnormalities. However, and particularly when tackling cyber issues there may be a requirement to commission the services of external cyber audit specialists.

  Deloitte have produced an excellent open source PDF in relation to cyber security and the role of the internal audit team at https://www2.deloitte.com/us/en/pages/risk/articles/cybersecurity-internal-audit-role.html.

- *The legal team*

  As with any other aspect of security management, the importance of a strong legal team cannot be overstated, whether it is in support of the board's approach to cyber governance and how this impacts the day-to-day activities of staff and management, or whether it is constructing a legal case against a potential cyber perpetrator. Additionally, the legal team will be involved in cyber when a breach occurs. It is very likely that all communications will be run past the legal team before being released to the media or a regulator. The communications team normally crafts any breach notifications with the CISO. Legal also works with the CISO's and Compliance Managers on corporate policies (Evans, 2019).

We are still focussing on cybercrime.

The Internet of Things

Simply put, the Internet of Things (IoT) is a group of devices with on/off switches that are configured to connect to the Internet and each other. Simple!

Devices which have hit the headlines recently have been smart fridges that monitor food contained within; smart heating and ventilating systems that can be controlled remotely by a smartphone; or most contentiously the smart meter, designed to monitor and in some cases manage the flow of electricity and gas to a domestic or commercial location. The one thing all of these entities have in common is a lack of security. Buy why?

Well, there are a number of issues when it comes to including built-in security with any device: flow impediment and cost.

If for example a smart fridge had to adhere to internal security protocols every time it was accessed, or requested to carry out an operation, for instance report on the use by date of a packet of butter; by the time security requirements had been met, the butter would be off! Equally, if the smart meter monitoring and managing power requirements were complete with firewalls and antivirus protection, the system would slow down, and communications with the service provider would almost be at a standstill; at least that is how the service provider portrays the lack of security within IoT appliances.

In terms of cost, smart meters and smart fridges are assembled at the lowest possible price in order that they may be competitive, and of course the producers will always argue that the consumer isn't that interested in security; service levels and cost of purchase are far important. Both arguments playing into the hands of the cyber hacker, who sees the smart devices and applications as an ideal means of accessing the Internet connectivity that such devices require.

In an article written by Nick Ismail on 22 January 2018, the author argues that the Internet of Things (IoT), the ability of everyday devices to connect and transfer data to each other, is already carving out a place in the consumer market, with devices like smart home locks, thermostats, lighting, and energy monitors.

The latest research also claims that 29% of organisations have already implemented IoT solutions, and this is expected to surge to 48% by the end of 2018, as businesses are increasingly sold on the cost-savings and productivity-enhancing benefits of IoT.

Ismail then goes on to argue that with the IoT bandwagon rushing full steam ahead, few vendors or customers are pausing to consider the enormous security risks associated with the devices. The influx of additional entry points into an organisation's network, plus a current lack of security standards for IoT devices, means there is a gaping hole in the perimeter of any home or business that has installed IoT devices.

Consider the operating systems for such appliances. How do you upgrade the OS in a wall-mounted air conditioning unit that's connected wirelessly? Or a smart light bulb? If you can't upgrade an operating system, how can you attempt to patch any vulnerabilities?

Then, when you are hacked (and it is when, not if), where does that leave you? You now have a 'dirty' corner of your network, and all it takes is for another hacker to connect to that 'dirty' corner to repeat the process. It's a case of vulnerability after vulnerability. By 2020, it is estimated that 25% of cyberattacks will target IoT devices.

Worryingly however, *a recent survey by price comparison website MoneySupermarket indicates UK consumers are aware of the perils associated with IoT devices – but the apparent convenience, security and cost-saving benefits appear to outweigh the risks.*

The research shows more than three-quarters of UK consumers are fearful of connected home technology, citing concerns about hacking and unapproved data collection. But the same survey forecasts that there will still be 25–30 billion devices worldwide by the early 2020s.

The real concern here is that whilst consumers (domestic and commercial) espouse fears of a lack of security, particularly when it involves cyber connectivity, the temptation to elect for greater convenience of use normally has the final say.

It is impossible to accurately forecast the damage that may be done by cybercrime globally in the next decade, but I is likely to be somewhere around $6–10 trillion annually.

Cybercrime can and does impact all walks of life, including of course all aspects of critical national infrastructure.

Exercise Brave Defender – task 7: cybercrime and the cyberthreat

Synopsis

Intelligence has been received that the likelihood of an attack against the Britcom plc IT network has risen, with sources informing you that it is probable that the company will be subjected a series of malware breaches, including the potential for a ransomware attach, and distributed denial of service attacks.

You are tasked with advising the executive board on the most effective means of defending the company network against the above onslaughts.

3.8 Critical national infrastructure

Pause for thought

What is meant by the term 'critical national infrastructure'?

The Centre for the Protection of National Infrastructure (CPNI) argues that *National Infrastructure are those facilities, systems, sites, information, people, networks and processes, necessary for a country to function and upon which daily life depends.*

It also includes some functions, sites and organisations which are not critical to the maintenance of essential services, but which need protection due to the potential danger to the public (civil nuclear and chemical sites, for example).

In the UK, there are 13 national infrastructure sectors: chemicals, civil nuclear communications, defence, emergency services, energy, finance, food, government, health, space, transport and water. Several sectors have defined 'sub-sectors'; emergency services, for example can be split into police, ambulance, fire services and coast guard.

Not everything within a national infrastructure sector is judged to be 'critical'. The UK government's official definition of CPNI is:

> Those critical elements of infrastructure (namely assets, facilities, systems, networks or processes and the essential workers that operate and facilitate them), the loss or compromise of which could result in:
>
> a)   Major detrimental impact on the availability, integrity or delivery of essential services – including those services whose integrity, if compromised, could result in significant loss of life or casualties – taking into account significant economic or social impacts; and/or
>
> b)   Significant impact on national security, national defence, or the functioning of the state.[54]

It is very clear that the protection of critical national infrastructures is crucial for the safety of a community or nation state, and that resources have to be found to protect such services. However, before we begin to look at how we can protect critical infrastructures, we need to spend some time looking at threats, vulnerabilities and impact measurements. One of the greatest vulnerabilities is interdependency.

Interdependency

Interdependency means that a number of elements of the critical national infrastructure are reliant upon the infrastructure chain being resilient. For instance, should a number of power generating plants (power stations) be successfully attacked concurrently, it may mean that elements of the national health service, hospitals and ambulance facilities are without power and therefore unable to operate at maximum performance levels.

Equally, water filtration and supply may be impacted because the pumps require electrical power, and if they don't have sufficient back-up, water supplies and sewage services are going to grind to a halt. Of course, national infrastructures such as data centres, communications hubs, and water supply facilities are likely to have reserve systems such as uninterruptible power supply (UPS) and backup generators. They may have even solar or wind power, but this form of supply is only going to represent a small percentage of the electricity required, and for a limited time.

If a number of communications hubs are rendered inoperative because of a distributed denial of service (DDoS), national communications are going to be interrupted for an extended period.

The stark reality of the situation is that the sheer interdependency of critical infrastructure is its greatest vulnerability, offering those with criminal or terrorist intent a powerful target, which if not adequately defended, will easily be defeated. So, the next area that we must examine are the risks to critical infrastructure, and how they are assessed and measured.

Risk and critical infrastructures (CI)

In terms of measuring risk to critical infrastructure, the first issue we must consider are the current threats and vulnerabilities that serve to cause damage to those assets.

Threats to critical infrastructures

It is logical to argue that there are basically two central types of threats that may, if not controlled, impact critical infrastructures, and they are:

Physical threats

Physical threats can appear in two distinct forms, natural or man-made.

Natural threats to critical infrastructures can take many forms, but probably the most damaging are hurricanes and tsunami floods. Of course, during the planning stage of any CI installation, the threat envelope is taken into consideration during the risk assessment phase, and all types of natural threats are examined. However, history informs us that man's propensity to 'cut corners' and mother nature's ferociousness often means that defences may be useless, and that lives are often lost, property is destroyed, and lessons are never learned.

Probably one of the most damaging aspects of the critical infrastructure impact analysis is the harm that could be inflicted on national communications provision, not just for ensuring that the nation can talk but also for defending against the cyberthreat. If a national communications service is disabled, even for a short time, this will allow criminals, terrorists, and enemy states to carry out an attack that may not be recovered from.

Also of critical importance is the provision of electrical power and the safety of nuclear powers stations, but of course that shouldn't occur at a nuclear facility in an advanced nation, such as Japan for instance. Unless, of course, the power station is built on a coastline which is vulnerable to high tides and the occasional tsunami.

Fukushima Daiichi

On a coastal plain in Japan's North East, hemmed in between a ridge of forested mountains to the west and sandy beaches that edge the Pacific Ocean, sit the towns of Futaba and Okuma. These quiet burgs had relied on fishing and farming for generations but wanted to reinvent themselves and take part in the post-war boom. In the Autumn if 1961, the town councils of Futaba and Okuma both unanimously voted to invite TEPCO, the Tokyo Electric Power Company, to build a nuclear power station on the border of the two towns.

To win the towns' acceptance, the Japan Atomic Energy Commission and TEPCO reinforced the notion that nuclear power stations were absolutely safe. Citizens need not fear, because nothing would go wrong. Construction of the Fukushima Daiichi Nuclear Power Station's first reactor began in 1967, and it began supplying electricity in 1971.

In a country as prone to earthquakes and tsunamis as Japan, building nuclear reactors on the coast may seem like pure folly. But the government was confident that it had assessed the geological risks, as well as the myriad other risks related to siting a nuclear power facility, and had prepared for them. Fukushima Daiichi engineers had estimated that the largest tsunami that could probably hit the plant would be about 10 feet high, and when, in 1970, Japan established a regulatory standard for tsunami height, the government found Fukushima to have met this new standard. More than three decades later the Japan Society of Civil Engineers raised the worst-case estimation for Fukushima Daiichi to about 19 feet, and TEPCO voluntarily elevated some equipment installations near the harbour. The plant was assumed to be well out of harm's way and untouchable by even the angriest ocean.

So when on 11 March 2011, a massive tsunami rolled in from the Pacific and inundated the Fukushima Daiichi Nuclear Power Station, when the facilities electrical systems went off and stayed off, when the emergency cooling systems faltered and failed, and when the three operating nuclear reactors started to boil away their coolant, the utilities and the government and the people of Japan were unprepared.

In Tokyo, cabinet members reached for the nuclear emergency response manual and flipped through it, looking for instructions on what to do in such a dire situation. But those instructions didn't exist. According to the emergency response manual, this situation could never occur (Bricker, 2014).

Man-made threats, on the other hand, are premeditated and are consciously designed and instrumented to maximise any impact on critical infrastructures. It is safe to argue that the intention of a man-made attack against critical infrastructures is designed to ensure destruction of property and services, and ultimately loss of life. For the purpose of this book we will focus on the most concerning threat to critical infrastructure, and that is terrorism.

- *Terrorism*

   In terms of a terrorist attack, there is likely to be the perception that this will be in the form of a physical frontal assault, or perhaps a placed improvised explosive device (IED) which will wreak physical damage on the facility, and of course that has to be a consideration that we will discuss. But we also need to understand that groups such as al-Qaeda and Islamic State who are capable of such attacks, have also been planning to deliver a cyber campaign against critical infrastructures. So, in this subchapter we will examine the threats from terrorist organisations that may consider the options of physical and cyberattacks against CIs.

Physical

Attackers who have identified critical infrastructure as legitimate targets have one aim, and that is to physically damage or destroy as much of the infrastructure as possible, and if that means fatalities, well so be it. It is of course a significant bonus if critical infrastructure interdependency is also impacted, as that means there will be greater damage to the nation.

The terrorist is of course is presented with a number of options in relation to the weapons systems available for him or her to carry out a physical attack against a CI.

- *Improvised explosive device (IED).*

   The IED will be covered on detail in the following chapter, but suffice it to say that this particular weapons platform is tried and trusted by international terrorist groups, with levels of success unparalleled over the years of its deployment. It can be placed, contained in some form of container such as a rucksack or a briefcase, or it may be delivered in the form of a vehicle-borne IED, with the device placed in the delivery platform, which is the car or truck.

- *Incendiary devices*

   The incendiary device was probably most effective when used by the Provisional Irish Republican Army (PIRA) during the period 1970 to 1990, in what was referred to as 'the troubles'. Incendiary weapons, incendiary devices, incendiary munitions, or incendiary bombs are weapons designed to start fires or destroy sensitive equipment using fire (and sometimes used as anti-personnel weaponry), which use materials such as napalm, thermite, magnesium powder, chlorine trifluoride, or white phosphorus. Though colloquially often known as bombs, they are not explosives but in fact are designed to slow the process of chemical reactions and use ignition rather than detonation to start and or maintain the reaction.[55]

- *Rocket-propelled grenades (RPG)*

   The rocket propelled grenade (RPG) is essentially a rocket launcher that fires a projectile complete with warhead at a target. The missile isn't guided in any way, and historically that has been its greatest flaw, however, it does have a good track record of success.

The RPG is a relatively basic weapons systems, but the RPG-7, which is Russian built, has been successfully used by a plethora of global terrorist organisations for decades, and there is no reason why it could not be used against perhaps a gas/oil installation or a power station.

- *Marauding terrorist attacks*

Marauding terrorist attacks are fast-moving, violent incidents where assailants move through a location aiming to find and kill or injure as many people as possible. Most deaths occur within the first few minutes of the attack, before police are able to respond.[56]

Mumbai

Probably the highest profile marauding terrorist attack in recent years took place in Mumbai, India in 2008, when ten terrorists entered Mumbai and proceeded to attack 12 coordinated shootings and bombings which lasted for four days. Attackers targeted a train station, hotels, restaurants, a police station and a hospital. Hostages were taken at some locations and eight explosions were reported over the four days. The hostage crisis in the Taj Mahal Palace Hotel ended with a raid on 29 November.[57]

As a result of the attack, 166 people were killed and 600 injured.

Paris

On 13 November 2013, Multiple attacks took place across Paris killing 137 including seven perpetrators. Three terrorist teams composed of at least nine attackers carried out six separate attacks. One team of three detonated outside of the Stade de France at different times, killing only one civilian. Another team of three attacked bars and restaurants across Paris, one detonating his vest in a restaurant at Boulevard Voltaire. The final team took hostages at the Bataclan theatre, massacring attendees of a concert while holding them hostage. All three detonated during the raid of the Bataclan.

These are two examples of many such attacks that have taken place over the years, and inevitably the focus, quite correctly in my opinion, has been on the number of bystanders, because that is exactly what they were, have been killed during the attacks. I am not supporting the idea that such an attack may take place against a power station or a data centre, because I don't believe a great deal would be gained by the terrorist, except of course for publicity reasons.

National authorities should be concerned that the same levels of energy could be generated to attack a number of CI installations simultaneously, with the terrorist aim being to capture hostages in order to operationally take over the installation. The successful capture of a number of power stations may mean the national grid of that country would be incapacitated, with a massive loss of power to interdependent CI installations. Equally, a similar attack against a number of data centres, with the aim of destroying the structure and data held, may be catastrophic.

Of course, you may believe that this is science fiction, but unfortunately I remind you of that allegedly unforeseen day in September 2001, when an act of terrorism took place, against the most powerful country on the planet. Three thousand innocent individuals were killed as the result of an attack, which equally, the day before would have been seen as an act of science fiction; we ignore worst-case scenarios at our peril.

- *Sabotage and the insider threat*

    The *Cambridge Dictionary* argues that sabotage is to *damage or destroy equipment, weapons, or buildings in order to prevent the success of an enemy or competitor.*[58] The worrying aspect of this scenario is the fact that sabotage from within is probably the easiest means of attacking a critical infrastructure location, with the reason being that the saboteur under such conditions will be convinced that he or she understands the vulnerabilities of the system, and they will ultimately have the opportunity to carry out the attack.

    An insider is someone who (knowingly or unknowingly) misuses legitimate access to commit a malicious act or damage their employer. These days, most insider acts involve IT exploitation termed 'Cyber Insider'.[59]

    Varonis[60] support CPNI by saying that an insider threat is a security risk that originates within the targeted organisation. This doesn't mean that the actor must be a current employee or officer in the organisation. They could be a consultant, former employee, business partner, or board member.

    Thirty-four percent of data breaches in the 2019 Verizon Data Breach Investigations Report involve internal actors. According to the 2019 Varonis Data Risk Report, 17% of all sensitive files were accessible to every employee. So what do these statistics tell us? Insiders have the capabilities, motivations, and privileges needed to steal important data – which makes it a CISO's job to identify and build a defence against all of those attack vectors.

    Anyone who has insider knowledge and/or access to the organisation's confidential data, IT, or network resources is a potential insider threat.

- *Chemical, biological, radiological or nuclear (CBRN) weapons*

    The ultimate threat to CI has to be the result of a CBRN attack. So let us break that down, with an understanding of what is meant by CBRN.

- **Chemical**

    The Organisation for the Prohibition of Chemical Weapons (OPCW) says that a chemical weapon is a chemical used to cause intentional death or harm through its toxic properties. Munitions, devices, and other equipment specifically designed to weaponise toxic chemicals also fall under the definition of chemical weapons.

    Further, a common conception of a chemical weapon (CW) is of a toxic chemical contained in a delivery system such as a bomb or artillery shell. While technically correct, a definition based on this conception would only cover a small portion of the range of things the Chemical Weapons Convention (CWC) prohibits as 'chemical weapons'.

    Under the CWC, the definition of a chemical weapon includes all toxic chemicals and their precursors, except when used for purposes permitted by the Convention – in quantities consistent with such a purpose.[61]

- **Biological**

  Most biological weapons systems are designed to deliver life-threatening diseases such as bacteria, fungi, toxins, and so forth – any known disease that is harmful to man.

  Biological weapons are normally referred to as the prime delivery system used in non-conventional warfare, with the perception of the use of weapons of mass destruction (WMD) being used on a battlefield to cause the annihilation of enemy forces. However, that is not to say that the same type of weaponry could not be used in a more restricted environment such as a power station of a water filtration centre to cause maximum casualties on a long-term basis.

- **Radiological**

  The ease of recovery from [a radiological] attack would depend to a great extent on how the attack was handled by first responders, political leaders, and the news media, all of which would help to shape public opinion and reactions.

  Making the Nation Safer National Research Council (2002)

  Radiological effects normally follow the detonation of some form of nuclear weapons and are left dispersed across large areas for a significant period of time. If ingested in way by humans, animals and wildlife, death is almost certain. However, one of the greatest concerns recently has been the detonation of what is referred to as a 'dirty bomb' by a terrorist organisation.

  A "dirty bomb" is constructed by the combination of conventional explosives and some form of radiological material. When the IED is detonated there is the normal effect of a bomb explosion, with the damage that can inflict, and this is added to by the spread of radiological contamination. Whilst of course this may pale into insignificance when compared to a military-grade nuclear attack, but a "dirty bomb" strategically detonated in, let us say, a busy city centre would create havoc. The immediate impact of the explosive device, perhaps supported by shrapnel (nails, concrete, etc.) and the lingering radiological contamination would mean that the area would be exposed for a number of years.

- **Nuclear**

  The ultimate and most dreaded scenario in the context of an attack against a critical infrastructure must be the use of a nuclear weapon by a terrorist organisation, because of the devastation and long-term effects. I am not suggesting for one minute that a terrorist will ever be able to deliver a nuclear weapon in conventional warfare terms (i.e. using either an aircraft or a missile), but the use of a placed tactical nuclear weapon must be considered.

  The considered opinion of the majority of counterterrorism experts throughout the world is that the likelihood of a terrorist group being able to deliver a tactical nuclear device is extremely low, and that nation states should be concentrating their resources on the battle against conventional terrorist warfare.

  A nuclear terrorist attack would have grave consequences, but it is currently not a realistic or viable threat given that it would require a level of sophistication from terrorists that has not yet been witnessed (Ward, 2018).

I do not disagree with the above argument, and from a risk perspective that makes a great deal of sense; however, as I have previously argued, we dismiss worst-case scenarios at our peril.

The main points of consideration to be taken from this section are not the individual definitions of chemical, biological, radiological, or nuclear (CBRN) weapons, but rather the fact that should such weapons fall into the hands of international terrorists, they could be used against any critical infrastructure with devastating effects.

Cyber

Critical infrastructure has been reliant on information technology for some time, and it has always been recognised that if the cybercriminal or cyberterrorist is able to hack a CI IT system, they will have access to information and data that can be used to attack and potentially severely damage or destroy the remainder of a critical infrastructure. Attacks such as malware and DDoS have been the prime platforms which have aided the cyber attacker. However, that landscape has begun to change with the convergence of IT and OT systems.

Information technology (IT) systems are designed to carry digital information which is the platform for most electronic systems today. Current IT systems can deliver data very quickly, with bandwidths (volume of the transmission) being incomparable to only a few years ago, and if an IT system is successfully attacked by a hacker it can cause untold damage to business. Operational Technology (OT) enables machinery to be managed and monitored remotely, so there is less of a need to man control rooms and alarm centres, however it is probably more critical because an attack may lead to loss of life.

Historically, the OT remained separated, or "air-gapped", from the internal IT networks connected to the Internet; however, this is now changing dramatically. For a number of reasons, predominantly speed and cost, organisations are transmitting IT and OT signals along the same telemetry infrastructure, and that means of course that if a hacker is successful at breaching a network, he or she is not only in a position to attack the IT framework, but also the OT infrastructure. Organisations and companies need to think long and hard about this coordination of IT and OT data transmission.

The protection of critical infrastructure (CI)

The first step in the protection of critical infrastructure is a recognition of what the impact of a successful attack may be. What damage can be done, and who will be affected. Only then can protective measure be undertaken. Once this has been achieved, any element of critical infrastructure has to be protected in an equivalent manner to other physical assets, and their supporting digital processes.

The protective approach begins with a security risk assessment (SRA) during which all assets will be identified, with threat and vulnerability assessments being carried out. As part of the SRA, some form of operational requirement should be specified, with my preference being the CPNI Operational Requirements 1 and 2 (see www.cpni.gov.uk/operational-requirements).

Once the SRA has taken place, a security survey (see page 116–136) of all physical and digital systems should be carried out to determine what systems are fit for purpose, and to pay attention to those that are not.

The next phase of the protection program is to upgrade or replace those systems that have been identified as not fit for purpose, with the CPNI OR 2 being used in support.

This is probably the most difficult part of the programme, because there is likely to be a budgetary requirement for replacement systems, and of course that means convincing the chief finance officer that it is in the best interests of the organisation to invest in security (yet again!). Far too often, even though compelling evidence may have been submitted, funds for upgrades or replacements are withheld, and that can be critical, verging on disastrous.

Cyber-NHS and ransomware

In May 2018, the British National Health Service (NHS) was attacked, it is believed by North Korean cyber hackers using a piece of malware, referred to as 'WannaCry', also known as ransomware, because the attackers demanded payment to have the software removed.

The NHS IT system at that time was using Windows XP, an operating system that was 17 years old and was recognised as being prone to malware attacks; but despite a number of warnings from independent cyber specialists the NHS refused to upgrade to Windows 10, and the successful attack, closing down 200,000 NHS computers, caused 19,000 appointments to be cancelled. The cost of the attack was £20 million, and the consequent clean-up and upgrade cost a further £72 million.

I have not viewed the IT risk assessment carried out before the attack, if indeed one was in existence, but it is likely that one of the recommendations would have been to upgrade all operating systems to a platform that would robustly defend the NHS IT system against this form of attack; and it is equally likely that the upgrade didn't take place because of the financial austerity measures in place at the time.

Of course we all possess a PhD in hindsight, and it is extremely easy to criticise the management of an event with post incident evidence, however, I am convinced that had there been an effective IT SRA carried out, supported by a robust business case, the WannaCry attack may not have occurred, but had it taken place, it probably would have failed, or at least have been mitigated.

As previously mentioned, and as evidenced in the WannaCry scenario, probably the greatest threat to any critical infrastructure derives from the cybercriminal or terrorist, whose sole intent is to destabilise or destroy the Critical Infrastructure by attacking one or all of the following three support mechanisms:

* **Information Technology (IT)**

    The term 'information technology' has been used, probably since the 1970s, with the advent of personal computing, and describes how technologically, information and data can be managed quickly, effectively and under some circumstances, securely. Today, IT systems are the backbone of all systems, whether they are physical or digital. In the WannaCry example, once the NHS had been infected, with at least 200,000 computers being temporarily disabled, staff were forced to resort to the use of paper and pen; I am sure somewhat reluctantly, but at least that was the contingency option and I assume they were competent in the use of hard copy. I was travelling in the US in 2012, and I decided to hire a motor vehicle from an international car hire firm for the final leg of my journey. I booked the vehicle online, with an agreed time and date (one week in the future) for me to pick up my means of transportation. On the arranged day, I duly arrived at the car hire location, only to be informed that the company IT system 'was down' and the branch manager was waiting for IT support to have it up and running again, sometime later that day. When I asked him what his IT contingency plans were, he stared at me as though I had just asked the most bizarre question. The contingency was to wait for IT, 'and no, we don't resort to paper and pen; it's not what we do. This after all the 21st century'.

Of course, critical infrastructures will be protected by international standards such as ISO 27001 (Information Security Systems), BS 11200 (Crisis Management), ISO 22301 (Business Continuity), and so on, and that is fine. However, I'm sure the NHS was also protected by similar standards, but they didn't prevent the WannaCry attack.

The criminal is very aware of the reliance on sound IT systems in use by all organisations today, and critical infrastructure is no different. If an IT system can be successfully attacked, there will be overwhelming results from the loss of information.

- **Operational technology**

The main problem that must be faced by the management teams at any critical infrastructure site is that whilst a breach of IT security tends to mean a loss of data and information, which will of course be detrimental to the operational effectiveness of the plant. A violation of OT security may mean injury to personnel, perhaps even fatalities because safety systems are reliant on OT.

The UK National Cyber Security Centre points out that where cyber security for IT has traditionally been concerned with information confidentiality, integrity and availability, OT priorities are often safety, reliability and availability, as there are clearly physical dangers associated with OT failure or malfunction. Many businesses strive for improved OT process efficiency and reliability for their customers, which often results in increased connectivity to enterprise technologies and the Internet. This convergence has the potential to increase system vulnerabilities, but can be addressed by adopting sound risk management principles, which are the same regardless of the underlying system type. Furthermore, many OT environments form part of the UK's Critical National Infrastructure, so disruption to services that they control is potentially of concern.[62]

The main hurdle as far as OT security is concerned is convergence – convergence with networking interfaces that draw cybercriminals, and almost encourage hacking. Historically, operational technology has required a physical human presence to manage the systems that required OT, generally meaning that there would be isolated control rooms, in which a workforce would operate the switch gear and control devices to ensure that the technology required was operating correctly. Meaning that to attack such systems the criminals and terrorists would require access to the control room, or perhaps the spider web of cabling and pipework, in order to do any damage. Recently, and of course it was inevitable, such OT systems have been able to be operated and managed remotely through the use of networking interfaces, leading to a convergence of IT and OT infrastructures. So instead of burgling the control room, or physically attacking cables and pipes, which was never simple, all that is required is a seasoned cyber hacker who will attack the IT network, allowing access to the operational technology systems. Maximum devastation without moving from the office or bedroom. Job done.

- **Supervisory Control and Data Acquisition (SCADA)**

    A SCADA system gathers information, such as where a leak on a pipeline has occurred, transfers the information back to a central site, alerting the home station that the leak has occurred, carrying out necessary analysis and control, such as determining if the leak is critical, and displaying the information in a logical and organised fashion.

    SCADA systems can be relatively simple, such as one that monitors environmental conditions of a small office building, or incredibly complex, such as a system that monitors all the activity in a nuclear power plant or the activity of a municipal water system.[63]

    So as with IT and OT systems, SCADA is critical for the operational effectiveness of a critical infrastructure, and it needs to be protected at all times.

    In the first instance, whether it is IT, OT, or SCADA, there needs to be a recognition that all network interfaced systems need the same cyber protection within critical infrastructure as with any other organisation. Processes such as security awareness, protection against all manner of malware threats, and support from senior management to ensure that all resources available are committed to the protection of networked critical infrastructure.

Exercise Brave Defender – task 8: critical national infrastructure

Synopsis

As mentioned within the chapter, telecommunication is very much an integral element of a nation's critical infrastructure. Much like the national power grid, the country relies on a communications and data flow network that must be rigorous enough to continue all operations under all circumstances.

Task

Britcom has a number of data centres (DC) throughout the world, and in anticipation of one or a number of DCs being included in a critical national infrastructure, the executive board has tasked you with compiling a report in relation to the minimum physical and digital standards each DC will need to be compliant with.

   You are to write the report, which will be divided between physical and digital standards in such a way that all board members will understand. Bullet pointed notes will suffice.

3.9 Terrorism and counterterrorism

Definitions and identification of terrorism

> **Pause for thought**
>
> In your own words, define terrorism.

Where to begin.

First things first. Nobody has an absolute right to push theirs or anybody else's defini-tion of terrorism, as defining this abhorrent act is too complex. I will, however, offer a number of opinions and arguments during this section, some of which you may agree with and others that you are less likely be persuaded by.

I suspect that if you asked a number of random passers-by on any street corner what their definition of terrorism was, you would probably receive answers such as "People who want to kill us to take over the government" or "Zealots who want to push their religious beliefs on to us", or perhaps "Lunatics who just want to kill innocent civilians".

Memories are very short, and although thousands of people, on both sides of the divide were killed during what was referred to as 'the troubles' in Northern Ireland between 1969 and 1998, visons are blurred in terms of what the Provisional Irish Republican Army (PIRA) or the Ulster Defence Association (UDA) stood for. It is possible that because of the hor-rendous terrorist attacks by al-Qaeda against the Twin Towers of the World Trade Center in New York on 11 September 2001 and the recent atrocities carried out by the Islamic State Group in Syria that people may be tempted to believe that terrorism is relatively new.

However, terrorism is as old as civilisation, and as new as this morning's headlines. For some, it seems obvious that individuals and organisations have used terrorism for millen-nia, whilst others insist that real terrorism has only been around for decades. Both camps are right – up to a point. The weapons, methods, and goals of terrorists constantly change, but core features have remained since the earliest times: Clodius Pulcher, the Roman patrician who used murderous gangs to intimidate his opponents; the dagger-wielding Sicarri of Judea, who hoped to provoke war with the Romans; twelfth-century assassins who killed and terrorised their Muslim rivals; medieval scholars who quoted scripture to justify killing rulers – all these are examples of terrorism, and all predate the advent of the word 'terrorism' in revolutionary France (Law, 2016).

However, that still doesn't take us any closer to defining terrorism, an exercise that is one of the most difficult to carry out in the pursuit of understanding what this phenomenon is.

A definition recommended by Walker and Osborne (2010), which mirrors that offered by the FBI as an operational definition, is 'the use of serious violence against persons or property, or threat to use such violence, to intimidate or coerce a government, the public or a section of the public, in order to promote political, social or ideological objectives'.

The legal definition as found in the UK Terrorism Act 2000 states that 'terrorism' means the use or threat of action where:

1   It involves serious violence against a person, involves serious damage to property, endangers a person's life (other than that of the person committing the action), cre-ates a serious risk to the health or safety of the public or a section of the public, or is designed seriously to interfere with or seriously to disrupt an electronic system;
2   It is designed to influence the government, or an international government organisa-tion, or to intimidate the public or a section of the public; and
3   Is made for the purpose of advancing a political, religious, racial or ideological cause.

The United States has defined terrorism under the Federal Criminal Code. Title 18 of the United States Code defines terrorism and lists the crimes associated with terrorism. Section 2331 of Chapter 113(B) defines terrorism as

activities that involve violent . . . or life-threatening acts . . . that are a violation of the criminal laws of the United States or of any State and . . . appear to be intended (i) to intimidate or coerce a civilian population; (ii) to influence the policy of a government by intimidation or coercion; or (iii) to affect the conduct of a government by mass destruction, assassination, or kidnapping; and. . . (C) occur primarily within the territorial jurisdiction of the United States.

The European Union defines terrorism for legal/official purposes in Art. 1 of the Framework Decision on Combating Terrorism (2002). This provides that terrorist offences are certain criminal offences set out in a list comprised largely of serious offences against persons and property which,

> given their nature or context, may seriously damage a country or an international organization where committed with the aim of: seriously intimidating a population; or unduly compelling a Government or international organization to perform or abstain from performing any act; or seriously destabilizing or destroying the fundamental political, constitutional, economic or social structures of a country or an international organization.

So although there is such a diversification of terrorism definitions on a global scale, the fact of the matter is that there are still a number of groups and organisations in existence that see themselves as responsible for changing, by whatever means necessary, the methods that governments act and control their populations and cultures; they are often referred to as terrorists, and they originate from a variety of cultural and geographical locations.

The psychology and rationale of terrorism

The first questions that are constantly asked after a terrorist attack are "Why did they do that?" and "Why do they want to be terrorists?"

* Why did al-Qaeda kill 3,000 people in New York on 11 September 2001?
* Why did four young Muslims kill 58 people in a suicide attack on the London transportation systems in July 2005?
* Why did Boko Haram kill 67 innocent civilians in a restaurant in Nigeria in July 2005?
* Why did Islamic State murder 300 migrants in Libya in January 2016?

The answer is far from simple, but if terrorism is ever to be defeated, we must try to understand what compels the terrorist to commit, in the eyes of innocent bystanders, murder for political, perhaps religious, and certainly ideological reasons.

John Horgan (2005) postulates that very often, it seems that the goal of terrorism is simply to create widespread fear, arousal and uncertainty on a wider, more distant scale than that achieved by targeting the victim alone, *thereby* influencing the political process and how it normally be expected to function. Horgan goes on to explain that an important and alternative defining feature of terrorism is that for terrorists there is a distinction to be made between the immediate target of *violence and terror* and the overall target of *terror*; between the terrorists immediate victim (such as the person who has died from a bombing or a shooting) and the terrorists *opponent* (which for many terrorist movements represent a government.

As far as I am concerned, Horgan has explained the terrorist rationale very clearly.

When contemplating the phrase "One man's terrorist . . .", it becomes fairly obvious that there is certainly no simple definition or pen picture of a terrorist. However, what is self-evident is the fact that through the centuries, bands or groups, and at times individuals, who are disincentivised are consumed with the belief that the only way to change tyrannical governments or defend against an invading force is through the use of political violence – but why attack innocent civilians?

Let's take a look at the Middle East.

There has been conflict between Arab countries and the Jewish race for centuries, but in relatively recent times this confrontation came to a head during the Six-Day War of 1967, when the Israeli Defence Forces, after heavily defeating the armed forces of Egypt, Syria, and Jordan, invaded and occupied the Jordanian West Bank, including Jerusalem; beginning what has now been over 50 years of armed conflict in that area. Palestinians who previously occupied the West Bank claim sovereignty, and Israel, having constructed hundreds of homes for their people in the West Bank, will not surrender the spoils of war.

Israel has invaded Lebanon on a number of occasions (1978 and 1982) in an effort to destroy Shia Muslim resistance and create a buffer zone to protect the civilian population of northern Israel. However, after the invasion in 1982, the world witnessed the birth of a new resistance organisation that was to challenge the state of Israel to this day, and in my opinion Israel really only has itself to blame for the upsurge of Arab resistance.

However, as Norton (2007) explains, even if Israel had not launched its invasion of southern Lebanon in 1982, the young would-be revolutionaries among the Shia would have pursued their path of emulating Iran's Islamic revolution. Undoubtably, however, the invasion pushed the Shia further in this direction, creating conditions for the establishment and flourishing of Hezbollah. Former Israeli Prime Minister Ehud Barak put the matter succinctly in 2006: "When we entered Lebanon . . . there was no Hezbollah. We were accepted with perfumed rice and flowers by the Shia in the South. It was our presence there that created Hezbollah" (*Newsweek*, 18 July 2006).

As Barak's comment suggests, by occupying Lebanon rather than promptly withdrawing, Israel wore out its welcome and provided a context for Hezbollah to grow.

Another Israeli prime minister, Yitzhak Rabin, who was assassinated in 1995, made precisely the same point in 1987, speaking of how Israel had let the "genie out of the bottle".

Since the invasions, I am sure Hezbollah would protest that the Israeli Defence Forces (IDF) are responsible for the deaths of many Arabs (accusing the IDF of state terrorism), and that they (Hezbollah) must protect their people. Hezbollah might further argue that as they do not possess powerful armed forces to combat the Israelis, the only recourse they have is to carry out long-range rocket attacks against Israeli cities and close-quarter suicide operations, with injured and dead Israeli civilians being collateral war damage.

To the populations of cities in Israel of course, such attacks, accompanied by Arab suicide bombers who attack synagogues during holy days, are carried out by terrorists, because in the name of Allah, they murder innocent Israeli men, women, and children. Hezbollah believe this is the only means at their disposal to deter the IDF from attacking Arab counties and their people.

One man's terrorist is another man's freedom fighter.

Of course, people clearly don't wake up in the morning thinking that without any provocation or malice, they would become terrorists. No, terrorism scholars will tell you that terrorists are generally taken on a journey towards terrorism, and that is known as radicalisation.

Radicalisation and de-radicalisation

Just a thought

In your own words, define the terms 'radicalisation' and 'de-radicalisation'.

Radicalisation

The psychology of terrorism is the subject of a great deal of academic debate. It is widely accepted that extremist beliefs are exceptional and develop over time in particular social and political circumstances. It is this period of development which provides an opportunity to identify where extremist beliefs are emerging. The way in which people move towards extremist beliefs is often referred to as 'radicalisation'. It is simply a process by which people adopt an interpretation of religious, political, or ideological beliefs that may ultimately, but not necessarily, lead to their legitimising the use of violence through acts of terrorism (Walker and Osborne, 2010).[64]

Radicalisation unfortunately is too often labelled as a process only used by Islamic fundamentalist extremists, but that is an inaccurate portrayal of a tactic that, it is probably correct to say, has been used since extremist organisations realised that generally the young and vulnerable in their immediate communities were easy targets.

The National Society for the Prevention of Cruelty to Children (NSPCC)[65] says that 'radicalisation is the way a person (normally young and vulnerable)[66] comes to support or be involved in extremism and terrorism. It's a gradual process so young people who are affected may not realise what's happening'.

The organisation then goes on to warn that radicalisation is a form of harm. The process may involve:

- Being groomed online or in person
- Exploitation, including sexual exploitation
- Psychological manipulation
- Exposure to violent material and other inappropriate information
- The risk of physical harm or death through extremist acts.

Anyone can be radicalised, but there are some factors which may make a young person more vulnerable. These include:

- Being easily influenced or impressionable
- Having low self-esteem or being isolated
- Feeling that rejection, discrimination, or injustice is taking place in society
- Experiencing community tension amongst different groups
- Being disrespectful or angry towards family and peers
- Having a strong need for acceptance or belonging
- Experiencing grief, such as loss of a loved one.

Indicators that a child is being radicalised include:

- Becoming disrespectful and intolerant of others
- Becoming more angry

- Avoiding discussions about their views
- Using words and phrases that sound scripted
- Becoming isolated and secretive
- Not wanting to anyone else to know what they are looking at online.

From 1969 to when the Good Friday Agreement was signed in 1998, there had been continuous conflict which began in Northern Ireland, and later extended to the UK mainland and Europe. The Provisional IRA were prepared to take their fight, as they saw it, to the British wherever insurgency was required. In order to achieve what was in fact military resistance, the Provos (as they were often referred to, sometimes as a badge of honour) needed finance, weapons and ammunition, and logistics on a grand scale. Finance was provided in abundance by sources in the Republic of Ireland, the US and even Australia, but manpower was home-grown; and it was generally achieved by some form of radicalisation.

Youngsters in West Belfast or Londonderry would belong to families that had been involved in insurrection against the British for decades, and there was an expectancy for young boys (mainly) to follow in their fathers' footsteps and fight for the Fenian cause at an early age.

Of course, it was recognised that a teenager, probably still attending school, would eventually be accepted or even relied upon to engage in a firefight with British soldiers, or perhaps plant an improvised explosive device (IED) near a police station or military establishment; but that would come later. There was a recruitment and training process, during which the newly radicalised youth would work his or her way through an informal rank and status structure. This would mean that the new recruit would probably begin life as an apprentice terrorist by hanging around street corners, reporting on army and police movements in their sector of responsibility. Invariably, if sufficient progress was made, the apprentice would move through a series of responsibilities, such as driving, delivering IED component parts and other weapons to senior members, until the day came when they would be accepted into an active service unit (ASU), consisting of no more than four members, and be instructed to carry out a more responsible task, such as planting the IED or engaging police and military targets.

In Palestine the situation has been very similar, but instead of the enemy being the Royal Ulster Constabulary (now the Police Service of Northern Ireland) or the British Army, the target for Islamist fundamentalist extremists was (is) the Israeli Defence Force (IDF) and any vulnerable Israeli targets available.

In the UK, during the last two decades there has been a massive increase in Islamist radicalisation, mainly targeting young Muslim students away from home attending university. University students have been identified by groups such as Jamat-e-Islami led by Abul Ala Mawdudi as being not only vulnerable, but also being in possession of an appetite to learn (otherwise, why are they attending university?). Of course, UK universities have a reputation for encouraging free thought and freedom of speech, and it is therefore totally logical for extremist organisation, through the manipulation of individuals and groups, to be successful at delivering radicalisation programmes.

In one of the most open and honest books written about radicalisation from the point of view of the victim or target, is the book *The Islamist*, written by Ed Husain (2007). Husain describes his early life when, as a Muslim living in the UK amongst a very strong nuclear family, dominated by his father and a Muslim preacher referred to as his Grandpa, when, as a member of the Young Muslim Organisation (YMO) he was swayed and indeed radicalised by two particular extreme Islamist groups, Jamat-e-Islami, and Hizb ut–Tahrir.

These particular Islamist organisations believed in the distinction between Muslims who worshipped and paid homage to the Muslim religion and extremist Muslims who believed that Islam should not just be a religion but should dominate politics, government, and ideology in all Muslim communities. Hizb ut–Tahrir (Hizb), with its violent extremist views, brought Husain into direct conflict with the family that he loved, and initially he was prepared to forgo his family loyalties in favour of his new Islamist peers. That was until, in his own words,

> Just as I had become a member of the HIZB over a period of time, my departure from the organisation did not occur on a specific date. Attraction and commitment to extremism have always been part of a gradual process. My first move away was to disassociate myself from the '*halaqah*',[67] a move prompted by the taking of an innocent life, Omar Bakri's[68] subsequent deceit, and my horror when I realised how poisonous was the atmosphere I had helped to create. Most important of these was the murder – the Hizb's idea had led to the belief that the life of a *kafir*[69] was of little consequence in attaining Muslim dominance. I could not bear to be associated with such ideas any longer. I was frightened of where they might lead. Did I really want to follow a credo that led to violence and murder? I had advocated the ideas of Muslim domination, confrontation and jihad, never for one moment thinking that their catastrophic consequences would arrive on my doorstep. It had all seemed abstract and remote, relevant for Bosnia or the Middle East, not Britain.

De-radicalisation and disengagement

As a result of the overwhelming preoccupation with uncovering the process of radicalisation into terrorist activity, little attention has been paid to the related yet distinct processes of disengagement and de-radicalisation from terrorism. This continuing neglect is ironic because it may be in the analysis of disengagement that *practical initiatives* for counterterrorism may become more apparent in their development and feasible in their execution. While a variety of de-radicalisation initiatives worldwide are currently receiving enormous interest from afar, it is inevitable they will be subjected to intense scrutiny regarding their alleged outcomes and claimed successes.

A more immediate challenge, however, is to assert some conceptual and terminological clarity. While *de-radicalisation* has become the latest buzzword in counterterrorism, it is critical that we distinguish it from *disengagement* and stress that not only are they different, but that just because one leaves terrorism behind, it rarely implies (or even necessitates) that one become 'de-radicalised'. One of several implications arising from this distinction may be a more realistic appraisal of how our knowledge and understanding of the disengagement processes (and not undefined and poorly conceptualised de-radicalisation efforts) may be put to effective use in the short- to medium-term development of research agendas (Horgan, 2005). So, having established a relationship between disengagement and de-radicalisation, we now need to understand what radicalisation programmes are available.

It is safe to say that Husain was radicalised by a very powerful extremist organisation, Hizb ut–Tahrir, and he was probably seen as quite an easy target because he was already a devoted follower of Islam, and he had almost no social life until he began to pray at a number of mosques that had been infiltrated by the Young Muslim Organisation (YMO) and Hizb ut–Tahrir.

He was extremely fortunate to have the support of his family and the strength to deny extremist Islamists when he was being coerced to carry out acts of political violence and murder. In a sense, Ed Husain disengaged himself from the extremist groups that he had been associated with and then de-radicalised himself. He was very fortunate; not all radicalised targets are so lucky.

Having researched the concept of de-radicalisation, I am of the opinion that individual nation states define and react to de-radicalisation in a number of ways, and the term 'de-radicalisation' is incredibly blurred, primarily because it is extremely difficult to measure the results of any de-radicalisation programme.

One such programme that is held in high esteem is the Prevent programme in the United Kingdom, but even this established programme is far from clear in its aims and objectives; it is certainly not the definitive de-radicalisation programme that it is published as being.

In section 3.8 of the preface to the official UK government document covering Prevent,[70] the definition reads as 'Prevent is part of our counter-terrorism strategy, CONTEST. Its aim *is to stop people becoming terrorists or supporting terrorism*'.

So here is an ambiguity, because as mentioned, the vast numbers of referrals to the Prevent programme describe it as a de-radicalisation strategy, but it appears that it was designed to identify and rehabilitate radicalisation targets before they were drawn into whatever extremist group they were attractive to.

So, my argument is this. It is far more effective to identify radicalisation targets before they are 'captured', because once they are drawn into an extremist organisation, such as Hizb ut–Tahrir or Islamic State, it is incredibly difficult to positively disengage and then de-radicalise the terrorist. Better to prevent than repair.

Terrorist methods of operation and attack platforms

"You have to be lucky all of the time, we only have to be lucky once".[71]

As terrorism has developed over the centuries, so has the terrorist's method of operation and weapons of choice. Intrinsically, the terrorist will choose whatever weapon is available to him or her, after examining the defensive posture of the target.

Before an attack, the terrorist active service unit (ASU) will carry out a reconnaissance of the target and its location; for all intents and purposes this will be a risk assessment. Unless the method of attack is that of a suicide bombing, the terrorist wants to carry out the attack and make a safe escape. It is during the research and reconnaissance phases of the attack that the terrorist will (if it is within their gift) choose the most appropriate weapons system for the attack.

Let us now take a look at a number of terrorist organisations and the methods of operation favoured by them.

- *The Sicarri (Jewish Daggermen)*

  The Sicarri were a group of Jewish zealots, who in AD 70, took it upon themselves to evict the Roman army from Judea by means of what may be seen as the first suicide attacks. Their method of operation was to discreetly enter a Roman camp and try to kill as many Roman soldiers as possible, by stabbing and slashing with a small curved knife known as the sicarri, before they were slain by what they believed was an invading force.

- *The French Revolution*

The reign of terror, or 'the terror', was brought upon the people of France during the French revolution (1793–94). The terror was instigated as a deterrent to any French citizens who may have been considering defection to foreign hostile forces that had surrounded France at that time.

During the terror, the Revolutionary Committee, led by the Jacobean Maximillian de Robespierre, was responsible for the execution of 17,000 French men, women and children, whilst 10,000 of their fellow French citizens died in prison after being incarcerated without trial. The guillotine was the favoured method of execution.

Robespierre is believed to have said when asked his opinion of terrorism:

> Terror is only justice: prompt, severe and inflexible; it is then an emanation of virtue; it is less a distinct principle than a natural consequence of the general principle of democracy, applied to the most pressing wants of the country.

- *Guy Fawkes and the gunpowder plot*

In 1605, Guy Fawkes and a group of Catholic conspirators planned to kill King James of England and his parliamentary colleagues because they believed that the king was purging Catholics in England by having churches burned to the ground and all Catholic priests deported to France and Spain.

The conspirators, since referred to as terrorists, planted almost forty barrels of gunpowder (high explosives) in the cellar of the Houses of Parliament, with the intention of killing all within. Fortunately for the parliamentarians, and unfortunately for Fawkes et al., the explosives were discovered by an alert guard, and Fawkes was arrested. He and his colleagues were detained in the Tower of London, and under the orders of the king were tortured until they confessed. After a short trial, in January 1606 they were hung, drawn and quartered, with their heads placed on the railings surrounding the Houses of Parliament as a warning to other aspiring terrorists.

New wave terrorism

In the twentieth and twenty first century, three organisations have dominated the headlines in terms of terrorist attacks, and they are the Provisional Irish Republican Army (PIRA), al-Qaeda, and Islamic State. Although PIRA is no longer operational (theoretically), the group has had such a significant impact on modern terrorism that it would be remiss to ignore their 'contribution' to this section. The term 9/11 does and will always strike fear into the hearts of Western countries, as that was the day when the world changed, thanks to al-Qaeda. Islamic State has achieved more military success than any other terrorist organisation, certainly in the last ten centuries.

The Provisional Irish Republican Army

The Provisional Irish Republican Army (PIRA) was born in 1970 when the Official Irish Republican Army (IRA) refused to engage the Royal Ulster Constabulary in defence of Roman Catholics in West Belfast and Londonderry.

In his book *The Provisional IRA: From Insurrection to Parliament*, Mc Kearney (2011) argues that unlike other parts of the United Kingdom, Northern Ireland had a quasi-colonial tradition where one section of the community (Unionists) participated enthusiastically in policing the other (Republicans). He says that it required no con-spiracy to bring great numbers of Protestants into action for what they perceived as defence of the regime. And, as in other parts of the world, where one community takes it upon itself to police the other, the consequences are typically destructive.

So a mood of insurrection by Catholics (Republicans) was beginning to gather momentum, and when others retreated, armed Republicans moved forward with cer-tainty. Mc Kearney argues that if they (PIRA) had not worked out a comprehensive strategy (and they had not), they still appeared to act with assuredness and certainty. While others, advocating reform were trying to gauge whether to appeal to Britain, or attempt to pressurise the London government from without, the Provisional IRA simply said that they intended to arm and fight.

The latter stages of the twentieth century saw the Provisional Irish Republican Army (PIRA) engaging the Crown forces of Great Britain, not only in Norther Ire-land but also on the European mainland.

Initially this consisted of PIRA gunmen, hiding behind crowds of people in Belfast and Londonderry, using them as a human shield whilst they would fire one shot or maybe two from relic rifles at the police and army, before disappearing into the shad-ows and rabbit warrens of Republican areas.

By the early 1970s, PIRA and their political arm, Sinn Fein, had negotiated with Muammar Gadhafi, who was the prime minister of Libya, and he was more than prepared to sell them modern arms, such as Russian-made Kalashnikov AK-47 assault rifles and US-produced general purpose machine guns (GPMG). With this upgraded armoury now in the hands of the Republican terrorists, UK Crown Forces became the targets of far more sophisticated sniper and ambush attacks, and by the mid 1980s PIRA was quite prepared to engage the British Army in firefights using weapons and military tactics honed over the previous 15 years.

Once again, in the early 1970s PIRA began to purchase explosives from Gadhafi, usually Eastern European–made Semtex, which was not only extremely powerful but also very difficult to detect. Initially the PIRA improvised explosive devices (IED) were detonated by command wire, which meant that an electrical current was sent along a cable, to an electric detonator, which activated the main charge (Semtex) of the device, causing a massive explosion and fragmentation.

PIRA then began to use Timer and Power Units (TPU) in their IED's, consisting of a timer and battery which, when the timer ran down would once again fire the detonator, causing the explosion. The original timer was a mechanical device that wound down from 59 minutes to detonation, and this was later replaced by a light emitting diode (LED) timer, infamously used when PIRA attacked the Grand Hotel in Brighton in October 1984, whilst the UK government was in situ. This meant that the terrorist was in a position to hide an IED and make its getaway before it exploded.

The pièce de résistance for PIRA IED attacks was the use of remote controlled (RC) devices. A receiver, usually a cell phone, would be attached to the device, and when a particular signal was sent to the receiver, it would trigger an electronic circuit, which would activate the device.

The final weapon in PIRA's armoury was the improvised mortar. PIRA designed a number of homemade mortars which could be fired from the back of a vehicle. This weapons system was not only devastating in terms of damage inflicted but it was also accurate, robust with a good range.

On 7 February 1991, the Provisional IRA attacked 10 Downing Street, whilst the prime minister, John Major and his cabinet were discussing the Gulf War. Three Mark 10 homemade mortars were fired from a Ford Transit van, with one of the missiles landing in the back garden and the other two narrowly over flying the building. Evidence in the van was destroyed by the back blast of the fired mortars.

Al-Qaeda

Al-Qaeda, literally translated, means 'the base', and when the Soviet Union invaded Afghanistan in 1979, Osama bin Laden and his former university lecturer, Ayman al-Zawahiri, recruited about 40,000 Arab fighters to help their fellow Muslims in the fight against the invading forces. Bin Laden's fighters were then referred to as the Mujahideen, later to be re-named al-Qaeda. Bin Laden was later to be held responsible for the death of 3,000 US citizens on 11 September 2001, when a group of al-Qaeda terrorists highjacked three commercial airliners before crashing them into the North and South Towers of the World Trade Center in New York, and the Pentagon just outside Washington, DC. After Bin Laden was killed, command of al-Qaeda was handed over to Zawahiri.

Whilst Osama bin Laden was commanding his forces during the conflict with the Soviet Union in Afghanistan, there is evidence that he was utilising the experiences gained by PIRA, and textbooks were found describing weapons systems and tactics that had been written by PIRA members whilst incarcerated in prisons in Northern Ireland.

The al-Qaeda weapon of choice initially was the improvised explosive device (IED), which the group used successfully on a number of occasions, mainly against the US and Israel; the group later used a form of attack unforeseen by Western intelligence.

The World Trade Center, New York

On the morning of 26 February 1993, a massive truck bomb ripped a hole almost 30 metres (100 feet) across the B-2 level of the parking garage beneath the World Trade Center's North Tower. The blast wave was so powerful that it penetrated five stories of the reinforced concrete building. In addition to causing structural damage, the explosion destroyed or heavily damaged hundreds of vehicles in the garage. That such a powerful explosion killed only six people is nothing short of a miracle, for the attackers had a goal much more grandiose.

They wanted to topple the North Tower onto the South Tower to destroy them both and kill thousands. Had a device of the same magnitude been detonated at street level during rush hour, it would have likely killed scores if not hundreds of people and wounded perhaps thousands more. Al-Qaeda would eventually admit to carrying out the World Trade Center attack, but it was to be the prelude to probably the most atrocious and devastating terrorist attack in history.

Airborne

Much has been written about the al-Qaeda attacks against the Twin Towers in New York and the Pentagon on 11 September 2001, but what is probably the most interesting, if not frightening aspect of the attack was the method of operation and the weapons used. This atrocity was to alter the perception of terrorism, and the limits of the terrorist's capability and capacity to attack beyond the limits of civilised imagination.

If you had suggested such an attack on 10 September 2001, you would either have been laughed at or arrested under the Mental Health Act (1946). Nobody would have believed you, but God help the souls of those who perished – it happened.

According to the 9/11 Commission Report (2002), the chronology of the attacks on 11 September 2001 is as follows.

- *North Tower*

  At 08:46:40, hijacked American Airlines Flight 11 flew into the upper portion of the North Tower, cutting through floors 93 to 99.

- *South Tower*

  At 09:04:11, hijacked United Airlines Flight 175 hit 2 WTC (the South Tower) from the south, crashing through floors 77 to 85.

- *The Pentagon*

  At 09:37, the west wall of the Pentagon was hit by hijacked American Airlines Flight 77, a Boeing 757. The crash caused immediate and catastrophic damage. All 64 people aboard the airliner were killed, as were 125 people inside the Pentagon.

Islamic State

Holding a number of names, such as the Islamic State of Iraq and the Levant (ISIL), and the Islamic State of Iraq and Syria (ISIS), the organisation generally recognised as Islamic State (IS) sprang to notoriety in 2014 when it won a number of hard-fought military campaigns before being in control of large swathes of Iraq and Syria. IS attempted to fill the vacuum produced by the civil wars fought in the two countries, which were in a state of disarray.

The prime aim of IS was to introduce Sharia law across the region, and carve out for itself a caliphate, which is recognised as an Islamic state under the leadership of a caliph, a political and religious leader who is identified as being the successor to the Prophet Muhammad.

IS took global nations by surprise and was able to mount a number of serious military campaigns, until they took control of and identified the area from Aleppo in Syria to Diyala in Iraq as its caliphate, which was ruled by the cleric Abu Bakr Baghdadi. The cleric killed himself and his two children on 26 October 2019 whilst being pursued by US Special Forces.

Islamic State made a name for itself generally as a military fighting force, and during its short military existence was renowned for its primitive ruthlessness and its propensity to murder Western hostages in front of the world's media.

Weapons systems and their use

- *The improvised explosive device (IED)*

  Going back perhaps as far as the Guy Fawkes gunpowder plot, the vast majority of terrorist organisations have at some time used an IED. Whether it was in its most basic format, consisting of a power source, a detonator and an explosive substance, or whether initiation is by means of a command wire, timer or remote control, the IED has always been an effective means of delivering an explosive terrorist attack. It is relatively simple to construct, and depending on the amount and type of explosives used, extremely effective. The IED over time has been used in a variety of ways.

- *The letter/book IED*

  This form of attack was used extensively through the 1960s and 70s, mainly by groups such as the Italian Red Brigades and the German Baade Meinhof group. The components of the letter and book bombs were very similar to other IEDs but on a smaller scale. Both forms of delivery were designed and constructed to generally attack individuals, who upon opening the letter/book would initiate the explosive charge, and this would either kill or maim a single person. Both means of delivery were unstable, and through the use of x-ray machines, used by postal services were relatively easy to discover. Letter IED's were used to attack members of the Greek Parliament in 2016 but were unsuccessful.

- *The parcel IED*

  A deceptive description because this type of explosive device can be delivered in a number of forms; anything from a small parcel to a briefcase, a suitcase or a rucksack. The major of advantage, from a terrorist perspective is the ease at which a parcel IED can be delivered. A parcel can be left on a reception desk, a briefcase may be left in an office environment, and a suitcase or rucksack can be deposited in a busy train station, bus terminus, or airport. The means of initiation of this form of explosive device is likely to be either a timer connected to the detonator or a remote-control signalling system detonated some distance away from the device.

  Another advantage the terrorist has when deploying the parcel bomb is lethargy, because security teams, and often the police are today so often tasked with investigating suspect devices (parcel, suitcase, rucksack, etc.); and it is a human frailty to become lethargic and 'switch off', thinking "This is bound to be another false alarm, I may as well take a look inside". Wrong, because that is exactly what the terrorist wants and expects.

  Later in this section we will examine a method of managing a situation where a suspect device is found, prior to the arrival of the emergency services. This is referred to as the six Cs.

- *The vehicle-borne IED*

  This form of IED delivery platform is probably the favoured method of attack for those terrorist groups capable of delivery. Whether it is an under vehicle IED booby trap, as used so successfully by the Provisional IRA, or a heavy goods vehicle packed with high explosive used in the Middle East, the vehicle-borne IED has unfortunately been an extremely successful means of attack for the terrorist.

Lebanon

On 18 April 1983, the US embassy to the Lebanon was attacked in West Beirut. A vehicle packed with up to 2,000 pounds of high explosives, belonging to the Islamic Jihad terrorist organisation, sponsored by Iran, burst through the main entrance of the US compound, before stopping and exploding outside of the main building. Sixty-three people were killed and 120 were injured, including the ambassadors of the US and UK.

On 23 October 1983, at 622hrs, a heavy goods vehicle (HGV) packed with 2,000 pounds of high explosives was driven into the US Marines barracks in Beirut, where the explosives were detonated. The vehicle was driven by a member of the Lebanese based Hezbollah, and the attack was responsible for the deaths of 241 US military personnel.

On the same day, a Hezbollah pick-up truck, laden with high explosives, was driven into the French military compound in Beirut by a Hezbollah suicide bomber. The explosion killed 58 French soldiers.

In February 1984, all US military personnel were re-patriated to the USA.

Nairobi and Dar Es Salaam

On 07 August 1988, Egyptian Islamic Jihad carried out two simultaneous attacks against US embassies in Nairobi and Dar es-Salaam. Vehicles were parked outside the embassies, and at 1030hrs, the explosives contained in the vehicles were detonated by a timer. As a result of the attacks, 213 people were killed in Nairobi, with 4,000 injured, and in Dar es-Salaam 11 people were killed with 85 being injured.

- *The under-vehicle booby trap (UVBT)*

  The Provisional IRA almost perfected this form of device and were probably more successful with its deployment than any other terrorist organisation. That said, the environment in which PIRA operated was certainly conducive to this method of attack, because generally access to targets for the terrorists was relatively simple; a car parked outside of a house, or on an insecure driveway. The UVBT was normally contained within a wooden box which was slightly larger than a novel.

  Inside the container would be the standard components of an IED, that is to say an explosive substance, a detonator and some form of initiator. The initiator could either be a timer or perhaps a means of collapsing an electrical circuit to energise the detonator, causing an explosion. The UBVT would normally have two powerful magnets taped to the IED container, and the device would be very quickly attached to the underside of the car, at a point in between the front and rear wheels because that was the easiest way to attach it quickly. Of course, with the UVBT being placed in the centre of the vehicle it was easy to see upon examination of the underside of the car, and during the troubles, all soldiers and police officers would regularly have to search their vehicles for UVBT's. When my sons were 8 and 5 years old, respectively, we lived in Northern Ireland where I served as a Royal Military Policeman, and my boys Karl and Joe at such early ages could and had to be able to recognise an explosive device under the family car.

Colchester 1989

Of course, PIRA knew that soldiers and police officers in Northern Ireland searched their vehicles every day, but the terrorist organisation wasn't sure if the same could be said for British soldiers on the mainland – England, Scotland and Wales. They were soon to find out and act accordingly.

Colchester in 1989 was one of, if not the largest, British army garrison towns in the UK, holding close to perhaps 10,000 soldiers at any one time. Of course, the British army was continually vigilant and aware of the UVBT threat throughout the United Kingdom, and Colchester was no exception. Every day, soldiers would search the undersides of their vehicles before leaving for duty, or before perhaps taking their children to school. Intelligence informed us that the current terrorist method of operation (MO) was consistent, and we were to check for UVBT's attached to the steel chassis, between the front and rear wheels.

At 1023hrs on 19 November 1989, Andy Mudd, who was a staff sergeant in the Royal Military Police serving in Colchester searched under his car, a Volkswagen Golf, before setting off on a shopping trip with his wife Maggie. As he turned the ignition key, and the car moved slightly forward, there was huge explosion from underneath the vehicle and Andy was seriously injured by the blast, losing both legs and two fingers. Maggie received superficial injuries. Andy says that he 'took a quick look', but I had known him for nine years, and he is an extremely bright and precise guy. If the UVBT had been placed in the expected location on the car, he would have seen it.

Intelligence sources believe that Andy had been observed by the IRA for a number of days, and the terrorists were aware of his search patterns, so they probably placed the device under the wheel arch where it couldn't be seen. It is believed the terrorists attached a fishing wire to the centre of the front offside wheel, connecting it to a dowel rod inside the UVBT container. The vehicle only needed to move forward less than half an inch, and the dowel rod would be removed, completing an electrical circuit feeding the detonator, and the rest is history.

The lesson learned from this cowardly attack against an honest and very brave man were that the terrorist must never be taken for granted, because remember:

You have to be lucky all of the time, we only have to be lucky once.

Andy survived the attack, and opted for life in a wheelchair, as opposed to wearing two prosthetic legs, because "They were bloody uncomfortable".

Bravo, Andy Mudd.

- *The secondary device*

    It is critical to understand the fact that terrorist active service units (ASU) do not carry out their attacks on a wing and a prayer. Whilst military units will always make contingency plans for a worst-case scenario, the terrorist ASU and their intelligence sources will look for vulnerabilities and weaknesses in the 'enemy's' defence.

    Such weaknesses may include poor physical defence, such as ineffective access control or electronic systems that are not fit for purpose. However, the one area that the terrorist unit has always looked for is apathy and pattern setting.

    In terms of close or executive protection, apathy and pattern setting are two weaknesses or vulnerabilities that the close protection officer or bodyguard will have had instilled in him or her since training; and that is generally communicated to the person being protected (the principle).

However, once again – and this was made evident when PIRA attacked and almost killed Andy Mudd – the terrorist knows that very often the intended target will search the same place at the same time in the same location. Andy was following intelligence briefings given to him by a credible source, so he had no choice other than to carry out the same search procedures every time he went to his car. So as far as PIRA was concerned, he was a credible and very easy target.

Another method of exploiting this particular weakness is by placing a second IED in an area where the terrorist believes that the police or military are likely to take shelter once an IED has been discovered elsewhere.

Warrenpoint

The first attack

On 27 August 1979, the British Army in Northern Ireland had more soldiers killed in a single attack than in any other counter-insurgency operation since the Second World War. This was the first time a so-called 'secondary' attack had been carried out by the Provisional IRA.

At 1640hrs on 27 August 1979, a convoy of British Soldiers being transported in a convoy consisting of a Land Rover and two four-ton vehicles along the Newry Road near Warrenpoint, in County Down were attacked by PIRA.

The terrorists had hidden an 800-pound improvised explosive device (IED) in bales of hay, placed on a flatbed trailer to the side of the road, and as the military convoy passed the trailer, the explosive device was detonated remotely by two terrorists hiding behind bushes, in the Republic of Ireland, across the Newry River. Six soldiers were killed and a number were injured in the explosion.

The second attack

The IRA had been monitoring British Army tactics for some time, and they were aware of the fact that during or after an attack, British soldiers would always try to hide behind what was referred to as 'hard cover', were they would form an 'all-round defence' and an incident control point (ICP).

They were correct.

After the first explosion, surviving soldiers helped their injured comrades to the shelter of a stone wall, where they called for re-enforcements and medical help; whilst setting up the ICP. It wasn't very long before the Quick Reaction Force (QRF) arrived at the scene of carnage in a Wessex helicopter and began to deploy defensive tactics to protect the wounded soldiers and defend the location.

By 1742hrs, all injured personnel had been carried onto the Wessex, and it was intended to take them as quickly as possible to the nearest hospital, but just as the aircraft was taking off, PIRA detonated another 800-pound bomb, which was hidden behind the stone wall at the ICP. In the resulting explosion a further 12 soldiers were killed and the Wessex was badly damaged, but not destroyed.

That was a secondary or 'come on' attack

Lessons were learned from the attacks against 2 Para at Warrenpoint in August 1979, and all British army strategic thinking and training from that day took into account the change in terrorist strategies. Of course, something would be remiss if such important lessons were missed by a professional army that is expected to be able to adapt in order to defeat the enemy. However, such lessons have not been so readily accepted by organisations and corporations operating in city centres or in business parks.

Just a thought

A new building has been constructed in a busy business park in the UK Midlands. The unit will probably hold 500 people at any one time. Where do you think the evacuation assembly point will be located?

Not surprisingly, when compiling an evacuation strategy for a standalone building in a business park, the first priority is the evacuation and safety of staff in the event of a fire. Building evacuation procedures will be drawn up, normally beginning with clearing the building in an orderly and controlled manner with the use of a fire alarm, and a strict evacuation route which will lead staff to the external evacuation assembly point (EAP). The EAP is more often than not to be found at the nearest car park, and for the evacuation in the event of a fire that is fine. However, if the building is being evacuated because a suspect bag has been found in reception, fire safety evacuation is not fit for purpose, and here are the reasons why.

First of all, let us look at this situation through the eyes of the terrorist, who wants to wreak as much havoc as possible.

The terrorist really has two choices. He or she can plan their attack in the hope of killing as many people as possible by placing an IED in a crowded area of the building, assuming the blast will kill or seriously injure those located in, let say, the ground floor reception area.

An alternative means of attack is by the use of a secondary device, placed at the evacuation assembly point, which is of course a car park in the case of a business park, or a crowded street should the target building be located in a busy city centre. If it is in the car park, an option for the terrorist is to locate his vehicle containing a remotely controlled IED central to the EVP to cause maximum disruption. In a busy city centre street, the option is to place the IED either in a parked car or perhaps in a waste bin; either will cause mayhem and destruction.

I have carried out security surveys in numerous locations such as those above, and one of the tasks required by the client is for the security surveyor to review policies, plans and procedures; which includes of course the evacuation procedures strategy. It is fair to say that, mainly because of health and safety law and procedures, in the vast majority of surveys, there have been very clear instructions relating to the evacuation of a building in the event of fire, reflecting the paragraphs above.

However, even today it is rare to find evacuation procedures dealing with a bomb threat. If a suspect bag is found or a credible telephone bomb warning is received, the fire alarm is normally sounded, and staff are corralled to either the car park or busy street, to perhaps where the real danger lies.

My advice in this situation is twofold:

1   Never evacuate past a suspect bag or device. Always have arrangements in place for staff to exit the building via a route that does not take them anywhere near the bag or parcel.
2   If evacuation to an external EAP is believed appropriate, send a member of the security team if possible, to carry out a cursory search of the car park/street prior to the arrival of staff. Of course, there is absolutely no guarantee that a secondary device will be discovered, but before any terrorist attack is carried out, it is likely that the terrorist will be watching and noting security procedures in place. Being diligent and being seen to be diligent in carrying out a search or 'sweep' may cause the attacker to have second thoughts and cancel the attack.

•   *The six Cs*

In the previous section where we covered the secondary device, the suspect bag or case left in a busy reception was mentioned, and in that section, we jumped forward to a point where the bag had been deemed suspect; but how did that happen?

I cannot emphasise strongly enough the importance of always calling the emergency services, in whatever country pertains, if you believe that a bag, briefcase, or suitcase may contain an IED. I believe that I am safe in arguing that no police force will ever criticise a member of the public who is acting with regards to the safety and security of himself and fellow citizens.

However, one has to be brutally realistic when considering emergency service response, in that, within a busy city centre or a business park that is some distance from the nearest police station, response is unlikely to be immediate, and the onus is likely to be on the security team to manage the situation, and there must be a strategic approach to manging suspect devices. In the military and a number of police forces, it is known as the 6 Cs, standing for:

Confirm:

It is highly unlikely that the bag or case under scrutiny will have wires protruding from a seam, neither is it likely to be ticking. I don't mean for one instance here mean to sound flippant about this subject, because my experience tells me that there is nothing more important than the protection of life. Unfortunately, fictitious programmes transmitted on a variety of media platforms often portray the suspect IED as a crude device with red wires and bundles of dynamite; nothing could be further from the truth.

Today's terrorist is no fool, and he or she will deliver an IED in a format that will be almost invisible, and one that will blend in with the environment identified by the attacker. There are, however, a number of elements, which when examined may be able to give the security manager or whoever is in command of the incident some guidance about his or her course of action if a potentially suspect bag is found.

- The current national terrorism threat level
  According to the UK Security Service, MI5, at the time of writing this book the current terrorism threat level is severe, meaning an attack is highly likely. The only level higher is critical, which means that an attack is highly likely in the near future.[72] Whilst this is not substantial evidence that a terrorist attack is about to take place, it is a good indicator of the current threat environment.

- Location
  The bag or parcel has been found unattended in a busy reception area, with a populated building in the centre of the city; an ideal target for maximum disruption.

- Placement
  The bag or parcel was not in that location ten minutes earlier, and nobody saw it being placed.

- Ownership
  Despite loudspeaker announcements, the use of CCTV and questioning those in the vicinity, ownership of the bag or parcel cannot be ascertained.

  Taking into consideration all of the above, and maybe a telephone warning, the person in charge of the scene may think there is sufficient evidence for confirmation that the bag or parcel may contain an improvised explosive device (IED). If so, he or she should consider the next course of action.

Clear

The person in charge or incident commander now has a series of decisions to make, and they must be made quickly.

- To evacuate or invacuate.
  During the early days of the 'troubles', that is to say the problems in Northern Ireland when the Provisional IRA was at its peak, it was natural to evacuate a building if a suspect device had been located within. However, once outside the building, those evacuating were at severe risk of being injured or killed by flying glass, with up to 85% of injuries from an explosion being the result of flying glass.[73] Of course the technology of glass production has made leaps and bounds since the 1970s when windows were protected by curtains and blinds. Today, windows can easily be protected from blast by the installation of anti-shatter film (ASF).
  The Centre for the Protection of National Infrastructure (CPNI)[74] argue that if it is not possible to upgrade and install protective glazing, such as laminated glass, into existing buildings, the use of ASF may be applied as a retrofit measure to mitigate the glazing hazard inside a building as a result of an external blast or impact.
  As a mitigation measure, ASF is usually applied in a 'daylight' application, meaning that the film is applied to the inside face of the glass with a 1–3 mm gap between the edge of the film and the frame. This allows the liquid used in the application of the ASF film to the glass surface to be pushed to the edge and wiped away, leaving a daylight area around the perimeter of the film.

The mitigation provided by daylight applied ASF is dependent on the size of the window, the thickness and type of glass, the thickness and tear resistance of the ASF product, and the quality of its application. Therefore, it is important to determine the specification of the existing glazing in order to prepare the specification for the daylight applied ASF installation.

However, a significant percentage of new buildings being constructed, particularly in city centres today, include predesigned invacuation areas.

An invacuation is a safe location within a building that has been designed and constructed to act as a refuge area if there is the possibility of an IED in the building. History as taught us that a significant percentage of casualties and fatalities are normally caused by flying glass as the result of the detonation of an IED. Too often, people evacuating from the building are caught in the blast and are injured or killed by glass shrapnel.

If the decision is made to evacuate the building, the incident commander must take into consideration the route to the evacuation assembly point (EAP), not past the suspect bag or parcel, and if possible, have the EAP swept (searched) in terms of a secondary threat.

Remember to continue to keep the emergency services informed of all actions if they have yet to arrive at the scene. Do not use a mobile phone or handheld radio within 200 metres of the suspect bag or parcel, as there is a chance that it may detonate the device if it is remotely controlled.

Once the building is empty, we enter the next phase of the operation.

Cordon

If the military are forced to protect an area of land, perhaps because there has been some form of military incident, or the police are protecting the scene of a crime, they will put a cordon in place. That is to say, using all of their facilities, soldiers, police officers, bollards, tape, and so forth to afford 360-degree protection of the area or building, allowing nobody to enter the cordoned-off location on grounds of safety or the protection of evidence.

For the police and the military it is relatively easy operation, because generally logistics will not be an issue, and if the cordon is on military property, or at the scene of a crime protected by the police, they have the authority to prevent anybody breaching the perimeter cordon.

Security officers and members of the public generally have neither the provisions and logistics nor the authority to implement and then protect a cordon. Nonetheless a cordon must be put in place to stop, or at least to try to stop anybody entering the potential danger area. The cordon should be at least 200 metres away from a suspect parcel or bag, and 400 metres away from a suspect vehicle.

This is the moment when the incident commander hopes and prays that the emergency services will arrive, or volunteers will step up to the plate to help implementation of the cordon.

Once a cordon is in place, the next phase of the operation begins.

Control

As mentioned earlier, the police will have the resources and authority to maintain the integrity of the cordon. They will have personnel resources and the law on their side. Our incident commander will probably have neither. Those maintaining the cordon cannot physically stop anybody entering the location inside the cordon, as to physically manhandle may constitute assault. The wisest option is to warn anybody wishing to enter the scene that there is a suspect bag or parcel that may contain an IED inside, and that they are putting their lives, and potentially the lives of those nearby, in danger.

Check

Although this phase of the 6 Cs generally tends to fall fifth or sixth within the definition, in reality, as soon as a suspect bag or parcel (or any other method of delivering an IED) is discovered, checking for secondary devices should begin immediately. In the building reception area, the invacuation or evacuation route and the final destination, which is likely to be the evacuation assembly point (EAP).

Remember Warrenpoint, where the Provisional IRA killed 18 soldiers, 12 of whom were killed by a secondary device.

Communicate

As with checking for secondary devices, communication of the situation should be constantly taking place in order that those manning the cordon and the emergency services are aware of the current state of play. Remember it is advised not to use either a cell phone or a handheld radio within 200 metres of any suspect device, as the use of such devices may transmit on the same frequency as a remotely controlled IED.

The 6 Cs do of course have vulnerabilities, but the process offers a person or team a strategy that is tried and tested, and at the very least will prove that those in charge of the situation have a plan to enact until the emergency services arrive at the scene.

• The suicide bomber

Pedahzur and Perliger (2006) ask the question why do guerrilla groups make use of suicide attacks when this entails sacrificing their activist members? A preliminary answer is that this is the most efficient way to achieve the highest number of victims. While the average number of victims in a shooting attack is 3.32, and those in a remote-control explosive attack is 6.92, the average number of victims harmed by a suicide bomber wearing an explosive belt is 81.48. When the suicide bomber is driving an explosive laden car, the number of victims rises to an average of 97.81. Thus it is only natural that guerrilla groups or terror organisations which are interested in increasing the effectiveness of their acts of violence will turn to suicide attacks.

The volatile subject of suicide bombings or suicide missions has been discussed and debated, at probably every level of society, and there are a multitude of opinions and arguments relating to why a human being would seek to fatally attack innocent civilians; knowing only too well that he or she will perish during, or shortly after such an attack.

There are some wild and fanciful notions about why suicide bombers should choose to kill themselves whilst attacking their enemies, with theories such as 'they are all brain washed' or 'It is an easy way to meet Allah', and other generally unresearched reasons for this terrorist method of operation.

One of the most effective means of ascertaining why a person commits a crime is to ask him or her their reasons; that is relatively straightforward and has been the basis for academic research for some time. With suicide bombers of course, that is impossible, unless they are interviewed before they carry out the act.

However, Ami Pedahzur (2005), an Israeli social scientist researching suicide terrorism and commenting on revenge argues that the desire for revenge is indeed known as one of the most powerful forces that can drive a human to commit horrific acts. And yet, the deeper I probed into the study of suicide terrorism in the Palestinian arena, as well as in other locations, I realised that this argument sheds light on only part of the phenomenon whose explanations are immeasurably more numerous and complex.

This section of the book will examine the methods of operation and rational behind a number of high-profile terrorist organisations that have historically carried out suicide attacks. Of interest is the fact that although they waged war against, in their eyes, an Imperialist invading army for several decades, the Provisional IRA never sought to include suicide missions in the strategies and tactics whilst fighting the British army.

Kamikaze

Suicide missions were not invented or indeed first carried out by either al-Qaeda or Hezbollah, although both groups have rendered maximum publicity for suicide attacks during the last 20 years. Without scouring history, probably the best-known suicide fighters were Kamikaze (translated as 'divine wind') pilots of the imperial Japanese army and navy towards the end of the Second World War. Their aim was to sink an enemy warship before it could attack Japanese assets; this would be achieved by the Japanese pilot deliberately crashing his (yes, men only) aircraft into (normally) a US warship – and the bigger, the better.

Since the earliest recorded period of Japanese history, a warrior's self-destruction was accepted as a release from shame, an act of honour and courage, and an ultimate proof of integrity (Morris, 2975 in Gambetta, 2005). Kamikaze pilots knew that of course they would be killed during their attack against the enemy of Japan, but it was an honourable way to die, and their immediate family would receive credit on their behalf.

According to Hill in (Gambetta, 2005), from October 1944 to August 1945 over 3,000 Japanese army and navy pilots died attempting to crash their planes into allied ships. Such pilots are credited with the sinking of at least 30 naval vessels during the Second World War and being responsible for damaging hundreds more.

The Middle East

It is fair to say that, with the exception of 9/11 and the underground attacks in London on 7 July 2005, media focus in terms of suicide attacks has focussed mainly on conflict in the Middle East, reporting on the troubles between Israel and its surrounding Arab nations during the period 1981–2003. A number of insurgent or terrorist organisations using suicide tactics have been involved in the Middle East conflict with Israel, and by association the allies of Israel – mainly the US.

Hezbollah

Hezbollah, meaning 'Party of God', is a Shia military and political organisation that was formed in the Lebanon in 1982, as a direct result of what was seen by many as the invasion of Lebanon by the Israeli Defence Forces (IDF). The organisation has been very closely linked to Shia Iran, from whom it drew ideological and cultural strength, with the Shia state contributing to Hezbollah's finances and weapons stocks.

Hezbollah is reputed to have been among the first Islamic resistance groups to use tactical suicide bombing in the Middle East, and early bombings attributed to the group (e.g. the Tyre truck bombings and the 1983 Beirut barracks bombing) inspired other militant extremist groups to adopt the tactic for their own purposes. Jeffrey Goldberg wrote in *The New Yorker* that during this period Hezbollah quickly became the most successful terrorist organisation in modern history, serving as a role model for terror groups around the world, and virtually inventing the multipronged terror attack when, early on the morning of 23 October 1983, it synchronised the suicide bombings, in Beirut, of the United States Marine barracks and an apartment building housing a contingent of French peacekeepers. Those attacks occurred just 20 seconds apart.[75] In total, 366 soldiers and support staff were killed as the result of the two suicide attacks.

Between 1983 and 1986, Hezbollah are believed to have carried out at least 36 suicide attacks in Beirut and Southern Lebanon.

- On 18 April 1983, the group attacked the US embassy building in West Beirut. Using a US purchased truck loaded with 2,000 pounds of high explosives, the driver parked the vehicle alongside one of the main walls before detonating the explosives in the vehicle, killing him and 63 other innocent civilians.
- Hezbollah synchronized suicide bombings in Beirut on 23 October 1983, as described earlier.
- Between 1982 and 1985, the terrorist group (as seen by most global nation states, particularly the US and the UK) carried out 11 direct attacks against targets in Israel.
- 1985 to 1986 saw Hezbollah carry out 20 suicide missions against the Israeli Defence Forces, and their supporting paramilitary group the South Lebanon Army (SLA).

The logic of Hezbollah's attacks, certainly from their perspective would be that they were defending Shia Muslims in the Lebanon from a hostile force which was heavily armed, and they (Hezbollah) having no equivalent ordnance only had the suicide option that would force the invading army from the soil of the Levant.

Al-Qaeda

The attacks by al-Qaeda terrorists against the World Trade Center on 11 September 2001, in which over 3,000 people were killed, have been extensively documented and reported, because the use of two commercial airlines to attack high-rise buildings in the US was never for one second foreseen. Quite naturally, if members of the public, particularly in the US were asked for an association with al-Qaeda, I suspect a significant percentage of those questioned would relate the terrorist organisation with 9/11 and probably little else.

However, al-Qaeda has an infamous track record for suicide bombings, with 9/11 in their eyes being their greatest achievement.

- On 7 August 1998, Osama bin Laden's al-Qaeda organisation bombed American embassies in Nairobi, Kenya, and Dar es-Salaam, Tanzania. The attacks utilised massive truck bombs that nearly destroyed the embassies and devastated the surrounding neighbourhoods. The bombings ultimately killed 224 people and injured many thousands more. The trucks were both driven by suicide attackers and the bombs were delivered only a few minutes apart, beginning with the first blast in Nairobi at approximately 1035hrs. Each of the truck bombs contained more than a ton of explosives.

  In Nairobi, the blast sheared off the face of the embassy and completely destroyed a neighbouring seven-story office building that contained a secretarial college. The toll was 213 dead, among them 12 Americans. Hundreds of people were blinded by flying glass and it took rescuers two days to free all the people buried in the rubble and debris.

  As deadly as the attacks were, they could have been worse. In Nairobi, an accomplice to the suicide bomber failed in his task of raising the drop bar that prevented entry into the embassy parking lot. Because of his failure the bomber was unable to get his vehicle close enough to destroy the building entirely.[76]

- The MV *Limburg* (formerly the MV *Maritime Jewel*) was a newly designed crude oil tanker that was launched in the year 2000. She weighed 157 gross tons and was capable of cruising at a speed of 15 nautical miles per hour.

  On 6 October 2002 the *Limburg* was sailing from Iran to Malaysia carrying 397,000 barrels of crude oil, and when she weighed anchor in the Gulf of Aden she was rammed by a fast, high-explosive-laden dinghy, piloted by two terrorist members of al-Qaeda. The dingy struck the *Limburg* on her starboard side almost dead centre and exploded, killing one crew member and injuring 12 more. Approximately 90,000 barrels of crude oil were discharged into the Gulf waters.

  Al-Qaeda claimed responsibility for the attack on the Jehad.net website, which has since been shut down. Abd al-Rahim al-Nashiri, who allegedly also masterminded the USS *Cole* bombing, was charged by US military prosecutors for planning the attack. Osama bin Laden issued a statement, which read:

  > By exploding the oil tanker in Yemen, the holy warriors hit the umbilical cord and lifeline of the crusader community, reminding the enemy of the heavy cost of blood and the gravity of losses they will pay as a price for their continued aggression on our community and looting of our wealth.[77]

  Had the *Limburg* not been so robustly constructed, with design features that included a double-skinned hull, it is likely that more fatalities would have ensued, and potentially 357,000 barrels of crude oil could have been discharged into the Gulf of Aden causing one of the world's greatest environmental terrorist attacks.

Al-Shabaab

Harakat al-Shabaab al-Mujahideen, more commonly known as al-Shabaab ('The Youth'), is a terrorist, jihadist fundamentalist group based in East Africa. In 2012, it pledged allegiance to the militant Islamist organisation al-Qaeda. In February 2012, some of the group's leaders quarrelled with al-Qaeda over the union and quickly lost ground. Al-Shabaab's troop strength was estimated at 7,000 to 9,000 militants in 2014. As of 2015, the group has retreated from the major cities; however, al-Shabaab still controls large parts of the rural areas.

Al-Shabaab began as the armed wing of the Islamic Courts Union (ICU), which later splintered into several smaller factions after its defeat in 2006 by Somalia's transitional federal government (TFG) and the TFG's Ethiopian military allies. The group describes itself as waging jihad against "enemies of Islam" and is engaged in combat against the Federal Government of Somalia and the African Union Mission to Somalia (AMISOM). Al-Shabaab has been designated as a terrorist organisation by Australia, Canada, the United Arab Emirates, the United Kingdom and the United States. As of June 2012, the US State Department has open bounties on several of the group's senior commanders.[78]

The group has been responsible for a number of atrocities in the region:

- Kampala, June 2010

  The 11 July 2010 Kampala attacks were suicide bombings carried out against crowds watching a screening of the 2010 FIFA World Cup Final match at two locations in Kampala, the capital city of Uganda. The attacks left 74 dead and 71 injured. Al-Shabaab, an Islamist militia based in Somalia that has ties to al-Qaeda, claimed responsibility for the blasts as retaliation for Ugandan support for the African Union Mission in Somalia (AMISOM).

- Mogadishu, 23 March 2019

  Al-Shabaab carried out a two-pronged attack by using a marauding weapons assault and by detonating a vehicle borne IED in the centre of the city, killing 15 civilians.

- Mogadishu, 25 July 2019

  This was yet another suicide bombing in which seven people were killed inside a government building, with the mayor being lucky enough to escape. This was the first time that al-Shabaab had used a female suicide bomber.

  Whether the suicide attacks constitutes a young recently radicalised Muslim man detonating an explosives vest in a restaurant, or perhaps a seasoned suicide terrorist who parks a vehicle laden with high explosives alongside a government building killing himself and dozens of innocent bystanders, the suicide attacker is probably the most dedicated operative in whatever organisations he or she is fighting for.

Cyberterrorism

Up to this point it has been relatively straightforward describing methods of operation and weapons platforms used by global terrorist organisations, but when it comes to cyberterrorism there is the problem of recognition and integrity. Although with terrorism it is difficult to reach a consensus about exactly what constitutes the act, and how we recognise a terrorist; there is agreement that terrorism in a number of forms does exist, and there are several organisations intent on bringing down governments through ideological and political means, and often the threat of violence.

Members of the public, through twenty four hour media access can visualise two aircraft crashing into high rise buildings, or a vehicle exploding after an improvised explosive device (IED) has been detonated; but we can't see information being stolen or data manipulated in an effort to carry out an attack against society, including government, commerce and industry. Yes, we are probably all aware of the dangers to personal information if our PCs, laptops and credit cards are hacked: we lose money.

However, what we must now come to terms with is the fact that we live in such a high-tech environment where there is interdependency in relation to our critical national infrastructures. Which means that if a power generating plant is taken out of action by whatever means, the knock–on effect (interdependency) may mean that hospitals have reduced or no power, and water filtration plants might not be able to operate. Communications subject matter experts will argue that through the intervention of uninterruptible power supply (UPS) systems[79] and standby generators, prior to re-connection of the electricity grid, will supply sufficient power. However, even the connection of a standby power supply to a hospital often requires the support of Internet communications technology (ICT), and there is another vulnerability for the hacker to attack.

We have reached a point, certainly in most developed countries, where we understand how to prevent or mitigate physical attacks, whether they emanate from criminal gangs' intent on committing general crime, or terrorist organisations committed to attacking us using recognised means such as weapons and explosives. We are protected by defence in depth, and target hardening and sophisticated integrated security systems that will prevent or slow down a burglar/terrorist intent on attacking our locations.

A well-illuminated brick wall topped with barbed wire and patrolled by professional security officers is no match for a terrorist with advanced cyber skills . . . and that's a problem! The issue of course is how the security sector deals with threats, cyberthreats in particular.

However, we need to add perspective to the argument, in that cyber terrorism is still in its infancy, and 31,300 is roughly the number of magazine journal articles written so far that discuss the phenomenon of cyberterrorism. Zero. That's the number of people who had been physically hurt or killed by cyberterrorism at the time this book went to press (Singer and Friedman, 2014). Cyberterrorism can be equated to other severe threats, such as standard methods of terrorism, a tsunami or an earthquake; they are low likelihood but high impact. But of course, with the speed of growth of ICT, and that fact that a significant percentage of terrorists today hold some form of academic qualification,[80] it can be credibly argued that the likelihood of a cyberterrorism attack is reducing, perhaps exponentially.

However, this is far too critical a situation to merely speculate and hope that cyberterrorism either doesn't exist, or it will disappear overnight. Let's be crystal clear: the worries over vulnerabilities in critical infrastructure to cyberattack have real validity. From 2011 to 2013, probes and intrusions into the computer networks of critical infrastructure in the United States were up by 1,700%. And the worries of cyberterrorists harming this infrastructure are certainly a real concern. For instance, in 2011 a water provider in California hired a team of computer hackers to probe the vulnerabilities, known as a penetration test, of its computer networks, and the simulated attackers got into the system in less than a week (Singer and Friedman, 2014).

Irish terrorism

As I write this book, the United Kingdom (UK) is preparing to exit the European Union (EU), after what has been referred to as a Brexit (British exit) referendum held in June 2016, during which 52% of UK voters decided that now is the time for 'independence'.

What theoretically should have been a straightforward series of negotiations between the UK and the EU after three years descended to a number of major disagreements over one aspect of the withdrawal agreement – the future of the border between the Republic of Ireland (RoI) and the UK (Northern Ireland).

> Without examining in detail what is referred to as 'the backstop',[81] it is enough to say that neither side wishes to return to the previous status quo, when during 'the troubles'[82] there was a hard, re-enforced border between the two states.
>
> Until the Northern Ireland peace agreement, which was signed on 10 April 1988, the border between the RoI and the UK (Northern Ireland) was often seen as a flash point in the conflict involving the Irish Republican Army (IRA) and UK Crown Forces. Very often, Active Service Units (ASU) of the IRA would emerge from the Republic, before moving North to carry out some form of attack against either the Protestant community in Northern Ireland, or the Crown Security Forces (British Army and the RUC), before fleeing south over the border where they felt relatively safe. Neither the RUC nor the British Army had authority to carry out what was known as a hot pursuit, that is pursuing the terrorists over the border of another sovereign state, so the border on the northern side was heavily enforced with aggressive Observation Posts (OP's) every couple of miles, and twenty four seven armed patrols.

When the peace agreement was signed, all border crossing check points were removed, and free passage of movement between the two countries was approved. This placated the politicians and population of the Republic of Ireland and the Nationalists in the north, because it allowed for free and safe passage between the North and South. Unionists in the North were also content because PIRA at long last had promised peace on the island. Brexit has now been agreed, with the UK, the Irish republic and the EU promising never to construct a hard border again, because there would have course be the possibility of a return to 'the troubles'.

The troubles

The British Army deployed to Northern Ireland, or Ulster to be more precise in support of the Royal Ulster Constabulary (RUC) in 1969, because the Northern Ireland police service was struggling to maintain law and order in Londonderry and Belfast. Initially the British Army was tasked with the protection of the Roman Catholic or Nationalist population in those cities, because on an almost nightly basis they were attacked by the Protestant or Unionist inhabitants, and the RUC, it is alleged, were not providing sufficient levels of protection to the Nationalist community that would guarantee their safety.[83]

This was the beginning of a period that was always going to be recognised, and referred to as 'the troubles', which saw the Provisional Irish Republican Army (PIRA), from their perspective, defending Roman Catholic Republicans, who primarily were arguing and fighting for equal rights, and as a secondary consideration, a united Ireland.

This was certainly not the first time that the Irish Republican Army (IRA) as it was then known, had been involved in such an insurgent situation.

The Fenians

On 17 March 1858 an organisation was founded in Dublin by a railway engineer called James Stephens. It was St Patrick's Day. Within a few years this mutated into the Irish Republican Brotherhood, although that name was never employed as 'Fenians'. This referred to a mythical band of pre-Christian Irish warriors, or the Fianna, roughly similar to romantic English legends about the knights of King Arthur.

For the English it meant a dastardly gang of murdering desperados. Fenianism encompassed a range of activities, with harmless conviviality and labour activism at the legal end of the spectrum, through to rural disturbances, insurrection and terrorism on the illegal margins. The general goal (of the Fenians) was the disenthralment of the Irish race and the achievement of an Irish republic through violent struggle, all this within a broader context of Gaelic cultural self-assertion to which there has been some allusion. The strategy, ultimately derived from the 1798 Wolfe Tone rebellion, was to transform British imperial difficulties into Irish opportunities.

The Fenians, or Irish Republican Brotherhood (IRB), were at the historic core of, and mythologised model for, what became the Irish Republican Army (IRA). Ironically, the success of the (not entirely) opposed constitutional tradition in getting the British government to concede Irish Home Rule in 1914 had already engendered a blocking Unionist response – the formation in 1913 of the Ulster Volunteer Force (UVF). Outrageous British government acquiescence in this first paramilitary army – with its links to the Conservative Party and the British armed forces – contributed to the creation in Dublin of the Irish Volunteers, elements of which would fuse with the IRB to become the IRA (Burleigh, 2009).

The Fenians were to be at the forefront of Irish insurrection for six decades, and their success was to be the catalyst for the next phase in the emerging civil war in Northern Ireland, which would last for over 40 years. More than 3,500 people were killed in the conflict, of whom 52% were civilians, 32% were members of the British security forces, and 16% were members of paramilitary groups.[84]

Partition

Probably the final stage which pre-empted the troubles in Ireland and Northern Ireland was partition. The island of Ireland was partitioned in 1920, partly due to a combination of British duplicity, the insecurities, fears, and desires of Ulster unionists, and the delusions and dashed hopes of Southern Irish republicans; and partly because the likely alternative to a border was civil war. In subsequent decades the border was cemented by aggressive political ideology, economic policy, and harrowing violence before its potency was tempered by a peace process and economic and political pragmatism. Its future, since the British electorate voted to leave the EU in June 2016, has been under a focus not witnessed in decades, as it is the UK's only land border with another European country (Ferriter, 2019)

1969 – the Apprentice Boys march

On 12 August 1969, during a 15,000 strong Protestant Apprentice Boys march in Derry, intended to trumpet Protestant superiority over Catholics, B-Specials[85] attempted to enter the densely populated Catholic Bogside area of the city, but were prevented from doing so by barricades erected by residents who feared that their homes were about to be attacked. Catholics used petrol bombs to keep the police at bay. Two days of rioting followed, which became known in the nationalist community as the 'Battle of the Bogside'. Catholics established 'Free Derry' in the Bogside, a self-policed 'no-go' area, preventing state security forces from entering. The violence quickly spread to Belfast, where Catholics rioted in solidarity and in order to further stretch police resources. Protestant mobs responded by launching a pogrom, setting fire to hundreds of Catholic homes. Catholics living in Belfast's Bombay Street were forced out of their homes and saw their entire neighbourhood burned to the ground. The RUC responded to the deteriorating situation by spraying the remaining Catholic homes with bullets from heavy calibre Browning machine guns mounted on armoured vehicles. Eight Catholics were killed in the violence.

Faced with the prospect of a collapse into anarchy of its oldest colony, on 14 August 1969 the British government at Westminster sent troops to Derry to restore order. Additional troops were sent to Belfast the next day (Shanahan, 2009).

There are of course many versions of the beginning of the troubles in Northern Ireland, initiated this time in August 1969, but the fact of the matter is that as the result, perhaps perceived, that the Catholic community was under fire, the Provisional Irish Republican Army (PIRA) was established, and was to become one of the most effective and atrocious terrorist organisations on the planet.

The Provisional Irish Republican Army (PIRA)

In his book *Irish Republican Terrorism and Politics*, Rekawek (2011) discusses the development of the Provisional Irish Republican Army (PIRA) in Londonderry and Belfast in the summer of 1969, when it was clear that the Official Irish Republican Army (OIRA) had neither the stomach, political enthusiasm nor the capacity to bridge the gap in terms of protecting Roman catholic families from the believed onslaught of Protestant Unionist forces, including the RUC and the British Army.

Rekawek discusses an incident in August 1969, when inhabitants of the Protestant, working class Shankhill district of West Belfast literally invaded the neighbouring Catholic Falls [road] in one of the worst displays of Northern Irelands sectarianism (Moloney, 2007). This incident was the result of the earlier riots in Derry where both communities clashed in the aftermath of the Apprentice Boys of Derry's (a solely Protestant organisation) annual 12 August march. The riots in Belfast were instigated in order to ease the pressure on civil rights activists and the nationalist population fighting with the security forces in Derry's 'battle of the Bogside'. In reaction to this, the Belfast Protestants rampaged through side streets leading to the Catholic falls. Thus, the Northern Irish Troubles began.

The events of this violent August led to the creation of the PIRA, a new and truly reformed IRA, which has been playing a pivotal role in Northern Irish history and politics ever since. In the orthodox, pro-Provisional narrative of events, the downgraded, unprepared IRA, which should have defended Belfast's Catholics from the protestant onslaught, stood idly by and failed to perform its duties. Graffiti of 'I.R.A. = I Ran Away' was to appear on the walls of the Falls, and the Catholic community was to turn its back on the pre-1969 Irish Republicans.

The commanders of the latter-day PIRA (often referred to as the Provo's), such as Gerry Adams and Martin McGuinness, had two dreams or aspirations: the removal of all British presence from Northern Ireland and the re-unification of the North with the Republican South. Violence (internal and external) was certainly an option.

In the first instance, the Provos, with no faith in the rule of law as applied by the RUC, had to ensure that order was established throughout all Republican areas, urban and rural; and if that meant punishing their own people, then so be it. PIRA was determined to rule with an iron fist.

At the lower end of the criminal scale, through the auspices of the PIRA Army Council, anybody within Republican areas found guilty of breaking the law, or socially acceptable rules would be punished, with the punishment meted out being measured on a sliding scale. For example; unemployment levels in Republican areas was generally high, primarily because it was difficult for a Roman Catholic to find work in a public organisation such as the Council or the police, and almost impossible for a Republican to be offered employment by a Protestant employer. That of course meant that there were ever-growing numbers of young people unemployed, and that gave them time on their hands, with not a great deal to occupy their empty days. In the 1970s and '80s, the criminal offence of illegally taking and driving a motor vehicle, or as the locals named it 'joy riding', was a daily occurrence, and though it was a criminal offence that often ended in serious injury and fatalities, the RUC were reluctant to enter a Republican area to enforce the law; so it was left to the Provos to fill the void left by the police service. PIRA, through their own grapevine, made it very clear that any person found joy riding in a Republican area would be punished, and that normally meant for a first offender the punishment would be a beating. If the criminal continued, the punishment would increase to perhaps a broken ankle or knee cap, and if that was no deterrent, the joy rider would be taken to an alley way, and would receive a single bullet fired through the back of his[86] knee, and he would never walk properly again. Beatings and knee-capping, as it was called were relatively common, and to a certain extent general crime in Republican areas was low. If it was believed that a member of the Nationalist community was fraternising with the RUC or Crown Forces, they would be publicly punished, some time by means of tarring and feathering. If a Republican was found to be passing on information to the security forces, it would probably mean the death sentence, which would be a single bullet fired through the back of the head of the 'traitor'.

By the late 1980s, tension in all areas of Northern Ireland was at its highest levels, with tit for tat killings taking place all too often.

The corporal killings

British Army corporals Derek Wood and David Howes were killed by the Provisional IRA on 19 March 1988 in Belfast, Northern Ireland, in what became known as the corporals killings. The undercover soldiers – wearing civilian clothes, both armed with Browning high power pistols and in a civilian car – accidentally drove into the funeral procession of an IRA member. Three days before, loyalist Michael Stone had attacked an IRA funeral and killed three people. Believing the soldiers were loyalists' intent on repeating Stone's attack, dozens of people surrounded and attacked their car. During this, Corporal Wood drew his service pistol and fired a shot in the air. The soldiers were then dragged from the car and taken to a nearby sports ground where they were beaten, stripped and searched. They were then driven to nearby waste ground where they were shot dead.[87]

What was not made public at the time was the fact that after they were beaten almost to death, they both received over 100 knife wounds to their backs before being shot several times at a waste ground in front of several young families. A local Roman Catholic priest, Father Alec Reid, attempted to save the lives of the young British soldiers, but he was unable to, and at the end performed the last rites for them.

PIRA certainly oversaw the killings, sending a very strong message to anybody with intentions of attacking their community.

PIRA external operations

• **The Brighton Hotel bombings**

The Brighton hotel bombing was a Provisional Irish Republican Army (IRA) assassination attempt against the top tier of the British government that occurred on 12 October 1984 at the Grand Brighton Hotel in Brighton, England. A long-delay time bomb was planted in the hotel by IRA member Patrick Magee, with the purpose of killing Prime Minister Margaret Thatcher and her cabinet, who were staying at the hotel for the Conservative Party conference. Although Thatcher narrowly escaped the blast, five people connected with the Conservative Party were killed, including a sitting Conservative MP, and 31 were injured.

Margaret Thatcher was the primary target of the PIRA, and she survived. After the attack PIRA released the following, now infamous statement.[88]

Today we were unlucky, but remember, we only have to be lucky once; you will have to be lucky always. Give Ireland peace and there will be no war.

During its campaign against the British Crown Forces, the PIRA was responsible for a number of atrocities, what they would call successful attacks. There was one particular attack against the PIRA and in their eyes, innocent Irish people that was unforgivable, and would kindle terrorist attacks in the future.

• **Bloody Sunday – 30 January 1972**

Thirteen people were killed and 15 people wounded after members of the Army's Parachute Regiment opened fire on civil rights demonstrators in the Bogside – a predominantly Catholic part of Londonderry – on Sunday, 30 January 1972.

The day became known as Bloody Sunday — one of the darkest days of the Northern Ireland Troubles.

About 15,000 people gathered in the Creggan area of Derry on the morning of 30 January 1972 to take part in a civil rights march. The march began shortly after 1500hrs and the intended destination was the city centre.

However, Army barricades blocked marchers.

The majority of demonstrators were instead directed towards Free Derry Corner in the Bogside.

After prolonged skirmishes between groups of youths and the Army, soldiers from the Parachute Regiment moved in to make arrests.

Just before 1600hrs, stones were thrown and soldiers responded with rubber bullets, tear gas, and water cannon. Two men were shot and wounded.

At 1607hrs, paratroopers moved to arrest as many marchers as possible.

At 1610hrs, soldiers began to open fire.

The British army provide evidence that 21 soldiers fired their weapons on that day, firing 108 live rounds, and 13 Republicans were killed as the result of the gunfire.

- **Bloody Friday – 21 July 1972**

On this day, the IRA detonated 19 bombs in and around Belfast city centre, killing nine people and injuring 130.

The IRA insisted that ample warnings had been given and the intention was not to kill civilians, however the warnings were inadequate and imprecise. The bombing was to give the British government a warning it was still in business. Ten days after Bloody Friday, in the biggest British military operation since Suez, 12,000 soldiers with bulldozers and tanks entered what were considered the no-go areas of the province.

There have been many terrible events in the history of Northern Ireland's conflict, but few have seared the collective consciousness of its people as those on Friday, 21 July 1972, a day that became known as Bloody Friday.

By the end of the day, the IRA's Belfast brigade had detonated at least 20 bombs across the city.

In just 75 minutes of violence, nine people were dead and some 130 more were mutilated, injured, and mentally scarred by what they had witnessed.

From the outset, the IRA's bombing of the city caused widespread chaos and stretched the security forces to the limit.

Such was the scale of the attack, witnesses at the time remember seeing people running in all directions, not knowing where the bombs were being detonated.

As one report at the time described the scene, "it was impossible for anyone to feel perfectly safe".[89]

- **The Birmingham pub bombings – 21 November 1974**

While the shooting and bombing continued relentlessly at home, the IRA had already started to extend its campaign to England.

It targeted pubs frequented by off-duty soldiers. Bombs in Guilford and Woolwich killed six people and injured many more. This new campaign was to have a horrific climax when bombs went off without warning in two Birmingham pubs: 19 people were killed and 182 were injured. Britain was shocked at the carnage and the way in which the 'war' in Northern Ireland was being brought home with such savage ferocity.[90]

The Provisional Irish Republican Army has never officially admitted responsibility for the Birmingham pub bombings, although a former senior officer of the organisation confessed to their involvement in 2014. In 2017, one of the alleged perpetrators, Michael Hayes, also claimed that the intention of the bombings had not been to harm civilians, and that their deaths had been caused by an unintentional delay in delivering an advance telephone warning to security services.

Six Irishmen were arrested within hours of the blasts, and in 1975 sentenced to life imprisonment for the bombings. The men – who became known as the Birmingham Six – maintained their innocence and insisted police had coerced them into signing false confessions through severe physical and psychological abuse. After 16 years in prison, and a lengthy campaign, their convictions were declared unsafe and unsatisfactory, and quashed by the Court of Appeal in 1991. The episode is seen as one of the worst miscarriages of justice in British legal history.

The Birmingham pub bombings were one of the deadliest acts of the troubles, and the deadliest act of terrorism to occur in England between the Second World War and the 2005 London bombings.[91]

- **Warrington bomb attacks – 20 March 1993**

Perhaps the most unnecessary and brutal attack carried out by the PIRA was in Warrington, England.

The IRA exploded two bombs concealed in litter bins in Warrington, when the town was packed with Saturday shoppers.

Inadequate warnings were given, and two young boys were killed in the blasts and 51 people were injured. Public revulsion was on a scale similar to Enniskillen but remarkably an unauthorised secret meeting between the IRA and British intelligence officers went ahead. The Warrington bomb seemed to make the meeting even more urgent if the violence was ever to stop.[92]

Shortly before midday on 20 March 1993, the Samaritans in Liverpool received a bomb warning by telephone. According to police, the caller said only that a bomb had been planted outside a Boots shop. Merseyside Police sent officers to branches of Boots in Liverpool and warned the Cheshire Constabulary, who patrolled nearby Warrington. About 30 minutes later, at about 1225hrs, two bombs exploded on Bridge Street in Warrington, about 100 yards (90 m) apart. The blasts happened within a minute of each other. One exploded outside Boots and McDonald's, and one outside the Argos catalogue store. The area was crowded with shoppers. Witnesses said that shoppers fled from the first explosion into the path of the second. It was later found that the bombs had been placed inside cast-iron litter bins, causing large amounts of shrapnel. Buses were organised to ferry people away from the scene, and 20 paramedics and crews from 17 ambulances were sent to deal with the aftermath.

Three-year-old Johnathan Ball died at the scene. He had been in town with his babysitter, shopping for a Mother's Day card. The second victim, 12-year-old Tim Parry, was gravely wounded. He died on 25 March 1993 when his life support machine was switched off, after tests had found only minimal brain activity. Fifty-four other people were injured, four of them seriously. One of the survivors, 32-year-old Bronwen Vickers, the mother of two young daughters, had to have a leg amputated, and died just over a year later from cancer.

The Provisional IRA issued a statement the day after the bombing, acknowledging its involvement but saying:

Responsibility for the tragic and deeply regrettable death and injuries caused in Warrington yesterday lies squarely at the door of those in the British authorities who deliberately failed to act on precise and adequate warnings.

A day later, an IRA spokesman said that "two precise warnings" had been given "in adequate time", one to the Samaritans and one to Merseyside Police. He added:

"You don't provide warnings if it is your intention to kill". Cheshire's assistant chief constable denied there had been a second warning and said:

Yes, a warning was given half an hour before, but no mention was made of Warrington. If the IRA think they can pass on their responsibility for this terrible act by issuing such a nonsensical statement, they have sadly underestimated the understanding of the British public.

A piece on BBC North West's *Inside Out* programme in September 2013 speculated that the bombing may have been the work of a "rogue" IRA unit, which was supported by the IRA but operated independently and who used operatives who were from England to avoid suspicion. The programme also examined a possible link between the attack and British leftist political group Red Action, though nothing was ever proven.[93]

There is no question that since the PIRA took on the mantle, so called, to protect Roman Catholics in Northern Ireland, their tactics altered dramatically, with the focus being defeat of British Crown Forces in Northern Ireland, and the return of sovereignty of the Island of Ireland to the Irish people. Whilst they fought a brutal and intransigent war of insurrection, they were unsuccessful in terms of both of their objectives; but it was close.

Jihad

This is probably one of the east understood terms of reference in the study of terrorism.

Martin (2006) discusses the subject of jihad in some detail in his book *Understanding Terrorism* first by explaining how he sees the topic.

The concept of jihad is a central tenet in Islam. Contrary to the misinterpretation common in the West, the term literally means a sacred 'struggle' or 'effort' rather than an armed conflict or fanatical holy war. Although jihad can certainly be manifested as a holy war, it more correctly refers to the duty of Muslims to personally strive "in the way of God".

This is the primary meaning of the term as used in the Qur'an, which refers to an internal effort to reform bad habits in the Islamic community or within the individual Muslim. The term is also used more specifically to denote a war waged in the service of religion.

Regarding how one should wage jihad, Martin goes on to explain that the *'greater' jihad* refers to the struggle each person has within him or herself to do what is right. Because of human pride, selfishness, and sinfulness, people of faith must constantly wrestle with themselves and strive to do what is right and good. The *'lesser' jihad* involves the outwards defence of Islam. Muslims should be prepared to defend Islam, including military defence when the community of faith is under attack.

The precipitating causes for the modern resurgence of the armed and radical *Jihadi* movement are twofold: the revolutionary ideals and ideology of the 1979 Iranian Revolution and the practical application of jihad against the Soviet Union's occupation of Afghanistan. Some radical Muslim clerics and scholars have concluded that the Afghan jihad brought God's judgement against the Soviet Union, leading to the collapse of its empire. As a consequence, radical jihadis fervently believe that they are fighting in the name of an inexorable force that will end in total victory and guarantee them a place in Paradise.

Of course, considerable numbers of non-Muslim's believe that this jihad is a base for terrorist activities.

Islamic Jihadi terrorism

According to Khan (2011), the Islamic 'jihad' or 'holy war' stands for *fighting in the cause of Allah.*

Over 3,500 people were murdered during the troubles in Northern Ireland, a conflict that lasted for four decades. During the al-Qaeda terrorist attacks against the Twin Towers on 11 September 2001, at least 3,000 innocent souls were lost. It is impossible to evidence exactly why Osama bin Laden decided to attack the United States, with explanations such as:

- *The alienation of Muslim immigrants in the West.* Three of the four 9/11 pilots and two key planners, Ramzi bin al Shibh and Khalid Sheikh Mohammed, became more militant while living in the West.
- *US foreign policies in the Middle East, in particular its support of Israel.* By Bin Laden's own account, this is why al-Qaeda is attacking America. His critique has never been cultural; he never mentions Madonna, Hollywood, homosexuality, or drugs in his diatribes. US support for Israel, especially the support it gave to Israel's invasion of southern Lebanon in 1982, first triggered Bin Laden's anti-Americanism, which during the 1980s took the form of urging a boycott of US goods. He was later outraged by the 'defiling' export of 500,000 US troops to Saudi Arabia after Saddam Hussein's invasion of Kuwait in 1990.
- *Bin Laden was an astute tactical leader and rational political actor fighting a deeply felt religious war against the West.* Like others before him, Bin Laden has made a rational choice to adopt terrorism as a shortcut to transforming the political landscape.

However, what is clear is that Bin Laden signed a number of fatwas against the United States.

Osama bin Laden authored two fatwas in the late 1990s. The first was published in August 1996 and the second in February 1998. At the time, Bin Laden was not a wanted man in any country except his native Saudi Arabia, and was not yet known as the leader of the international terrorist organisation al-Qaeda. Therefore, these fatwas received relatively little attention until after the August 1998 United States embassy bombings, for which Bin Laden was indicted. The indictment mentions the first fatwa and claims that Khalid al-Fawwaz, of Bin Laden's Advice and Reformation Committee in London, participated in its communication to the press.

Bin Laden's 1996 fatwa is entitled "Declaration of War against the Americans Occupying the Land of the Two Holy Places". This document is sometimes called the *Ladenese epistle*, a term derived from Bin Laden's surname. It is a long piece and complains of American activities in numerous countries. It was faxed to Arab-language newspapers internationally but particularly in the England. It first appeared in the London-based Arabic paper *Al-Quds Al-Arabi.*[94]

The attacks against on 9/11 were carried out by al-Qaeda operatives, under the command of Osama bin Laden, and all of the attackers came from the Middle East (Egypt, Lebanon, Saudi Arabia and the United Arab Emirates). All belonged to the Islamic faith, and it is likely that all attackers believed that they were fighting to enforce a holy jihad.

Mainly because of extensive media coverage of terrorist attacks by groups such as al-Qaeda, Islamic State and Hezbollah, there is confusion, certainly amongst Western populations about the true nature of Islam and Islamic jihad. Far too often, the likes of Osama bin Laden and his mentor Ayman al-Zawahiri have quoted the Qur'an and Islamic Jihad, which from their perspective meant attacking and killing as many infidels[95] as possible.

However, groups such as al-Qaeda and Hezbollah, who quote Jihad as the justification for attacking infidels, are often called into question, as it appears that Jihad can mean a number of things.

Speakers at a counter-terrorism conference (February 19–21, 2008) organised by the East West Institute at Brussels repeatedly argued that the term 'jihad' must be disassociated from the violence of al-Qaeda because, for most Muslims, jihad "originally means a spiritual struggle and they don't want it hi-jacked anymore". Iraqi scholar Sheikh Mohammad Ali told the conference that "Jihad is the struggle against all evil things in your soul. . . . There is no Jihadi terrorism in Islam". Emphasising that Jihad can be a struggle *for the elimination of poverty, for education* or *for something very, very positive in life*, General Ehsan Ui Haq, the former chairman of Pakistan's Joint Chiefs of Staff, asserted that calling the terrorists jihadists is either reflective of a "lack of understanding of Islam "or unfortunately "an intended misuse" (Khan, 2011).

Extreme right-wing terrorism

Martin (2007) argues that right wing terrorists picture themselves as champions of an ideal order that has been usurped or attacked by inferior ethno-national interests or religious values. They faithfully believe that final victory will result in the natural assumption (or restoration) of power by the favoured group or belief. These uncompromising beliefs are typical among right-wing advocates who act on behalf of national groups, regional minorities, religious fundamentalists, or other groups with a distinctive identity. The identity is championed as being more legitimate, more sacred, or otherwise superior to other identities.

In a broader context, both violent and nonviolent activism on the extreme right possesses basic common characteristics. The following commonalities are typical elements found in right-wing movements and political parties.

- *Nationalism*: Only people belonging to a particular nationality have a right to reside within that group's country.
- *Racism*: The notion that there are natural and permanent differences between groups of people.
- *Xenophobia*: The fear of strangers or foreigners. In its current manifestation, it also posits the superiority of the group to which the fearful belong.
- *Antidemocracy*: An aversion to the democratic rules of the game; a rejection of the principle of equality; opposition to a pluralistic conception of society.
- *String state*: Support for militarism and for "law and order" against the threat of crime and chaos.

Left-wing ideologies

Leftist agitation is group oriented. Emphasis has traditionally been placed on creating a collective political consciousness – a class or nationalist consciousness within the championed group. On the far fringe left, this collective political consciousness is considered a pre-condition to successful revolution. Hence, indoctrination has been used by radical leftists to fashion a disciplined and motivated cadre group who represent the interests of the class or national group. At the vanguard of this struggle, then, are the political and military cadres – those that have been indoctrinated to engage in political agitation and armed conflict on behalf of the championed group. This concept of a politically disciplined cadre group has been applied by leftist extremists in many contexts, including non-violent agitation, guerrilla warfare, and terrorist campaigns.

Many leftists, especially Marxists, believe that capitalism inherently causes social and economic inequities that relegate working people and other groups (such as racial minorities) to subordinate political status. The political agenda on the left frequently reflects this fundamental principle.

State-sponsored terrorism

It is safe to argue that most people believe that acts of terrorism are carried out by either an inspired 'lone wolf' or an idealistic, probably religious group such as al-Qaeda, or when active, the Provisional Irish Republican Army (PIRA). However, in this section we will examine an area of terrorism that don't always receive the publicity that perhaps it should: state-sponsored terrorism.

I refer to Martin (2006) once again, because in my opinion his arguments and opinions are based on sound, robust research. When discussing state-sponsored terrorism, Martin argues that state participation in terrorist and extremist behaviour can involve either direct or indirect sponsorship and can be conducted in the international or domestic policy domains. State *patronage* refers to relatively direct linkages between a regime and political violence. State *assistance* relatively indirect linkages.

State patronage

State patronage for terrorism refers to active participation in, and encouragement of, terrorist behaviour. Its basic characteristic is that the state, through its agencies and personnel, actively takes part in repression, violence, and terrorism. Thus, state patrons adopt policies that *initiate* terrorism and other subversive activities, including directly arming, training, and providing sanctuary for terrorists.

State assistance

State assistance for terrorism refers to tacit participation in, and encouragement of, terrorist behaviour. Its basic characteristic is that the state, through sympathetic proxies and agents, implicitly take part in repression, violence, and terrorism. In contrast to state patronage for terrorism, state assistors are less explicit in their sponsorship, and linkages to state policies and personnel are more ambiguous. State assistance include policies that help sympathetic extremist proxies engage in terrorist violence, whereby the state will *indirectly* arm, train and provide sanctuary for terrorists.

In an article written by Dr Steve Hewitt, who is currently a senior lecturer in American and Canadian studies at the University of Birmingham, the author cites a journalist murdered in the Saudi consulate in Istanbul, allegedly by Saudi government agents; and an ex-Russian spy and his daughter poisoned with a nerve agent in Salisbury, apparently by Russian intelligence agents. What connects these two 2018 events is a concept that receives little attention in wider media and political discourses: state terrorism.

Hewitt further argues that authoritarian states do not have a monopoly on state terrorism. To try to stop protests against nuclear tests, French government agents bombed the Greenpeace ship, the *Rainbow Warrior*, in New Zealand in 1985, killing one person. Israel has spent decades targeting perceived threats, such as scientists active in Iran's nuclear programme, for death. In a case of state-sponsored terrorism, the American Central Intelligence Agency allegedly sponsored a car bombing in Beirut in 1985 in an effort to kill a cleric connected to Hezbollah. The explosion missed its intended target, murdering 80 people instead. And in 1998 a former MI5 agent, David Shayler, alleged that MI6 sponsored a 1996 assassination attempt on the then Libyan leader, Muammar Gaddafi, that missed its target but killed several other people instead.

On a larger and probably more controversial scale, we have examples where nation states have used the might of their military forces to attack innocent civilians; remember we are still talking about state terrorism. In terms of controversy, I refer to the interpretation of such actions.

- ### Israeli Defence Forces and Lebanon

  Operation Peace for Galilee
  In June 1982, the Israeli Defence Forces (IDF) invaded Lebanon in what was referred to as the Lebanon War. Israel deployed over 60,000 fighting troops, including 800 battle tanks, armoured fighting vehicles, artillery, and air power in the form of fixed-wing aircraft and combat helicopters such as the American-produced Cobra. Ostensibly, the reason for the invasion was to push the Palestinian Liberation Army (PLO), commanded by Yasser Arafat, from the Lebanese/Israeli border, where the PLO had been carrying out sporadic attacks against Israeli for a number of years. Israel's intention was to push the PLO as far north as possible, hopefully to Beirut, where the PLO would be trapped and would have to sue for peace.
  The IDF were successful in forcing the PLO to flee to Beirut, even though the Israelis took casualties from PLO rear-guard actions and from Syrian armed forces who certainly were not allies of the PLO but were still intent on revenge for the mauling they had taken on a number of occasions from the IDF. Once again, however, Syrian armed forces were no match for the Israelis, and they very quickly withdrew from combat, leaving the PLO to suffer the consequences of challenging Israel.
  Siege of Beirut had begun on 14 June: Israeli forces had completed the encirclement of the city the previous day. The Israelis chose to keep the city under siege rather than forcibly capture it, as they were unwilling to accept the heavy casualties that the heavy street fighting required to capture the city would have resulted in. Israeli forces bombarded targets within Beirut from land, sea, and air, and attempted to assassinate Palestinian leaders through airstrikes. The siege lasted until August, when an agreement was reached in August 1982. More than 14,000 PLO combatants evacuated the country in August and September, supervised by the Multinational Force in Lebanon, an international peacekeeping force with troops from the United States, United Kingdom, France, and Italy. About 6,500 Fatah fighters relocated from Beirut to Jordan, Syria, Iraq, Sudan, both North and South Yemen, Greece, and Tunisia – the latter of which became the new PLO headquarters.[96]
  The world stood by for the majority of the period when the IDF were bombarding the city of Beirut, and it is believed that up to 20,000 Lebanese were killed in this act of state terrorism. However, no atrocity committed by either side

matched a particularly horrific act of state sponsored terrorism, when the Israeli Defence Forces encouraged their Christian militia allies to attack a refugee camp in Lebanon.

- **Sabra and Shatila**

   Between 15 and 18 September 1982, depending upon who you believe, it is reported that between 800 and 3,500 Palestinians and Muslim Shiites were slaughtered inside a refugee camp in Lebanon: Sabra and Shatila. Israeli Defence Forces alleged that the two camps were holding areas of the Palestine Liberation Organisation (PLO), and this was an opportunity to once and for all eliminate the threat from what they referred to as a terrorist organisation.

   There is little dispute about the fact that PLO sympathisers were ensconced within the camps, but that is completely different to the allegation that PLO fighters occupied them.

   On 15 September, Israeli Defence Force troops surrounded the camps and set up roadblocks at all entrances and exits to prevent any of the occupants leaving. At the same time 1,500 fighters from the Christian militia known as the Phalange, which was allied to the Lebanese Kataeb Party, entered the camps, and after an initial skirmish, began what was later to be recognised by members of the United Nations as an act of genocide.

   Men, women, and children were brutally attacked and killed systematically whilst the Israeli Defence Forces looked on. It is alleged that Phalange fighters were using Israeli arms and ammunition and that during the hours of darkness, the IDF continually fired flares to illuminate the area.

   There is absolutely no question that this was state-sponsored terrorism. The IDF not only encouraged the Phalange to carry out an attack against innocent Lebanese civilians, but it equipped them to do so. I argue that whilst it was a barbarous act of murder, it was also an act of terrorism, because the Israelis sent a clear, terrifying message to all Muslims in the vicinity that it could be their turn next – terrorism in its rawest form.

- **The United States support of the Contras**

   The term 'contra' is short for *la contrarrevolución*, in English 'the counter-revolution'.

   From the late 1970s to the early 1990s, the socialist Sandinista National Liberation Front (SNLF), the government of Nicaragua, was involved in guerrilla warfare with a group of ultra-right-wing terrorist organisations collectively known as the Contras.

   The Contras were the various U.S.-backed and funded right-wing rebel groups that were active from 1979 to the early 1990s in opposition to the socialist Sandinista Junta of National Reconstruction Government in Nicaragua. Among the separate contra groups, the Nicaraguan Democratic Force (FDN) emerged as the largest by far. In 1987, virtually all contra organisations were united, at least nominally, into the Nicaraguan Resistance.

   During their war against the Nicaraguan government, the Contras committed numerous human rights violations and used terrorist tactics. These actions were frequently carried out systematically as a part of the strategy of the Contras. Supporters of the Contras tried to downplay these violations, particularly the Reagan administration in the US, which engaged in a campaign of white propaganda to alter public opinion in favour of the Contras while covertly encouraging the Contras to attack civilian targets.

From an early stage, the rebels received financial and military support from the United States government, and their military significance decisively depended on it. After US support was banned by Congress, the Reagan administration covertly continued it. These illegal activities culminated in the Iran–Contra affair.[97]

Exercise Brave Defender – task 9: terrorism and counterterrorism

Synopsis

You have received intelligence from the local counter terrorism unit (CTU) that there is a possibility of a terrorist attack against either the Britcom head office or the new data centre.

Task

The executive board has instructed you to write an article for the company intranet, advising members of staff about the threat of terrorism. You are first of all required to produce a bullet-pointed advisory sheet for the board offering advice and guidance about counterterrorism safety for all staff and management.

3.10 Aviation and maritime security management

There is absolutely no doubt that the events of 11 September 2001 – when 18 Middle Eastern terrorists representing al-Qaeda attacked and killed about 3,000 people in the Twin Towers of the World Trade Center in New York – was the deadliest aviation terrorist attack the world has ever known. As a result of the attack, aviation security was enhanced at all major airports throughout the world to a level never seen before, and 18 years on those standards have remained. However, what is not generally appreciated, certainly by the public at large, is the fact that 9/11 also had a dramatic impact on maritime security. After the Twin Towers attacks, the International Maritime Organisation (IMO) upon receiving intelligence information from a number of credible sources authorised the enactment of a regulation known as the International Ship and Port Facility Security Code (2004), which would alter the maritime security environment in a manner which has never been replicated. Although this chapter is devoted primarily to aviation and maritime security, there are supply chain issues which overlap both security areas, and they will be encompassed here.

Aviation security

Throughout most of the history of aviation, terrorists and criminals have used aircraft and airports to conduct many forms of unlawful activity. Examples include special interest groups or terrorists using aviation to gain geopolitical attention, and criminals using commercial or general aviation to smuggle contraband in one form or another. In these cases, aviation has provided a public stage for the former, and an expedient distribution channel for the latter. Aviation is essential to sustaining the economic viability of world commerce, the movement of people and cargo, and the flow of information and knowledge throughout society. Therefore, it is essential that those responsible for protecting the aviation industry are proactive in developing and implementing strategic and tactical systems that are effective in helping to mitigate criminal and terrorist activity.

The terrorist attacks in the United States on 11 September 2001 were designed to damage global security and the US economy – an economy reliant on aviation. A critical strategy for responding to terrorist threats is to moderate the response so it is appropriate and does not cause further deterioration to the economy or stability of a society. Terrorist organisations understand that they usually do not have the forces or resources to defeat an enemy in a traditional military conflict. Therefore, terrorists operate more asymmetrically, striking in ways that cause targeted countries or societies to incur loss of life, economic damage, changes in policies, or other effects. These attacks are usually designed with the hope that countries or societies will overreact in ways that further diminish the ability to protect or sustain safety and economic viability.

In addition to appropriate responses to terrorist or criminal attacks, those charged with protecting aviation must ensure that strategies and technologies remain current and viable for defending against new threats. Security practitioners employing outdated strategies and tactics create opportunities for terrorists to use these systems to their advantage. For instance, the 9/11 attacks showed ingenuity and were organised using modern technologies (the Internet, etc.) to defeat what was then a 1970s aviation security system (Price and Forrest, 2013).

So one of the many lessons learned from 9/11 was the need to technologically be aware of the opportunities presented to the attacker, whether that is a general criminal who wishes to steal or damage property, or the terrorist whose ambition and aspiration is to wreak havoc, culminating in death and destruction.

Ultimately, the worst-case scenario at any airport is an armed intruder accessing an aircraft, either whilst on the tarmac or in the air. To that end, defence in depth is a concept that was almost designed for aviation security, particularly from the perspective of an airport which has in itself a number of operational layers, consisting of:

- The environment surrounding the airport
- The perimeter
- The public areas
- The secure flight side areas
- The aircraft.

We must of course take into consideration the variety of targets in an airport (i.e. people, property (aircraft), goods etc.); a variety of targets that encourages a variation of threat platforms. In this section, as we would if we were carrying out a standard security risk assessment, identify:

- The assets requiring protection
- The threats to aviation
- Aviation security vulnerabilities
- The likelihood of an attack
- Mitigation strategies that can be applied

- The impacts of a number of different threats.

- **The assets.**

  The assets are numerous, with the protection of life always being at the forefront of any defence strategies. Of course, that is also the priority of the terrorist, but if that is not possible he or she will probably be content to cause as much damage and panic as possible. Ultimately the terrorist wishes to achieve as much publicity as possible, and a successful terrorist attack will always catch the attention of the world's media, and that type of negative publicity is going to create maximum damage to the brand and reputation of the airport or airline.

- **Threats**

  Threats to an airport or aircraft are diverse and are very much dependent on what the criminal or terrorist wants to gain from the attack. At the lower end of the scale there will be the opportunist criminal's intent on making some form of living from stealing; whether that is from retail outlets in the concourse areas, or from fellow travellers, the opportunist will strike at their convenience. At the upper end of the scale we are of course considering a terrorist attack, which may be in the form of a physical assault (including the use of IEDs), or perhaps the intention is to take down the airport IT network. Once again, it depends on what the terrorist hopes to achieve.

- **Vulnerabilities**

  The most critical vulnerability within any commercial aviation environment is the fact that there is no barring of public access to the main land side areas (i.e. arrivals and departures). The reason for that of course is the sheer volume of movement by vehicle and on foot, and over the years, unfortunately there have been a number of attacks by terrorist groups making the mist of the vulnerability.

  Some examples of recent attacks:

  - 22 March 2016 – Brussels

    Two suicide bombers, allegedly fighting on behalf of ISIS, attacked travellers at Brussels International Airport, Belgium. The terrorists detonated their devices in the main departure's concourse, killing 31 people and injured 270.

  - 29 June 2016 – Istanbul

    A number of terrorists opened fire against security personnel at Istanbul International Airport, and shortly after the firefight there were a series of explosions as suicide bombers detonated their IEDs. Forty-one people were killed and 198 were injured. The Turkish government blamed ISIS for the atrocities.

  - 21 December 1988 – Lockerbie, Scotland

    A Boeing 747 flying from Frankfurt to New York via London was destroyed by a bomb, killing all on board and 11 people on the ground (270 deaths in total), when large sections of the aircraft crashed onto residential areas of Lockerbie, Scotland. The bomb was made from PETN and RDX high explosives concealed in a radio cassette player. Libyan intelligence officer Abdelbaset al-Megrahi was convicted in connection with the bombing. Prior to 9/11, this was the worst recorded terrorist attack against an aviation target.

- **Likelihood**

  As with any form of attack, whether we are considering a low level criminal act or a terrorist attack against a major travel hub, forecasting the likelihood is the most difficult area of the process; because that is exactly what we are trying to do – forecast the future. Key to measuring the likelihood of an attack is intelligence about current threat vectors, taking into consideration the importance of the asset, any vulnerabilities that could be exploited, and the various individuals or groups that pose the greatest threat. Historical statistical evidence in relation to previous attacks can complement gathered evidence but should not be relied on as a sole source of evidence.

- **Mitigation**

  Ideally, airport authorities and security teams would like to be able to prevent every attack against an airport or an airplane, but that is never going to happen, because the criminal or terrorist makes the choice about where and when the attack is going to take place. This is where defence in depth and the three Ds (deter, detect and delay) offer support, and of equal importance is the integration of all security systems; physical, electronic, processes and human resources. Two other crime prevention methods that have been successful in offering protection to an airport, and ultimately to an airplane are Crime Prevention Through Environmental Design (CPTED) and Situational Crime Prevention (SCP).

- **Impact**

  The impact of an attack, whether it is theft from an expensive retailer or the result of a terrorist attack, is relatively straightforward to calculate. In the aftermath of some form of attack, calculation can be made to measure the impact. It may be the result of an audit which informs the retailer that a certain amount of stock has been stolen, or perhaps the calculation of lives lost, or injuries received as the result of a terrorist attack. However, they are the immediate impact calculations, but impact is very often not as straightforward as it seems immediately after the event. For example, on 5 July 2007, four young Muslim males from Leeds acting as suicide bombers attacked the London transport system, killing 59 commuters and injuring hundreds more. Of course, of immediate concern was the recovery of those killed and ensuring that injured personnel received medical attention immediately. However, that wasn't the total impact, because for much of that day all transport services ground to a halt and cellular communications were unavailable. However, far more important was the next step, which was to ensure that all involved in the attack, the emergency services and survivors received some form of counselling for the psychological scarring that was to ensue.

Maritime security

International terrorism

Prior to the enactment of the International Ship and Port Facility Security Code (2004), or the ISPS Code as it was to be known, maritime legislation and regulation was centred around safety, with very little thought being given to ship and port security, particularly from a terrorism perspective. Yes of course there was minor crime, such as theft, smuggling and criminal damage, but the thought of al-Qaeda attacking a container vessel on the high seas or within a container terminal was fantasy – until 9/11, when it was realised that in fact, a liquefied natural gas (LNG) vessel or a cruise liner would be ideal targets for any terrorist organisation needing the oxygen of publicity. Prior to the enactment of the ISPS Code, two terrorist attacks took place, which in many people's opinion validated acceptance of the Code.

MV Limburg

On 6 October 2002, the *Limburg* was carrying 397,000 barrels (63,100 cubic metres) of crude oil from Iran to Malaysia and was in the Gulf of Aden off Yemen to pick up another load of oil. She was registered under a French flag and had been chartered by the Malaysian petrol firm Petronas. While she was some distance offshore, suicide bombers rammed an explosives-laden dinghy into the starboard side of the tanker. Upon detonation, the vessel caught fire and approximately 90,000 barrels (14,000 cubic metres) of oil leaked into the Gulf of Aden. Although Yemeni officials initially claimed that the explosion was caused by an accident, later investigations found traces of TNT on the damaged ship.

One crew member was killed and 12 other crew members were injured. The fire was extinguished, and four days later *Limburg* was towed to Dubai, United Arab Emirates. The ship was renamed *Maritime Jewel*, bought by Tanker Pacific, and repaired at Dubai Drydocks from March to August 2003. The attack caused the short-term collapse of international shipping in the Gulf of Aden and as a result, cost Yemen $3.8 million a month in port revenues.[98]

Al-Qaeda in Yemen later claimed responsibility for the attack.

USS Cole

The USS *Cole* bombing was an attack against a guided missile destroyer of the United States Navy, on 12 October 2000, while she was being refuelled in Yemen's Aden harbour.

Seventeen US Navy sailors were killed and 39 injured in the deadliest attack against a United States naval vessel since the USS *Stark* incident in 1987.

The organisation al-Qaeda claimed responsibility for the attack against the United States. A US judge has held Sudan liable for the attack, while another has released over $13 million in Sudanese frozen assets to the relatives of those killed.

Although the ISPS Code does not apply to military vessels, the attack against the *Cole* and the *Limburg* is proof, if it were needed, that al-Qaeda certainly had the capacity and appetite to carry out such attacks.

The ISPS Code

The aim of the ISPS Code is to offer all ships over 500 gross tonnage sailing in international waters, or any port facility (PF)[99] serving such vessels the advice and guidance on how to carry out an effective risk assessment to lower the likelihood of or mitigate a terrorist attack.

In accordance with the Code in 2004, every ship that met the requirements would have a ship security assessment (SSA) and onboard ship security survey (OSSS) carried out and be issued a ship security plan (SSP) and an international ship security certificate (ISSC) that would expire after seven years. Every vessel that holds an ISSC must also recruit a ship security officer (SSO) who will be trained and qualified in relation to the ISPS Code.

Every port facility will have a port facility security assessment (PFSA) and port facility security plan (PFSP), which is renewed every three years, and each PF must recruit a port facility security officer (PFSO) who is also trained and qualified in relation to the Code.

The introduction of the ISPS Code also heralded several pieces of legislation and initiatives, primarily American, designed to assist maritime security and land-based logistics.

Maritime Transportation Security Act (MTSA) of 2002 – USA

The Maritime Transportation Security Act of 2002 (MTSA) (Pub. L. No. 107–295) was enacted by the 107th US Congress to address port and waterway security. It was signed into law by President George W. Bush on 25 November 2002.

This law is the US implementation of the International Ship and Port Facility Security Code (ISPS). Its full provisions came into effect on 1 July 2004. It requires vessels and port facilities to conduct vulnerability assessments and develop security plans that may include passenger, vehicle and baggage screening procedures; security patrols; establishing restricted areas; personnel identification procedures; access control measures; and/or installation of surveillance equipment. The Act creates a consistent security program for all the nation's ports to better identify and deter threats.

Developed using risk-based methodology, the MTSA security regulations focus on those sectors of maritime industry that have a higher risk of involvement in a transportation security incident, including various tank vessels, barges, large passenger vessels, cargo vessels, towing vessels, offshore oil and gas platforms, and port facilities that handle certain kinds of dangerous cargo or service the vessels listed above.

MTSA also required the establishment committees in all the nation's ports to coordinate the activities of all port stakeholders, including other federal, local and state agencies, industry and the boating public. These groups, called Area Maritime Security Committees, are tasked with collaborating on plans to secure their ports so that the resources of an area can be best used to deter, prevent and respond to terror threats.[100]

Container Security Initiative (CSI) – US

CSI addresses the threat to border security and global trade posed by the potential for terrorist use of a maritime container to deliver a weapon. CSI proposes a security regime to ensure all containers that pose a potential risk for terrorism are identified and inspected at foreign ports before they are placed on vessels destined for the US. CBP has stationed teams of US CBP officers in foreign locations to work together with our host foreign government counterparts. Their mission is to target and pre-screen containers and to develop additional investigative leads related to the terrorist threat to cargo destined to the United States.

The three core elements of CSI are:

- Identify high-risk containers. CBP uses automated targeting tools to identify containers that pose a potential risk for terrorism, based on advance information and strategic intelligence.
- Pre-screen and evaluate containers before they are shipped. Containers are screened as early in the supply chain as possible, generally at the port of departure.
- Use technology to pre-screen high-risk containers to ensure that screening can be done rapidly without slowing down the movement of trade. This technology includes large-scale x-ray and gamma ray machines and radiation detection devices.

Through CSI, CBP officers work with host customs administrations to establish security criteria for identifying high-risk containers. Those administrations use non-intrusive inspection (NII) and radiation detection technology to screen high-risk containers before they are shipped to US ports.

Announced in January 2002, CSI has made great strides since its inception. A significant number of customs administrations have committed to joining CSI and operate at various stages of implementation.

Customs Trade Partnership Against Terrorism (C-TPAT) – USA

The Customs-Trade Partnership Against Terrorism (C-TPAT) is a voluntary supply-chain security program led by US Customs and Border Protection (CBP), focussed on improving the security of private companies' supply chains with respect to terrorism. The program was launched in November 2001 with seven initial participants, all large U.S. companies. As of 1 December 2014, the program had 10,854 members. The 4,315 importers in the program account for approximately 54% of the value of all merchandise imported into the US.

Companies who achieve C-TPAT certification must have a documented process for determining and alleviating risk throughout their international supply chain. This allows companies to be considered low risk, resulting in expedited processing of their cargo, including fewer customs examinations.[101]

Although on the surface the C-TPAT initiative may appear to be distinct from maritime security, it should be noted that the vast majority of containers entering the USA arrive via a coastal port, having been transported by sea; there is the connection.

World Customs Organisation (WCO) Framework of Standards to Secure and Facilitate Trade (SAFE)

The purpose of the framework is to enhance security and facilitation in global trade, which of course includes aviation and maritime security.[102]

The SAFE Framework rests on two pillars: customs-to-customs network and customs-to-business partnerships. It is furthermore complemented by a capacity buildings programme, the so-called Columbus Programme. Core elements of the SAFE Framework are:

- Harmonising advance cargo information
- Introducing risk management approach

- Sending country's customs inspection of high-risk containers by customs authorities
- Benefits program for compliant traders.

The SAFE Framework of Standards is a set of recommendations to the customs organisations, which include issues as:

- Integrated customs control procedures for Integrated Supply Chain Management
- Authority to inspect cargo and use modern technology in doing so
- Risk-management system to identify potentially high-risk shipments
- Identification of high-risk cargo and container shipments
- Advance electronic information on cargo and container shipments
- Joint targeting and screening.

Many countries have introduced national measures based on the SAFE Framework and work together through mutual recognition of each other's programmes. Part of the SAFE Framework is the authorised economic operator (AEO).[103]

Authorised Economic Operator (AEO) – EU

In an effort to mimic C-TPAT in the USA, the European Union (EU) introduced an initiative named the authorised economic operator (AEO).

An AEO is any European organisation recognised by the World Customs Organisation (WCO) involved in the global supply chain, with the aim of moving goods across national boundaries with as little resistance as possible at border points.

National revenue bodies throughout Europe are responsible for AEO certification, which is based on the financial validity and security standards. All applicants must be able to evidence two things:

- It is financially sound and meets all of the tax and revenue criteria for the country in which it is registered.
- Security standards throughout the organisation meet those standards demanded by the revenue.

Although the aforementioned pieces of legislation, regulations and initiatives are aimed at the prevention or mitigation of the risk of terrorism, it must be added that perhaps, and certainly to date, the prophecies made after the 9/11 attacks appear not to have had substance so far. That said, given the enormous importance of maritime trade, there are significant concerns as to the ramifications of a possible attack. There are a few well-known examples of maritime terrorism: the hijacking of the Italian cruise ship *Achille Lauro* by the Palestine Liberation Front in 1985; the al-Qaeda attacks on the *USS Cole* in 2000 and the French oil tanker *Limburg* two years later; and the bomb explosion on the Filipino *Superferry 14* in 2004, perpetrated by Abu Sayyaf.

One can assume that due to the low frequency of maritime terrorism that it would not be a priority to allocate resources to defend against them. On the other hand, in comparison to the total number of terrorist incidents in the same period, instances of maritime terrorism are relatively small and therefore [perhaps] less alarming.

Compared with land-based incidents, maritime terrorism represents a very small percentage of overall terrorist attacks. In 2003, the Aegis Research and Intelligence Database estimated between 1999 and 2003 that maritime targets represented less than one percent of all terrorist attacks. A similar analysis of the RAND terrorism database supports these figures; of the 40,126 terrorist incidents recorded between 1968 and 2007, only 136 (0.34%) were against the maritime domain. Not only are the maritime numbers very low, but maritime terrorist incidents of any significance have also not occurred for some years. The last major maritime attack was the bombing of the *M/V Limburg* while it was underway near Yemen in 2002.

Since then, maritime attacks have tended to be fairly small in nature, consisting largely of bombings near port facilities or suspicious activities involving barges. There has been only one attack against a ship since the *Limburg*; the attack on the *M Star* in the Strait of Hormuz in 2010. The low incidence of maritime terrorist attacks is despite the fact that a number of very active terrorist groups have known maritime capabilities. At the same time, nations spend billions of dollars annually, protecting their ships, port facilities, and related maritime infrastructure from attack. This raises the question of how real the threat of maritime terrorism really is. Would these funds be better spent elsewhere, or are they a vital protection against a potential period of greater maritime terrorism in the future?[104]

Maritime security – piracy

Amazingly, if you asked a member of the public in most countries today their views on piracy, they would probably refer to illegal copying of DVDs or downloading music; or perhaps paint a picture of Johnny Depp like a pirate of the Caribbean, complete with eye patch, and maybe even a parrot perched on the right shoulder. However, between 2003 and 2010, what may be defined as 'modern day' pirates were rife in the Straits of Malacca and off the coast (up to 200 nautical miles) of Somalia.

According to Britannica.com, for many people the term 'pirate' conjures up images of the so-called 'golden age' of piracy, in the 17th and 18th centuries, along with legendary pirates such as Blackbeard or Captain Kidd or their fictional equivalents such as Long John Silver or Captain Jack Sparrow. But piracy is a much more universal phenomenon. Any time people have used the sea for military and commercial purposes, there presumably has been some form of piracy.

A privateer was a pirate with papers. As the name suggests, privateers were private individuals commissioned by governments to carry out quasi-military activities. They would sail in privately owned armed ships, robbing merchant vessels and pillaging settlements belonging to a rival country. The most famous of all privateers is probably English admiral Francis Drake, who made a fortune plundering Spanish settlements in the Americas after being granted a privateering commission by Elizabeth I in 1572.

Generally, because they were private entities, and therefore not subject to the same rules and regulations of national naval forces, privateers were able to push the boundaries and extend their influence on a global perspective.

Of course in the 16th century, young boys aspired to become Drake-like buccaneers who would sail the high seas at the behest of the king or queen of England, in the *Golden Hind*, with a ship's company, armed with cutlass and blunderbuss, who were relatively loyal to their Captain, and interested in one thing, and one thing only: Spanish gold.

The pirates sailing in and around the Straits of Malacca and off the coast of Somalia were of course a different breed. There was no *Golden Hind* – rather they would sail a small, fast motor boat known as a skiff.[105] There may be a leader, but he would be no Francis Drake or Walter Raleigh, rather he would command the ship either because of the hierarchy in the village were the crew originated, or he was the most adept to survive in a fight. There would be no cutlass or blunderbuss, instead every pirate would be armed with a Russian-made Kalashnikov AK-47 high-powered assault rifle, with on board support from a heavy calibre general purpose machine gun capable of firing 600–1,000 rounds (bullets) per minute at a range of up to 800 metres. Huge fire power. In 2008/9, pirate skiffs began to operate, supported by mother ships which would be responsible for the management of all operations and logistics. Perhaps four to five skiffs would operate at any given time, and what defence their targets had[106] was very thin on the ground when deployed against four or five fast, heavily armoured attack vessels.

Pirates running through the Straits of Malacca were generally quite sophisticated, perhaps sponsored by a hostile state, and primarily interested in taking over the target vessel. This may have been a container ship or general cargo carrier, and the hijackers would demand, and normally be paid, a ransom for the ship and her crew.

Somalian pirates, on the other hand were a different breed altogether. Normally originating from extremely poor villages where they had been simple fishermen, Somalian prates resorted to piracy because the waters off the coast of Somalia had been fished dry by South Korean vessels, 5,500 miles from their home waters. Somalians would argue that they were faced with two choices; to rob merchant ships or allow their families to starve to death.

In recent times, 2009 was a significant year with Somali pirates attacking over 200 vessels, successfully hijacking over 40 ships. This was at a time when the area was policed by an international naval task force.

In 2011, the fight against maritime piracy changed. Until then, the world's navies were primarily charged with providing the bulk of anti-piracy protection, and individual ships were encouraged to do their part in deterring piratical acts by employing the industry's 'best management practices' – a set of primarily passive defence measures. But in early 2011, the International Chamber of Shipping (ICS), the main trade association for the shipping industry, announced that it had changed its previous stance opposing the use of armed guards on ships. Instead, it stated that the decision of whether to hire armed guards should be left to ship owners and their flag states.

States embraced the new policy position, and many began authorising their cargo ships to carry armed guards to help protect them when travelling through pirate-infested waters. The reason for the change was simple: the world's navies had managed to prevent many pirate attacks after they began patrolling the Gulf of Aden and Indian Ocean in 2008, but they simply could not control enough of the high seas to make travel safe for all. By 2012, some 60% of cargo ships employed armed guards. Hiring the guards is not cheap; it cost a ship owner about $60,000 for a four-person team to accompany travel through the Gulf of Aden. On the other hand, the evidence suggests that no ship protected by private armed guards has been the victim of a successful pirate attack.

The levels of piracy attacks have dwindled dramatically since 2015, and as already argued, maritime terrorism when carried out effectively can be disastrous for the target or victim, but the likelihood of a maritime terrorist attack in contrast with a land attack is slim. However, one of the greatest fears in relation to maritime security is the nexus between piracy and maritime terrorism. There is little evidence of such a collaboration to date, maybe because there is little trust between piracy groups and terrorist organisations, or perhaps the cultural chasm between the two threats is too great; it impossible at this moment in time to know. One thing is quite certain, if such a relationship ever materialised, with skilful seamen being financially and logistically supported by al-Qaeda or Islamic State, merchant vessels would face a significant risk whilst sailing the high seas.

Exercise Brave Defender – task 10: aviation and maritime security

Synopsis

Due to a recent upgrade requirement, there is a need to transport a number of mainframe computers from Tokyo to London. You have been tasked with advising the Executive Board about the most secure means of transportation.

Task

Decide on whether the equipment should be shipped or flown from Japan and present your evidence to the Board in the form of a report which argues for your choice of transportation.

3.11 Supply chain security management

Before we begin to examine supply chain security management, we need to have a good understanding of what is meant by supply chain management, but that is no easy task.

One definition is that supply chain management is the movement of goods or produce from the location of production to the ultimate end user. The supply chain begins at the point where the raw supplies are converted to commercial products, moving through a series of transport hubs, until it reaches its final destination.

Another and more detailed version is that in commerce, supply chain management (SCM), the management of the flow of goods and services, involves the movement and storage of raw materials, of work-in-process inventory, and of finished goods from point of origin to point of consumption. Interconnected, interrelated or interlinked networks, channels and node businesses combine in the provision of products and services required by end customers in a supply chain. Supply-chain management has been defined as the "design, planning, execution, control, and monitoring of supply-chain activities with the objective of creating net value, building a competitive infrastructure, leveraging worldwide logistics, synchronizing supply with demand and measuring performance globally".[107]

Intermodal transportation

To complicate this even more we need to discuss the term 'intermodal', which refers to how the product is transported, and although there is the perception that everything travels in a huge container vessel from A to B; that is not necessarily the case.

To define intermodal transport in a few words, it may be argued that it is the combination of different means of transport using a single container. In general, adaptable containers are used to transport all kinds of goods by different means of transport. In this way, the freight forwarding process is faster and more efficient.

This process allows for transportation in several ways: land transport (road or rail) and maritime or river transport. By the fact that the transport is done on several vehicles to reach its final destination, it is also called multimodal.

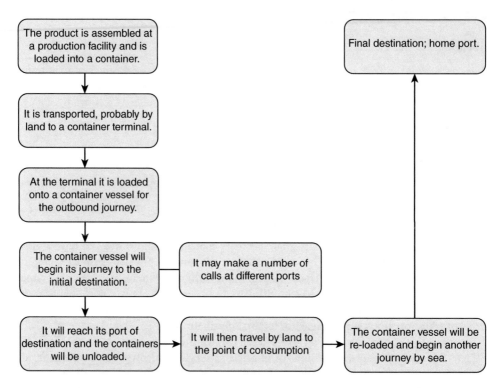

Figure 3.10 The production and transportation of a consumer product without detailing the specification of the product or defining in detail the intermodal journey. From that very generalised scenario it is difficult to envisage any level of risk, however from the following case study we should be able to visualise how and why security risk management is required within the supply chain.

So combined or intermodal traffic is characterised by the use of at least two different means of transport to move the goods, without a change of container being made.

Figure 3.10 describes the journey of a product from home port to point of consumption, and then the return journey.

Operation Extended Reach

Arguably the most expensive commodity in the world today is lithium, with the price of a kilogram rising from $3 in 2005 to $10 per kilogram in 2010. Now it is not only the fact that lithium is an expensive commodity that is increasing in value by approximately 25% per annum, but it is a critical ingredient not just for smartphones, which are designed around it, and it is the most important ingredient (lithium carbonate) in smart, light energy efficient batteries for electric cars.

So, for the purposes of this case study we are going to examine the security and risk implications of a consignment of lithium being transported from one of the world's largest producer of the commodity, Chile, to the United Kingdom, which is currently the world leader in battery technology.

Operation Extended Reach

The MV *Hampton Bridge* is a 42,527-ton dead weight bulk carrier, flying the flag of Malta. She was constructed in 2013 and will be responsible for carrying boxed lithium from Santiago, Chile, to Pontevedra in Spain, for onward transmission to London, UK. The *Hampton Bridge* will carry the lithium in sealed airtight containers, with each box being worth approximately $5,000.00 in street value, and there will be 1,000 containers in the hold. Each box can be handled by two people. More important than the street value of the contents of each box is the fact that the batteries being produced in the UK are totally reliant on lithium as the main ingredient.

Phase one: production facility to port

The lithium containers will be transported from the processing site to the port by a fleet of four sealed container vehicles, with the journey being mainly poorly maintained roads and tracks. The movement to the port will take approximately six hours, with a stop that is favoured by truck drivers, in the middle of the journey. Each vehicle will have only a driver, and will not have any form of communication, other than the cell phone belonging to the driver.

Phase two: containment

The container vehicles arrived at their port destination at 2000hrs, and they were able to unload their containers into a secure container terminal that is compliant with the International Ship and Port Facility Security Code (ISPS). The containers will stand on the dockside until they are loaded onto the *Hampton Bridge* at 0800 the following morning. All containers are secured with Radio Frequency Identification (RFID) seals and are held in a well-lit area of the terminal.

Phase three: from Chile to Spain

The distance from Chile to Spain is 6,783 miles, and cruising at a speed of 30 knots per hour, the *Hampton Bridge* will arrive at Pontevedra in Spain approximately 220 days later. The cargo will be held in a sealed hold, with only the ship's master and ship security officer having access to the lithium. The vessel will be refuelled at sea and will be stationary for approximately eight hours.

Phase four: containment

The ship will dock at Pontevedra and will be held for 24 hours at a non–ISPS Code berth, whilst she is loaded with timber for unloading in London. During this period the crew of the *Hampton Bridge* will be responsible for her security, with the assistance of a land-based security company. During the day there will be a watch of four security officers/ship's company, and during the night that will be reduced to one security officer and one member of the ship's crew on watch.

Phase five: Spain to the UK

The distance from Pontevedra to London is just over 600 miles, with a steaming time of 20 days.

Phase six: unloading and onward journey

The *Hampton Bridge* arrived at London at 0600hrs, and her cargo of Lithium was unloaded and on the road by 0930hrs. Once again four container vehicles are used for the journey from East London to Newport, Wales, which with a break will take approximately five hours. As always, the drivers will stop at Moto Chieveley Services near Newbury, as this is a favourite service stop for all HGV drivers.

Phase seven: completion of journey

At approximately 1500hrs, the four container vehicles, complete with (hopefully) 1,000 cases of Lithium will arrive at the battery production facility in Newport, which is their destination – some 240 days after sailing from Chile.

Earlier in this section, and in Chapter 1 of the book we discussed security risk management, and now is the perfect opportunity, having read the above case study, to introduce security risk management to the supply chain.

ISO 28000 (2007) covers security management systems for the supply chain, and in the abstract, the standards says that ISO 28000:2007 specifies the requirements for a security management system, including those aspects critical to security assurance of the supply chain. Security management is linked to many other aspects of business management. Aspects include all activities controlled or influenced by organisations that impact on supply chain security. These other aspects should be considered directly, where and when they have an impact on security management, including transporting these goods along the supply chain.

ISO 28000:2007 is applicable to all sizes of organisations, from small to multinational, in manufacturing, service, storage or transportation at any stage of the production or supply chain that wishes to:

1   Establish, implement, maintain and improve a security management system
2   Assure conformance with stated security management policy

3 Demonstrate such conformance to others
4 Seek certification/registration of its security management system by an accredited third-party certification body; or
5 Make a self-determination and self-declaration of conformance with ISO 28000:2007.[108]

There are legislative and regulatory codes that address some of the requirements in ISO 28000:2007.

It is not the intention of ISO 28000:2007 to require duplicative demonstration of conformance.

Organisations that choose third-party certification can further demonstrate that they are contributing significantly to supply chain security.

A critical requirement for the standard is for accredited parties to demonstrate through a risk assessment process that they have a credible means of introducing a security risk management programme that will protect all aspects of the organisational supply chain.

We will now examine once again the component parts of risk management by reflecting on the lithium journey from Chile to Newport.

As a reminder of the principles of the risk assessment and risk management process, we need to understand the following component parts of risk and build them into the case study.

- **Assets**
  An asset is anything of value belonging to an organisation that holds value, and therefore requires protection.

  - **Case study**
    There are of course a number of assets to choose from in the case study. There are the vehicles and crews used to transport the product by land. There is the *Hampton Bridge* and her crew, who have braved the high seas to move the lithium from Chile to London, and of course there is the lithium itself, which is at the centre of all supply chain operations within the case study. There is the brand and reputation of the transportation company, because although it is intangible, should the operation fail, for whatever reason, the company's brand and reputation will be in ruins.
    Asset: Lithium

- **Threats**
  A threat is any action which may culminate by damaging or harming the asset. It can also be defined as a combination of capability and intent: for example I am going to kill you or steal your lithium!

  - **Case study**
    The threats against the product are numerous, and we will look at some of them on an individual basis.

    - **Espionage** and theft of information protocols, that is the commercial theft of research and development information in relation to all aspects of the lithium process. The threat of commercial espionage is extremely high, particularly with the aid of insider operatives.
    - **Theft** whilst in storage, containment or in transit. The product (lithium) is probably at its greatest threat when the final processing stage is complete, and

it has value. On the road, there is the threat of hijack and theft of the product, and whilst on the high seas there is the possibility of pilferage by the ship's crew.

- **Criminal damage and arson**. Perhaps the easiest way to attack the product is by either causing physical damage or setting it alight. If it cannot be stolen, commercial competitors and organised criminals may decide it is to their advantage for the product to be destroyed.
- **Assault**. Whilst not a direct threat to the product, it is very possible that either drivers or security personnel may be harmed by a potential criminal who is attempting to either steal or destroy the lithium.

- **Vulnerabilities**
A weakness in the system that can be exposed by a threat.

  - **Case study**
  As with threats to the product, vulnerabilities are many, with the following most pertinent:

    - **The human element.** From the moment Lithium processing begins to the time when it is delivered to the consumer, there will be human involvement, and with any high value product there is always the vulnerability of human involvement. Whether the threats are espionage, theft, criminal damage/arson or assault, there will be human interaction, and at present it is impossible to prevent such an influence, but the risk holder must be aware of this vulnerability at all times.
    - **Physical protection.** No system is tamper proof, and therefore if the standards of physical protection are not fit for purpose, the perpetrator will use this vulnerability to attack the asset. Lithium will be contained in sealed boxes, and whilst on the road or at sea, will be further protected within robust, sealed and secured steel containers. That is not say, however, that such precautions cannot be breached; and that quantifies the importance of an effective security risk assessment and operational requirement.
    - **Policies plans and procedures.** From vetting of personnel, through to the risk assessment and crisis management planning, policies, plans and procedures need to be robust, and they need to be exercised on a regular basis. They also need to be effectively communicated to all stakeholders, in order that all documentation is fully understood and may be adhered to and acted upon under all circumstances and at any time of day.
    - **Information technology.** Too often the Achilles' heel of any process or system. Owners of the system are sometimes inclined to either ignore the threat in the belief that their IT systems and networks are effectively protected. Or perhaps there is the opinion that because the systems have never been attacked, it is unlikely that they will be now. Both assumptions are wide of the mark, and indeed they increase the vulnerability of the product. The entire processing and movement project will be reliant on IT support, and that of course will be known by the criminal or terrorist, who if successful in hacking the network will have total access to all aspects of the programme.
    - **Ineffective communications.** This can be the greatest vulnerability of any programme, because if those involved do not have a complete understanding

of the overall picture, and what is expected of them, any programme can very quickly determinate to a level where there is significant risk to the asset. The transportation of the processed lithium from Chile to Wales will have involved several hundred stakeholders, operating at various levels of management and responsibility, and they need a 24/7 understanding of exactly where they fit in and what their roles are. Communications requirements must involve not only those active in the project itself, but also specialist personnel who are responsible for risk and crisis management communications, this must be from the 'top down'.

- **Likelihood**
The chance or probability that an event will occur or not.

  - **Case study**
  Whilst the definition of likelihood is extremely simple, the measurement of the concept is exceptionally complex. In terms of risk, the assessor technically, is attempting to predict future events, and a trap that is far too often fallen in to is following the temptation to measure the future, purely by calculating events in the past. For instance, because a number of container vehicles have been hijacked in a particular location during a defined period of time historically, it is (somewhat naively) argued that container vehicles travelling through the same location are also likely to be attacked. I argue that it is impossible to predict likelihood with any level of certainty, but it is probably the most important act of any risk assessment, and it has to be treated as such.

  In order for an effective likelihood assessment to be achieved, whilst utilising the case study, we need to consider the following areas:

  - **The asset.** In this case we are looking at the protection of the product, which is processed lithium. The question that must be asked is why is the asset important, and what are we protecting it from, because thinking like a criminal (remember that idea?) we need to understand the value of the lithium, and why anybody would wish to steal or damage it.
  - **The threat.** We must have an effective understanding of the threat (espionage, theft, criminal damage/arson or assault), and we need to consider and examine the credibility of those threatening the asset (organised criminals, opportunists, state actors, terrorists, etc.). For this we need to have access to the most sophisticated selection of intelligence analysis, and this may mean courting police and state security services or procuring private intelligence information and data.
  - **Vulnerability.**
  If the risk owner can identify a vulnerability in the system, then there is a good chance that the criminal/terrorist will identify the same weakness, and be encouraged to attack, as and when it suits him or her. In terms of the case study, we have already observed a number of critical areas that could be exposed as vulnerabilities, and they need to be treated as a matter of urgency.

- **Impact**
The consequences of a successful attack against the asset. For example one of the many impacts that resulted after the attacks on 9/11 was the loss of life.

- **Case study**
  To a certain extent the impact of an attack against the processed lithium is dependent on the aims of the aggressor. That is to say, the attacker will have a predetermined aim of what he or she is trying to achieve. The attack may be in the form of either criminal damage against the production facility, with the aim of ensuring that the project is slowed down, if not cancelled, with a huge impact in terms of finance and brand and reputation. The attack may take place whilst the asset is being transported on land, and it may be in the form of a vehicle hijack, with the potential impact being injuries or fatalities of the drivers and a loss of the product. Once again there will be a concurrent financial impact, and damage to brand and reputation. Potentially the most critical impact will be felt if the research and development programme is attacked in the form of an IT breach, because there is every possibility that critical sensitive information and data will be stolen, with once again financial and brand and reputation concerns. Whichever means of attack is successful, there will be consequential impact that may take years to recover from.

- **Risk treatment**
  Risk treatment relates to the measures taken to control risk once it has been analysed, and risk values are known.

  - **Case study**
    It is generally accepted that there are four ways to treat risk, and they are to *accept, avoid, reduce*, or *transfer* the risk. Using the case study profile, we will examine the four means of risk treatment.

    - Accept
      As the result of the security risk assessment in relation to the processing and movement of lithium, it has been agreed that an attack against the asset whilst being transported on land is possible. If such an act of aggression took place, the executive board is comforted with the assurance that the product will be transported by using four sealed container vehicles, with the vehicles using individual routes to the consumer in Newport, Wales. The likelihood of all four transporters being successfully attacked is low, and the Board is prepared to accept the risk, which after all means of treatment have been utilised is referred to as 'residual risk'. The action of risk acceptance also fits into the organisations risk appetite. Risk acceptance.
    - Avoid
      Risk avoidance is probably the most complicated of the four risk treatment methods, because inevitably it attracts organisational politics an upheaval. Once again we will utilise the case study to examine how risk avoidance may be an option, albeit an uncomfortable option. The contract to process, transport and hand over the boxed lithium to the battery manufacturers in South Wales is worth approximately $20 million, with a profit margin of 22%, meaning a pre-tax profit of approximately $3.4 million, which is a substantial percentage of the company's annual turnover and pre-tax profit, and as the global security manager having been informed by a number credible intelligence sources that the asset will be attacked at sea, with a

strong possibility of the *Hampton Bridge* being hijacked, with the potential for a complete loss of product, and even more concerning, the possibility of a loss of life.

The dilemma now of course is that you have to convince the executive board to avoid the risk by cancelling the contract, or at least postponing it, which will bring with it heavy financial penalties, and damage to the brand and reputation of the company. You may believe your intelligence sources, but how do you convince the board of this credibility? Risk avoidance.

- Reduce
  By far the most generic form of risk treatment is that of risk reduction. That is to say, we understand the risk factor for the movement of the product, and in order to reduce it we introduce a series of risk reduction methods, or control measures. I relation to the movement of lithium by land, which is believed to carry the greatest risk, the control measures we will introduce are:

  - Ensure that all container vehicles travel by separate routes.
  - All vehicles will have two means of communication.
  - There will be a two-man crew.
  - The police will be aware of all four journeys and will be furnished with route information.
  - Every container will be protected by a radio frequency identification (RFID) seal.

  The preceding precautions and control measures will not of course guarantee that no attack will take place; rather they should reduce the likelihood of a successful act of aggression, thus reducing the risk.

- Transfer
  This is the element of risk treatment that is common but is rarely discussed. The cost of the contract will be approximately $20 million, and that does not include capital and operational expenditure that will cause costs to rise. In order that the company involved in the transportation of the product is protected for all circumstances, an appropriate level of insurance will be arranged, and should damage be inflicted on the operation, the company will be supported by its insurance brokers.

Therefore, any logistics operations carried out within the global intermodal supply chain is critically reliant on the effectiveness of a robust risk assessment process, that should be aligned with the operations being carried out by the organisation.

Exercise Brave Defender – task 11: supply chain security management

Synopsis

As the result of a recent IT security risk assessment it has been decided by the executive board, advised by the chief information officer (CIO) and the chief information security officer (CISO) that a network upgrade is required. This is going to be a substantial investment, and computer hardware, such as servers and routers are going to have to be ordered direct from the manufacturer in Japan.

> Task 1: Once the CIO/CISO have identified the equipment required from the supplier in Japan, you are to complete a security operations plan for the safe and secure transportation of the hardware from the following locations.
>
> 1 The hardware will be produced and stored in Nagoya.
> 2 The closest commercial seaport is Nagoya
> 3 The nearest freight airport is Haneda Airport, Tokyo.

The consignment will consist of eight containers approximately $2 \times 2 \times 2$ metres.

> Task 2: Advise the CIO/CISO which is the safest and most secure way of transporting the hardware, by sea or by air.
>
> Task 3: Consider which security risk management standards will be appropriate for the operation.

3.12 Hostile environment awareness

Notwithstanding the above political initiative, which stretches the definition of a hostile environment, the world has always been a dangerous place to live and work, including immigrants to the Americas, or the New World as it was known, Prisoners of Mother England who were shipped off to Australia, or even Christian missionaries who very often gave their lives for a religious belief in countries such as China, Africa and Russia. However, in recent times, particularly since the events of 9/11 and the resulting wars in Iraq and Afghanistan, life in what have been termed hostile areas has been incredibly difficult and dangerous. As a result, hundreds, if not thousands of Hostile Environment Awareness Training (HEAT) training courses have been written and delivered for journalists, corporate businesspeople, and VIPs who have to either exist in those areas or travel through them. The aim of this sub-chapter is not to replicate such training courses, but rather it is to assist the reader in understanding what is meant by hostile environment awareness.

Interestingly, if you search for the term 'hostile environment', you will find answers such as:

- 'In United States labour law, a *hostile work environment* exists when one's behavior within a workplace creates an environment that is difficult or uncomfortable for another person to work in, due to discrimination.'[109]

Hostile countries and regions: The influence of local warlords and militias

Just prior to and quickly after hostilities ceased in Iraq and Afghanistan, and in other war-torn areas such as Libya and Syria, there became a need for travel to those areas for purposes such as media coverage, business development, and for operations carried out by non-governmental organisations (NGO) such as Oxfam, the Red Cross, and so on. Of course, regions which are post conflict tend to generate turf wars, which are fought by baronial individuals pursuant in vacuuming as much profit from the devastated country as possible, and the last thing they want is bad publicity or threats from external financial institutes. They tend to recruit for their own militias, bringing pressure on standing governments, either financially or in military terms, very often by issuing bribes, or threatening blackmail, not being afraid to resort to kidnap and ransom, or close quarter assassination (CQA).

Beirut

Beirut is the capital city of Lebanon, with a population of about 360,000, and from a religious perspective has always been split between Muslims (54%) and Christians (40%), with the remainder being divided between Druze and other Christian denominations.

During the period 1975–1990, Lebanon was devastated by a civil war not seen in the region for centuries, during which it is believed that 120,000 people lost their lives. I was serving in the British Royal Military Police during that period, and in December 1984 I deployed to West Beirut to lead the close protection team at the British Embassy, under the stewardship of Sir David Myers, who was probably the wisest person that I ever had the honour to serve.

The ambassador, his staff and my team lived at various locations in West Beirut, which was probably the most dangerous city in the world at that time. What absolutely astounded me upon my arrival was that embassy staff, despite extremely high levels of kidnapping of foreigners, went about their everyday life as though they were posted to Kensington or York, including the often frequenting of the Commodore Hotel, which was the last standing hotel in West Beirut, and populated by the world's media, all others, including the Holiday Inn, the Phoenicia and the St George being destroyed during the fighting.

There was an unwritten agreement between the fighting militias such as the PSP and Hezbollah that if reporting of the war by global media was not to blame the militias, the Commodore would remain standing, and intact. It was seen as a safe refuge, and because generally, reporting on the conflict was balanced it was left alone. The Commodore also had a tactical and geographical advantage, and the BBC reporter Robert Fisk wrote during the conflict:

> If the Commodore had not been there, the Israeli invasion would not have been so well reported

Of course, that would never be allowed today in Iraq or Afghanistan.

Another aspect of the period post conflict, particularly in Iraq, was the rise of the private military security company (PMSC). The PMSC has been covered earlier in this book, but suffice it say that the involvement of such organisations in hostile regions generated an almost ghost industry interestingly referred to as 'the circuit'.

The circuit consists of PMSCs that employ almost totally former British soldiers, predominantly teeth arm infantrymen, who drift from contract to contract in a constantly dynamic environment which changes on an almost daily basis, known as the circuit. A significant percentage of the work carried out by such operators is close protection, sometimes referred to as executive protection, and in this role the protection teams are deployed to ensure the safety of expatriates who are contracted to work in a hostile environment.

Very often, prior to deployment in a hostile area, the expatriates will participate in some form of hostile environment training, to make them aware of what they should expect to be exposed to once deployed overseas.

For the purpose of this book I searched for appropriate hostile environment training, known as Hostile Environment Awareness Training (HEAT) in an attempt to discover exactly what such a training course consist of.[110]

It would appear that the following topics and subject are consistently taught on a HEAT course.[111]

- *The personal risk assessment*: Because there are so many variables when considering threats and vulnerabilities, the delegate will be offered a range of risk assessment techniques, which can be adapted for individual environment. During this part of the course, the delegate should also be mentored in relation to the appropriate prevention and mitigation approaches required to reduce or avoid the risk.
- *Information and data security management*: In any environment, the protection of information is critical, but more so in a hostile region, where criminals and terrorists will benefit from receiving sensitive information. During this part of the course the impact of losing or having information stolen should be demonstrated, followed by advice and guidance on how to ensure such information remains secure.
- *Cultural awareness and understanding*: Far too often, Western businesspeople and contractors fail to understand the criticality of cultural awareness, which could vary from shaking the hand of a female without consent to a lack of empathy in relation to religious beliefs. In this section delegates will be made aware of a number of cultural differences, and how they should be managed.
- *Conflict management*: Closely related to cultural awareness and understanding, conflict management training deliverers an awareness of conflict escalation, and how such potential escalation should be managed before it spirals to a level where injuries are received, and perhaps loss of life.
- *Captivation management*: One of the most frightening aspects of living and working in a hostile environment is the prospect of being taken hostage, even after a risk assessment has been carried out. When taken captive, the hostage is too often unaware of what to expect, because it is likely that he or she knows nothing about their captors. In this part of the training course students will be taken through a number of scenarios and cases studies that will give them the skills to manage a captivation situation should it occur.
- *Improvised explosive device (IED) awareness*: In a significant percentage of those hostile environment where expatriates find themselves living and working, there is always the risk that they will be exposed to unexploded ordnance (explosives and ammunition) and suspect devices and packages. During this section of the training course delegates will be shown a number of different types of explosives, weapons and ammunition and the impact that can have. They will also be advised on the actions that should be taken (the 6 Cs) if they are exposed to any form of suspicious situation.
- *Medical training*: During a tour of duty in a hostile environment, it is likely that expatriates will encounter some form of medical situation, which may be in the form of a road accident, a gunshot wound, or the results of a detonated explosive device. During the course, delegates will be trained in a range of medical and first aid skills.
- *Safe travel planning and management*: Driving in a developed country with the use of a GPS device when encountering motorways or safe A roads is relatively straightforward. Travelling along a sandy potholed road with little or no road information is not so simple. During this part of the course students will be taught how to carry out a

managed route recce and understand the safe means of travelling along unprepared roads in a hostile environment.

- *Anti-surveillance drills*: Unless it is an opportunistic attack, the vast majority of acts of aggression carried out against foreigners will have been practiced and surveilled. It may be that the foreign contractor walks or drives to work every day at the same time, using the same route, which is easy for the aggressor. During this section students will be taught a range of anti-surveillance skills, such as not setting patterns or being aware of surveillance techniques, which will make it difficult for the aggressor to plan his or her attack.
- *Residence and hotel security*: Whether the expatriate lives in in a private residence or a hotel, there will be times when he or she is vulnerable to attack in pace of abode. This art of the training course will offer advice and guidance about ensuring that the residence or hotel area is safe, and that the occupant understand what action is necessary should they encounter any firm of attack outside of their work environment.

Hostile awareness training and management is critical in a world that probably has more post conflict regions than at any time in recent history. It will vary dependent on the region, the threats, and the nature of the training and protection requirements, but there is no doubt that it is important in all matters relating to security and risk management.

Exercise Brave Defender – task 12: hostile environment awareness

Synopsis

Two members of the executive board, male and female (the chief operations officer (male) and the finance director (female)) are required to travel to Libya to open discussions with the fledgling Libyan government about the possibility of signing a contract to supply cloud and land communications for that country.

> Task: Write a hostile environment awareness report to submit to the Board in preparation for the forthcoming trip. Take into consideration (at least) the following issues:
>
> 1 Is HEAT required; if it is what subjects would you like to be included in the training?
> 2 How will the two directors be transported to Libya?
> 3 What accommodation should be arranged for the visitors?
> 4 Will they require executive protection, and if so, in what form?

3.13 Strategic business awareness

It could be argued that this sub-chapter epitomises the rationale behind the book, in that a major concern of the private security sector today is that security management is unaware of the business requirements of the organisation they are supporting. But what does that mean?

Without wishing to reconstitute a number of points already made in the book, the fact of the matter is that for too long security managers have almost relied on the generosity of the board in general, and the chief finance officer in particular, for funding support.

Whilst the security function may be aware of what is required in terms of the security budget, it is common for the strategic objectives of the security department to be mis-aligned with those of the business.

I am certainly not advocating a loss of focus in terms of the protection of organisational assets, rather my argument is that there has to be a more robust cohesion in relation to what the organisation requires in order for the business to grow, and how it may be protected. If the business does not grow, there is a receding need for asset protection, and if there are poor levels of security risk management support, it is unlikely the business will develop. I argue that there is a symbiotic relationship here.

So what is meant by the term business awareness, and why does it include the security manager and his or her team?

Business awareness is one of the key skills that all strands of management must possess, and it comprises three distinct areas:

- A total understanding of what is required for the manager to be able to carry out their core activities, as seen by the internal functions of the department (the team), and by external proponents within the organisation (other teams). How is the security manager perceived by his or her team, and how are they judged by other supporting functions?
- A full appreciation of how the organisation is being supported by its functions and how it is impacted by internal and external influencing factors.
- An understanding of the context in which the core values and responsibilities (security) of the department support the business. Is the department a business enabler or a barrier to business growth?

The first point is relatively straightforward, insofar as the security manager is concerned, because he or she will have responded to some form of recruitment campaign, and although this may be a contentious remark, I am confident that the majority of forward thinking organisations are clear about what is required in terms of asset protection, which is still the formal requirement of a security function. That is to ensure the safety of all organisational assets through risk awareness and risk management response.

The second and third points, however, are far from transparent.

Britcom plc

The organisation critical to this exercise is, as I am sure you will recall, an international communications company that is in the process of consolidation and development, in a market that is dynamic and challenging to say the least. At the heart of Britcom's business portfolio, and indeed the current unique selling point is a secure cloud-based means of protecting customer information and data. An emphasis on the context of the term 'secure cloud'.

Once again, I am confident in the ability of the security department, which includes information security and cyber protection functions to make safe the facilities of the cloud-based communications system. My concern, however, is does the security department understand the *business and commercial operations* needed to develop and maintain such an advanced high technology service.

This is yet another contentious area for discussion, because whilst there may be arguments in favour of the security team understanding the intricacies of developing and selling such technological innovations, a more primitive view is likely to be that the security team is formed to protect the business, not develop it. Security is for security, not sales.

Perhaps unsurprisingly, I sit somewhere in the middle, believing that there is merit to both sides of this argument, and here is my philosophy.

Businesses today are expecting every facet of the organisation to contribute to its development, that includes the security function; and of course, that, from a business perspective makes absolute sense. However, it must be remembered that from an operational, tactical and strategic perspective, *the core function* of any security department is to ensure the safety and security of the assets belonging to the organisation that the security department supports and protects.

Think about this potential problem from the perspective of the executive board of a large corporation.

When a Blue Chip or FTSE 100 company begins the process of recruiting a head of security, the human resources department are not instructed to seek candidates holding a master's in business administration (MBA), or a bachelor's degree in engineering or sales. Rather the candidates for this particular role will be required to possess a higher education qualification, perhaps an MSc in a security related discipline. Applicants will also have to demonstrate a strategic awareness of security risk management, the law, physical and electronic security systems, workplace investigations, and so on.

There is also a strong possibility that candidates will be required to deliver added value skills, and that may include an understanding of health and safety legislation, and perhaps a second language, dependent upon the geographical location.

However, the core requirement will be to demonstrate advanced skills and knowledge in relation to security and risk management.

Once recruited, the head of security will be required to very quickly come to terms with the functionality of other departments, primarily so he or she may be able to understand the relationships between the security department and other teams.

This functional adjustment is critical in terms of avoiding a 'silo' mentality, otherwise the security department could quite easily be perceived as functioning independently of the remainder of the organisation, with aims and objectives that are not in alignment with the aims and objectives of other departments, and are therefore alienated from the company's strategic, tactical and operational momentum. Once again the security department is going to be seen as the team that actually inhibits growth, as opposed to the function that enables business development, part of the bigger team.

There is no doubt that it is absolutely crucial for all members of the security department to be able to demonstrate an understanding of the financial and business operations of the organisation. However, a balance must be struck, with an understanding that whilst such a business acumen is of course a major advantage, the core function of the security manager and his team is to protect the organisation and secure its assets.

Exercise Brave Defender – task 13: security business awareness

Synopsis

The executive board have offered the opportunity for middle and senior managers within the business to apply for representation of their function; and this includes you, the security manager.

Task

In less than 500 words, draft a biography of yourself, arguing why you should be offered a seat on the board. Emphasise the following:

- Your current value to the organisation in terms of your current role.
- What added value you can bring to help grow the business.
- An example of a recent business case submitted by you.
- Your unique selling point.

3.14 Fraud and fraud investigations

The increasing globalisation of fraud continues, driven by an enhanced international communications infrastructure, increased accessibility to the Internet, poor levels of regulation and under-resourced law enforcement capabilities in some countries (Betts, 2017).

Concern – 2018

PWC, in their annual report, produced as the result of a global survey which included 7,200 respondents from 123 different states, titled:

Pulling fraud out of the shadows: The biggest competitor you didn't know you had

PwC's 2018 Global Economic Crime and Fraud Survey

PwC announced a series of extremely concerning statistics for 2018, including the facts that:

- 49% of organisations globally said they've been a victim of fraud and economic crime – up from 36%
- 64% of respondents said losses due directly to their most disruptive fraud could reach USD 1 million.
- 52% of all frauds are perpetrated by people inside the organisation.
- 31% of respondents that suffered fraud indicated they experienced cybercrime.

In a telling section of the PWC economic crime survey, organisations were asked:

> "Has your organisation experienced any fraud and/or economic crime within the last 24 months?" Here is how those respondents answered:

Figure 3.11 shows an increase in economic crime in all seven regions, with Latin America suffering most with an increase of just over 47% during the timescale.

Spending on counter fraud measures has also increased over the same time scale, with 42% of respondents saying their companies had increased spending on combatting fraud and economic crime over the past two years (up from 39% in 2016).

- 44% of respondents said they plan to boost spending over the next two years.

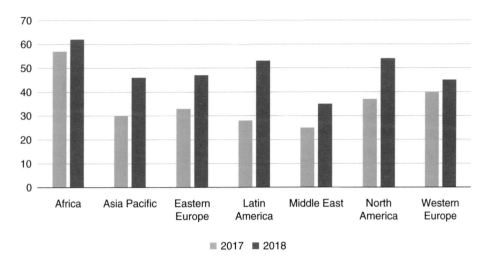

Figure 3.11 Reported economic crime

If you are involved in financial security within an organisation, or perhaps whether you are just interested, go to www.pwc.com/gx/en/services/advisory/forensics/economic-crime-survey.html#cta-1 and download the PWC report.

Fraud

In the UK, when describing the enormity of problems relating to fraud, the National Crime Agency says that "fewer than 20 per cent of incidents of fraud are actually reported so the true figure may be much higher. This means that the scale of fraud is very significant, but that under-reporting also hampers our understanding of the threat".[112]

There are a vast number of elements that are related to the crime of fraud, such as forgery, corruption, theft, collusion and so on.

The Chartered Institute of Public Financing and Accountancy (CIPFA) define fraud as:

> Any intentional false representation, including failure to declare information or abuse of position that is carried out to make gain, cause loss or expose another to the risk of loss.

- **Intentional false representation:**

  This relates to deception when offering personal information, generally when an application is being completed.

- **Failure to declare information.**

  - Dishonestly fails to disclose to another person information which he is under a legal duty to disclose; and
  - When there is the 'intention' not to provide relevant and legally required information to make a gain in some form.

- **Abuse of position that is carried out to make gain, cause loss or expose another to the risk of loss.**

  - Occupies a position in which he is expected to safeguard, or not to act against, the financial interests of another person;
  - Dishonestly abuses that position; and
  - Intends, by means of the abuse of that position –

    - To make a gain for himself or another; or
    - To cause loss to another or to expose another to a risk of loss.

  - A person may be regarded as having abused his position even though his conduct consisted of an omission rather than an act.[113]

Types of fraud

A vast number of publications have been made available relating to fraud, all of which will meticulously detail the huge number of ways in which a fraudster can overcome his or her victim; but the volume of fraud by type is too great to include in this book. Instead we shall examine several types of fraud that are more likely to be deployed against individuals and businesses today.

The first and probably most common means of form is identity theft.

Identity theft

Pause for thought

You receive a telephone call at home one evening, and the caller announces that she is employed by your bank, and that she would like to speak to you about your account. However, she informs you that before the conversation can commence, she needs to 'go through' your security details. What will be your response?

Identity theft is the deliberate use of someone else's identity, usually as a method to gain a financial advantage or obtain credit and other benefits in the other person's name, and perhaps to the other person's disadvantage or loss. The person whose identity has been assumed may suffer adverse consequences, especially if they are held responsible for the perpetrator's actions. Identity theft occurs when someone uses another's personally identifying information, like their name, identifying number, or credit card number, without their permission, to commit fraud or other crimes.[114]

According to Action Fraud,[115] a record 172,919 identity frauds were recorded in 2016 more than in any other previous year, according to Cifas, the UK's leading fraud prevention service.[116]

The Information Commissioners Office (ICO)[117] offer this stark warning:

Your identity is one of your most valuable assets. If your identity is stolen, you can lose money and may find it difficult to get loans, credit cards or a mortgage.

Your name, address and date of birth provide enough information to create another "you". An identity thief can use a number of methods to find out your personal information and will then use it to open bank accounts, take out credit cards and apply for state benefits in your name.

However, despite the high profile of one of the most publicised crimes in the world, Acoca (2008) in Gill (2014) questions the lack of statistical evidence available when she argues that:

Identity theft (whether offline, or online) has failed to attract the attention of statisticians. Most data are from the United states; statistics from Europe do not exist, except for the United Kingdom. When data are available, they often do not cover identity theft as an independent wrong.

As Acoca has quite correctly (in my opinion) argued, although identity theft is statistically lean, it is nevertheless a very high-profile crime that can impact anybody; literally anybody. Interestingly there are generally two approaches to researching this form of crime (as with any other) and that is from an academic perspective, and from the viewpoint of the practitioner.

For example, Pontell and Geis in Gill (2014) after discussing legislation (or rather a lack of legislation), perpetrator and victim typology and global identity theft conclude that:

Identity theft is a newcomer to the roster of criminal behaviours that are being given serious attention throughout the world. Its extent apparently has grown precipitously; in part, it appears, because those who come to practice it find it easy, impersonal, profitable and relatively (not completely of course) risk free. In an ironic way, identity theft has filled gaps left by robbers who have abandoned the practice and bemoan the fact that previously excellent targets – the suit and tie folks – no longer carry large amounts of cash but have come to depend on credit cards.

On the other hand, Betts (2017), perhaps from a more practical perspective, points to the fact that identity theft happens when fraudsters access enough information about someone's identity (e.g. their name, gender, date of birth, current or previous address) to commit identity fraud. Identity theft can take place regardless of whether the fraud victim is alive or deceased. Batts goes on to say that identity fraud can be described as the use of that stolen identity in criminal activity to obtain goods or services by fraud.

Fraudsters can use identity details to:

- Open bank accounts
- Obtain credit cards, loans and state benefits
- Order goods
- Take over existing accounts
- Take out mobile phone contracts
- Obtain genuine documents such as passports and driving licences, and from my personal experience,
- Obtain insurance (or at least attempt to).

Criminals commit identity theft by stealing personal information. This is often done by taking documents from the rubbish, or by making contact with the victim and pretending to be from a legitimate organisation. Other identity thefts occur when insiders steal personal information or penetrate data bases holding private information. The first victims may know of it may be when they receive bills or invoices for things they have not ordered, or when they receive letters from debt collectors for debts that are not theirs (Betts, 2017).

However intelligent and street wise the identity fraudster may think himself or herself may be, they are not guaranteed to be successful if you and I carry out a few extremely basic security tasks, such as:

- Always cross shred personal information.
- Thinking about the pause for thought at the beginning of this section, never give security or personal details over the phone unless you absolutely sure that they will be secure. Certainly not as the result of an unsolicited telephone call or email.
- There's no excuse these days for not examining all of our bank and other statements, either in hard copy or electronically. If anything, suspicious is perceived, the bank or financial institute must be contacted immediately.
- Change all passwords and codes as often as possible, perhaps on a monthly basis, and ensure that all of the passwords used are complex. Do not use birthdays, regimental numbers, house addresses, and so forth, as the fraudster will find such security extremely easy to breach.
- Take care of your credit and debit cards. Never hand them over, and if possible secure them in a carbon case that cannot be penetrated by an RFID scanner.
- Think twice before using a contactless card, as such cards are less secure than a chip and PIN variation.
- If you are in the UK and you believe that you have been the victim of identity fraud, contact Action Fraud on 0300 1232040 or on www.actionfraud.police.uk.

Whilst identity fraud through identity theft has an enormous impact, there are of course many other types of fraud that can bring devastation to personnel and organisations alike. In the next part of this section we will examine a number of other types of fraud currently being perpetrated.

Electronic fraud

Electronic fraud, which is the use of computer technology and the Internet, probably has a greater rate of growth than any other form of fraud, and it can impact in a number of ways. Below are a list of fraud opportunities taken by the criminal.

- **Account takeover**

  This is probably one of the most common forms of fraud today, it is certainly the fastest growing type of fraudulent offence, and anybody can be the victim.

  Opening an unknown email attachment or staying on the telephone too long when the caller s unknown are the two most common forms of account take over, as the criminal normally acquires sufficient information to take over. Unfortunately, common is the action of a fraudulent caller claiming to represent the bank of the victim, who is asked to pass his or her security details over the phone.

Don't do it. If you don't know who you are talking to, don't release any personal information.

- **Bank card fraud**
  According to ActionFraud, bank card and cheque fraud happens when criminals steal cards or chequebooks and gain access to funds in an account.

  Criminals steal bank cards or cheque book; or they obtain card or account details, allowing them to take money from an account or run up credit in the name of the account holder. He or she will usually notice this by seeing unfamiliar transactions on their statements, or suddenly finding that the overdraft limit or credit limit has been exceeded and card is refused when a purchase is attempted.

  Here are some of the ways a fraudster could steal money:

  - The ATM.
    A relatively common means of committing ATM fraud is to have a card recognition system illegally installed within the ATM, and as the card is legally inserted, all details will be captured, and used later by the thief. Another means is to have a miniature camera positioned above the ATM, which will photograph the card details as cash is being withdrawn, and once again the details will be used, probably online, at a later date. Always check the ATM for perhaps any protruding slot lips which may mean that a device has been illegally installed, equally, before taking the card from a pocket, examine the ATM, looking for what may appear to be some form of lens. If you are suspicious, don't use the ATM and report it to the cash provider.

  - Counterfeit cards.
    Generally referred to as 'skimming', this is where once again the thief steals the card details, either by the use of some form of device at an ATM, or perhaps at a hotel or restaurant when the card is taken away for payment. There is also a recent piece of equipment which allows the thief to skim the card whilst it is inside a wallet, inside a pocket. Never allow a member of staff at a retail outlet, and that includes hotels, pubs, restaurants, and so forth to remove the card to a place where it cannot be seen. There are carbon card holders on the market that will prevent the card from being skimmed.

  - Contactless cards
    Contactless cards have been in use for some time now, and they use quite standard RFID technology, which allows the RFID tag built into the card to be read by the host, enabling reader to make some form of transaction, whether is it purchasing goods, or withdrawing cash, without chip and PIN security. Although this is an extremely convenient means of transaction, it is fraught with security issues. If a contactless card is lost and found, or should it be stolen, it can be used by anybody as there is no requirement

to prove ownership of the card, which is achieved by the use of a (hopefully) secure Personal Identification Number (PIN) when the card is legitimately used. Whilst writing this book, I made an enquiry about how many times a found or stolen contactless card can be used before it is flagged as illegal. I was informed that the limit was £150, and for any transaction after that PIN and chip is required. However, I was offered the option of receiving a new card without contactless functionality.

The financial sector

The financial services sector is an important part of many economies. In the United Kingdom it assumes a huge contribution to the economy, accounting for 7.9% of UK GDP (gross domestic product), it accounts for 11.6% of tax receipts, employing over a million people, with a further 967,000 in professional services link to this sector. Some of the key parts of the financial services sector include insurance, pensions, personal banking services and commercial banking services. In the UK financial services also have a significant global dimension, attracting substantial foreign investment, generating a trade surplus of over £47 billion (The City UK, 2013).

There are a wide range of criminal activities which occur in the financial services sector. They range from a robber holding up a bank with a firearm, cybercriminals seeking to hack into the bank's computers to steal funds, to complex frauds perpetrated by the financial services sector against their own customers. Fraud alone is estimated to cost the financial services sector over £5 billion per annuum.

Criminal behaviours in this sector will broadly be grouped under the following headings.

- *Traditional 'ordinary' crimes against the financial services sector*: a variety of criminal behaviours largely perpetrated against the financial institutes which, when the perpetrator is identified, are normally processed through the criminal justice system if there is sufficient evidence and resources.
- *Grey crimes against the financial services sector*: a multiplicity of criminal behaviours which, when the perpetrator is identified, are usually settled through private or regulatory mechanisms. Very rarely there may also be a criminal prosecution, but that is not the norm.
- *Grey crimes by financial institutions against society and their customers*: these involve a range of criminal behaviours undertaken by financial institutions, largely dealt with through private and regulatory mechanisms. Very rarely there may also be a criminal prosecution, buy that is not the norm (Button and Tunley in Gill, 2014)

Investment fraud

Often referred to as 'scams', investment fraud is generally aimed at the vulnerable in society. Criminals will carry out extensive demographic research, before targeting their victims en masse. The criminals will promise substantial returns on fictitious investments, which may involve stocks and shares, commodities, and so forth. Cash up front will be demanded of course, and the victim very rarely sees his or her money again, let alone a return on investment (ROI).

The police will rarely involve themselves in this form of crime, and recommend victims report their plight to Action Fraud on www.actionfraud.police.uk.

Exercise Brave Defender – task 14: fraud

Synopsis and task

Taking into consideration the fact that the offence of fraud has increased in all areas of business recently, the board of Britcom has requested you to investigate possible threats to the business, outlining three critical areas of fraud, and how they may be countered.

3.15 Retail loss and prevention methods

Beck in Gill (2014) says that rarely is the topic of retailing far from the top of news agenda – not least because of the inflated role the sector now plays in the economies of countries across the world. Measures of consumer confidence, sales and retailer profits are routinely scrutinised by governments and the 'market' alike, to get a sense of the overall wellbeing (or not) of an economy – if people are shopping, then all is deemed well with the world. This is perhaps not surprising, when the scale of the sector is considered. Within the United Kingdom, retailing now accounts for approximately 22% of the GDP, earning about £381 billion for the country in 2018.

The UK retail sector accounts for one-third of consumer spending in the UK.[118] The most common term for loss within the retail sector is known as shrinkage.

The term shrinkage can be quite deceiving, but it is generally thought of as being the result of theft, however that is not truly accurate. Shrinkage is divided into two areas and can include the following means of discrepancy:

* *Known shrinkage*

  Price reductions: Authorised by the store manager
  Wastage: Authorised by the store manager
  Discovered theft: Theft being investigated.

* *Unknown shrinkage*

  Unrecorded waste: Products that have been disposed of without authority
  Undiscovered theft: Location of goods that is unaccounted for
  Undeclared reductions: Possible collusion between a member of staff and a member of the public.

For the purpose of this book we will consider retail shrinkage as the accepted general term for retail loss.

According to report commissioned by Tyco Retail Solutions in 2018, called *The Sensormatic Global Shrink Index*, 1,120 respondents reported a shrinkage rate of 1.82% across 14 countries and 13 retail verticals in the survey conducted during 2017–18. The cost of shrinkage amounts to $99.56 billion for retailers, globally. The four regions involved in the survey, with their shrinkage percentages were:

* United States (1.85%)
* Europe (1.83%)

- Latin America (1.81%)
- Asia Pacific (1.75%)

Survey respondents globally (81.61%) report shrinkage represents up to 2.99% of total annual sales. In terms of financial impact, the top three countries show that shrinkage in 2017–18 were:

- United States ($42.49 billion)
- China ($13.52 billion)
- UK ($7.45 billion)

Table 3.4[119] shows shrinkage figures by type of outlet.

What is interesting from table is the fact that despite having the lowest measurement in terms of percentage (1.73%), shrinkage at hypermarkets and superstores, because of the foot flow and volume of sales, was three times that of its nearest peer group (supermarkets and neighbourhood stores at $8.96 billion) with a loss through shrinkage of $24.16 billion.[120]

The British Retail Consortium (BRC)

In the UK the lead organisation for the study of and research into retail is the British Retail Consortium (BRC), which publishes a detailed annual report relating to crime trends over the previous 12 months. In its introduction for the year 2018/2019,[121] the BRC worryingly announced the following:

This year's key findings are:

- The combined cost of spending on crime prevention and losses from crime to the industry is £1.9 billion;
- Every day, including weekends, 115 colleagues are attacked, with many more threatened, across the industry;
- Knives are seen as the most significant type of weapon;
- More than £700 million was lost to customer theft alone;
- Although retailers are spending 17% more on cybersecurity than last year, nearly 80% of the retailers surveyed have seen an increase in the number of attacks and/or breaches; and
- Around 80% of respondents describe the police response to retail crime as poor or very poor, with opinions generally better for violence than customer theft or fraud.

The report covers the following crime areas within the retail sector.

Table 3.4 Shrinkage figures

Type of outlet	2017–18 Shrink as a % of sales	Shrinkage value ($ billion)	Rank, based on shrinkage percentage
Fashion and Accessories Stores	1.98%	4.12	1
Department Stores	1.84%	3.37	2
Consumer Electronics Stores	1.82%	4.44	3
Supermarkets and Neighbourhood Stores	1.79%	8.96	4
Hypermarkets and Superstores	1.73%	24.16	5

Context and trends

The BRC's Retail Crime Survey has, for the fourth successive year, shown a growth in the direct cost of crime. Applying a sample group to the entire industry, this year's figure stands at just under £900 million, an increase of 28% (not adjusted for inflation), over the previous years. Broken down, this total is distributed between five principal areas of crime committed against the retail sector.

Percentage annual increase is shown in brackets.

1   Customer theft: £663 million, growth of £160 million (32%)
2   Fraud: £163 million, growth of £8 million (5%)
3   Robbery: £15 million, growth of £9 million (173%)
4   Burglary: £15 million, growth of £1.5 million (11%)
5   Criminal damage: £3.4 million, growth of £0.2 million (6%)

What is also interesting in the report is the fact that retail crime prevent spending has increased from just over £250,000 in the fiscal year 2015/16 to marginally over £1million for the period 2017/18. It also means that the industry is spending more than £100 million on crime prevention methods than it is losing to crime.

Violence and abuse

The BRC reports 115 members of staff being abused every day, with annual a total during the reporting period of 42,000 violent incidents. What is extremely interesting in this section of the report, and you of course can judge the validity of this for yourself, is that the BRC no longer discriminates between what they refer to as 'violence with injury' and 'violence without injury'. The argument being that 'the impact violence can have even where there is no immediately obvious physical injury. Emotional harm can be as serious a problem as physical injury, even if it may not be immediately apparent.'[122] I am not convinced that inflicting a major injury on a member of staff by use of a knife should be included in the same statistical category as that member of staff being informed that he or she were going to be 'beaten up after work'; but you must decide for yourself, based on your own judgements.

What cannot and should not be ignored, if the survey is factually correct, is the increasing use of knives as a weapon of first choice. It would appear that overwhelmingly staff are reporting that the greatest threat to them is the violent use of a knife, followed by inflicting a wound with the use of a syringe,[123] and last by the use of firearms.

Theft and damage

What is interesting to me about this section is that overall there has been a near 40% increase in theft and damage, with the report arguing that this is 'largely driven by 'Customer Theft' which represents just over 98% of all types by number of incidents.' However, in percentage terms, when measuring theft, there has been a 33% increase in customer theft, whilst it appears that staff theft has increased by 129%. However, nowhere in the report does it make comparisons between volumes and values of theft, in terms of customer and staff inclusion, and whilst it is relatively easy to research customer theft, staff theft is conveniently inconspicuous by its absence.

Fraud

According to the BRC, fraud against retail outlets increased by 5% when compared to the year 2017/18, but no figures were available. However, the latest Office for National Statistics (ONS) crime figures reflect the evolving challenges of combatting financial fraud today, revealing a 12% increase in overall fraud in 2018 compared with the previous year, based on the Crime Survey for England and Wales (CSEW).

The three most prevalent forms of fraud endured by the retail sectors are:

- *Card not present:* That is to say that the card is not presented to the retailer, rather the details are communicated over the Internet or by phone, normally being information about the legal owner that has been stolen.
- *Refund:* This pertains to a situation where the retailer has a 'no refunds' policy, and the criminal will return possibly stolen items in exchange for other goods which they are not legally entitled to. This is also sometimes referred to as a 'refund scam' or a 'whitehouse scam'.
- *Insider:* Often referred to as internal fraud, but it falls under the category of the insider threat, and there are three ways for the insider to achieve his or her goals:

  - First, there is *opportunity*, which fits in with the Routine Activity Theory (RAT) and is enhanced by the fact that employees believe they know the system so well that it easy (from their perspective) commit the offence of fraud. This is eased if there is no suitable guardian, and the funds are there for the taking.
  - Standards of living may be enriched by the act of fraud, particularly if the criminal or his/her partner is living to a standard of living that they now rely on, and they are under *pressure* to continue with a lifestyle that they have become used to.
  - Finally, there is *self-justification*, meaning that in the eyes of the employee/fraudster, the company owes them. I may be that data analyst believes that she is undervalued, or perhaps it is payback time for all the extra hours he has worked unpaid. Or may be as simple as believing that the organisation wouldn't miss the tiny sum being stolen.

Cyber

This is an extremely weak section of the report, which focusses on investments made in combating the cyberthreat, and a meek reference to types of cyberattacks suffered by the industry. That is concerning, because I am convinced that the retail sector is no less vulnerable to the cyberthreat than any other sector of industry. In fact, because of the increase in online sales over the last couple of years, I would argue that if anything, the sector is more threatened than a number of other areas.

There are a number of ways in which a cybercriminal may choose to attack a retailer.

- **Point of sale systems attacks**

  Probably the greatest threat to retail point of sale (PoS) systems is from a malware attack, and to refresh your memory, malware, or malicious software is designed to gain easy access to a computer system, and then once accessed create mayhem on that system by taking over or deleting files. One of the highest profile incidents involving malware being introduced to a point of sale system, was the attack against systems owned by Target, the giant US retail outlet.

In January 2014, cybercriminals managed to install malware onto the PoS terminals at Target shops throughout the US, and it would appear that the attackers were able to gain access to information belonging to 110 million customers. It has never been verified if the information and data was used in criminal activities, but it was the most audacious retail IT attack in US history.

- **Payment card skimming**

  Payment card skimming is unfortunately on the rise, particularly in a retail environment. Very simply put, the criminal will install a piece of equipment over the card reader that is concealed, and when the card, credit or debit, is inserted the system will copy the card details for use at a later date. If the stolen details are to be used online, it is simple for the criminal because he or she is in possession of all the details they need. It may be more appropriate for the criminal to have a replica card made with the legal owner's details embossed on the clone card, and until the theft has been discovered, the criminal will use the card as many times as possible. Card skimmers are also used at ATMs where they are inserted within the slot provided for the card holder to complete the transaction, and once again all details on the card are stolen and used at a later date. Occasionally, fraudsters will install a mini covert camera at the ATM which will photograph or film transactions.

- **Denial of service (DoS)**

  A denial of service attack occurs when a computer or server is overwhelmed by the volume of traffic it is attempting to process; the volume being orchestrated by a malicious attacker. Because the computer has a finite memory and processing speed, once the buffers are full it will halt all processing, meaning that the legal user can no longer access files or process information.

There are two types of DoS:

- Buffer overflow attacks

  The buffer system within a central processing unit (CPU) is designed to absorb a percentage of data (normally 20%) prior to it being fed to the hard drive. This allows the hard drive to operate smoothly as it is not processing all of the information at once. A buffer attacker will assign a data pathway that ensures that the buffer receives more data than it can handle, the data overflows to the hard drive, which slows down or stops operating.

- Flood attacks

  This is to quite literally overcome the capacity of a server by sending to it more packets of data than it can process, the attacker will be in possession of greater bandwidth than the victim and the server will stop operating.

- **Distributed denial of service (DDoS)**

  DDoS attacks target the subsystems that handle connections to the Internet, such as web servers. Their vulnerabilities are based on the principle that responding to an incoming query consumes computational and bandwidth resources. If someone were to call your phone incessantly, you would first lose the ability to concentrate, and then lose the ability to use your phone for any other purpose. Similarly, in the cyber world, if the attacker can overwhelm the connection link, the system is effectively removed from the Internet. It is fairly easy to defend against a single attacker against a fixed source: one just has to block the sender, just like blocking an annoying callers' number. In a distributed denial of service attack, the attacker uses a botnet of thousands or even millions to overwhelm the victim. It is the equivalent of having thousands or even millions of people trying to call your phone. Not only would you get nothing done, but the calls you actually want to receive wouldn't easily get through (Singer and Friedman, 2014).

The Beijing Olympics

When the Chinese government only wanted positive news to surround the 2008 Beijing Olympics, Chinese patriotic hacker forums made negative news by providing tutorials on how to launch a DDoS attack against the CNN website (they were upset by its reporting on riots in Tibet). Things escalated in 2010 when patriotic hackers from Iran and China – two ostensible allies in the real world – got into an escalating series of retaliatory attacks after www.baidu.com (the Chinese version of Google) was hit by the "Iranian Cyber Army".

- ### IoT vulnerabilities

    We have already covered the Internet of Things, which as I am sure you will recall is when a system is hacked via a smart piece of electronic equipment known as 'smart devices', such as smart electricity and gas meters, or a virtual digital assistant (VDA) such as the Amazon Echo or Alexa, devices that can control a range of home systems by voice command. These are smart devices or appliances that have no inbuilt security to prevent hacking. Any retail outlet that is reliant on such devices exposes systems such as point of sale (PoS) and radio frequency identification (RFID) configurations to external hacking.

- ### Threats to the supply chain

    We have already covered supply chain security in an earlier sub-chapter of the book, and it is important to emphasise that whether it is a high street clothes outlet or a shopping centre electronics shop, all retailers are reliant on the global intermodal supply chain being secure.

Retail loss prevention

Like any other organisation that is reliant sales, retail loss prevention is far too often seen, although with some justification, as nothing more than a cost centre. In fact, in retail, the loss prevention function is at times viewed as a business disabler, because there is the perception that secure cabinets and rear store areas are seen as barriers to sales. The retailer is often prepared to accept loss if it encourages sales.

Case Study – A UK retailer.

In the run-up to Christmas in 2007, a large UK electronics retailer decided to carry out a unique sales experiment, which initially was far from popular with staff and management.

The retailer in question ran store operations in 236 locations throughout the UK with an annual turnover then of just over £100 million.

The sales director managed to convince the executive board that the following strategy would increase sales.

It was decided that in all stores, boxed DVD players would be located just inside the shop to make it convenient for shoppers to pick up the box, take it to a sales terminal, pay for the product and leave the store. This was in comparison to the recognised system whereby the customer would order the goods from the sales terminal, and then wait until a member of staff was available to pick it from the warehouse to the rear of the store and bring it to the sales terminal where it would be processed. The argument being that this would be far more convenient for customers, and such convenience would stimulate sales.

Of course store management teams were initially incredibly reluctant to adopt the system, referring to it as 'pick and nick' reminiscent of the sweet counter sales strategy of 'pick and mix', where the sweets are spooned into a paper bag, before being weighed and paid for.

There were visions of local thieves popping into the store, picking up a boxed DVD player, then disappearing out of the front door, never to be seen again.

At the end of the Christmas period, the loss prevention controller was asked to carry out a survey of any increase in shrinkage due to the theft of DVD players, and unsurprisingly at the end of the period it was proven that 4.1% of the DVD players had been stolen, a huge increase in theft. However, when the sales director sponsored a survey to make sales comparisons over the period, it appeared that there had been a huge increase in sales of boxed DVDs to the value of 27.6%.

Of course, the increase in sales didn't impress individual store managers, who were extremely parochial, and took the increase in theft very personally.

The company sales director of course was very pleased with the tactic because she was interested in one aspect of store operations, and that of course was sales. Job done.

The same company barred the installation of sounders that activated if the warehouse door was breached, because in the words of the sales director, 'The high decibel sound was off putting for customers trying to concentrate on what they were going to buy next!'

There is no magic formulae when considering loss prevention methods except to argue that it is very much dependent on risk acceptance and the cost-benefit analysis.

In my experience there are three types of criminals who are prepared to carry out, or at least attempt to carry out an attack against the retail outlet.

- Members of staff
- Organised criminals
- Opportunist criminals.

Members of staff

In 2017–18 there was an increase in staff theft by a huge 179%,[124] and Beck (2014) in Gill argues that globally, internal theft accounted for 35%, with 45% of losses in the United

States being caused by internal theft, which should be a major concern for the retail industry. However, in my opinion, it isn't necessarily the rise in crime that should be addressed, rather it is the question 'why?' For what reasons do staff believe it is appropriate to steal from their place of work?

Hollinger and Clark (1983) in Gill (2014) argue that such theft should be referred to property deviance, which relates to incidents where staff steal or purposefully damage the assets of the employer. We are still left asking the question, 'why?'

Beck (2014) once again offers a number of reasons why members of staff commit property deviance. In the first instance he argues that staff may be under some form of financial pressure to steal; they may have built up personal debt, may have a drug or gambling addiction, or may simply have developed a lifestyle that is beyond their current income's capability to meet. Beck then argues that an explanation may be that dishonest employees may have low morale and levels of loyalty to the organisation – they feel poorly treated in various ways by their employer and hence steal to compensate for this (Altheide et al., 1978; Ditton, 1977; Greenburg, 1997; Hollinger and Clark, 1982; Mars, 1974, 1982, 2000). The third reason for this dishonesty, Beck suggests, is that organisational culture can influence the likelihood of employees stealing, in particular 'learned behaviour' from other employees (Curtis, 1979; Hollinger and Clark, 1983; Kamp and Brooks, 1991; Kresevich, 2007). However, there are two other arguments which tend to explain why employees steal from their employer:

- Opportunity

    Related to Situational Crime Prevention and Routine Activity Theory is opportunity, which is to say that employees, particularly in a retail environment are surrounded on a daily basis by produce that that may be insecure, located in an area often frequented by the employee. Whether that employee is an accountant or auditor with access to cash, or perhaps the rear store supervisor who is responsible for the acceptance and securing of produce that is easily and illegally moved on, or as referred to in the retail world; CRAVED:

    - **C**oncealable
    - **R**emovable
    - **A**vailable
    - **V**aluable
    - **E**njoyable
    - **D**isposable.

- Overconfidence

    Of course, confidence very often develops into arrogance, which is often related to carelessness. The rear door supervisor, who on a daily basis handles produce that is supported by paperwork and documentation that he or she has been processing for many years, and they know that process 'back to front', and it can easily be defeated (or so they think). The sales colleague who has been managing the point of sale terminal for 'God knows how long' is bored to the point of believing that the system is easily beaten (perhaps!). The cashier who is responsible for moving money around the business, especially to and from the bank is his own Nick Leeson:[125] a rogue trader who will never be caught.

The problem for this type of offender of course is that the belief that only he or she knows the system is inaccurate, because eventually the errors, through arrogance and pomposity, made in their attempt to commit the perfect crime, will be discovered, and this is where criminology can help the retail loss prevention manager who can utilise Situational Crime Prevention, which will reduce the ease at which the crime is committed, and increase the risk to the criminal of being apprehended.

Organised criminals

It could be argued that organised criminals make their own opportunities, and with their knowledge of the industry, at least their perceived knowledge, and very often collusion from inside, they are extremely difficult to investigate and prosecute. Organised criminals, and those belonging to organised crime syndicates are generally not interested in a 42" smart television stolen from a high street outlet, rather they immerse themselves in the theft of high ticket price goods, such as expensive clothing, watches and jewellery, and top-end electronic goods in volume that cannot be traced. By their very nature, organised crime syndicates will decide where and when to strike. It may be the cashier who is clumsily moving £10k to the bank by himself, at a time and on a route that is used twice per week. Equally, the syndicate may identify a member of staff with influence who has some form of need, be it drugs or gambling, and they will move in to help the member of staff, who at first trusted his new friends, until they begin to make demands, and it is too late for him to turn back time; he has fallen into their trap, and there is no going back.

Opportunist criminals

Rather like a predator animal that will wait until its victim makes a mistake or shows its soft underbelly, before he or she strikes, the opportunist criminal may watch and wait until they see an opportunity to attack, or they may be fortunate enough to walk into a store where there is an unlocked cabinet containing jewellery or perfume, because the member of staff responsible for that area has been called away in a hurry and forgo to lock the cabinet. Bingo. Alternatively, the opportunist may study the security in a store, before realising that at 1000hrs until 1200hrs there are no security guards, or in the middle of the afternoon staff numbers are at a minimum because sales at that time are slack. More common is the fact that the entry/exit tagging system (electronic article surveillance) is constantly false alarming, or at least when it sounds there is no reaction except for a 'It's OK mate, on you go' from either staff or the extremely bored security guard; and this happens at every store in that chain. It's his birthday and Christmas all rolled into one.

Mitigation

In many respects, the introduction of mitigation techniques in a retail environment is very similar to those systems implemented as crime prevention processes in other environments, such as banking, production, and so forth. We can discuss theories and concepts such as Situational Crime Prevention (SCP), Crime Prevention Through Environmental Design (CTED) and Target Hardening, as we have done earlier in the book, and they of course have a place; but experience tells me that the most important mitigation process in any environment is having a positive security culture. Easier said than done, I hear you saying.

Pause for thought

What is meant by the term 'security culture'?

The Centre for the Protection of Infrastructure (CPNI) argues that developing and sustaining an effective security culture is an essential component of a protective security regime and helps mitigate against a range of threats that could cause physical, reputational or financial damage to organisations. *Security culture refers to the set of values, shared by everyone in an organisation, that determine how people are expected to think about and approach security.* Getting security culture right will help develop a security conscious workforce and promote the desired security behaviours you want from staff.[126]

"Security culture refers to the set of values, *shared by everyone in an organisation*, that determine how people are expected to think about and approach security".

As I said earlier, easier said than done.

Experience tell me that whilst the security manager and his team, and the executive board (perhaps) appreciate the security requirements of the organisation, and by association have generated a loose security culture within those two arenas; there is no guarantee that the remainder of the workforce understands the concept.

An example being the operator in a busy call centre, whose finances are dependent on the number of new customers she signs up on a daily basis. I am pretty confident that if she was approached to take part in a survey to estimate the security culture of the company, her input would be minimal; because "Security isn't my job, I leave that to the security guards".

So the security guard is asked his opinion about the security culture in the company, and he replies: "How do I know? That is way above my pay scale. Ask my supervisor".

We question the security supervisor, and he says. . . . Yes, I think you know where we are going with this, don't you?

The single point of failure for any organisation attempting to establish an effective security culture, is the call centre operator or the security guard who cannot verify that culture because they have never been advised how to. It's all about communication!

Pause for thought

In your opinion, what are the first steps an organisation must take to understand the level of security culture?

Irrelevant of size, strength or sector, there has to be a stakeholder survey carried out to ascertain if a security culture exists, and if it does, how resilient is it?

Very often this type of survey is beyond the scope or skill levels of the internal security function, and the task may have to be outsourced to a subject matter expert (SME) who has experience in this field. Another major advantage of outsourcing is that of neutrality, without the internal security function being accused of swaying the survey recipients towards a positive result, inferring that the security culture is in existence and is robust.

Mixed method research will be used and will take the form of quantitative survey questionnaires and qualitative semi-structured interviews involving all stakeholders.

Once the results of the survey have been collated and analysed, the organisation will have a clearer idea of the robustness of its security culture.

Involve the right people with the right approach

On too many occasions in the past, organisations have attempted to introduce, or change a particular culture by holding the sword of Damocles over the heads of the workforce or population. However, whether it is the introduction or alteration of a culture, it is undoubtedly an exercise in change management, and that isn't always received with a great deal of either sympathy or empathy. And of course, change management handled unprofessionally can have disastrous results.

Venice and the unions

In 2005 a large maritime security project was carried, sponsored by the Port of Venice Authority. The project involved a series of maritime risk assessments, throughout thirty-five port facilities, the aim was to have each port facility certificated in conformity with the approaching International Ship and Port Facility Security Code (ISPS). The project was divided into two phases. The first phase, which was the physical examination of all security systems at each facility, was managed without any negative issues.

Phase two, however, was to prove more difficult and potentially disastrous.

One vulnerability discovered during the risk assessments was the low level of access control, with workers being able to access all of the facilities without the use of any form of access control card. It was decided by the project team and the Port of Venice Authority to issue new photographic RFID identity cards to the workforce of just over 4,000 stevedores without union consultation. However, before the distribution of the cards took place the Port Authority saw sense and opened up discussions about the new ID cards with the very active and powerful union. This was an immense security culture change and had discussions not taken place it could have led to an all-out strike which would have cost the port millions of euros.

The right people

It may be argued that this is the most critical stage of the introduction of any form of culture, whether it is risk, sales, H&S or security; this is all about trust, and as I have said on so many occasions, it is also all about communication.

One of the most significant security culture introduction is the implementation of an international standard such as ISO 27001 (Information Security Management Systems), ISO 28000 (Supply Chain Security Management Systems) or ISO 31000 (Risk Management Systems). Perhaps perceptually, management is introducing this particular standard to reduce manpower, or to introduce greater levels of social intrusion, and to the workforce this is a management initiative that has one aim and one aim only, and that is to suit the needs and personal requirements of the manager! Therefore, a culture change management team that represents all facets of the business is critical.

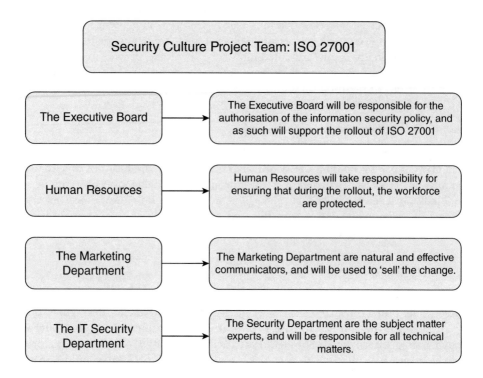

Figure 3.12 The security culture project team

All of the above international standards have a clause which states that management support in the introduction of the standard is crucial, and that argument can be made when relating to the introduction or alteration of a security culture. Momentum must be generated from within the board room, and communications emanating from that lofty place must be accurate, honest and worded using language that isn't seen as threatening by the workforce, and that is where human resources will add value to the project team. The marketing function will also be a valuable ally in the team, because marketing tends to be able to communicate effectively at a range of levels (normally better than the security department!), and they will be viewed as neutral. Every member of the project team will have individual value, as seen in Figure 3.12.

Resistance

People will inevitably resistant any new theory or concept, and until ISO 27001 is seen as a practical enhancement to working practices, that is all it will be: a concept or theory. Inevitably the IT security department will be perceived to have an agenda, because perhaps the vast majority of the workforce do not understand IT to the same degree as the security department, and therefore there will be level of mistrust. This is where HR and the marketing department will reflect their true value.

Choose activities and topics

For our example we have chosen the introduction of an international standard, and that will require a series of training modules to ensure that all those performing within the standard understand what is expected from them and their working practices.

It may be that the security culture project team have indicated a greater need than compliance with a single standard; international or otherwise. There may have been an attack or a series of security incidents that have concerned the board, and the security culture project team has been instructed to introduce a security training programme that will offer more effective security work practices, and that may mean two forms of security training.

- *High level training*: This form of training will be aimed at and inclusive of all stakeholders directly involved in some form of security function. It should incorporate all of the security work-based operations carried out within the organisation, and it must be a formally recognised training programme that includes learning outcomes and assessment criteria.
- *Low level training*: In reality this should be delivered to staff and management operating in the organisation, and it should consist of a security knowledge and awareness programme that will advise and guide personnel about how they can contribute to the security landscape.

Plan and execute

During the planning and execution phase, there should be a detailed programme that includes the following:

- Clearly defined and communicated aims and objectives
- Functions and departments to fit the high and low levels of training
- Clearly defined activities, and a plan of their progress
- Some form of measurement strategy that will inform the progress of the programme
- Management support objectives.

The above programme, if delivered effectively, will allow the security culture projects team to manage every phase, and to be constantly aware of the progress and any issues encountered during the delivery.

Exercise Brave Defender – task 15: retail loss and prevention methods

Synopsis

The board of Britcom plc has made a strategic decision to develop the retail portfolio of the business, beginning with a destination outlet at a major outdoor shopping centre in South West England. There is a vacant property that has been identified as a potential location for the shop, which is the chosen destination for the sales team. Your task is to:

1   Analyse the location from a security perspective, in order to advise the board accordingly. Consider the following aspects of defence in depth:

    a   The environment
    b   Physical and electronic security systems required

    c   Retail shrinkage policies, plans and procedures
    d   Manned guarding requirements
    e   Liaison with other retailers and law enforcement.

3.16 Workplace investigations

Pause for thought

In any investigation, whether it is carried out in the workplace or at an external environment, what is the most important rule to keep in mind at all times?

The intention of this sub-chapter is not to define the differences between criminal and civil proceedings, rather it is to guide the reader through the processes required to carry out an investigation in the workplace.

Of critical importance is the fact that a person must be presumed innocent until proved guilty, and guilt cannot be proven without evidence.

Evidence

The Cambridge Dictionary defines evidence as:

One or more reasons for believing that something is or is not true.

Examples being:

The police have found no evidence *of* a terrorist link with the murder.
    Several experts are to *give* evidence on the subject.

So endless rumours about Joe exaggerating his expenses or Elly taking cash from the till are just that; rumours. Until credible evidence is submitted for legal examination, Joe and Elly are innocent of any crime.

The term 'evidence' is used to indicate the means by which any fact or point in issue may be proved or disproved. Specific types of evidence are discussed later in this section and there are differences between preparing evidence for criminal cases and civil matters.

Two key terms must be considered when obtaining information for use as evidence:

- 'Admissibility' – evidence will be admissible if it relates to the facts of the matter at hand *and* has been properly obtained;
- Weight of evidence – if the investigator can demonstrate the authenticity and reliability of the information, then it will have greater evidential weight or credibility (Darroch-Warren and Gill, 2010).

There are various types of evidence, and once again it is imperative for all investigators to be skilful in processing different categories of evidence. Let's take a look at this myriad of legal differentiation.

- **Original or secondary evidence:**

  - Original evidence normally refers to documentary evidence, and in this scenario it is always best evidence to provide the original letter or report.
  - Secondary evidence refers to a copy of the original evidence, perhaps in the form of a photocopy or a photograph of the original.

- **Real evidence:**

  Real evidence refers to some form of object that may have been used in the commission of a crime, such as a weapon, a letter, a vehicle; something that is tangible and can be used. The weapon or the letter can be passed around the court and be examined by the defence and prosecution. Whilst real evidence is significant in its importance it is usually supported by witness evidence. That is not to say that it is not non-admissible by itself, but that is extremely rare.

- **Documentary evidence:**

  Documentary evidence is any evidence that is, or can be, introduced at a trial in the form of documents, as distinguished from oral testimony. Documentary evidence is most widely understood to refer to writings on paper (such as an invoice, a contract, or a will), but the term can also apply to any media by which information can be preserved, such as photographs; a medium that needs a mechanical device to be viewed, such as a tape recording or film; and a printed form of digital evidence, such as emails or spreadsheets.

  Normally, before documentary evidence is admissible as evidence, it must be proved by other evidence from a witness that the document is genuine, called "laying a foundation".[127]

- **Oral evidence:**

  Oral evidence is evidence spoken to the court by a witness. It can cover any or all of the following; what the witness:

  - Heard
  - Saw
  - Tasted
  - Touched
  - Smelt
  - Felt.

- **Circumstantial evidence**

  Hearsay evidence is evidence that tends to prove a fact, although not directly. It is the assessment of information from the scene of a crime that might point to a perpetrator, but it is insufficient on its own in a court of law to gain a conviction.

  Example:

  James was seen lying on the street with blood flowing from a cut to his neck. John stood above him holding a knife dripping with blood. Although the act wasn't witnessed, it could be inferred that John stabbed James in the neck.

- **Hearsay evidence**

  Hearsay evidence is evidence tendered that has been said by a third party, and not by a witness to an incident. Sometimes referred to as "he said, she said". For example, whilst giving testament during a trial, Joe said that Charlie told him that he had seen Elly taking cash from the till. Joe wasn't a witness to the alleged offence, but he had been informed that Elly was guilty of theft. That is hearsay.

- **Opinion evidence**

  Opinion evidence can be offered by anybody in a court of law, whether they be expert or lay, and dependent on the level of complexity, the judge will decide what is admissible and what is not.

  Digital evidence

  Simply put, digital evidence is any evidence that is captured and held on any form of electronic or digital piece of equipment. A good example may be a hard drive, or even a network that has stored digital information and data which relates to a crime. If not surrendered, the law enforcement agency will seize and hold the equipment for as long as necessary in order to retrieve admissible evidence to be used in a court of law.

- **CCTV evidence**

  The Code of Practice, produced by the Information Commissioner's Office (ICO), applies to all CCTV systems in the UK, and before any CCTV evidence is provided for a court of law there must be confidence that it is in compliance with the Code, and it must conform with all data protection legislation. CCTV evidence can be used in a court of law or a tribunal, but if it doesn't comply with the above, it is likely to be seen as inadmissible.

- **Forensic evidence**

  The use of scientific means to unearth credible evidence is known as forensics, with the two focal points of investigation and forensic research being blood and DNA. Blood and DNA samples can be taken from suspects during an investigation, and such samples will be compared with any blood or DNA evidence found at or nearby the scene of the crime. The evidence is admissible in almost any court of law and has a history of successful convictions. A major advantage is that forensic evidence can link a suspect to not only one offence, but potentially a series of crimes.

Legislation

It is important at this stage to understand that, certainly in the UK, there are two types of law: civil law and criminal law.

Civil law

Civil law is a branch of the law. In common law legal systems such as England and Wales and the United States, the term refers to non-criminal law. The law relating to civil wrongs and quasi-contracts is part of the civil law, as is law of property (other than property-related crimes, such as theft or vandalism). Civil law may, like criminal law, be divided into substantive law and procedural law. The rights and duties of persons (natural persons and legal persons) amongst themselves is the primary concern of civil law. It is often suggested that civil proceedings are taken for the purpose of obtaining compensation for injury, and may thus be distinguished from criminal proceedings, whose purpose is to inflict punishment. However, exemplary damages or punitive damages may be awarded in civil proceedings. It was also formerly possible for common informers to sue for a penalty in civil proceedings.[128]

Issues involving civil law are generally dealt with at employment tribunals, the County Court and sometimes the High Court. Civil law cases are not dealt with at the Crown Court.

The standard of proof in civil law cases is judged on the balance of probabilities, which means that a dispute will be decided in favour of the party whose claims are more likely to be true. That is to say that although evidence has been submitted and accepted, it is not likely to be up to the standard required in a criminal case. The judge or the jury will hear evidence from either side of the dispute and will decide in their opinion, which of the two arguments is likely (not positively) to be true. A tough call.

Criminal law

The law society argues that criminal law sets out the definitions of criminal offences and the rules and procedures that apply when the police investigate an offence they allege has been committed; when the prosecuting authorities charge a person; and when he or she must appear in a criminal court. If they admit the offence or are found guilty, the court will impose a punishment, ranging from fines, community orders, and imprisonment.

Criminal law solicitors will help if a citizen is suspected or accused of a crime. When the police allege that he or she committed a criminal offence, solicitors can represent them to make sure that all legal rights are protected and to present the case in court to make sure the defendant is given a fair hearing.[129]

Criminal matters are dealt with at the Magistrates' and Crown Court – where they will be heard by a judge and jury, and at times a justice of the peace.

In criminal law situations, the standard of proof is higher than that of a civil case and is based on the premise that the case was proven beyond reasonable doubt. The *Legal Dictionary* defines this as:

> The standard that must be met by the prosecution's evidence in a criminal prosecution: that no other logical explanation can be derived from the facts except that the defendant committed the crime, thereby overcoming the presumption that a person is innocent until proven guilty.
>
> If the jurors or judge have no doubt as to the defendant's guilt, or if their only doubts are unreasonable doubts, then the prosecutor has proven the defendant's guilt beyond a reasonable doubt and the defendant should be pronounced guilty.
>
> The term connotes that evidence establishes a particular point to a moral certainty and that it is beyond dispute that any reasonable alternative is possible. It does not mean that no doubt exists as to the accused's guilt, but only that no Reasonable Doubt is possible from the evidence presented.[130]

Acts of Parliament

Before moving on to the mechanics of carrying out an investigation, it is worthwhile understanding that there are a number of pieces of legislation that need to be consider when preparing an investigation, because the investigator and possible his or her team need to know what crime has been committed, if any.

Here are the basic components of a number of pieces of legislation.

- **The Human Rights Act (1998)**

The Human Rights Act gives effect to the human rights set out in the European Convention on Human Rights. These rights are called convention rights.
Examples of convention or human rights include:

- The right to life
- The right to respect for private and family life
- The right to freedom of religion and belief.

Article 6 calls for a right to a fair hearing.

- **Data Protection Act (2018) and the General Data Protection Regulations (GDPR)**

Data protection is the fair and proper use of information about people. It's part of the fundamental right to privacy – but on a more practical level, it's really about building trust between people and organisations. It's about treating people fairly and openly, recognising their right to have control over their own identity and their interactions with others, and striking a balance with the wider interests of society.
It's also about removing unnecessary barriers to trade and co-operation. It exists in part because of international treaties for common standards that enable the free flow of data across borders. The UK has been actively involved in developing these standards.
Data protection is essential to innovation. Good practice in data protection is vital to ensure public trust in, engagement with and support for innovative uses of data in both the public and private sectors.
The UK data protection regime is set out in the DPA 2018 and the GDPR (which also forms part of UK law).[131]

- **The Police and Criminal Evidence Act (1984) (PACE)**

PACE sets out to strike the right balance between the powers of the police and the rights and freedoms of the public. Maintaining that balance is a central element of PACE.
The PACE codes of practice cover:

- Powers of stop and search
- Powers of arrest
- Powers of detention
- Codes of investigation
- Powers of identification
- Codes for interviewing detainees

- **The Criminal Procedures and Investigations Act 1996**

  The Criminal Procedure and Investigations Act 1996 is a piece of statutory legislation in the United Kingdom that regulates the procedures of investigating and prosecution of criminal offences.

  The Act provides the framework for mutual disclosure of information during the prosecution process – whilst aimed at law enforcement, certain sections will have a bearing on workplace investigations.

- **Public Interest Disclosure Act 1998**

  The Public Interest Disclosure Act 1998 (c. 23) is an Act of the Parliament of the United Kingdom that protects whistle-blowers from detrimental treatment by their employer. It protects employees who make disclosures of certain types of information, including evidence of illegal activity or damage to the environment, from retribution from their employers, such as dismissal or being passed over for promotion. In cases where such retribution takes place the employee may bring a case before an employment tribunal, which can award compensation.

  Under the Act a non-disclosure agreement (NDA) between an employer and employee, often a condition of compensation for loss of employment for some reason, does not remove a worker's right to make a protected disclosure (i.e. to blow the whistle). In 2019 a consultation was held on adding limitations on confidentiality clauses, following evidence that some employers used confidentiality clauses to intimidate victims of harassment or discrimination into silence, suggesting that the worker did not have the right to blow the whistle, take a matter to a tribunal, or even discuss with people such as the police, a doctor, or a therapist.

- **The Health and Safety at Work Act 1974**

  The Health and Safety at Work Act 1974 (HASAWA) lays down wide-ranging duties on employers. Employers must protect the 'health, safety and welfare' at work of all their employees, as well as others on their premises, including temps, casual workers, the self-employed, clients, visitors, and the public. However, these duties are qualified with the words 'so far as is reasonably practicable'. This means that employers can argue that the costs of a particular safety measure are not justified by the reduction in risk that the measure would produce. But it does not mean they can avoid their responsibilities simply by claiming that they cannot afford improvements.

  The Act contains powers for the Health and Safety Executive (HSE) to enforce these employer duties and penalties for non-compliance.

  The onus is on the investigator, or investigations team to be full cognisant of all local criminal and civil law that may impact the investigation.

The investigation

The term 'successful investigation', therefore, can mean a number of things – on the one hand it can refer to an investigation that leads to a conviction. On the other hand, 'successful' may mean identifying culprits, applying internal disciplinary measures, justifying dismissals, facilitating civil litigation, or simply initiating revision of policies and procedures (Gill et al., 2006).

A proper investigation enables the employer to uncover the facts which will help it to reach a decision as to whether or not there has been malpractice or even criminality. It also secures fairness for the employee by providing that person with an opportunity to respond to the allegations being made. If misconduct has been established, then such investigation will allow an opportunity for the employee to put forward factors which might mitigate the seriousness of the disciplinary offence and therefore the outcome of the disciplinary hearing.

The main principles which apply to workplace investigations concern:

- Natural justice
- Fairness, objectivity and impartiality
- Consistency and proportionality
- Legal compliance (Darroch–Warren and Gill, 2010).

Gill (2007) argues that prior to embarking on a lengthy and perhaps costly investigation, careful consideration needs to be made as to the veracity of the allegation in the first instance. Some incidents can be dealt with informally as they may be petty, malicious and without foundation, little or no evidence to support a formal investigation.

Gathering the facts from the outset and establishing the validity of the complaint may sound obvious, but employers frequently fail to substantiate the matter. Such a failure can lead to adverse consequences in terms of injustices, as well as impacting adversely on the organisation as a whole, for example industrial action, risk to reputation, and negative media coverage.

It is the emphasis on there being a reasonable belief in the truth of the allegation which may drive the need for a more extensive investigation than the employer first thought. The benefit of taking advice at an early stage and appointing the right person to lead an investigation is not just the value to be added in solving the problem but the remedial lessons which get learned, and the know-how exchanged on the way.

The decision to investigate may depend upon:

- *The nature of the allegation*: Who is alleging what, against who?
- *The need for criminal prosecution*: It may be a serious offence that may result in more than internal discipline, perhaps the police will be involved, and that may result in a criminal prosecution.
- *Regulatory compliance/corporate governance requirements*: The allegation may be related to some form of non-compliance issue, or perhaps an offence against the corporate governance of the organisation, as laid down by the executive board or senior management team.
- *Risk to the organisation's reputation*: The allegation may relate to an offence, that is proven could have an impact against the brand and reputation of the organisation, which could affect share price and so forth.
- *Expectations by other stakeholders (such as unions or shareholders)*: If the alleged offence is made public, and there is a need for fairness, particularly in the eyes of employees or shareholders, a formal investigation may be required.

At the point of deciding that an investigation is required it must be decided who will lead the investigation – there may for example be a *conflict of interest*, such as personal friendships; does the proposed 'investigator' have the competency, knowledge, resources or indeed time required to undertake a thorough investigation? (Darroch–Warren and Gill, 2010).

Planning

Unlike fictitious TV and cinema scenarios, an investigation doesn't take place as soon as the first hint of an allegation is received, neither does the process of investigation materialise because the informer (for lack of a better word!) is popular amongst the workforce and can do nothing wrong. Every investigation has to planned to the last detail, from the initial allegation, to the point when an outcome has been decided either at an employment tribunal or a court of law, as seen in Figure 3.13.

Procedural transparency

From its inception, every investigation has to be seen to be open, transparent, and fair. Justice has to be done, and it has to be seen to be done, in order that those involved and those witnessing the procedures can be clear that all procedures are fair.

The Advisory, Conciliation and Arbitration Service (ACAS) in 2009, published a set of guidelines, reproduced by Darroch-Warren and Gill (2010), referring to procedural

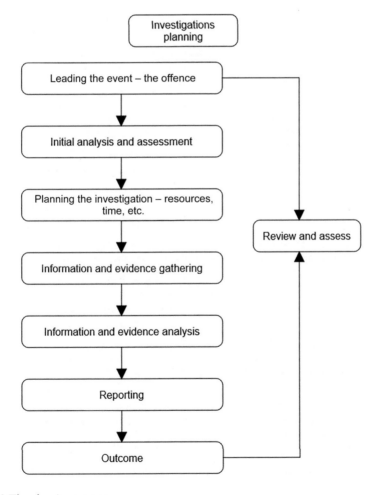

Figure 3.13 The planning process

fairness, which said that to be procedurally fair certain requirements need to be met. Employers should:

- Deal with issues promptly and not unreasonably delay investigations, meetings, decisions or confirmation of those decisions.
- Act consistently and fairly.
- Carry out sufficient investigations to establish the facts of the case before making a decision.
- Ensure that decision-makers do not have a direct interest in the case at hand
- Inform employees of the basis of the problem and give them an opportunity to state their case in response before any decisions are made.
- Allow employees to be accompanied at any formal disciplinary or grievance meeting.
- Allow employees to appeal against any formal decision made.
- Comply with the organisation's disciplinary processes and procedures.

(ACAS, 2009)

Procedural fairness benefits both the investigator and the person under investigation. Sound investigation procedure enables an investigator to properly check facts and identify the primary issues under investigation. If actions are taken that undermine the principle of procedural fairness, and that of natural justice, it is likely that these actions will be challenged during the legal process.

So whether the investigator is examining evidence relating to a procedurally incident, or the perpetration of crime, the investigation, from the very beginning has to be seen to be fair and just.

Never forget the criticality of the presumption of innocence.

Exercise Brave Defender – task 16: workplace investigations

Synopsis

Rumours have been circulating that the chief information officer (CIO) has held regular, but covert meetings with a senior network engineer from an opposing telecommunications company. Rumour has it that the CIO has been seen passing large envelopes to his erstwhile colleague in pubs and restaurants, and coincidently specialist services once only provided by Britcom are now being offered by the opposition.

The Britcom CEO has approached you and has asked you to investigate this 'rumour'.

Tasks

1 Carry out an initial investigation into this allegation.
2 If you believe that you have sufficient evidence, in cooperation with HR open a formal investigation into whatever offence(s) you believe has been committed.
3 Write a paper advising the CEO how you intend to achieve the above; talk him through your proposed actions.

3.17 Academic and vocational qualifications

On 11 May 2001, the Private Security Industry Act was accepted, introducing the Security Industry Authority (SIA), which would be the single point of contact for all matters relating to the regulation of the private security industry in the UK. This also brought about the licencing of all front-line security officers, door supervisors and public space surveillance (PSS) (CCTV) operators, meaning that from May 2001, front line officers would be required to receive 30 hours' training and pass two examinations before being issued their licences. I have since heard the repeated criticism that 30 hours is far from appropriate, but my argument is that before that date in May 2001, security officers in the UK learned every skill they needed 'on the job', and on far too many occasions that meant no training whatsoever.

This was a crucial juncture for the UK security industry, as it set the minimum standards for all front line security personnel, with the exception of security officers employed on a pay as your earn (PAYE) basis, employed as security officers 'in house'.

Today there are more training and education opportunities than ever before for personnel employed in the security industry, as the following pathways will illustrate:

SIA front line training

All front-line security officers will receive a minimum of 30 hours training which is divided into three sections:

Common security industry knowledge

This includes training in such areas as the law, Health and Safety, fire and emergency procedures, communications and good customer service.

Security guarding specialist module

In this module learners are taken through basic security officer duties such as patrolling, roles and responsibilities of the security officer, access control and search and technology.

Conflict management module

Here, students will study avoiding conflict, defusing conflict, and resolving and learning from conflict.

Speciality training for door supervisors, close protection officers, PSS operators, cash and values in transit officer, and key holding and vehicle immobilisation officers will be carried out taking into consideration the individual skill sets required.

The Regulated Qualifications Framework (RQF)

The England/Northern Ireland qualifications framework – The Regulated Qualifications Framework (RQF) – was launched by Ofqual (the Regulatory Body for England for all qualifications outside the Higher Education Qualifications Framework) on 1 October 2015. The RQF replaced the Qualifications and Credit Framework (QCF) for Vocational Qualifications and the National Qualifications Framework (NQF) for general/school qualifications.

The Framework is divided into a number of levels that represent individual qualifications criteria. See Table 3.5.

Table 3.5 QCF levels of competence

Entry	Entry level award
1	GCSE – grades 3, 2, 1 or grades D, E, F, G
2	GCSE – grades 9, 8, 7, 6, 5, 4 or grades A, A, B, C
3	A level
4	Certificate of higher education (CertHE)
5	Foundation degree
6	Degree with honours – for example bachelor of the arts (BA) hons, bachelor of science (BSc) hons
7	Master's degree, for example master of arts (MA), master of science (MSc)
8	Doctorate, for example doctor of philosophy (PhD or DPhil)

Within the security industry in the UK, the most common qualifications are:

- Front line licencing
- Level three certificate in security management
- Level four award in security management or managing security surveys
- Level five diploma in security management
- Level six risk and security management (BA honours)
- Level seven international security and risk management (BSc)
- Level eight professional doctorate in security risk management (DSRM).

In terms of pure academic study, the following options are available.

Foundation degree

A foundation degree is a combined academic and vocational qualification in higher education, equivalent to two-thirds of an honours bachelor's degree, introduced by the government of the United Kingdom in September 2001. Foundation degrees are available in England, Wales and Northern Ireland, offered by universities, by colleges that have their own foundation degree awarding powers, and by colleges and employers running courses validated by universities.

Foundation degrees must include a pathway for graduates to progress to an honour's degree. This may be via joining the final year of a standard three-year course or through a dedicated 'top-up' course. Students can also transfer to other institutions to take a top-up course or the final year of an honours course. It may also be possible for students to join the second year of an honours course in a different but related subject.[132]

Today a large number of all degrees are delivered online, by the use of a virtual learning platform (VLP).

Perhaps less attractive than either an MSc or PhD, a foundation degree in security management or security risk management is still available at a number of UK universities, and typically delivered on the course are modules which may include:

- *An introduction to security and risk*: This is where the learner is introduced to security and risk, perhaps for the first time. This is arguably the most important module in any security management degree because it is critical for the security professional to be able to distinguish between the two concepts and theories.

- *Leadership and management*: This is of particular importance because the learner needs to understand a number of different forms of management if they are ever going to effectively manage a team. The module should also point out the unique challenges of managing a team in an extremely competitive and dynamic environment such as security and risk.
- *Crime prevention*: The module should cover social and situational crime prevention, with topics such as Crime Prevention Through Environmental Design (CPTED) and Situational Crime Prevention (SCP). This may be the first time that learners have been introduced to the concept of criminology and its impact on security crime prevention.
- *Information and communications technology (ICT) and security*: This is a hybrid module because not only should it deliver knowledge about information technology and cybersecurity, which today is critical, but it should also include information about the importance of ICT based security technology systems such as CCTV and Automatic Access Control (AAC).
- *Crisis management (CM) and business continuity management (BCM)*: This is a fairly recent revelation for the professional security manager, who until quite recently has probably never been involved in either of the two disciplines. However, organisations and corporations are beginning to understand the relationship between security risk management and CM/BCM. The study of standards such as BS11200 (CM) and ISO 22301 (BCM) should be included in this module.
- *Business security management*: Traditionally, the role of the typical security manager has been to ensure the security and integrity of the assists belonging to the organisation, whether are property, information or even people. Today, because of functional integration within an organisation, the security manager must have at least a working knowledge of the business that employee him or her. During this module the student will be introduced to a number of business-critical concepts and theories and will participate in several business case studies.
- *Research and critical analysis*: The ability of a student to be able to carry out critically analysed, evidence-based research is crucial for all levels of academic study, and during this module the learner will be taken through a number of research models that will help him or her to critically research for their final project, which is likely to be a written dissertation.

Bachelor's degree (BA/BSc)

A bachelor's degree is a course of academic study leading to a qualification such as a bachelor of arts (BA), bachelor of science (BSc), or bachelor of medicine (MB).

It usually takes three or four years to complete full-time (normally four years if the student is doing a sandwich course, as this includes a year in industry or abroad). Some bachelor's degrees like medical courses can take longer. Learners can also study for a bachelor's degree part-time or through flexible learning.

The qualification is designed to give the undergraduate a thorough understanding of a subject. It helps the student develop analytical, intellectual and essay/dissertation writing skills.

As with the foundation degree, there are a number of options for learners wishing to study for a bachelor's degree in the UK, with examples being risk and security management (BA honours), or security management (BSc honours).

Master's degree (MA/MSc/MLitt/MPhil)

A master's degree (from Latin *magister*) is an academic degree awarded by universities or colleges upon completion of a course of study demonstrating mastery or a high-order overview of a specific field of study or area of professional practice. A master's degree normally (although not always) requires previous study at the bachelor's level, either as a separate degree or as part of an integrated course. Within the area studied, master's graduates are expected to possess advanced knowledge of a specialised body of theoretical and applied topics; high-order skills in analysis, critical evaluation, or professional application; and the ability to solve complex problems and think rigorously and independently.[133]

In terms of security, the master's degree is by far the most popular, and is taught either in a classroom setting or via the VLP, by a high number of universities in the UK. Titles such professional security management, risk, crisis and disaster management and international security and risk management are extremely attractive to the student and potential employer/client.

PhD

A PhD, or doctorate of philosophy, is recognised as being the highest level of degree a student can achieve, allowing successful candidates to be recognised as experts in their particular fields of research.

This is research as opposed to taught study and will take between four and six years to complete. Work is assessed by way of a written thesis of between 60,000 and 80,000 words presented to a university senate. The researcher will have to orally defend his or her work before being awarded a PhD.

Both the master's degree and the doctorate require levels of commitment that will probably be alien to a percentage of learners, particularly mature students who have not studied for some time. However, there are no short cuts or easy options for either of the disciplines, and anybody contemplating such levels of study and research must be prepared to go the extra mile under all circumstances.

Chartered status

The Register of Chartered Security Professionals was established under a Royal Charter issued to the Worshipful Company of Security Professionals in the UK and launched in 2011.

* Registrants use *CSyP* as a post nominal.
* Being admitted to the Register and becoming a CSyP is a means of being recognised and continuing to represent the highest standards and ongoing proficiency. It is the gold standard of competence in security.
* CSyPs have to comply with a Code of Conduct, a Professional Disciplinary Code, and also complete continuous professional development each year.
* Applications to the Register are managed by the Security Institute on behalf of the Worshipful Company of Security Professionals. Licenced organisations are the Security Institute and ASIS UK Chapter 208 who can both mentor and support CSyP applicants.

- The Register of Chartered Security Professionals is recognised across the UK, including the Association of Security Consultants (ASC), International Professional Security Association (IPSA) and the Centre for the Protection of National Infrastructure (CPNI)[134]

Achieving Chartered Status is the pinnacle for any professional security manager.

ASIS International

Once known as the American Society of Industrial Security, ASIS International is probably the largest security institute in the world, and it offers its members a number of security qualifications that are very attractive to employers, particularly in the US, the UK and Europe. The qualifications are:

- **Certified Protection Professional (CPP)**

  The Certified Protection Professional (CPP) is considered the 'gold standard' for security management professionals. This certification validates your knowledge in all areas of security management. Eligibility requirements include seven to nine years of security experience and three years in responsible charge of a security function.

- **Physical Security Professional (PSP)**

  The Physical Security Professional (PSP) demonstrates your knowledge in physical security assessments, application, design, and integration of physical security systems, and implementation of security measures. Eligibility requirements include a high school diploma, GED equivalent, or associate degree AND six years of progressive experience in the physical security field OR a bachelor's degree or higher AND four years of progressive experience in the physical security field.

- **Professional Certified Investigator (PCI)**

  The Professional Certified Investigator (PCI) certification provides demonstrable proof of an individual's knowledge and experience in case management, evidence collection, and preparation of reports and testimony to substantiate findings. Requirements include a high school diploma or GED equivalent and five years of investigations experience, with at least two years in case management.

There has never been a better time as far as education and training are concerned for the todays professional security manager, and it is incredibly refreshing, as a long-serving member of the industry and as a higher education tutor, to see the increase in numbers of applicants at all levels of education and training.

3.18 Conclusion

If you are reading this section, I hope that you have enjoyed the book. As I said at the beginning, I believe that is a book worth writing, and if you have taken anything away with you, then it was worth all the sweat, blood, and tears that went with the authorship.

So long and stay proud.

Notes

1 M. Gill (2014) *The Handbook of Security*. Basingstoke, Palgrave Macmillan.
2 The Islamic Revolutionary Guard Corps (IRGC) is tasked with preserving the Islamic Republic of Iran and the ideals of the 1979 revolution. The IRGC combines traditional military roles with a relentless focus on supposed domestic enemies. The IRGC is Iran's primary instrument for exporting the ideology of the Islamic Revolution worldwide. It is rigidly loyal to Iran's clerical elite. The IRGC is Iran's main link to its terrorist proxies, which the regime uses to boost Iran's global influence. www.counterextremism.com/threat/islamic-revolutionary-guard-corps-irgc Accessed on 09 October 2019
3 https://medium.com/@sbwoodside/defence-in-depth-the-medieval-castle-approach-to-internet-security-6c8225dec294.
4 Rational Choice Theory, which was founded by Gary Becker (1986), will be developed later in the book.
5 U. Beck (2007) *World at Risk*. Cambridge, Polity Press.
6 The Royal Society (1992) *Risk: Analysis, Perception, Management*. London, The Royal Society.
7 K. J. Engemann (Ed.) (2018) *The Routledge Companion to Rusk, Crisis and Security in Business*. London, Routledge.
8 Author's insertion.
9 Published by the Centre for Risk Research, Stockholm School of Economics.
10 The business in every case.
11 To ensure that best practice is achieved when assessing security threats to organisational assets.
12 www.bbc.co.uk/news/business-44385710.
13 www.theguardian.com/business/2019/nov/19/tsb-it-meltdown-report-computer-failure-accounts, accessed on 21 November 2019.
14 www.hse.gov.uk/corpmanslaughter/about.htm.
15 www.gov.uk/terrorism-national-emergency, accessed on 4 October 2019.
16 It is recommended for the purpose of the exercise, going forward, that you create a file that can be updated as you progress through the exercise.
17 Author's note.
18 Author's note.
19 https://en.wikipedia.org/wiki/Coaxial_cable, accessed on 12 October 2019.
20 www.computerhope.com/jargon/c/cat5.htm, accessed on 12 October 2019.
21 https://uk.rs-online.com/web/c/safety-security-esd-control-clean-room/cctv-security-surveillance/cctv-monitors/, accessed on 12 October 2019.
22 www.cpni.gov.uk/system/files/documents/2c/80/Guide-to-PIDS.pdf, accessed on 21 January 2020.
23 www.cpni.gov.uk/system/files/documents/2c/80/Guide-to-PIDS.pdf, accessed on 21 January 2020.
24 https://en.wikipedia.org/wiki/Lock_and_key, accessed on 21 January 2020.
25 https://en.wikipedia.org/wiki/Proximity_card, accessed on 21 January 2020.
26 https://en.wikipedia.org/wiki/Radio-frequency_identification, accessed on 22 January 2020.
27 This is covered in greater detail later in the book.
28 At the time of writing the book this is aspirational but will be pursued.
29 International Standards Organisation and British Standards European Norms.
30 www.police.uk, accessed on 12 October 2019.
31 Security resilience – Organisational resilience: Principles and attitudes (2017).
32 Author's insertion.
33 www.theirm.org/the-risk-profession/risk-management.aspx.
34 ISO 31000 Risk Management-principles and guidelines.
35 Mark Twain (1835–1910). www.goodreads.com/quotes/807622-never-let-the-truth-get-in-the-way-of-a.
36 Author's insertion.
37 https://en.wikipedia.org/wiki/Company_secretary.
38 Author's insertion.
39 Author's insertion.
40 To be covered in the next section.
41 https://en.wikipedia.org/wiki/Fifth_Amendment_to_the_United_States_Constitution.

42 https:// www.ifrc.org/en/what-we-do/disaster-management/about-disasters/what-is-a-disaster/, accessed on 8 October 2019.

43 www.unisdr.org/we/inform/terminology, accessed on 8 October 2019.

44 www.ifrc.org/en/what-we-do/disaster-management/about-disaster-management/, accessed on 14 October 2019.

45 www.salford.ac.uk/research/case-studies/case-studies/environment-and-sustainability/the-centre-for-disaster-resilience, accessed on 25 January 2020.

46 www.whatsnextcw.com/learning-best-japanese-earthquake-proof-buildings/, accessed on 15 October 2019.

47 https://en.wikipedia.org/wiki/Business_continuity_planning#Business_continuity.

48 https://en.wikipedia.org/wiki/Chief_information_security_officer.

49 Use the following website: www.police.uk.

50 RSA Cyber Security Conference in Evans (2019).

51 A consensual hallucination that felt and looked like a physical space but actually was a computer-generated construct representing abstract data (Gibson, 1984 in Gill 2014).

52 www.ncsc.gov.uk/section/advice-guidance/all-topics?topics=cyber%20threat&sort=date%2Bdesc&start=0&rows=20, accessed on 21 October 2019.

53 https://en.wikipedia.org/wiki/Strategy, accessed on 25 January 2020.

54 www.cpni.gov.uk/critical-national-infrastructure-0, accessed on 04 November 2019.

55 https://en.wikipedia.org/wiki/Incendiary_device, accessed on 11 January 2020.

56 www.cpni.gov.uk/marauding-terrorist-attacks-0, accessed on 11 January 2020.

57 https://en.wikipedia.org/wiki/List_of_marauding_terrorist_incidents, accessed on 11 January 2020.

58 https://dictionary.cambridge.org/dictionary/english/sabotage, accessed on 11 January 2020.

59 www.cpni.gov.uk/insider-threat, accessed on 11 January 2020.

60 www.varonis.com/blog/insider-threats/, accessed on 11 January 2020.

61 www.opcw.org/our-work/what-chemical-weapon, accessed on 11 January 2020.

62 www.ncsc.gov.uk/guidance/operational-technologies, accessed on 12 January 2020.

63 www.webopedia.com/TERM/S/SCADA.html, accessed on 12 January 2020.

64 *Blackstone's Counter Terrorism Handbook*.

65 https://learning.nspcc.org.uk/safeguarding-child-protection/radicalisation/, accessed on 22 September 2019.

66 Author's insertion.

67 A *halaqa* (Arabic: حلقة 'circle / ring') in Islamic terminology is a religious gathering or meeting for the study of Islam and the Quran. https://en.wikipedia.org/wiki/Halaqa, accessed on 23 September 2019.

68 Omar Bakri Muhammad is a Syrian Salafi Islamist militant leader, born in Aleppo, Syria. He was instrumental in developing Hizb ut-Tahrir in the United Kingdom before leaving the group and heading to another Islamist organisation, Al-Muhajiroun, until its disbandment in 2004.

69 Kafir is an Arabic term meaning 'infidel', 'rejector', 'disbeliever', 'unbeliever' or 'nonbeliever'. The term refers to a person who rejects or disbelieves in God or the tenets of Islam, denying the dominion and authority of God, and is thus often translated as 'infidel'. https://en.wikipedia.org/wiki/Kafir, accessed on 23 September 2019.

70 https://assets.publishing.service.gov.uk/government/uploads/system/uploads/attachment_data/file/97976/prevent-strategy-review.pdf, accessed on 23 September 2019.

71 An announcement by the IRA after the failed attempt to kill British Prime Minister Margaret Thatcher at the Grand Hotel, Brighton in 1984.

72 www.mi5.gov.uk/threat-levels.

73 https://en.wikipedia.org/wiki/Flying_glass.

74 www.cpni.gov.uk/system/files/documents/e5/ca/ASF-blast-mitigation-Daylight-application.pdf.

75 https://en.wikipedia.org/wiki/History_of_Hezbollah#Hezbollah_during_the_Lebanese_Civil_War_(1982–1990).

76 http://origins.osu.edu/milestones/august-2018-1998-east-african-embassy-bombings, accessed 26 September 2019.

77 https://en.wikipedia.org/wiki/Maritime_Jewel.

78 https://en.wikipedia.org/wiki/Al-Shabaab_(militant_group), accessed on 29 January 2020.

79 Which in reality are larger batteries supplying direct current, which is converted to alternating current, for a number of hours.

80 Fifteen of the 19 terrorists responsible for the attacks on 9/11 originated from Saudi Arabia. Three were trained pilots, and it is likely that a significant number of the attackers would have studied at university.

81 A means of providing an alternative means of border control, without the use of formal physical check points.

82 To be explained later.

83 It was a rushed operation to deploy the British Army to Ulster, with the Emergency Powers Act offering power and authority to young British soldiers who were expected to be transformed into police officers overnight, with no police or law enforcement whatsoever. Police officers are trained to maintain law and order, British soldiers were trained to kill; the two were incompatible.

84 https://en.wikipedia.org/wiki/The_Troubles.

85 The Ulster Special Constabulary (USC; commonly called the "B-Specials" or "B Men") was a quasi-military reserve special constable police force in Northern Ireland. It was set up in October 1920, shortly before the partition of Ireland. It was an armed corps, organised partially on military lines and called out in times of emergency, such as war or insurgency (https://en.wikipedia.org/wiki/Ulster_Special_Constabulary).

86 Joy riders were predominantly young males.

87 https://en.wikipedia.org/wiki/Corporals_killings.

88 https://en.wikipedia.org/wiki/Brighton_hotel_bombing.

89 http://news.bbc.co.uk/2/hi/uk_news/northern_ireland/2132219.stm.

90 www.bbc.com/timelines/z2wyvcw.

91 https://en.wikipedia.org/wiki/Birmingham_pub_bombings.

92 www.bbc.com/timelines/z2wyvcw.

93 https://en.wikipedia.org/wiki/Warrington_bombings.

94 https://en.wikipedia.org/wiki/Fatawā_of_Osama_bin_Laden.

95 'A person who does not accept a particular faith.' www.dictionary.com/browse/infide.

96 About 6,500 Fatah fighters relocated from Beirut to Jordan, Syria, Iraq, Sudan, both North and South Yemen, Greece, and Tunisia – the latter of which became the new PLO headquarters (see Note 97).

97 https://en.wikipedia.org/wiki/Contras#U.S._military_and_financial_assistance.

98 https://en.wikipedia.org/wiki/Maritime_Jewel.

99 A port facility is that area of a port, such as a container terminal, or a gas terminal that provides a service to ships.

100 https://en.wikipedia.org/wiki/Maritime_Transportation_Security_Act_of_2002.

101 https://en.wikipedia.org/wiki/Customs-Trade_Partnership_Against_Terrorism.

102 Author's insertion.

103 http://tfig.unece.org/contents/wco-safe.htm.

104 https://www.fairobserver.com/region/north_america/maritime-terrorism-how-real-threat. Accessed on 23 March 2020.

105 A very light, fast leisure vessel capable of moving at up to 80 mph.

106 Normally consisting of high-pressure water hoses operated from the bridge, and perhaps barbed wire along the rail.

107 https://en.wikipedia.org/wiki/Supply_chain_management. accessed on 27 January 2020.

108 ISO 28000 (2007) Specification for security management systems for the supply chain. Licensed to Charles Swanson.

109 https://en.wikipedia.org/wiki/Hostile_work_environment, accessed on 13 December 2019.

110 This is based on a cross section of commercial HEAT courses delivered in the UK for global delegates.

111 The topics are taken from a number of websites, and the author has offered an explanation of each subject based on his experience and academic qualifications.

112 www.nationalcrimeagency.gov.uk/what-we-do/crime-threats/fraud-and-economic-crime, accessed on 26 December 2019.

113 https://cfps.hscni.net/information/the-fraud-act/, accessed on 27 December 2019.

114 https://en.wikipedia.org/wiki/Identity_theft.

115 www.actionfraud.police.uk/, accessed on 14 January 2020.

116 www.actionfraud.police.uk/news/identity-fraud-reaches-record-levels, accessed on 29 December 2019.

117 https://ico.org.uk/, accessed on 14 January 2020.

118 www.retaileconomics.co.uk/library-retail-stats-and-facts, accessed on 15 December 2019.

119 Figures courtesy of Tyco Retail Solutions on https://shrinkindex.sensormatic.com/wp-content/uploads/2018/05/Sensormatic-Global-Shrink-Index.pdf, accessed on 14 December 2019.

120 https://shrinkindex.sensormatic.com/wp-content/uploads/2018/05/Sensormatic-Global-Shrink-Index.pdf, accessed on 28 January 2020.

121 https://brc.org.uk/media/404253/brc-annual-crime-survey-2019.pdf, accessed on 15 December 2019.

122 https://brc.org.uk/media/404253/brc-annual-crime-survey-2019.pdf, p. 16, accessed on 15 December 2019.

123 This may be HIV related, but there is no evidence to support such a theory.

124 British Retail Consortium Retail Crime Survey. https://brc.org.uk/media/404253/brc-annual-crime-survey-2019.pdf, accessed on 12 December 2019.

125 Nicholas William "Nick" Leeson (born 25 February 1967) is a former English derivatives broker famous for bringing down Barings Bank, the United Kingdom's oldest merchant bank, into bankruptcy. A rogue trader who made fraudulent, unauthorised and speculative moves, his actions led directly to the 1995 collapse of Barings Bank, for which he was sentenced to a term of imprisonment.

126 www.cpni.gov.uk/developing-security-culture, accessed on 23 December 2019.

127 https://en.wikipedia.org/wiki/Documentary_evidence, accessed on 27 December 2019.

128 https://en.wikipedia.org/wiki/Civil_law_(common_law)#cite_note-7, accessed on 28 January 2020.

129 www.lawsociety.org.uk/for-the-public/common-legal-issues/criminal/, accessed on 27 December 2019.

130 https://legal-dictionary.thefreedictionary.com/beyond+a+reasonable+doubt.

131 https://ico.org.uk/for-organisations/guide-to-data-protection/introduction-to-data-protection/some-basic-concepts/, accessed on 27 December 2019.

132 https://en.wikipedia.org/wiki/Foundation_degree, accessed on 26 December 2019.

133 https://en.wikipedia.org/wiki/Master%27s_degree, accessed on 26 December 2019.

134 https://security-institute.org/csyp/, accessed on 26 December 2019.

Bibliography

Abrahamsen, R., and Leander, K. (2016) *Routledge Handbook of Private Security Studies*. London, Routledge.

Abrahamsen, R., and Williams, M. C. (2011) *Security Beyond the State*. Cambridge, Cambridge University Press.

ACAS. (2009) *Code of Practice 1 – Disciplinary and Grievance Procedures*. Available at: http://www.acas.org.uk/CHttpHandler.ashx?id=1047

Adams, J. (1995) *Risk*. London, Routledge.

Altheide, D. L., Adler, P. A., Adler, P., and Altheide, D. A. (1978) The Social Meanings of Employee Theft. In J. M. Johnson and J. D. Douglas (eds.), *Crime at the Top*. Philadelphia, JB Lippincott.

Ambler, S. W. (2018) *Security Threat Models: An Agile Introduction* [Online]. Available at: www.agilemodeling.com/artifacts/securityThreatModel.htm, accessed on 19 April 2019.

Augustine, N. R., et al. (2000) *Harvard Business Review on Crisis Management*. Cambridge, MA, Harvard College.

Beck, A. (2014) *Understanding Loss in the Retail Sector*, M. Gill (ed.). London, Palgrave Macmillan.

Beck, U. (2007) *World at Risk*. Cambridge, Polity Press.

Bell, M. G. H. (2007) *Risk Management in Port Operations, Logistics and Supply Chain Security*. London, Informa Press.

Bennet, S. (2012) *Innovative Thinking in Risk, Crisis and Disaster Management*. Farnham, Gower.

Berube, C., and Cullen, P. (2013) *Maritime Private Security*. London, Routledge.

Betts, M. J. (2017) *Investigation of Fraud and Economic Crime*. Oxford, Oxford University Press.

Blumler, J. G., and Gurevitch, M. (1988) *The Crisis of Public Communications*. London, Routledge.

Bodemer, N., and Gaissmaier, W. (2015) *The Sage Handbook of Risk Communication*, H. Cho (ed.). California, Sage Publications.

Borodzicz, E. (2005) *Risk, Crisis and Security Management*. Chichester, John Wiley and Sons.

Bricker, M. K. (2014) *The Fukushima Daiichi Nuclear Power Station Disaster*. Oxon, Routledge.

Burke, J. (2004) *Al Qaeda: The True Story of Radical Islam*. London, Penguin.

Burleigh, M. (2009) *Blood and Rage: A Cultural History of Terrorism*. London, Harper Perennial.

Calder, A., and Watkins, S. (2008) *IT Governance: A Managers Guide to Data Security and ISO 27001/ISO 28002*. London, Kogan Page.

Caralli, R. A., Allen, G. H., and White, D. W. (2011) *CERT Resilience Management Model (CERT-RMM): A Maturity Model for Managing Operational Resilience*. Upper Saddle River, NJ, Addison-Wesley.

Chapple, Flatly and Smith (2011). Crime in England and Wales 2010/11 Findings from the British Crime Survey and police recorded crime (2nd Edition). London, Home Office Science Group. https://assets. publishing.service.gov.uk/government/uploads/system/uploads/attachment_data/file/116417/ hosb1011.pdf Accessed on 23 April 2020.

Cho, H., Reimer, T., and Mc Comas, K. A. (2015) *The SAGE Handbook of Risk Communication*. London, Sage.

Clark, A. (2014) *Disaster and Emergency Management Systems*. Hull, Amazon.

Clarke, R. V., and Felson, M. (2008) *Routine Activity and Rational Choice: Advances in Criminological Theory*. London, Transactions.

Cole, G. A. (1996) *Management Theory and Practice*. London, Letts Educational.

Covello, V. T. (1991) Risk Comparisons and Risk Communication: Issues and Problems in Comparing Health and Environmental Risk. In R. E. Kasperson and P. J. M. Stallen (eds.), *Communicating Risk to the Public*. Kluwer, Dordrecht.

Covello, V. T., Von Winterfieldt, D., and Slovic, P. (1986) Communicating Scientific Information About Health and Environmental Risks: Problems and Opportunities From a Social and Behavioural Perspective. In V. T. Covello, A. Mighissis, and V. R. R. Uppuluri (eds.), *Uncertainties in Risk Assessment and Risk Management*. New York, Plenum Press.

Crowe, D. T. (2013) *Crime Prevention Through Environmental Design*. Oxford, Butterworth-Heinemann.

Curtis, B. (1979) *How to Keep Employees Honest*. New York, Lebhar-Friedman Books.

Darroch-Warren, A.D. I., and Gill, D. J. (2010) *Good Practice Guide for Workplace Investigations*. Caldecote, The Security Institute.

De Bruin, W. B., Fischoff, B., Millstein, S.G. and Halper-Felsher, B. L. (2000) (de Bruin Organizational Behavior and Human Decision Processes. Elsevier, www.sciencedirect.com/science/article/abs/pii/ S0749597899928686 Accessed on 23 April 2020).

Denyer, D. (2017) *Organizational Resilience: A Summary of Academic Evidence, Business Insights and New Thinking*. BSI and Cranfield School of Management. Available at: https://www.cranfield.ac.uk

Dillon, B. (2014) *Blackstone's Emergency Planning, Crisis and Disaster Management*. Oxford, Oxford University Press.

Ditton, J. (1977) *Part Time Crime: An Ethnography of Fiddling and Pilferage*. London, Macmillan.

Dombrowski, W. R. (1995) Again and again: Is a disaster what we call a 'disaster'? Some conceptual notes on conceptualising the object of disaster sociology. *International Journal of Mass Emergencies and Disasters*, *13*(3), 241–254.

Drucker, P. F. (2007) *The Practice of Management*. London, Routledge.

Engemann, K. (2018) *The Routledge Companion to Risk, Crisis and Security in Business*. London, Routledge.

Evans, A. (2019) *Managing Cyber Risk*. London, Routledge.

Felson, M. (1998) *Crime and Everyday Life*. Thousand Oaks, CA, Sage.

Fennelly, L. J. (2013) *Crime Prevention Through Environmental Design*. Oxford, Butterworth-Heinemann.

Ferriter, D. (2019) *The Border: The Legacy of a Century of Anglo-Irish Politics*. London, Profile Books.

Fink, S. (2002) *Crisis Management: Planning for the Inevitable*. Lincoln, iUniverse.

Fischer, J. R., Halibozek, E. P., and Walters, D. C. (2013) *Introduction to Security*. Oxford, Butterworth-Heinemann.

Fischhoff, B., Millstein, S. G., and Halpern-Felsher, B. L. (2010) *Verbal and Numerical Expressions of Probability: "It's a Fifty-Fifty Chance"*. Available at: www.ncbi.nlm.nih.gov/pubmed/10631071, accessed on 31 January 2020.

Gambetta, D. (Ed.) (2005) *Making Sense of Suicide Missions*. Oxford, Oxford University Press.

Gill, M. (2006) *A Handbook of Security*. London, Palgrave.

Gill, M. (Ed.) (2014) *A Handbook of Security; Second Edition*. London, Palgrave Macmillan.

Gourley, R. (2018) *The Cyber Threat*. ISBN: 1501065149.

Graham-Smith, F. (1992) *Risk Analysis, Perception, Management*. London, The Royal Society.

Greenburg, J. (1997) The STEAL Motive: Managing the Social Determinants of Employee Theft. In R. Giacalone and J. Greenburg (eds.), *Antisocial Behaviour in Organisations*. Greenwich, JAI Press.

Held, D., Mc Grew, A., Goldblatt, D., and Perraton, J. (2016) *Global Transformations, Politics, Economics and Culture*. Cambridge, Polity Press.

Hollinger, R. C., and Clark, J. P. (1982) Employee deviance: A response to the perceived quality of the perceived work experience. *Work and Occupations*, *9*, 97–114.

Hollinger, R. C., and Clark, J. P. (1983) *Theft by Employees*. Lexington, Lexington Books.

Horgan, J. (2005) *The Psychology of Terrorism*. Oxon, Routledge.

Hubbard, D. W. (2009) *The Failure of Management*. Hoboken, NJ, John Wiley and Sons.

Husain, E. (2007) *The Islamist*. London, Penguin.

The Institute of Risk Management (IRM). (2020) Available at: www.theirm.org/the-risk-profession/risk-management.aspx , accessed on 21 December 2019.

ISPS Code. (2003) International Maritime Organisation (IMO).

Jones, S. (2001) *Criminology*. London. Butterworths.

Kamp, J., and Brooks, P. (1991) Perceived Organizational Climate and Employee Counterproductivity. *Journal of Business and Psychology*, *10*(4), 447–458.

Kean, H. T. (2002) *The 9/11 Commission Report*. New York, W. W. Norton.

Kevin Peachy. (2017) *TSB Admits 1,300 Accounts Hit by Fraud Amid IT Meltdown*. Available at: www.bbc.co.uk/news/business-44385710

Khan, M. A. (2011) *Islamic Jihad: A Legacy of Forced Conversion, Imperialism and Slavery*. The USA, Felibri.com.

Kresevich, M. (2007) *Using Culture to Cure Theft*. Available at: http://www.securitymanagement.com/article/using-culture-cure-theft?page=0%2CO, accessed on 13 February 2009.

Law, R. D. (2016) *Terrorism a History*. Cambridge, Polity Press.

Macauley, T. (2009) *Critical Infrastructure: Understanding Its Component Parts, Vulnerabilities, Operating Risks and Interdependencies*. London, CRC Press.

McCrie, R. D. (2007) *Security Operations Management*. Burlington, MA, Elsevier Butterworth-Heinemann.

Mc Kearney, T. (2011) *The Provisional IRA: From Insurrection to Parliament*. London, Pluto Press.

Mars, G. (1974) Cheats at Work: An Anthropology of Work-Based Crime. In P. Rock and M. Mc Intosh (eds.), *Deviance and Social Control*. London, Tavistock.

Mars, G. (1982) *An Anthropology of Work-Based Crime*. London, Allen and Unwin.

Mars, G. (2000) *Work-Based Sabotage*. Abingdon, Ashgate.

Martin, G. (2006) *Understanding Terrorism*. Thousand Oaks, CA, Sage.

Michaletos, I. (2009) *The Era of the Private Intelligence Agencies*. Available at: https://krypt3ia.wordpress.com/2009/03/10/6602/, accessed on 31 January 2019.

Millstein, S. G., and Halpern-Felsher, B. L. (2002) Perceptions of risk and vulnerability. *Journal of Adolescent Health*, *31*(Suppl 1), 10–27. https://doi.org/10.1016/S1054-139X(02)00412-3

Moloney, E. (2007) *A Secret History of the IRA*. London, Penguin.

Mueller, R. (2012) *RSA Cyber Security Conference*. San Francisco, CA. archives.fbi.gov (01 March 2012), accessed on 12 September 2018.

Murphy, M. N. (2011) *Somalia: The New Barbary?: Piracy and Islam in the Horn of Africa*. Chichester, Columbia University Press.

Newman, O. (1972) *Defensible Space: Crime Prevention Through Urban Design*. New York, Macmillan.

Newsome, B. (2014) *A Practical Introduction to Security and Risk Management*. Thousand Oaks, CA, Sage.

Norton, A. R. (2007) *Hezbollah*. Princeton, NJ, Princeton University Press.

Patterson, D. G. (2013) *Implementing Physical Protection Systems: A Practical Guide*. Alexandria, Virginia, ASIS International.

Pedahzur, A. (2005) *Suicide Terrorism*. Cambridge, Polity Press.

Petters, J. (2018) *Threat Modelling* [Online]. Available at: www.varonis.com/blog/threat-modeling/, accessed on 19 April 2019.

Pidgeon, N. F., Hood, C., Jones, D., Turner, B., & Gibson, R. (1992) Risk Perception. In *Risk: Analysis, Perception and Management. Report to the Royal Society Group*. London, The Royal Society.

Pidgeon, N. F., Kasperson, R. E., and Slovik, P. (2003) *The Social Amplification of Risk*. Cambridge, Cambridge University Press.

Price, C. J., and Forrest, S. J. (2013) *Practical Aviation Security: Predicting and Preventing Future Threats*. Chester, Butterworth-Heinemann.

Rekawek, K. (2011) *Irish Republican Terrorism and Politics: A Comparative Study of the Official and the Provisional IRA*. Oxon, Routledge.

Royal Society for the Prevention of Accidents. (1981) *Seat Belt Sense*. Birmingham, RoSpa.

Royal Society for the Prevention of Accidents. (1983) *Risk Assessment: A Study Group Report*. London, Royal Society.

Sennewald, C. A., and Baillie, C. (2015) *Effective Security Management*. Oxford, Butterworth-Heinemann.

Shanahan, T. (2009) *The Provisional Irish Republican Army and the Morality of Terrorism*. Edinburgh, Edinburgh University Press.

Sharp, J. (2012) *The Route Map to Business Continuity Management: Meeting the Requirements of ISO 22301*. London, BSI.

Sheffi, Y. (2017) *The Power of Resilience: How the Best Companies Manage the Unexpected*. Cambridge, MA, MIT Press.

Singer, P. W. (2003) *Corporate Warriors*. Ithaca, NY, Cornell University Press.

Singer, P. W., and Friedman, A. (2014) *Cyber Security and Cyber Warfare: What Everyone Needs to Know*. New York, Oxford University Press.

Sweet, K. M. (2004) *Aviation and Airport Security: Terrorism and Safety Concern's*. New Jersey, Pearson Prentice Hall.

Threat Horizon 2019: Disruption. Distortion. Deterioration. www.securityforum.org/research/threat-horizon-2019/

Thompson, M. (1980) The Aesthetics of Risk: Culture or Conflict. In R. C. Schwing and W. A. Albers (eds.), *Social Risk Assessment: How Safe Is Safe Enough?* (pp. 273–285). New York, Plenum.

Toft, B., and Reynolds, S. (2005) *Learning from Disasters: A Management Approach*. London, Palgrave Macmillan.

Ulmer, R. R., Sellnow, T. L., and Seeger, M. W. (2011) *Effective Crisis Communications: Moving from Crisis to Opportunity*. London, Sage.

Walker, C., and Osborne, S. (2010) *Blackstone's Counter Terrorism Handbook*. Oxford, Oxford University Press.

Ward, A. (2018) *Is the Threat of Nuclear Terrorism Distracting Attention from More Realistic Threats?* The Rand Corporation. Available at: https://www.rand.org/blog/2018/07/is-the-threat-of-nuclear-terrorism-distracting-attention.html, accessed on 21 March 2020.

Wheeler, A. (2019) *Crisis Communications Management*. Bingley, Emerald.

Wood, J., and Sheering, C. (2007) *Imagining Security*. Oxon. Routledge.

Zedner, L. (2003) Too much security. *International Journal of the Society of Law, 31*(3), 155–184.

Web addresses

https://en.wikipedia.org/wiki/*Birmingham_pub_bombings*.

https://en.wikipedia.org/wiki/*Coaxial_cable*, accessed on 12 October 2019.

https://en.wikipedia.org/wiki/*Fifth_Amendment_to_the_United_States_Constitution*.

https://en.wikipedia.org/wiki/*Flying_glass*.

https://en.wikipedia.org/wiki/*Hostile_work_environment*, accessed on 13 December 2019.

https://en.wikipedia.org/wiki/*Lock_and_key*, accessed on 21 January 2020.

https://en.wikipedia.org/wiki/*Maritime_Jewel*.

https://en.wikipedia.org/wiki/*Metropolitan_Police_Service*, accessed on 24 January 2020.

https://medium.com/@sbwoodside/*defence-in-depth-the-medieval-castle-approach-to-internet-security-*6c8225dec294.

https://uk.rs-online.com/web/c/safety-security-esd-control-clean-room/cctv-security-surveillance/cctv-monitors/, accessed on 12 October 2019.

https://www.ifrc.org/en/*what-we-do/disaster-management/about-disasters/what-is-a-disaster/*, accessed on 08 October 2019.

https://www.infosecurityeurope.com/__novadocuments/356893?v=636298498708300000, accessed on 21 March 2020.

www.computerhope.com/jargon/c/cat5.htm, accessed on 12 October 2019.

www.cpni.gov.uk/*critical-national-infrastructure*-0, accessed on 04 November 2019.

www.cpni.gov.uk/*developing-security-culture*, accessed on 23 December 2019.

www.cpni.gov.uk/*operational-requirements*.

www.cpni.gov.uk/system/files/documents/e5/ca/*ASF-blast-mitigation-Daylight-application.pdf*.

www.gov.uk/*national-minimum-wage-rates*.

www.gov.uk/*terrorism-national-emergency,* accessed on 04 October 2019.

www.hse.gov.uk/*corpmanslaughter*/about.htm.

www.mi5.gov.uk/*threat-levels*.

www.ncsc.gov.uk/*guidance/operational-technologies*, accessed on 12 January 2020.

www.ncsc.gov.uk/*section/advice-guidance/all-topics*?topics=cyber%20threat&sort=date%2Bdesc&start=0&rows=20, accessed on 21 October 2019.

www.police.uk, accessed on 12 October 2019.

www.salford.ac.uk/*research/case-studies/case-studies/environment-and-sustainability/the-centre-for-disaster-resilience*, accessed on 25 January 2020.

www.theguardian.com/business/2019/nov/19/*tsb-it-meltdown-report-computer-failure-accounts,* accessed on 21 November 2019.

www.webopedia.com/*TERM/S/SCADA*.html, accessed on 12 January 2020.

www.whatsnextcw.com/*learning-best-japanese-earthquake-proof-buildings/*, accessed on 15 October 2019.

Index

Note: Page numbers in *italic* indicate a figure and page numbers in **bold** indicate a table on the corresponding page.